ECONOMIC DEVELOPMENT IN A GLOBALIZED ENVIRONMENT:

East Asian Evidences

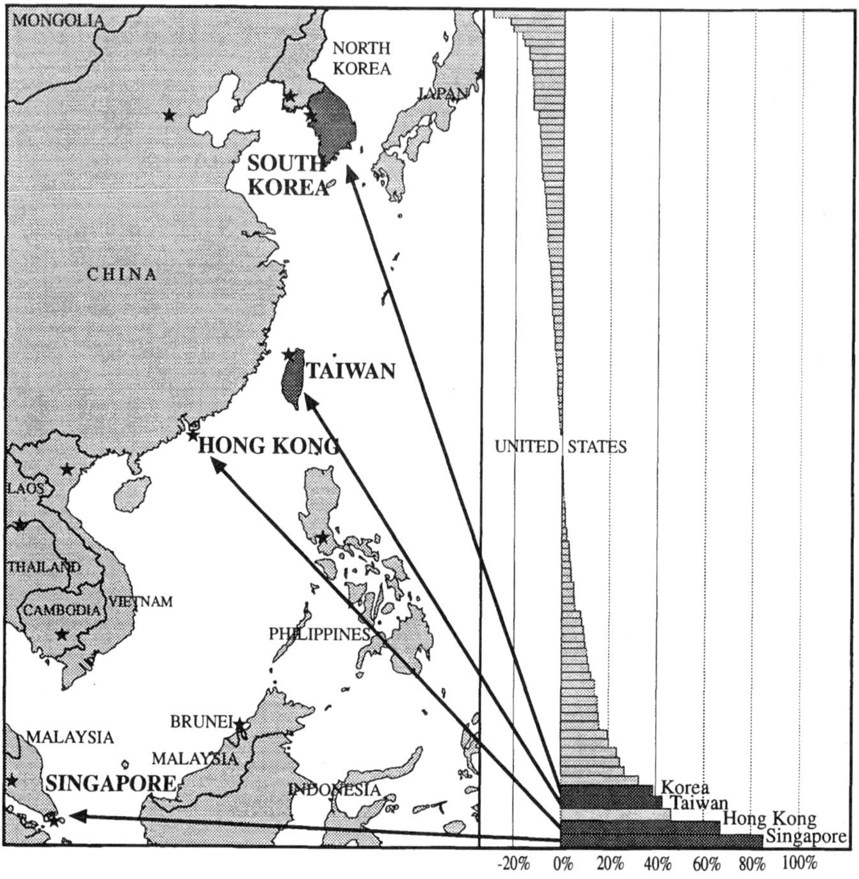

Change in per capita real income relative to the United States, 1960-1996

Economic Development in a Globalized Environment:

East Asian Evidences

Henry Y. Wan, Jr.

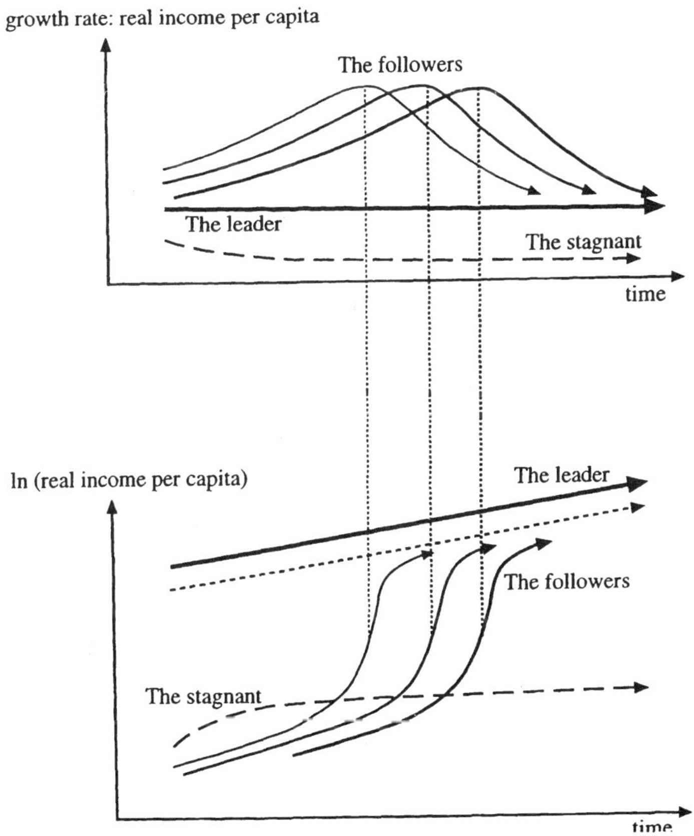

Library of Congress Cataloging-in-Publication Data

Economic Development in a Globalized Environment
By Henry Y. Wan, Jr.

A C.I.P. Catalogue record for this book is available from the Library of Congress.

ISBN 0-387-24205-8 (Paperback) ISBN 1-4020-7618-5 (Hardcover)

Printed in the United States of America.

9 8 7 6 5 4 3 2 1 SPIN 11372226

springeronline.com

To

Professor Shu-Jen Yang

Who introduced me to Economics

and

Mr. Morris Shimo Zhang

Who advised me to complete this volume

CONTENTS

PREFACE

This is a book on economic growth for the developing world. Among many volumes on the same subject, hopefully, here is a volume with a difference.

We adopt an integrated approach: theory is built on observations by inferences; evidence is assessed through analysis. The 'benchmark mechanism' forms the backbone of the theoretical discourse in Part 1; structured comparisons unify the development episodes in Part 2.

For us, economics is to be studied for relevance, and not for elegance. Insight we gain prepares policies to improve human welfare. We live in an interdependent world; policies are mostly made for a national agenda, with scanty coordination. To be tractable, economists identify causal mechanisms under simplified conditions. In most growth models, there is only one country. Literally speaking, they apply to either isolated states, whose time is long past, or a world in a unitary State, which may emerge, if ever, in some future century. No wonder such models approximate quite well the American scene, for which the 1956-7 Solow's studies were designed for. Outside influence – like Crisis 1997 – is usually modest. These models work far less well for other economies – as Solow warned – especially with the world market as their life line. To wit, the 2001 slowing down of the American economy spells the first-ever negative growth for both Singapore and Taiwan. To be sure, some of those simplified models illuminate crucially valuable mechanisms. Without their use, the compound economic interactions would appear so confounding that the economists' analysis might be no better than shrewd journalism. In our current context, the benchmark model is constructed on what was learned in an optimal growth model of Lau and Wan (1994).

The situation is quite similar in some other fields. Gone are the days of Da Vinci, when helicopters were designed with no concern about any power source. Today, to master the first principles of physics is obligatory for aeronautical engineers.

Yet it is far more than a small step between the principles of thermodynamics and actual airplane design. Nor is it trivial to transplant elegant findings in endogenous growth models to industrial policy. Take the theory of learning-by-doing for example. Chapter 3 below explains that although in logic, trade might retard growth for the developing economies (a finding many economists take note), yet in case after observed case, openness to the world market is the prerequisite condition for development.

Thus, there is a time for theory, also a time for empirical episodes – to provide both close support for policy making, and appropriate assumptions to make theory relevant.

Today, by and large, the world economy evolves by its technical dynamism. Since World War II, successful efforts in catching-up reflect effective acquisition of technology, through interactions with the developed world, where R. & D. activities are disproportionately concentrated today in the United States. In general, the mechanism works according to the theory of Gerschenkron. Yet one must face the question, why is it among economies at a similar stage, some seize the opportunities to catch up, while others remain mired in stagnation.

In truth, interactions do not occur in a vacuum. Those economies which have experienced sustained, rapid growth (mostly in East Asia) share common themes, but also exhibit considerable variation. The shared features suggest which factors are necessary for development. The differences are sometimes shaped by history and circumstances, or due to policy choice. Like chess openings, the merit of policy measures often depends on whether the subsequent play can build upon them as foundations.

To wring valuable information out of the historical record, we pursue structured comparisons among those few economies who have succeeded, and avoid the numerous unsuccessful cases: their diverse and idiosyncratic causes of failure may serve little purpose but as a distraction. Thus we avoid one key difficulty in cross country studies: with stagnant economies far outnumbering countries in robust growth, regression results may tell more about *how* development goes wrong than *which* policies get it right.

How does this volume differ from others in the literature? Some detailed discussion is in order.

A. The view from development economics. By the World Development Report, 2002, the world population is about six billion. Five sixths of these reside in economies with low or middle Human Development Index (HDI). Another 80 million live in the four Newly Industrialized Economies (NIEs) which are the most recent group of economies to achieve the high HDI.

Traditional development economics focus on the plight of not enjoying the status of high HDI; we emphasize the process of how to attain it.

B. The viewpoint of growth theory. For the past decade and a half, the cutting edge in macro-economics is the concept of endogenous growth, a theory pioneered by Shell (1966) and extended to development studies, as exemplified by Lucas (2002). To explore the distinction between the actual and optimal evolution for the ideal world economy, such studies often postulate a single 'social planner' for the world with myopia, or perfect foresight.

In contrast, this volume is written solely for the present world, in search of 'actionable' policies to be adopted by the national state. Thus, for us, the literature of endogenous growth provides intellectual stimulation, much more than specific policy analysis.

C. The viewpoint of trade theory. For observers of the world economy, it is well understood that in the last half a century, world trade has outgrown world production, also that economies enjoying sustained, rapid growth are typically those with medium income and gaining shares in aggregate world trade. This corroborates the statistical findings of Coe, Helpman and Hoffmaister (1997) on the trade-induced technology transfer. To us, it is by this mechanism, as much as by the classic gains of trade, that international trade has reshaped the economic world. This is so, even though in the trade literature, this aspect is conspicuous by its near-total absence.

D. The viewpoint of the area studies for East Asia. Traditionally, in-depth case studies are centered on one or two individual economies, either in isolation, or by pair-wise comparison. In contrast, our focus is the process of catching up, with those economies studied for evidence. Thus, Japan and Korea are compared to highlight the effect of institutions in policy setting: the inter-ministry check and balance in Japan versus presidential micro-management in Korea. Korea and Taiwan are compared to illustrate the alternative industrial structure for a developmental State: oligopolistic business groups versus monopolistically competitive SMEs. Taiwan and Hong Kong are compared to assess the need for government participation at different stages: the initial export expansion through labor intensive operations versus the subsequent industrial upgrading that involves high tech sectors. Hong Kong and Singapore are compared to focus on the relative risks of de-industrialization, under laissez faire or active government involvement. Singapore and Korea are compared to reveal that country size matters, for the need of multinationals in industrial targeting, but not for the possible use of industrial policy.

In our issue-oriented discussion, tailor-made theories and selected case studies are deployed to elucidate the catching up mechanism: *how* it functions, *what* it implies, and *why* it happens. The following examples make the point. Thus, our study of the catching up process does not stop at the gathering of statistical evidence. Conceptual underpinning receives equal attention. We anchor our study on the position of the technological leader: US now; UK in the past. This explains after World War II, the ease for Germany, or Japan, to overtake UK – an advanced follower by then - but not US, the technological leader.

In discussing the catching up process, the advantage of the one-good model is balanced by the warning about its limitation: its inability to explain the decline of Soviet growth, a victim of creative destruction: a falling behind (i. e., lack of catching up) through isolation.

The study of technology spill-over via direct foreign investment is backed up with both an examination of the nature of knowledge, in terms of information filters (like the σ-algebras in the probability theory), and the Wong-Watanabe example of technology transfer. This shows why the spill-over is a win-win outcome between the Northern firm and the Southern worker.

Other illustrations of our approach includes (a) the use of Hyundai's entry into the American car market to indicate that growth accounting understates total factor productivity growth when it is applied to NIEs like Korea, and (b) an integer-programming model to demonstrate the economics of the entrepôt: namely, the interaction between the modal choice between different shipping vessels and the cost-comparison between the coastal and cross-ocean routes. This explains how the Port of Singapore enjoys its advantage and why Malaysia is induced to compete for that niche.

In short, for questions involving policy action, analytical instruments are tailor-made when necessary, and only if it is necessary.

Moreover, by selective citations from policy makers, like Park Chung-Hee, Shirley Kuo, Mahathir, and Lee Kuan Yew, or businessmen like Tony Lo, and economic historians like Miyajima and Hikino, one can capture the perception of real life issues by decision makers and professional researchers far better than otherwise.

This book is designed for the use of research economists in several fields: development studies and growth, international economics and areas studies for Asia, as well as decision makers in business, government and international organizations. Complete with chapter summaries, problem set as well as a collection of general problems, the material can also serve as texts in special topic courses or assigned references in various related economic courses at the graduate or advanced college level.

We face an uncertain world where agents operate in decentralized markets and sign 'incomplete contracts'. *L'homme d'affaires* often holds the view that classroom economics can be lightly dismissed as irrelevant, because of its imperfection. This is so even though in matters of personal health, one would accept the equally imperfect opinion of physicians. To gain a more balanced perspective, we present exercise problems where economic theory and chains of close reasoning can give us unexpectedly sharp implications on issues with policy importance. For example, Problem 11, Chapter 2 shows that from the interactions of cultural affinity, political history and economic theory, one can predict *why* Korea and Taiwan are different in their directions of outward investment and patterns of change in trade flows, *what* such differences imply in acquiring foreign technology, and *how* their respective industrial policies might be justified accordingly.

In a class with a combined enrollment of advanced undergraduates and graduate students, the material of this volume has been class tested at Cornell, over nine years.

Finally, this book is also written for researchers in business, government, and various non-government organizations (NGOs). For their interest, one must take note of the Nobel Lecture of North (1994) in calling for a new institutional theory of development, based on history, to replace the current approach, based on 'neoclassical theory'. Space is obviously insufficient in this book for a *methodenstreit*, Round II[1]. Nonetheless, interested readers may consult Problem XIII (Institutionism) in the Appendix for General Review, where material in this book is related to the ambitious North Program, as we understand it. Problem XIV (The Argentina Project), same section, serves as the culmination.

Two more points need to be made. First, already today, we can represent analytically some of the topical themes in economic history, such as the 'keyboard study' (David, 1985) and The Industrial Revolution (Landes, 1994)[2]. Second, apart from any realization of the North Program, we can second the North view that researchers on development policy should be well versed in history. An analogy with other 'professional fields' today illustrates the case. Today, law school students are trained with the case method; medical curriculum includes clinic internship; military cadets analyze historic campaigns; aspired architects and engineers study designs of past masters. The rise of rigorous, sophisticated theories is no substitute

---

[1] Interested readers are referred to Richter (1996).

[2] A vintage typists model can explain the endurance of QWERTY. Cf. Wan (1994).

for baptism in reality. Thus, the inclusion of selected[3] historical narratives in this volume is not merely for expository illustration.

[3] Selection is needed. To wit, modern commanders no longer deploy war elephants.

ACKNOWLEDGMENTS

Many persons have enriched my background for this volume. A partial listing follows.

- In graduate school, as a research assistant to Robert Solow, my graduate school teacher, I had the opportunity to watch him doing research: being always concerned about the economic process behind the data, the model, the mathematics or statistics.
- On my return to Taipei, in 1961, S. J. Yang, my undergraduate teacher, then Secretary General, Academia Sinica, brought me to the Institute of Economics right at its preparatory stage. Serving as a correspondence researcher (also frequent visitor) to that institute over the last four decades has acquainted me with Taiwan's development process.
- In 1964, I came back to America and met Douglass North at the University of Washington, with his historical approach to economics. Pp. 357-8 represent my understanding of his influential work, then and later.
- In the 1970s and 1980s, I was a frequent visitor at the Chunghua Institution of Economic Research, then under the late Dr. S. C. Tsiang. The writing of newspaper articles for policy debates and exchange views with visitors from the Korean Development Institute had helped me to get some perspective on policy decisions.
- When teaching in Shanghai for the Ford Foundation Program, I had very valuable discussions with the Fudan University faculty about the economic issues facing the PRC.
- From the mid-1990s, when I went to Hong Kong for the Chinese Economic Association in North America (CEANA), I learned much in giving papers on the interactions between various Chinese economies.

- During my term as the Goh Keng Swee Professor at the National University of Singapore, I had the opportunity to offer public lectures on the Singaporean economy.
- My joint research with Murray Kemp over the decades, made me keenly aware that without compensations, the changing trade pattern can harm some individuals in an economy; in the short run, adjustment is likely to be costly. My colleague Jaroslav Vanek also reminded me about such possible side effects of globalization.
- My interactions with many Cornell colleagues at the East Asian Center and the Center for Sociology and Economics, like Sherman Cochran, Victor Nee, and Tzu-lin Mei have enriched my research with an interdisciplinary dimension.

Ever since my textbook *Economic Growth* appeared in 1972, Simone Clemhout encouraged me to write a sequel. By then the fastest ever growth rates in history were appearing – along the Northwest Pacific Rim. Such growth episodes are neither transient, often going on for three decades or more, nor negligible, having made the Japanese economy the World's second largest, nor understandable by neoclassic growth theory alone, according to Solow (2001: 283), the founder of that theory[4]. In existing single-country models, there is nothing to predict that fastest growth would occur around the Pacific, along the Northwest Rim, but not the Southeast Rim. Trade matters, but not in ways emphasized in the trade literature, though in my case, I can draw upon my joint work with Simone Clemhout on learning-by-doing for an open economy, and adapt it for repeated use in this volume. Overall, the inclusion of empirical data and the presentation of the material to a non-East Asian audience are neither easy nor entirely satisfactory. On these and other aspects, receiving constant, supportive advice from Simone (I am also privileged to be her spouse of 38 years) is certainly a reassuring help.

I have also drawn upon what is learned with my various co-researchers on related topics: Man-lui Lau, Van Hoang Pham, Yong-Chih Lin, Jason Weisman, Yeum Yeum Lim, Toshiyasu Kato, Chakrapong Uchupalanun, Erik Thorbecke, An-Ch Tung and Wing-Keung Wong. The last two as well as Kap-Young Jeong gave me valuable criticism on various chapters. Bettina Atten, Byung-Sun Choi, and Soon Teck Wong supplied valuable information and data. Successive classes of my students at Cornell University offered feedbacks, and very useful information in their term

[4] Thus, Solow gave us not only the coal of dynamic analysis, the spade of uniting theory with facts, but also the direction: for development economics, construct theories on one's own.

projects. Last but not the least, my Cornell colleagues like Kaushik Basu, David Easley, Tapan Mitra, Ted O'Donoghue, Uri Possen, Karl Shell, Salvador Ortigueira and Erik Thorbecke have gracefully served as my sounding board.

Andrea Williams-Wan, my daughter-in-law, offered me valuable organizational advice and help in editing and indexation; Vincent Wan, my son, provided me significant methodological perspective as a historian of science, specialized in another empirical but non-experimental discipline: paleontology.

Finally, in preparing the manuscript, thanks are due to the help of Jessica Vivian, Rebecca McCleary and the patient expertise and professional care of Henning Pape-Santos.

It is customary to stake the claim over all residual shortcomings in such an undertaking.

PART 1
GENERAL CONSIDERATIONS

Introduction to Part 1

In our integrated approach, we assess evidence and develop theory, side-by-side. Thus in Part 1, Chapter 1 introduces the benchmark model by using stylized facts distilled from data and Chapter 2 examines the East Asian environment where we draw our main body of evidence. Chapter 3 considers implications from a multi-sector context, and Chapter 4 emphasizes cross-economy interactions, thus extending the study of the benchmark model in two directions. Chapter 5 studies the role of the state by returning to the dynamic context. Based on the perspective developed in earlier discussions, we evaluate the major policy debates in the development literature. Chapter 6 considers uncertainty which is inherent in the framework of growth, as illustrated by the Asian experience in Crisis 1997.

In a quick reading, Chapter 2 may be postponed until a later time. Its appraisal of the influence of Confucianism and the experience and impact of Japan may be of interest on their own.

Chapter 6 specializes in the (international) financial aspects of growth, which can be skipped for those focusing on the 'real' economy. On the other hand, the study of the endogenous uncertainty arising out of the successful catching up efforts might be interesting to researchers in international macro-economics, in its own right.

Chapter 1

INTRODUCTION

A Theory For Catching Up

1. THE WORLD WE LIVE IN

For the five-sixths of mankind living in the developing world today, the late 20th century has brought reason for both distinct hope and gnawing concern. Over the last fifty years, some developing economies achieved the fastest growth rates ever seen in human history – in the course of a single generation joining the ranks of countries enjoying the highest levels of per capita income in the world. Other developing economies, however, have been left on the wrong side of a widening income gap; the world seems to have passed them by.[1]

We can identify here some factors relevant to the development successes that occurred after World War II. The socio-political and technological environment has changed profoundly over the last fifty years, and has in turn greatly influenced the possibilities for economic development. Without the wave of de-colonization that took place after World War II, for example, East Asian factories would not have been able to utilize Mideast fuel to compete against their former colonial masters, which had previously controlled such energy resources. Likewise, without the constellation of technological advances and socio-political changes that yielded greatly reduced rates for airfreight, Uganda would never have been able to supply cut flowers for the European market.

[1] See below for statistical evidence behind these statements.

The United States, as both the world's largest market and its largest post-industrial society, plays a particularly central role in the changes taking place in the global economy. The United States is a representative democracy with a large and financially independent retired population, and with no union-affiliated political party. Many voters favor cheap imports over sheltered shop floor jobs. The longest period of American prosperity was achieved in the face of an even longer spell of trade deficits. The relatively open American market has given rise to a globalized production system. It has dispelled the *export pessimism* that dominated development economics in the early post-World War II years.

Within this changing socio-political, technological, and economic environment, the experiences of the growing Asian economies, which have successfully entered the global marketplace, demands careful study. Economics is a non-experimental empirical science – as is, for instance, astronomy. By deploying a battery of calibrated instruments and close argument, astronomers have managed to deduce the content and structure of planets and satellites more than half a billion kilometers away from Earth. By marshalling the statistical evidence, closely examining case studies, and reasoning carefully, we economists should be able to ascertain the foundations of the process of economic development.

As a working definition, a development process shall be regarded as *successful* when per capita real income has undergone *sustained* rapid growth, say at 5% or more per year for a generation or longer (roughly 25 years). A growth record of 25 years implies some basic force for development is at work, and that the economy has not merely benefited from temporary windfalls. A growth rate of 5% per annum is clearly in excess of the growth rates of most developed economies (with the exception of Japan thirty years ago).[2] This growth rate therefore leads to a definite narrowing of the income gap with the developed societies – that is, to a 'catching up process.' To close the income gap is the fervent wish of most of the people in most developing societies today.

We can observe that, in real life, such *rapid* growth only occurs in an economy during some phase of its catching up process: West Europe after the Marshall Plan, for instance, and Japan before 1970. In particular, *the observed growth of the latecomer slows down when the gap narrows*. More

---

[2] The growth rates of per capita real income for some selected countries are as follows:

G 7	Canada	France	Germany	Italy	Japan	U. K.	U. S.
1990-7	0.8	1.0	0.7	1.0	1.4	1.9	1.7
NIEs	Hong Kong	Korea	Singapore				
1990-7	3.3	6.0	6.7				

Source: *World Bank Atlas, 1999.*

interesting still, in terms of per capita real income, none of the episodes of rapid growth have ended in another economy *overtaking* the United States, the leading developed economy. These facts are important. They help to reveal the nature and the process of such development, and we will return to them below.

Overtaking-the-leader is certainly neither ruled out by logic, nor unknown in history. After all, the U.S. *did* overtake the U.K. But, as we shall argue below, overtaking-the-leader is a much more demanding feat than narrowing the gap. At any rate, nothing of the sort has been observed for the past fifty years.

In truth, rapid technological progress is a double-edged sword. It empowers the *periphery* with modern know-how, but it also entrenches the incumbency at the *center*. As in the case of the horticulturists in Uganda, technology has lowered the threshold at which economies are able to join the supply chain and share some of the prosperity of the globalized economy. However, technology has also raised the hurdles in the race, making it more difficult for any latecomer to totally overtake the technological leader. Besides the United States, which country today can field *two* successful, competing teams to decode the human genome? Both of these aspects of technological progress underlie the 'benchmark model' that is presented below.

To characterize both the conditions conducive to the catching up process, and the policy regime*s* that allow that process to go on, the facts discussed above provide food for thought. By generally accepted reasoning, we believe that the growth episodes of East Asia are consistent with economic (and not solely cultural or historical) explanations. This view will be elaborated in Chapter 2, and revisited, economy by economy, in **Part 2** of this volume.

What factors have enabled economies to attain sustained rapid growth? We offer here some brief remarks, before an extended discussion in Chapter 3. None of the recent episodes of sustained rapid growth resulted from the discovery of mineral riches or the arrival of profitable cash crops – over time, for instance, OPEC-driven wealth has waxed and waned. The rapid growth episodes all involved the expansion of manufactured output and export. Social and political stability has been necessary, though obviously not sufficient. Typically, the early stages of such episodes are associated with abundant labor (hence low wages) and relatively high literacy.

These observations suggest that to *sustain* the *rapid* growth, one must sidestep the law of diminishing returns in both *production* and *world demand*, over the period in question. To delay the diminishing returns in *production*, one cannot rely on primary production, where 'land' in fixed supply sets the limit for growth. To postpone the diminishing returns in *demand*, one must serve a broad clientele by *exporting* one's product, and by producing *more valuable* varieties of *outputs*. For sustained growth, expanding export volume is not the answer. Korean growth started with an export boom in such goods as wigs of human hair. Even if there had been no fashion change phasing out demand for that product, certainly to sustain a rapid rate of growth on that trade alone, *the world is not enough*. One must not produce merely more of the same, but must produce more value out of the same inputs. This takes more human capital. Technical progress is necessary, but high saving rate is insufficient – history shows how futile was the high rate of Soviet forced saving.

Suppose an economy enjoys *reasonable* rates of both savings and technical progress. Is export still needed to *sustain rapid growth*? By logic, the answer seems to be "No." But although growth without export may be theoretically possible, such a scenario is not entirely plausible. After all, we are talking about growth rates much higher than the advanced economies for a generation or more. History shows that Soviet forced saving was ultimately futile for growth, while in the fast-growing East Asia, the rise of the saving/income ratio came *after* the rise in the growth rate. Thus, history is consistent with the view that, without both market discipline and technological advance, savings may go to waste, and that saving itself may be induced by investment opportunities provided by technological advances and market access. Documented cases also show that export can provide gains from the international division of labor, the prevention of resource misallocation due to monopoly, the inducement to capital formation, the acquisition of technology and improved market discipline against various types of government failures – from over-ambitious policy makers to the abuse of power and outright corruption by officials.

Since sustained rapid growth is observed in the four Newly Industrialized Economies (NIEs) of Korea, Taiwan, Hong Kong and Singapore, one may also ask: did high growth in these economies start with an export expansion? In their influential and thought-provoking studies, both Alwyn Young (1994, 1995) and Dani Rodrik (1995) answered this *empirical* question in the negative, against the views of both the 'orthodox' and the 'revisionist' schools. Yet assessing empirical evidence is always difficult, especially when sufficiently disaggregated data is scarce. We are convinced that much of the early East Asian growth represents Post World War II and Post Korean War reconstruction under massive external assistance, and would not have led to sustainable growth had there not been unimpeded trade (as in Hong Kong) or outward-oriented reform elsewhere.

As a corollary, specializing in manufacturing (rather than in the primary sectors) gives a dynamic advantage, because the skill accumulated is less product-specific, and may be adapted and upgraded for other pursuits.[3] Generally speaking, it is easier to transfer workers from the production of textile machines to the production of machine tools, than to transfer them from the tending of oil palms to the drilling of oil wells. This seems to explain why *literate* but *low-wage* labor is the usual ingredient in rapid development episodes.

The next issue is how to acquire the relevant labor skill today. This is a world where *technological progress is fast.* According to 'Moore's Law,' computer chips double their density every 18 months. The world is ever more closely connected in transportation and communication. Industries become footloose when the movement of both products and production factors become easy. Should one re-invent the wheel, or should one rather acquire technology from the more advanced societies, whenever possible?

Of course, the real choice is, *on what terms* skills are to be acquired. In general, there is *no free lunch.* Modern technical knowledge may come with an alien ethos deleterious to cherished native values. Foreign investment may degrade the environment and undermine political and economic sovereignty. The pursuit of export revenue may divert resources from the long-term national interest. Even economic transformation can polarize income distribution, impose hardship on the weaker members of the society, and tear apart families. So there are trade-offs to be weighed and externalities to be considered. In the next section we will discuss lessons that can be learned from the high-growth episodes about *how* technology is acquired, and *what* might be its cost.

The next topic is *how much* the government should be involved in development matters. There is no simple answer here, since both *market failure* and *government failure* are commonly observed. Much also depends upon *what* policy is applied, so that one might overcome market failure without risking government failure.[4] In Chapter 5, we shall present concrete examples and discuss some general guidelines about such matters.

Further questions one must address are the industrial structure and the resort to foreign savings. To these, nuanced answers are given in Chapter 6.

We are now in a position to offer a road map for the rest of **Part 1** of this volume, which is devoted to the following seven topics:

- The world we live in
- The 'benchmark path' for catching up

---

[3] Or to seize opportunity and deflect setbacks, as was done in Hong Kong. See Findlay and Wellisz (1993: 19-22).

[4] To grasp quickly the crux of the matter, one can consult Bhagwati (1999). To see how the same facts have led to a quite different interpretation, the passionate argument of Amsden (1999) – who *equally advocates trade* – provides a useful example. Our own discussion of the evidence is presented throughout this volume.

- Industrialization and human capital formation
- Channels for technology acquisition
- The proper role of the state
- The industrial structure
- Issues of borrowing for development

The first item will be reviewed once more in brevity, to motivate the investigation of the second item in the next section of this chapter. The other five will be treated in subsequent chapters.

Two Fundamental Facts

We now prepare the ground for some theorizing in the next section. To recapitulate, *two* fundamental facts about technology characterize the world we live in. *On the one hand*, advances in transportation and communication permit close interaction between spatially separated societies. This offers opportunities for an international division of labor in producing a broad range of final goods. As examples, by the 1980s, according to Doshi (1988:88), Singapore refined two-thirds of the aviation fuel used between California and the Persian Gulf; according to Meyers (1986), under the American trademark, The Limited, ladies' garments with an Italian design were made out of the khaki fabric from a Chinese factory and dyed in Hong Kong, tailored into pants in Hong Kong, shirts in Sri Lanka and shorts in Mauritius, and finally assembled in America for distribution, in record time. *On the other hand*, among different societies, the capability for research and development varies as much as one can possibly imagine. For example, the central processing units (CPUs) in most of the personal computers in use are designed by Intel and a few other firms, *all* American.

For a latecomer to industrialization, it is easy to join the worldwide supply networks for the multinational corporations, but it is well-nigh impossible to produce manufactured goods independently and self-sufficiently.

New technology and new goods appear in successive waves at an ever-quickening tempo, and they impact all aspects of our lives. A century ago, a radio was an electronic device, and an automobile was entirely a product of mechanical engineering. By the late 20th century, under the hood of every up-scale automobile are microprocessors – from the fuel injection system to the satellite link with the Global Positioning System (GPS). Like the digital television, the internet, and the GPS, the microprocessor was developed in the United States, but is used in every corner of the world.

Almost all the new inventions come from the developed economies, with the United States playing a disproportionately important role. A lion's share of scientists and engineers in the world are trained in the U.S. Out of this crop, the U.S. attracts the cream of the cream to its academic and research facilities. In field after field, from information technology to bioengineering to material science, the U.S. has the most and the best-equipped laboratories. This overwhelming advantage in science and technology is translated into a predominant position in world commerce. On top of all these advantages, patent laws, industrial standards, personal connections and brand loyalties all work to favor the entrenched establishments and firms operating out of centrally placed locations – most of which are in the United States.

For the time being, no other economy (or any likely combination of economies) can go it alone and match the United States in science and technology, or in product development. The Soviet bloc tried, with ephemeral success, but ultimate failure.

In the years immediately after World War II, many developing economies experimented with policies that de-emphasized interactions with the outside world. Nothing in principle prevents a 'de-linked' society from providing its members a decent, tranquil if very frugal livelihood. Significant economic achievement can be made by an economy essentially 'de-linked' from the outside world: both India and China, for instance, managed to free themselves from famine decades before their economic reforms brought them into closer contact with world markets.

However, regimes that prioritize self-sufficiency over trade tend to find the technological gap that faces them widening over time, leaving them isolated and defenseless when contact with the outside world eventually, and almost inevitably, occurs – witness the fate of the Aztecs. When products must suddenly face better substitutes in the marketplace, they suffer 'creative destruction.' Thus, after the fall of the Berlin Wall, the East German Trabant lost its previously protected market share to the West German Volkswagen, and all East Germans had to show for decades of forced savings was obsolete equipment for products without any demand.

Thus 'de-linking' strategies have fallen from favor in recent decades. Eventually, both India and China undertook economic reforms that expanded their interactions with the rest of the world. Likewise, President Cardoso of Brazil, a leading proponent of the '*Dependencia*' School decades ago, made a U-turn in policy after he came to power.[5]

2. THE BENCHMARK PATH FOR CATCHING UP

We now turn to the economies within the trading world. For a bird's eye view, one can associate the rate of growth of per capita (real) income of an

[5] See for example, Boeker (1993).

economy with the level of per capita (real) income of the same economy. Taking a cross-section of such paired data for all economies, the result has been summed up succinctly in Lucas (1988):

> *The mid-income countries grow the fastest, next the high-income countries, with the low-income countries growing the slowest.*

By and large, the world according to Lucas comes in three parts: the (developed) North, the (less developed) South, and the East (Asia with its mid-income economies).[6] How close the above characterization is to reality is discussed in Appendix 1.1.

We now distill a simple model from the Lucas quotation above. Let x be the per capita real income of an economy, and $y = (dx/dt)/x$ as the growth rate of x. The observed relationship at time t over all economies forms simply a time-dependent function:

(1.2.1) $$y = f(x; t).$$

What Lucas said may be represented as follows:

> *f is monotonically increasing in x until x^0, but monotonically decreasing beyond it.*

x^0 may vary with time t.

We next follow the view explained in Gomulka (1990) and postulate,

Assumption 1. (Time invariance) At any time t, the value of y depends only on the value of a ratio v, which is x divided by z, the highest per capita income of all economies (this is the U.S. over the period with which we are concerned).[7]

Assumption 2. (Constant growth of z)[8] The growth rate of z (the U.S. per capita real income) is approximately a constant, say, $(dz/dt)/z \equiv c < f(x^0, t)$.

The implication of Assumption 2 is that at t, an economy with a level of per capita real income x^0 grows faster than the economy with the highest per capita real income.

To simplify our analysis, we use Assumptions 1 and 2 to replace (1.2.1) with:

---

[6] Lucas attributed the differences in growth performance to the public good nature of knowledge, a theme started with Shell (1966) and Romer (1986). In this we concur. We further believe that the fact that sustained rapid growth only occurred in economies during their mid-income phase suggests this growth represents the cross-economy spillover of knowledge capital. Such growth is a feat that has not been replicated in already technically advanced economies. Likewise, the literature on endogenous growth offers stimulation but not answers to most of the operational questions about the catching up process.

[7] If cases like United Arab Emirates are excluded.

[8] This is the view of Tobin (1980).

(1.2.2)[9] $$(dv/dt)/v = y - c = F(v)$$

where v = x/z, a ratio often referred to as the 'relative per capita real income' (let us call it *'repcri'* for short). v = 1 means an economy has the same per capita real income as the 'leading economy.'

We next define:

(1.2.3) $$F^0 = \text{Max}_v\, F(v) = F(v^0) > c.$$

Figure 1.2.1 depicts the case where F is parabolic. This figure is a *'phase diagram'* for v. There is a stable equilibrium at v* and an unstable equilibrium at $\underline{v}$. Both are *steady states* where the value of v will stay forever, if it assumes either value. The arrow signs indicate that any v near v* but not equal to it must gravitate toward v*; any v near $\underline{v}$ but not equal to it must move ever farther from $\underline{v}$ over time.

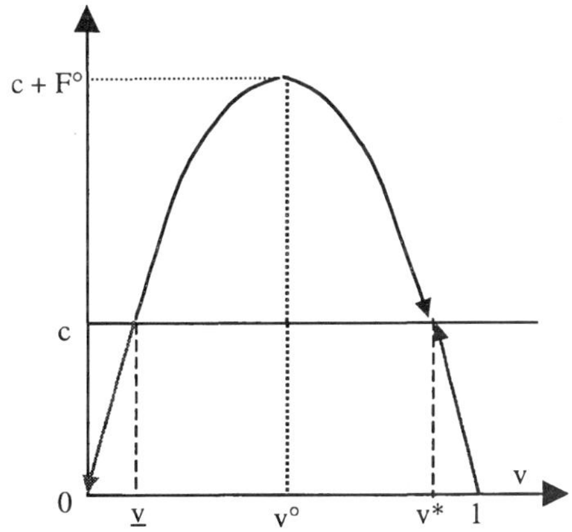

Figure 1.2.1 A phase diagram

The above diagram may be conveniently summed up by the following **four 'regularities':**

1. For those economies with a relative per capita real income lower than $\underline{v}$, they will lag increasingly behind the leading economies.[10]
2. For economies with a relative per capita real income between $\underline{v}$ and v*, their growth rate exceeds that of the 'leading economy,' c. The catching up process continues.
3. Over this phase, some stage of 'trend acceleration' is to be followed by an ultimate stage of 'trend deceleration.' The maximum growth rate, c +

---

[9] $(dv/dt)/v = d\log v/dt = d\log x/dt - d\log z/dt = y - c$.

[10] In fact, tragically, economies with the lowest income today can least afford to contain the AIDS crisis.

F^0, occurs at a point in time, t^o, where the repcri = v^0. The interval around t^o is often called the 'high growth period.'

4. The value of repcri may approach asymptotically some steady-state value, $v^* < 1$. Thus, the catching up process will never be complete at any finite time. The relative income gap will never be fully closed.

As we shall see below, in terms of the time paths of v(t), the facts captured include *both* the acceleration-then-deceleration mode of catching up with the United States by East Asia (incomplete though that may be), *and* the falling behind of most of the Latin American and sub-Saharan economies.

When v is within the interval, ($\underline{v}$, v^*), the relative per capita real income traces out a monotonically increasing function of time, t. The per capita real income is [Ce^{ct}] v(t) for some constant C, where the per capita real income of the leading economy is Ce^{ct}. In semilog scale, the slope of the time path is the growth rate.

Figure 1.2.2 displays the growth rate of an economy as a function of t. The time path is history-dependent.[11]

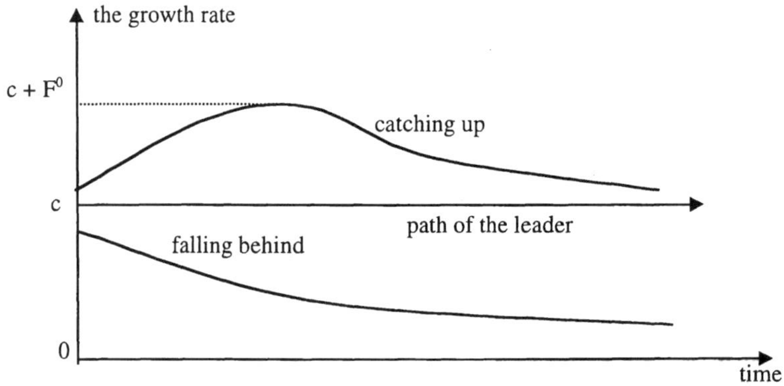

Figure 1.2.2 The different time profiles of growth rates

How the growth path will evolve depends critically on *what* initial conditions an economy is endowed with. For the very poor, even a partial closing of the gap is beyond their reach.

Next, in Figure 1.2.3, the level of per capita real income is plotted in semilog scale. It is now clear that even if an economy always enjoys some positive growth, it may still fall further and further behind the advanced economies. Also an economy that always grows faster than the leading economy may fail to completely close the income gap.

We must now stand back and take stock. Under Assumption 1, the catching up model postulates not only that the growth of the developing

[11] The moral: foreign aid, judiciously applied, can make a difference.

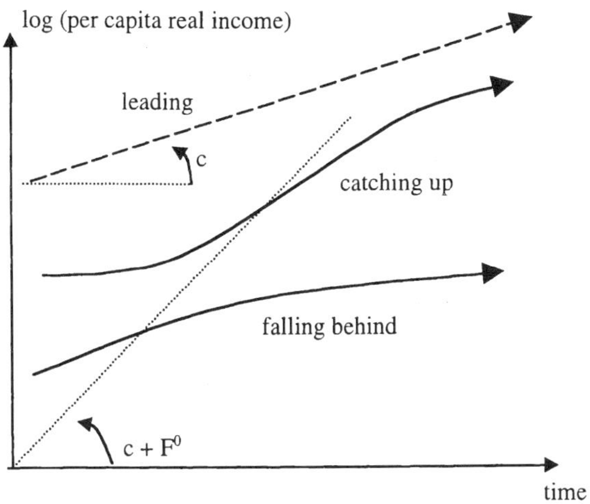

Figure 1.2.3 The different time paths of per capita real income in semilog

economy depends entirely upon certain interactions between the leading economy and that latecomer, but also implicitly that the *same* interaction exists for all developing economies. This implicit assumption ought to be relaxed. What is involved encompasses some mechanism of technology spillover. Of course, such a mechanism does not operate in a vacuum. It only functions within a proper environment, including the policy regime that allows for such interactions. All these will be extensively discussed later.

For the moment, suppose that for two developing economies, A and B, the catching up process has started with the same type of policy reform, which allows the process to take place at dates t_A and t_B, respectively, and $t_B > t_A$. Other things remain equal for these two economics.

The 'benchmark paths,' namely, the levels (in semilog scale) and growth rates of per capita real incomes of these two economies are then depicted in the upper and lower panels of Figure 1.2.4, aligned with each other. The relationship between the two latecomers is quite subtle and deserves careful consideration. This is done step by step.

By construction, the B-path is a diagonal shift of the A-path in the upper panel. The horizontal component of the shift represents the delay t_B - t_A, and the vertical shift corresponds to the growth over that delay by the leading economy, to which all followers in the catching up process relate. The two paths never cross. Thus, we have a cautionary tale to tell. Even though at t', and thereafter, the growth rate along the B-path always exceeds its counterpart along the A-path in the lower panel, yet in per capita real income terms, the B-path may never overtake the A-path. To be precise, both paths approach asymptotically the same dotted straight line (which is parallel to, but also uniformly lower than the leader's path). Thus the B-path approaches the A-path asymptotically, in that the ratio of per capita real income

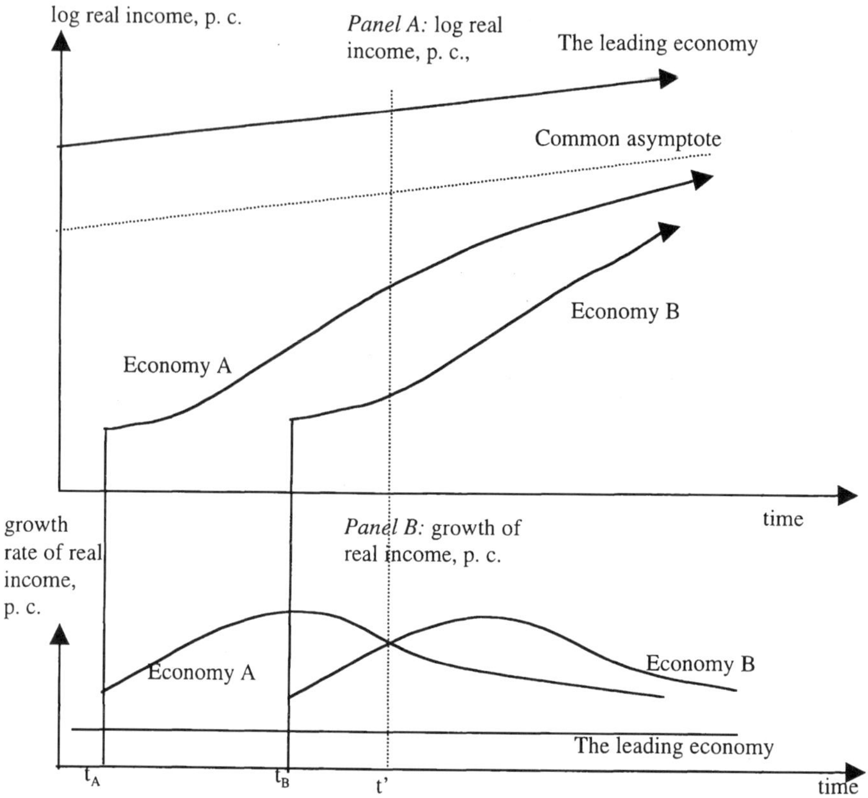

Figure 1.2.4 Catching up

incomes, B over A, will rise monotonically, ever closer to 1, but never exceeding it. Thus, one latecomer can fully catch up with another (in the ratio sense), but not with the leader. There is no overtaking, in either case. For developing economies with benchmark paths parallel to each other, they may be said to belong to the same 'convergence club,' in the literature on the convergence hypothesis. One may compare Barro and Sala-i-Martin (1995).

We hasten to add that the result, *one path is exactly such a diagonal translation of the other*, only holds true if the *same* spill-over mechanism for technology applies to both developing economies. If mechanisms differ, *one latecomer may overtake another latecomer, although neither one will ever overtake the leader. Both* the presence of economies falling behind *and* the taking over of some latecomers by others are inconsistent with the earlier version of the Convergence Hypothesis in Baumol (1986), but compatible with the 'benchmark model' introduced above.[12]

---

[12] When the function F may be economy-specific.

Two questions must be raised about the system (1.2.1)-(1.2.3). First, how well does the model agree with reality, and second, what are its methodological foundations?

Regarding the *empirical* question, Charts 1.2.1 and 1.2.2 display relative per capita real income v(t) for Japan and Argentina, based on the data from the Penn Table version 6.0.

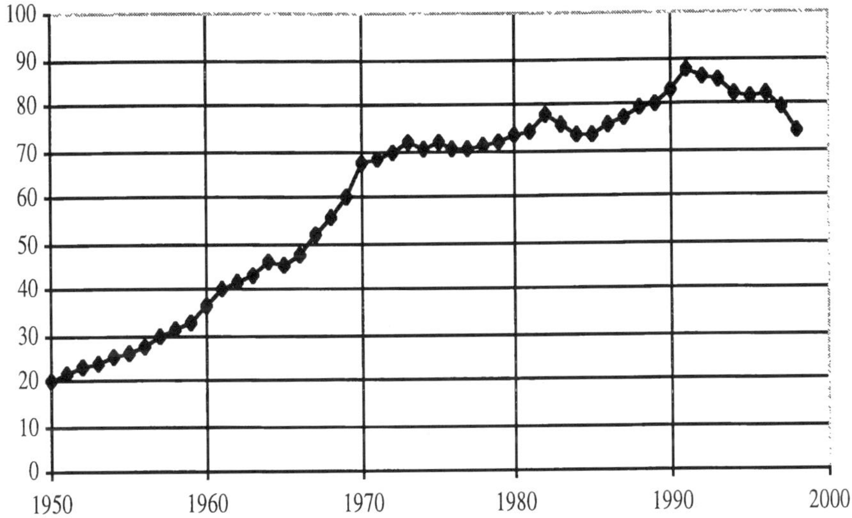

Chart 1.2.1 Repcri, Japan Source: PennTable 6.0

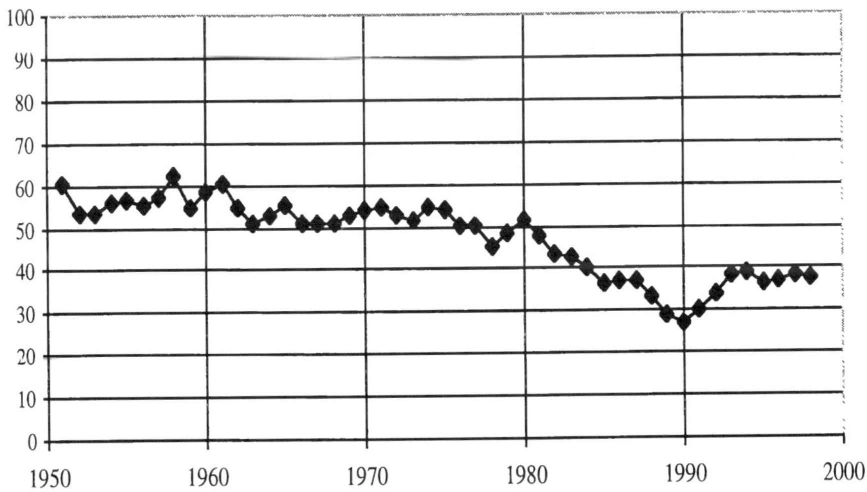

Chart 1.2.2 Repcri, Argentina Source: PennTable 6.0

For Japan, there is a clear catching up trend, but also a slowing down toward the end of the series, leaving the catching up incomplete. For Argentina, the trend of falling back is also unmistakable. It will be shown in Chart 2.1.2, next chapter, that in the spirit of the model here, Japan and Argentina must belong to different 'convergence clubs.' For quite some time, Japan managed to narrow the income gap between itself and the United States in terms of relative per capita real income. In contrast, at a higher initial figure of relative per capita real income, Argentina continued to lose ground relative to the U.S. This fact possibly reflects the dilemma facing a resource-based economy. Argentina must *either* accept a version of the 'Dutch Disease,' and allow its primary exports to keep wages at too high a level for the manufacturing industries to compete, *or* erect a protective trade wall, behind which its domestic industry may survive but will tend to weaken with respect to the rest of the world, lacking the incentive or the opportunity to keep up.

We must now return to the *methodological* matter. There are two ways to approach the issue, and both are analogous with neoclassical growth theory. The first is the utilitarian view. When Harrod and Domar studied the question of growth, they inherited from Keynes the assumption that the saving/income ratio is a constant, and the same hypothesis was adopted in Solow (1956). Keynes, in writing the General Theory, would claim his formulation descended from some mysterious Fundamental Psychological Law. Solow presumably justified its *use* by its *usefulness* in representing reality, just as he defended the aggregate production function. After all, the Keynes of General Theory was also the same Keynes of the Keynes-Ramsey Rule, who helped in the founding of the optimal growth theory, and Solow himself also joined Samuelson to generalize the Ramsey model to multiple goods.

Coming to the alternative approaches, note that when both technology and preference are loglinearized, as in Radner (1966), rational agents will invest a constant portion of the output. Thus, the simple descriptive device, with its exact, rigorous foundations, is also an approximation of reality. A similar antecedent comes from physics: the use of the Principle of Least Action does not mean physicists believe that Nature is lazy. Lau and Wan (1994) have anchored the system (1.2.1)-(1.2.3) on the social planner model. This provides an additional explanation of the phenomena of *the falling back by the poor* and *trend acceleration at the mid-income phase*: emulation being costly, the very poor society could not *and* would not learn fast.

Like a map leaving out details of secondary importance, so far we have outlined a theory as an idealization of reality.[13] As is the case in physical

---

[13] Thus, to contemplate gravity in the vacuum, Galileo first excluded the influence of the air he breathed. Of course, air drag had to be brought back later: gravity was studied then for the ballistics of a projectile.

science, this theory may be decomposed into various component hypotheses, each of which must be rejected or provisionally accepted on the strength of presently available evidence.

In this case, we can list below,

The five component hypotheses:

(a) The per capita real income of the leading economy reflects 'the best practice,' which progresses at its own pace;[14]

(a') That pace may be represented by a positive constant, $c > 0$, the growth rate of the per capita real income;

(b) The per capita real income of any other economy can be *usefully* written as the product of both the per capita real income of the leading economy and the value of the repcri of these two;

(b') The growth rate of the repcri, d logv/dt, may be again *usefully* approximated by the product of two terms, the first term g(v), represents 'the ability to learn' which is an *increasing*, *time-invariant* function of the repcri, v, and the second term stands for 'the opportunity to learn,' which increases (proportionately) with the difference between unity and the repcri, (1-v);

(b") ('Condition of proportionality') For concreteness, one imposes the requirement that g(v) is proportional to v.[15]

We then have:

(1.2.4) $$d \log v/dt = (4F^0)\, v\, (1 - v),$$

where the multiplicative factor is $4F^0 > 0$.

The postulation of proportionality is convenient, but not strictly necessary. Since this model is at most a first approximation to reality, we shall not relax that hypothesis, for the time being.

A Special Test of the Benchmark Model: The Record of East Asia

Note that hypotheses (a) and (b) together capture a version of the notion of innovation and imitation started by Schumpeter, applied at the economy level, while (b') dates back to the notion of 'technological backlog' in Gerschenkron (1952: 6):

---

[14] This approximates the notion of Kuznets (1982: 57), "at any given time, the worldwide, transnational stock of technology, sets a potential of full economic development – a level of per capita or per worker product."

[15] This is how Figure 1.2.1 is drawn. It is also analyzed in Appendix 1.2 below.

> *Industrialization always seemed the more promising the greater the backlog of technological innovations which the backward could take over from the advanced country.*

As the survey in Gomulka (1990) amply shows, the elements of such a theory were developed for events in Europe and the United States, well before the sustained, rapid growth of East Asia had caught the attention of economists.

Ironically, this catching up theory and the East Asian experience seem to be made for each other. On the one hand, the essence of the East Asian experience is best captured by the catching up theory, compared to all other theories.[16] On the other hand, among the recent histories of all regions of the world, East Asia seems to offer the clearest evidence supporting the catching up theory.[17] We shall next see why this is so.

In East Asia, four peoples have populated nine economies: Vietnamese in Vietnam, Japanese in Japan, Koreans in Korea, South and North, and Chinese in Macao, Singapore, Hong Kong, Taiwan and (Mainland) China. For Macao and North Korea, there was no policy change and thus there was no economic transition; the bursts of sustained rapid growth came forth in all the other seven after a sudden political shock.

Apparently, relative to the *change in policy environment*, political ideology, domestic market size, culture and ethnicity as well as the personality of leaders all *count little*. Thus, whatever the similarities and differences in location, history, culture, and so forth, in economic matters today, South Korea resembles Taiwan far more than it resembles North Korea.

Historically, the same Korean War that thrust Japan into re-industrialization to support the American war effort also re-oriented Hong Kong, which turned from serving the embargoed China as an entrèpôt, to supplying the rest of the world with light manufacture. The upheaval of 1960-61 switched South Korea from the confrontational diplomacy of Rhee to the export drive of Park. The 1958 reform marked Taiwan's sudden shift from warlike fervor to economic expansion under the *same* Chiang Kaishek. The separation from Malaysia in 1965 refocused the attention of Singapore from industrializing within a customs union to competing for foreign

---

[16] Germany's catching up with England was made famous by Veblen (1915). In that instance, technical innovation by Germans themselves may be argued to have been a major part of the story. For Taiwan or Singapore, the reliance of foreign technology certainly has been a more dominant feature of their success.

[17] In making up lost time, the East Asian economies of Japan, Korea and the PRC each registered surges of growth at rates never before seen in history. This was not quite the case for the U.S. or Germany during their industrialization period, presumably because they were never *that* backward initially, in relation to England, the technological leader at that time.

investment. The 1978 reform transformed China from mobilization under Mao's mass movements to the experimentalism of Deng. The 1985 reform started Vietnam's march from pragmatic isolation to accommodation with the West. Each of these socio-political changes shifts the F function in (1.2.2). As in music, there is a range of variations, but among them also lurks a common theme.

What makes the catching up theory operate with such vengeance in East Asia? To see this, one might borrow a leaf from medieval physics and extend the model. The effect of acceleration could be detected not when the lead ball was dropped near the ground level, but only when it was dropped from the height of '200 cubits' in Pisa.

A Variation of the Benchmark Theory: A Theory of *Artificial Ignorance*

To see *why East Asia appears 'miraculous,'* what we need is a slight extension of the basic catching up model. Above all, the essence of the catching up process is interaction – between an economy of the *informed* and an economy of the *uninformed*. The strength of the interaction depends on both the *capability*, what to learn with, v, and the *intention*, what may be learned, (1 - v).

The momentum for catching up is heightened when a labor force with a given level of literacy as well as discipline is 'artificially deprived' of information for production by a magnitude, Δ, until its sudden release due to a policy change. Thus, before that change, the *ability to learn* was not low. It assumed the particular value of v as expected. Yet due to an element of *arbitrary ignorance*, $\Delta > 0$ the initial ('virtual') *scope to learn* was kept artificially high, making it $1 - (v - \Delta) = (1 - v) + \Delta$. The factor of artificiality may be induced by warfare (as the case of Japan in World War II[18]), by policy, to avoid 'spiritual pollution' by some communist leadership, or by 'occupational distraction': serving the entrepôt trade in the case of Hong Kong, or the casino trade in the case of Macao. In the latter pair of European colonies, Hong Kong received the shock in the Korean War, but Macao faced no such challenge. It is usually said that, in economics, Nature does not perform experiments for mankind. Yet every rule has its exception. In East Asia, between the outbreak of the Korean War in 1950 and the Vietnamese Communist Party's decision for reform in 1985, a battery of

---

[18] See Saito (2000: 115).

nine experiments were conducted by Nature, to demonstrate the full power of the catching up process![19]

Moreover, in *two* ways the timing of East Asian industrialization differs from that of the European countries. First, with the advance of technology, the initial lead of the United States in high tech (say, over Korea) in the late 20th century was far more formidable than that of the British in engineering (say, over Germany) 100 or 150 years earlier. Compared with *then*, going it alone is much less feasible *now*. Second, in the former era, the British Imperial System monopolized world trade a good deal, but now American, Japanese and European businesses compete keenly against each other. Under an outward-oriented policy, the latecomers to industrialization have a better chance to prosper than in former times. That may explain the 'never look back' spirit in Asian reforms.

It is now time to conduct a number of,

General tests for consistency between hypotheses and observed reality

There are two types of 'reality checks,' namely,

I. Regarding the entire model, the facts are:

(α) The post-World War II experience of Japan fits all our four *regularities*,

(β) Experiences of the four Asian NIEs – Korea, Taiwan, Hong Kong and Singapore – are also consistent with the above-mentioned regularities.

(γ) The *widening gap* between the Soviet bloc and the OECD countries before 1989 suggests how much East Asian prosperity is due to the catching up mechanism, and not merely to the mobilization of inputs.

(δ) As we have just seen, the intensity of the East Asian pace in catching up can be explained by the *artificial ignorance* variation of the theory.

II. Regarding the component hypotheses, the facts are:

(α) During the initial expansion of trade and investment between East Asia and the U.S., the growth rate of per capita real income increases rapidly for the former but not for the latter [cf. component hypotheses (a) and (a')].

(β) In general, the East Asian economies have not surpassed the U.S. in per capita real income; ultimately, their rates of growth of per capita real income tend to decrease toward the U.S. rate [cf. component hypotheses (b) and (b')].

(γ) Economies enjoying sustained rapid growth are mostly the mid-income ones.

The words 'in general' and 'mostly' are inserted to take account of the fact that in terms of per capita real income, Singapore might exceed the

[19] Confucianism may perhaps matter in the presence of a literate and disciplined labor force.

United States, as does the United Arab Emirates, owing to the presence of 'hard core' poverty in the U.S., which is a large and diffuse society, while such poverty can be avoided in small states and those with oil wealth.

At a less formal level, economists arguing against the promotion of outward-oriented growth often claim that Japan and the NIEs succeeded because the world market was quite different at the beginning of their growth periods, and that their experiences would not be replicable now. However, apart from the temporary shocks of Crisis 1997, there is little evidence to support export pessimism.[20] Both the PRC and Thailand have enjoyed a decade-long prosperity, fueled by the expansion of manufactured exports. Their growth experience may be different from the experience of Korea and Taiwan, in one way or another, but neither faced export difficulty.

Referring now to Figure 1.2.4, lower panel, and assuming that Japan and Korea are represented as economies A and B respectively, the tapering off of the Japanese rate of growth, as time t approaches t', does not mean the passing of the Golden Age for manufactured export. To the contrary, the tried and true approach of the catching up process is now followed through by still another rising industrial power, Korea, which is experiencing its own phase of trend acceleration.

Test for the Usefulness of the Model — Isolating the Potent Element among the Trade Effects

The above analysis has one further interesting application. In principle, trade expansion may benefit all participants due to any or all of the following five effects:

- the *division of labor effect,* which reflects increased allocative efficiency;
- the *scale economy effect* in production, which is caused by trade creation;
- the *pro-competitive effect,* which results from reduced oligopolistic distortions;
- the *capital accumulation effect,* which means trading gains stimulate savings;
- the *transfer of technology effect*, which is a main focus here.

All these five effects are likely to be present in real life. Yet evidence also suggests that apparently, within the trade-development nexus, the most decisive factor is the last one, the spillover of the best practice spreading

[20] For a succinct clarification of the related issues, see Bhagwati (1998).

from the 'North' to the 'South.' This effect alone can have the following twin *testable implications*:

(i) (Across economies) North-South trade has raised appreciably the growth rate of the South, but not the North; and

(ii) (Over time) the increase in the Southern growth rate eventually tapers off.

The isolation of the most potent effects of trade is not just for intellectual curiosity, but is essential to the choice of policy regime for many developing economies.

The Limitations of the One-Good Models: On the Two 'Mega-events' of the 20th Century

We now hasten to place the benchmark model in perspective. At the turn of the millennium, one might speculate when posterity looks back, about what will be viewed as the two most important economic developments of the 20th century. We believe the top candidates will be:

A. The *rise and fall* of the centrally planned economies, and

B. The *acceleration and deceleration* of East Asia's efforts to catch up.

As our analysis suggests, we can all agree with Krugman (1994) that in the near term, neither Soviet Russia in the past, nor any East Asian economy at the present has yet posed any real threat to overtake the United States in per capita real income. The former utterly failed in catching up, while the latter can only achieve a partial success.

Nevertheless, there is a marked distinction between these two. As a first approximation to reality, our one-good analysis is *suggestive* of such a distinction, but fails to portray the matter in exact details. The decline in Russian real income per capita was not precipitated by any loss of technical efficiency. On the other hand, by its nature, *no* one-good model can depict the *creative destruction* dealt to the Trabant by the Volkswagen. That calls for a multi-good model, such as the one used by Clark (1993).

Nor is this the only limitation of the one-good model. At the heart of the catching up mechanism is the spillover of technology. *Contact* is the name of the game. Much of the contact takes place outside of academic exchanges and the dissemination of professional literature. It takes the form of the by-product of the movement of products (namely, *trade*) and productive factors (namely, *investment* and *migration*).

For the collection of solar power, the transmission of energy takes place through the circular flow of the working fluid. For the spillover of technology, the transmission of information takes place by exchanges of goods and services. There simply can be no representation of such exchanges in a one-good model.

Yet, as Koopmans (1957) explained, economic issues should best be analyzed with a sequence of models, rather than a model for all occasions. This serves as a natural introduction to the multi-good models of later chapters.

Recapitulation of Our First Approximation to Reality

We have presented a model with output per capita as the center of attention. The strength of this model lies in its simplicity. It highlights the following facts:

(a) Through the catching up approach, the latecomer can only partially close the gap with the leader, with no hope of overtaking the latter;

(b) Interaction with the leader and/or the others is essential for catching up; and

(c) The benchmark path marks a (dynamic) base line, with other factors causing systematic deviations from it.

The last point deserves some elaboration. Still another analogy may be helpful. It is well understood in pediatrics that the weekly rate of percentage weight gain by a child of 20 months is much slower than the rate of gain at 20 weeks, and both are much slower than at 20 days. That is just the nature of things. Yet in the American political debates of the late 1980s, the fact that the U.S. growth rate was lower than that of Korea was sometimes held as a sign of malaise. Few objections were raised by professional economists (or others) against such a specious comparison.

Similarly, the Japanese growth rate today has declined to a pace no higher than the other G7 countries (but not much lower either). Again, this decline has led some observers to believe that Japan is now an economic under-achiever. From what we just stated about the benchmark path, such an opinion also appears premature.

In principle, the insight gained from our model should remain intact in a multi-good version. Moreover, a fuller treatment must take account of *both* additional dynamic variables, each with its own 'law of motion,' *and* policy parameters, over which the society exercises its choice.

3. INSPECTION OF THE FOUNDATIONS OF THE BENCHMARK PATH MODEL

The benchmark path model may be a useful first approximation to reality, but what can be said about its foundations? Like much of the other research in economics (including the literature on catching up and convergence), this model is where *theoretical* reasoning is applied to *empirical* observations, hopefully to serve *policy* decisions. In econometric parlance, it is in the *reduced form*, and not a *structural relation*. The cogent questions are, (a) Can such a formulation be derived from some structural model, based on *theory*. Or, as in macroeconomics, does the model have some *micro-foundation*? (b) Can the *empirical* facts about capital formation and the changing 'labor input per capita' fit into such a theory? (c) How can *policy* (or the State) be brought back into the picture? In addition, one may also ask (d) What is the relationship between this theory and the literature of growth?

We now address these in turn.

The *Rational Pace* for Catching Up

To provide micro foundations for the catching up process, Lau and Wan (1994) set up a model of a developing economy where the representative agent maximizes the time integral of discounted utility. The rational pace for catching up is endogenously decided when learning is costly and haste means waste. Given the current income, the intertemporal trade-off is between (1) current consumption, hence current utility, and (2) *human capital formation,* which improves future income by speeding up the acquisition of foreign technology. It was established that, between a phase of *trend acceleration* and a phase of *growth slowing down*, the economy will have some 'high growth period,' and the relative per capita real income will approach asymptotically some proper fraction.

Physical Capital Formation

Although the causality of growth will be extensively discussed later in Chapter 4, a remark is in order about the relationship between the Lau and Wan model (hence the benchmark path) and various studies in the literature (such as DeLong and Summers, 1991; Kim and Lau, 1994; as well as Young, 1994 and 1995) which highlight the high investment in those East Asian economies enjoying high growth.[21] Empirically, there is much *complementarity* between physical and human capital formation, as was observed by Kim and Lau (1994). When heavy spending is made in physical capital, what is installed is usually not just tons after tons of steel plates but equipment with ever higher degree of complexity. Such equipment takes increasing levels of human capital to operate with any efficiency. Likewise,

[21] Lest the benchmark path model appear like a version of *Hamlet* without the Danish prince.

when increased human capital is brought to bear on production, new equipment is usually called for. Like the systems of power transmission and fuel ignition in an automobile, investment and the introduction of 'borrowed technology' are *both* indispensable parts of the virtuous circle in East Asia. In these economies, as Lucas (1988) observed, the process of catching up is accompanied by the continued introduction of *products never produced before in the economy.*[22] In upgrading the export mix from tungsten ores, then wigs, then to DRAMs (as Korea did), certainly *both* new skills *and* new equipment are needed.

The Factor of 'Labor Input Per Capita'

We now turn to the causal role of the changing 'labor input per capita,' pointed out in two well-known papers by Young (1994; 1995) as a significant cause for East Asian growth.[23] One can readily agree with his careful and meticulous calculations and still note that much of the increased East Asian labor supply is both endogenous, and induced by trade, just like physical capital formation.[24] Before the widespread use of electric appliances, women in most economies often quit jobs after marriage or childbirth. Everywhere, their marketable skill accumulated over periods far shorter than those of men. Naturally, when industrialization came, the initial comparative advantage of East Asian economies lay in goods produced by female workers, such as toys, plastic flowers, footwear, garments and the assembly of radios, TV sets and digital watches.[25]

Thus, much of the initial expansion of labor input per capita was due to the rise in female labor participation, sometimes working at home. Rising

[22] Strictly speaking, this can hardly be represented in a one-good model. Yet, this is another occasion confirming the view of Friedman (1953), that *descriptive accuracy* is not needed for *analytic relevance.*

[23] He apparently attributes such change to some autonomous demographic factors.

[24] For Taiwan, cash crop exports led to a rise in working days on the farm per hectare from 170 after World War II to 260 in the early 1960s (Ranis, 2002), while shoe export production even attracted aborigine villagers from offshore islands to Taiwanese cities (Shieh, 1992: 57).

[25] For illustration, consider three groups of industries that were important in Taiwan's export in 1975 (see Wan, 1978). The gender composition of their labor force was as follows:

Group of industries	Textile, garment and leather	Electric generators	Communication equipment
% female workers	70	63	72

working opportunities reduced the birth rate, and hence the dependence ratio, or increased the ratio of workers to total population.

Owing to the well-known quality-quantity trade-off in children, a drop in the birth rate comes with a rise in educational attainment for the next generation, as well as labor shortage for the labor-intensive industries. Both contributed to the exit of such industries and the upgrading of the industrial composition. It is true that much later, an aging population eventually causes the dependence ratio to rise again and the growth rate to taper off, as happened in Japan – but that comes long *after* the economy is fully developed.

Thus, outward-oriented development has both raised female employment opportunity, hence income, and reduced the birth rate, leaving households more income to save for capital formation as well. This lays the foundation for sustained growth. The proof of the pudding is that, regardless of the computed growth rate of total factor productivity,[26] the level of per capita income has ultimately risen to approach that of the developed economies, due to outward-oriented trade regimes. This is an outcome that would be welcomed with open arms from New Delhi, to Beijing, to Brasilia. History has shown us no better alternative.

Trade Regime as a Choice of the Policy Environment

In the last section, the function F(v) in equation (1.2.2) may be regarded as dependent also on some policy parameter, θ, and written as $F(v, \theta)$. As stated in the last section, the pride of place in the catching up model belongs to international interaction, which has multiple roles to play in reality. Each trade regime may be thought of as corresponding to one parameter value in some index set, say, Θ. For example, θ' may stand for import substitution, θ'' may denote export promotion, θ^0 may signify laissez faire, and so on. One may then proceed to specify how a policy change is going to shift the environment for technology transfer. In itself, the formalism is quite innocuous. It is the additional assumptions that matter. To be of practical use, detailed studies of specific policies will be discussed in a more disaggregated setting. We shall only use this formulation as a frame of reference to postulate the following two broad assumptions:

Assumption 3. For each parameter value θ, Assumptions 1 and 2 continue to hold.

Assumption 4. More international interaction means an upward shift of F for all values of v.

[26] To which we shall return later in Section 5.3.

Assumption 3 allows us to deduce the same four regularities as before under any policy. In conjunction with Assumption 4, one may conclude that by more active trade, an economy may secure a higher degree of technology acquisition and a higher value of v*, which means a more complete degree of catching up in the steady state. The analytical derivation is trivial and the interested reader may experiment with a multiplicative (or additive) scalar shift of the function F in Figure 1.2.1. Since the value $\underline{v}$ is also dependent upon the trade regime, in principle, the change of orientation in trade policy may reverse a 'widening gap' versus the advanced economies, to initiate the catching up process.

Much more important is to justify Assumption 4. To begin with, to *sustain* growth at a *rapid* tempo, the upgrading of the production mix should keep pace with the gains in production skill. It can hardly be constrained by the gradually shifting of the domestic consumption pattern. Instead, the transformation of the export mix often steps into the breach. The changing comparative advantage of Korea is instructive. The major Korean exports were minerals and seafood in the early 1960s, but oil tankers and computer chips by the late 1990s. To produce for the foreign market was essentially the key to success, not only for Korea but also for Singapore, Taiwan and Japan. Even for the PRC, with its billion-consumer market, trade remains crucial for similar reasons. Without trade, growth will prematurely grind to a halt against diminishing returns in production and demand, as happened in the former Soviets. It is trade that *lubricates* the onward charge.

On top of what has just been argued, technology spillover plays the lead in the catching up process in the late 20th century, with trade and foreign investment as the main channels for technology acquisition. Returning to the automobile analogy once more, for sustained rapid growth, international interaction is the *spark*, besides being just the *lubricant*. It is precisely for this reason that in the aftermath of 1989, policy-makers in Beijing continued their '*reform with an outward orientation*,' even though they knew full-well the political hazard to Asian Communism this orientation would pose after what had come to pass in Eastern Europe and the Soviet Union.

In fact, two more functions are served by international interaction. According to Lord Acton, power corrupts – and the monopolistic power of domestic producers sheltered by protective barriers is no exception. In the world arena, baptism under competitive fire is the surest means to cauterize corruption. More intrinsically, as we shall discuss next, in any decentralized system, capital formation feeds on both income and investment returns, and both are boosted by the international division of labor. Carrying further our driving analogy, international interaction is not only the *spark* and the *lubricant*, but also the *rust-proof agent,* as well as part of the *fuel.*

A methodological note is apropos here. Both trade and investment (in both human and physical capital) must be treated as endogenous in any realistic analysis. Thus, in an evaluation of policy regimes, one cannot simply ask whether trade *or* capital formation is the more potent. This is of course a simple variation of the well-known Lucas (1976) critique: higher levels of trade may induce more investment, and higher investment may allow for more trade. In short, growth accounting may be useful as part of the search for the source of growth. But one must keep the endogenous nature of such variables in mind.

Of course, everything has to be kept in balance, including even export promotion. Export may indeed bring forth social returns beyond the private returns, so that State promotion is justified *up to a degree*. But as we shall discuss in Chapter 6, and again in Chapter 7, when Korea coupled the export promotion program with directed credit, the unbridled thirst for investment funds led to the tapping of foreign savings, in loans denominated in foreign currency. Whenever temporary trade deficits develop, the economy is exposed to currency risks. The economy managed a narrow escape during the oil crisis. But finally the day of reckoning arrived during the Crisis of 1997.

The Paradigms of Growth Theories, 'Old' and 'New'

The pioneers of the 'old' growth theory, such as Harrod, Domar, Solow and Swan, came from the advanced industrial economies and focused on these economies in their initial writings. In particular, Solow (2000) refrained from applying his own pioneering work to development economics, in view of the complex forces at work there. The roots of the 'new' growth theory (or endogenous growth theory) go back to the study of Shell (1966) on the public good nature of knowledge. After Romer (1986) revived professional interest in information spillover, Lucas recognized the importance of spillovers to economic development and extended the application of growth theory to all economies, those developing as well as those developed.

Spillover involves two parties – the information donor and the recipient – and their asymmetric roles pose different types of problems for policy. It is generally taken for granted that developing economies will benefit from information spillover, as East Asia is seen to have done, and most of the attention of the 'new' growth theorists is devoted to the question of Shell and Romer: how to induce the donation of information, in spite of the benefits to the recipient and the relative lack of benefits to the donor. Relatively few studies are focused on the recipients. Yet for developing economies, attaining benefits from information spillover is hardly an easy task. How else can one explain that so few developing economies have enjoyed sustained, rapid growth? As Japanese economists have observed, it is especially difficult to effectively utilize spillover to launch new industries.[27]

As a complement to the growth literature, this volume is aimed at the question of how developing economies can take advantage of information and technology spillover to initiate their own catching up process. The key seems to be keeping the beneficial spillover coming by designing a win-win game.[28] A related strand in the literature is the convergence studies by Barro and Sala-i-Martin (1995), both among the different economies in the world and among the different regions of a single economy. Our interest is on the former case.

Policy Assessment

Having discussed how policy regimes enter into the catching up process, and how growth theory relates to technology spillover, we now close the circle and comment upon the use of growth accounting in evaluating the policy regime for a development state. Overall, the use of (growth) theoretic analysis and econometrics in economic development is certainly a welcome trend, bringing increasingly powerful tools to bear on policy issues. However, this still leaves the crucial task of drawing suitable policy implications from such exercises. As in health care, the development of powerful medicine is a complement to, rather than a substitute for, a physician who makes prescriptions based on clinical judgments. Some practical examples will demonstrate the point regarding the application of both theoretical and econometric methods to development.

It is the nature of theoretic research to identify a particular effect or mechanism. Its result is all the more elegant if it goes against common expectations. Simplifying assumptions are utilized so that the single cause effect can emerge with the greatest clarity. Nonetheless, fine theorists are rightfully cautious in translating their findings directly to policy proposals: some of the simplifying assumptions may not hold in real life. For example, on the issue of trade and learning – a topic to be extensively discussed below – Young (1991) reached one conclusion in a two-country model, then immediately pointed out that *an opposite outcome may obtain if the world contains three or more countries*.

In econometric studies, a research project is usually undertaken according to some model specification, provided there is enough data to

---

[27] See Itoh et al. (1991) and Miyajima et al. (1999).

[28] An example is explored in Van and Wan (1999), a micro-economic complement of Findlay (1978).

draw conclusions that are significant by some accepted statistical criterion. This often means the omission of all cross effect terms, including complementarity among various factors, to save the degree of freedom. The Lucas critique is rarely given the attention it deserves. An example of this is the application of 'growth accounting' we have just mentioned (and which will be elaborated in Chapter 5 below): capital formation is pitted against trade or some other factor, even though in any micro-based model, investment is an endogenous decision, influenced in part by trade and other factors.

In contrast, policy analysis is frequently the ultimate goal of the development economist. When one is making decisions in the real world, one does not have the luxury to pick and choose which issue to ignore, or which complication to assume away, just because the data necessary to reach an unambiguous conclusion is lacking.

For concreteness, consider once more the simultaneous growth of trade and per capita output in the case of Korea under President Park. Concomitant with its own human capital formation, Korea reinvented itself in less than 20 years. Take for example a wig-producing firm that transformed itself into an exporter of computer peripherals.[29] In the absence of increased trade, one can hardly expect that Korean households would be voracious consumers of wigs early on, only to metamorphose into eager collectors of computer peripherals within a single generation. Nor, without trade, could the Korean urban labor market accommodate so readily those rural females seeking city jobs. Had the State viewed trade with less enthusiasm, there would have been less income and less capital formation, quite aside from the effects of trade on demography as well as the technology spillover. For anyone doubtful of the potency of trade, it is enough to see what lack of trade did to a *Korean* economy: how the *same* planned economy of *North* Korea (or, for that matter, the same *market* economy of Finland) fared before and after the implosion of the Soviet Union, its primary trading partner.[30]

Thus, in the market economy of South Korea, where employment and savings were set by decentralized decisions, *export promotion* under President Park in one stroke caused (a) a higher rate of labor participation,

---

[29] See, for example, the change in product mix of a representative firm, the Handok Company, reported by Kim and Leipziger (1993): 95% in wigs in 1971 and 51% in computer related goods in 1985.

[30] The *value* of North Korean output probably declined with that of the Soviet Union, at its ultimate stage of existence. But the absolute decline of North Korean output seems to coincide with the virtual cessation of its Russian trade. The cause of the Finnish crisis is not certain, but the long and deep unemployment spell there (up to 20% for a time and lasting half dozen years) did coincide with the decline of the Soviet trade. See Wan (1998).

(b) a higher ratio of capital per worker, and (c) some gain in productivity. These mutually reinforcing advances were realized at more or less the same historical time, under a single change in policy regime. The Korean promotion of automobile export is a well-recorded and most instructive case. Guided by Park's 'Heavy Chemical Industry Drive' in the 1970s, Hyundai made heavy investments in order to *export* cars *in anticipation* of benefits from learning-by-doing. The plan was to meet the U.S. exhaust standard and to lose up to $1,000 per exported car as a starter, but eventually no loss was suffered.[31] The critical points are then:

1) The *expected* productivity gain had to come from *exporting* to the U.S. market ("Hyundai knew that unless it could enter the U. S. market ... it would have difficulty becoming ... efficient"[32]);
2) The *expectation was rational* since the gamble paid off even earlier than expected;
3) In preparation for export, massive physical investment was made in the 1970s *well in advance* of the entry into the U. S. market in 1986.[33]

In assessing the roles of trade, investment and productivity gain as causes of growth, the conclusions we reach are potentially important to the future of billions of the poorest people in the world. It is reasonable to hope that researchers should make explicit here how we should address the well-known argument of the Lucas critique. The Korean car industry seems to be a good case to start.[34]

What cannot easily be known is, given all the increasing returns, indivisibilities and so on, whether there exists any alternative policy by which one can secure mutually consistent advances that add up to the same (or higher) degree of growth of per capita income. In this case, again we can look for lessons from the actual Korean experience. To assess such questions related to the Heavy Chemical Industry Drive, it has been said that it needs, at the very least, a comprehensive simulation study – a project regarded as impossible to do well by Stern et al. (1995).

We do not claim that the policy option taken by President Park was superior to all alternatives. In fact, Dr. J. H. Yoo (1990) has argued that Taiwan did not do worse by selecting an outward-oriented policy of a somewhat different variety. But that alternative policy is not the creature of

[31] See pp.160-163 in Stern et al., 1995.

[32] Stern et al., 1995: 161.

[33] More specifically, much of the investment in the 1970s was made for productivity gain in the 1980s. A straightforward application of growth accounting will underestimate the Korean total factor productivity in the 1970s.

[34] See related issues in Van and Wan (1997).

speculation from academia. It is at least feasible, since it was practiced contemporaneously somewhere else. These matters will be taken up later.

Relationship with the Rest of the Volume

What we have presented so far is the general context for the process of catching up. By acquiring technical information from abroad, this process can improve the level of per capita income and narrow the 'North-South technology gap.'

Strictly speaking, the essence of the benchmark path is more qualitative than quantitative. The path experienced by Korea will not be an exact replay of what happened in Japan. What will happen in Thailand will not be merely a scaled-up version of the events in Korea or Taiwan. Like trees of the same species, the individual specimens may differ from one another in their structures of roots and branches, yet they remain sufficiently similar to be recognized as a species.

We shall deal with various questions related to the catching up process, using whatever type of analysis best suits the problem on hand: first theoretically in **Part 1**, issue by issue, then empirically in **Part 2**, economy by economy.

Overall, our inquiry is motivated by the actual experiences of selected economies in East Asia over the period from 1960 to the mid-1990s. Our choice is decided by two considerations:

(a) The *economies* on which we focus all have a successful track record for catching up. By the middle 1990s, each had either reached a par with the G7 economies in real per capita income, or was fast approaching this benchmark.[35]

(b) The *period* most interesting to us, in these economies, is their take-off phase (which started from the 1950s or 1960s). Their detailed evolution at that point in time, rather than their continued success now, probably holds more relevant insight for the less developed economies today.

Of course, one must still face the problem of replicability: are East Asian events mainly the consequences of East Asian special conditions? If that is the case, then their experience may be largely irrelevant elsewhere.

---

[35] The levels of per capita real income for some selected countries are as follows:

G 7	Canada	France	Germany	Italy	Japan	U. K.	U. S.
1997	21,750	22, 210	21,170	20,100	24,410	20,710	29,180
NIEs	Hong Kong	Korea	Singapore				
1997	24, 350	13,430	20, 230				

Source: *World Bank Atlas, 1999.*

This question is taken up in the next chapter. In order to keep a sharp focus on the catching up process, we shall leave out many other pressing issues in developing economies and interesting results in endogenous growth theory.[36]

[36] After all, Basu (1997), Ray (1998) and Aghion and Howitt (1998) have done a fine job in these areas.

APPENDIX 1.1 SOME STATISTICAL DESCRIPTION

Does our theory approximate reality? Having introduced the views of economists such as Lucas and Gomulka, we present below some statistical data for readers to make up their own minds.

For cross-economy comparison, we use the data from the World Development Index, which is released annually. Over the 24 consecutive years from 1975 to 1998, 110 economies have uninterrupted series of real per capita GDP.[37] To compute the repcri, the relative per capita real GDP, we must select an advanced economy as reference. The highest per capita real GDP for each of these 24 years comes from just 4 economies. Among these 4, it happens that the United States is the only one that has ranked among the top 4 places in all these 24 years. [38] Thus, in computing the relative per capita real GDP, there are grounds to state the level of all other economies as a fraction of the U.S. figure.

To provide a simple, numerical measure of how most of these economies have performed, we use the concept of income gap, $g_{it} = 1 - v_{it}$, for economy i at time t. To avoid the technicality in dealing with negative values of g_{it}, we shall exclude for now Switzerland, Luxembourg and the United Arab Emirates. Next, we plot the logarithmic value of the income gap g_{it} against time for the 106 economies, and the slope of this semilog time path gives the relative rate of gap reduction (or widening). Each least square trendline for such time paths yields, for an economy, a slope coefficient and an intercept. The former indicates the pace of proportional gap reduction (or widening) over the 24 years and the latter indicates the size of the average income gap. Charts A1.1.1a and A1.1.1b summarize data in Table A1.1.1 showing that (a) out of the 106 economies, only 42 have reduced the income gap, but (b) these include all the East Asian economies in the 106. In addition, (c) East Asian economies share a pattern with certain economies around Europe, such as Israel, Cyprus, Malta, Spain, Portugal, Ireland and Iceland. So in spite of the differences in history, culture, etc., some economic principle seems to be involved.

Next, Charts A1.1.2 is a scatter diagram which relates the slope coefficient to the constant term for these 106 economies. The relationship is none too obvious until we add trend lines to it. The quadratic trend line reveals what Lucas has remarked. The shrinking of the gap is most pronounced at the mid-income level. (See Problem XIV, p. 358, for more on Argentina.)

---

[37] On the basis of purchasing power parity (PPP).

[38] The other three are Switzerland, Luxembourg and the United Arab Emirates.

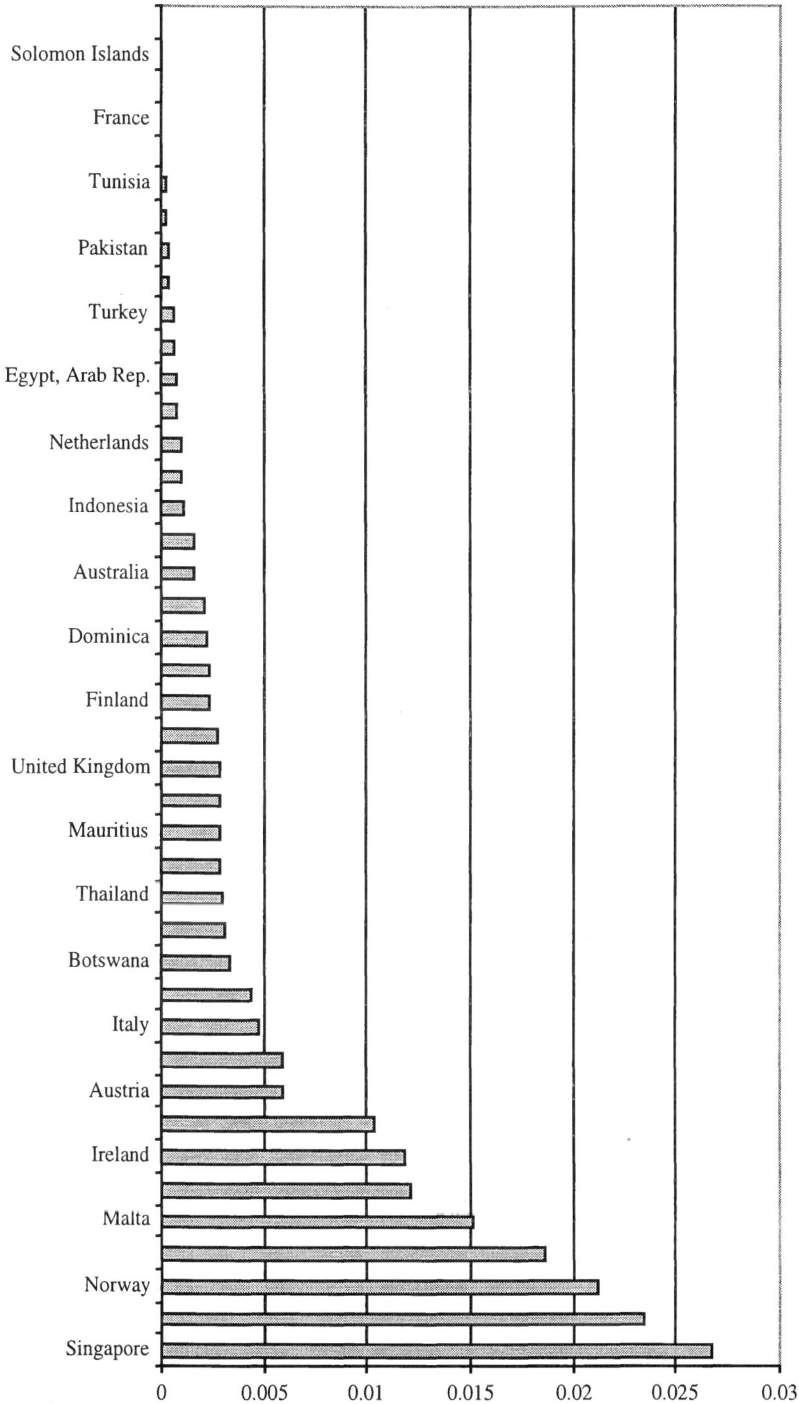

Chart A.1.1.1a Forty-two economies with shrinking gaps

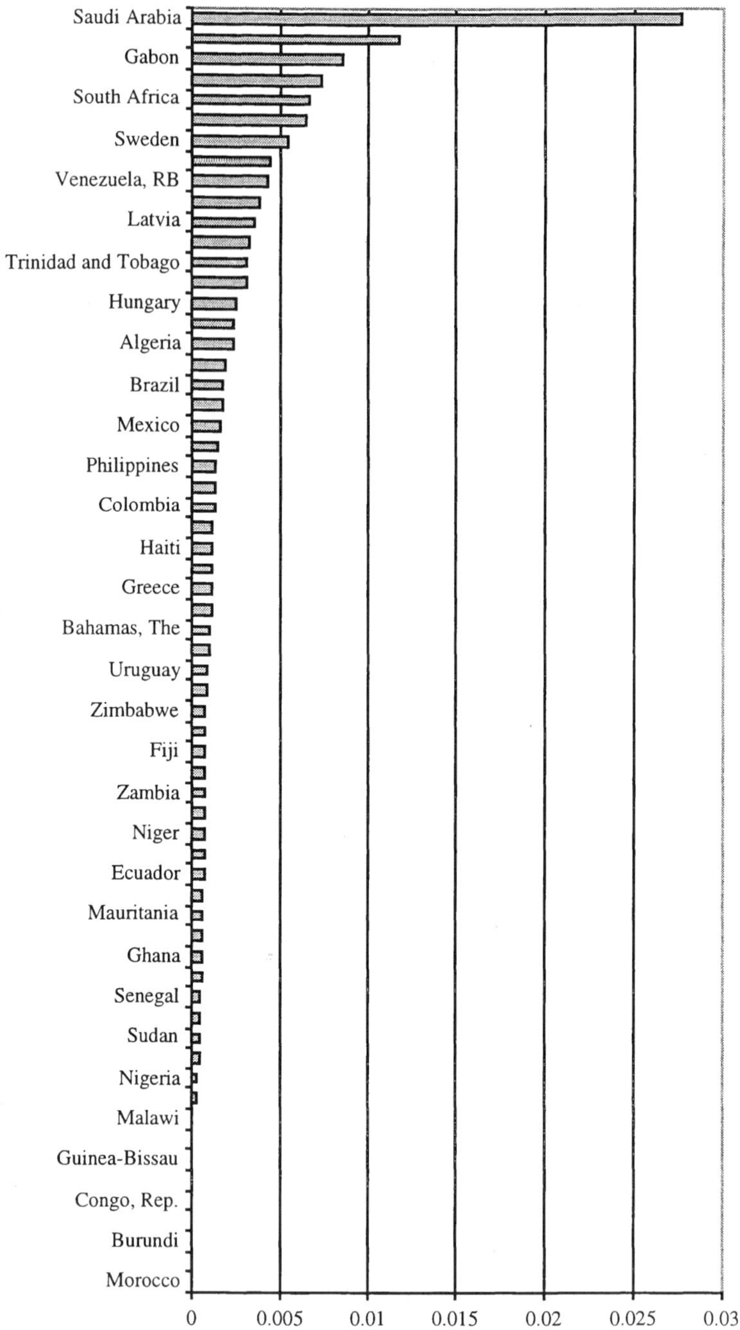

Chart A.1.1.1b Sixty-three economies with widening gaps

Table A1.1.1 Average rates of change of income gap, 1975-98

Economy	Slope	Gap	Economy	Slope	Gap
Singapore	-0.0267	reducing	Nigeria	0.0003	widening
Hong Kong, China	-0.0234	reducing	Papua New Guinea	0.0004	widening
Norway	-0.0212	reducing	Sudan	0.0004	widening
Japan	-0.0187	reducing	Gambia, The	0.0005	widening
Malta	-0.0151	reducing	Senegal	0.0005	widening
Cyprus	-0.0121	reducing	Cameroon	0.0006	widening
Ireland	-0.0119	reducing	Ghana	0.0006	widening
Korea, Rep.	-0.0103	reducing	Madagascar	0.0006	widening
Austria	-0.0059	reducing	Mauritania	0.0006	widening
Denmark	-0.0059	reducing	Sierra Leone	0.0006	widening
Italy	-0.0048	reducing	Ecuador	0.0007	widening
Portugal	-0.0044	reducing	Honduras	0.0007	widening
Botswana	-0.0034	reducing	Niger	0.0007	widening
Malaysia	-0.0031	reducing	Paraguay	0.0007	widening
Thailand	-0.003	reducing	Zambia	0.0007	widening
Belgium	-0.0029	reducing	Central African Republic	0.0008	widening
Mauritius	-0.0029	reducing	Fiji	0.0008	widening
Seychelles	-0.0029	reducing	Syrian Arab Republic	0.0008	widening
United Kingdom	-0.0029	reducing	Zimbabwe	0.0008	widening
Chile	-0.0028	reducing	Togo	0.0009	widening
Finland	-0.0024	reducing	Uruguay	0.0009	widening
Israel	-0.0024	reducing	Panama	0.001	widening
Dominica	-0.0023	reducing	Bahamas, The	0.0011	widening
Spain	-0.0021	reducing	Costa Rica	0.0012	widening
Australia	-0.0017	reducing	Greece	0.0012	widening
China	-0.0016	reducing	Guatemala	0.0012	widening
Indonesia	-0.0011	reducing	Haiti	0.0012	widening
Iceland	-0.001	reducing	Jamaica	0.0012	widening
Netherlands	-0.001	reducing	Colombia	0.0013	widening
Belize	-0.0007	reducing	Cote d'Ivoire	0.0013	widening
Egypt, Arab Rep.	-0.0007	reducing	Philippines	0.0013	widening
Sri Lanka	-0.0006	reducing	Guyana	0.0015	widening
Turkey	-0.0006	reducing	Mexico	0.0016	widening
India	-0.0004	reducing	El Salvador	0.0017	widening
Pakistan	-0.0004	reducing	Brazil	0.0018	widening
Swaziland	-0.0003	reducing	Congo, Dem. Rep.	0.0019	widening
Tunisia	-0.0002	reducing	Algeria	0.0023	widening
Bangladesh	-0.0001	reducing	Peru	0.0023	widening
France	-0.0001	reducing	Hungary	0.0025	widening
Lesotho	-0.0001	reducing	Nicaragua	0.0031	widening
Solomon Islands	-1.00E-04	reducing	Trinidad and Tobago	0.0031	widening
Nepal	-1.00E-05	reducing	Romania	0.0032	widening
Burkina Faso	9.00E-05	widening	Latvia	0.0036	widening
Morocco	0.0001	widening	Iran, Islamic Rep.	0.0038	widening
Benin	0.0002	widening	Venezuela, RB	0.0042	widening
Burundi	0.0002	widening	Argentina	0.0044	widening
Chad	0.0002	widening	Sweden	0.0054	widening
Congo, Rep.	0.0002	widening	Canada	0.0065	widening
Dominican Rep.	0.0002	widening	South Africa	0.0066	widening
Guinea-Bissau	0.0002	widening	New Zealand	0.0074	widening
Kenya	0.0002	widening	Gabon	0.0085	widening
Malawi	0.0002	widening	Georgia	0.0117	widening
Mali	0.0003	widening	Saudi Arabia	0.0276	widening

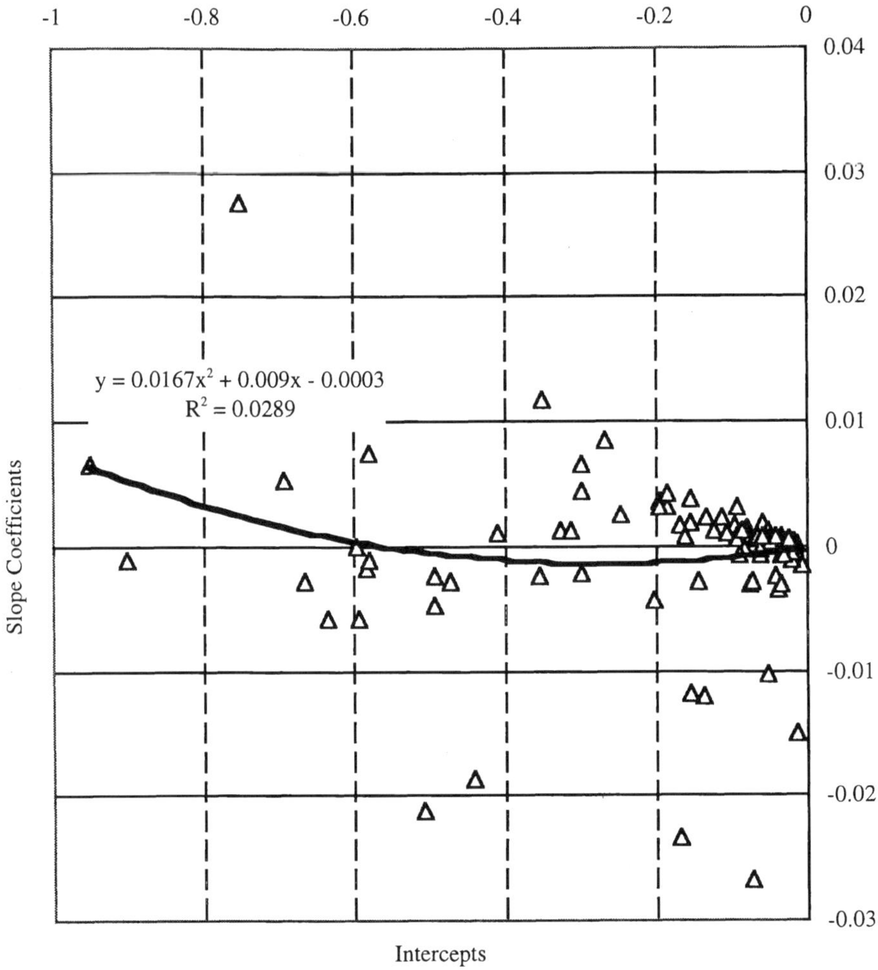

Chart A1.1.2 Least square trend for catching up, 106 economies

The above discussion follows the axle-and-spokes worldview inspired by Gerschenkron. The growth in the rest of the world depends crucially on economic interaction with the technological leaders. The latter must be a single economy to compute the country-specific repcri, and America is the convenient proxy. For a cross-economy comparison over a period of 24 years, the average rate of change of the income gap gives a convenient scalar measure, even if its computation has set aside economy-specific factors, like the short growth season of the Finnish Arctic agriculture or the deep water of the Port of Singapore at the choke point of the Malacca Strait.

The scatter diagram reveals the subtle truth in the observations of Lucas. A cross-checking with the tabulated data also highlights East Asian growth. Of all the eight economies with a slope coefficient less than -.01, four

(Singapore, Hong Kong, Japan and Korea) are the East Asian examples of Lucas (1988).[39] Their similarity with Malta, Cyprus and Ireland further indicates that the economics of spillover, rather than any Confucian ethos, is more relevant here.

To get longitudinal information, one would like to have longer statistical series. For this one can use the additional information from the Penn World Table 5.6. Here, we shall focus on the three miracles after World War II: the (West) German, the Japanese and the Korean. Rather than being distracted by the fluctuations of the annual data, we shall simply take the data of the decennial years. This yields Chart A1.1.3 below.

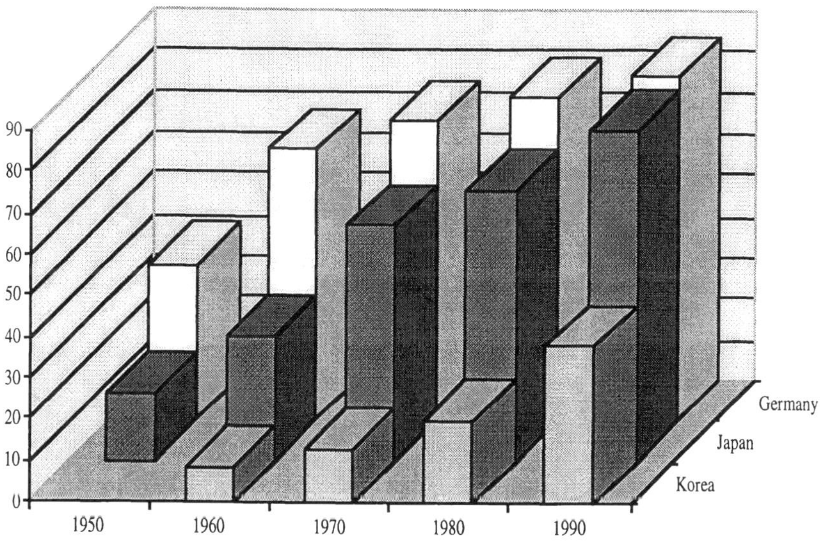

Chart A1.1.3 The three miracle economies

Clearly, one can see in the case of Japan, there is both a phase of accelerated catching up, but also a phase of tapering off. In comparison, one can clearly see the similar patterns of the other two cases, even though the German case happened earlier, beginning with the Marshall Plan and the Korean case took off later, after the recovery from the Korean War.

One might desire some reassurance that the use of two data sources (Penn Table and World Development Index) and the selection of only the decennial years have not introduced misleading artifacts. For this purpose, we provide below the Japanese data in Chart A1.1.4. Suffice to say, both the splicing and the selection have not distorted the over-all pattern.

---

[39] In contrast to Hong Kong, Taiwan's absence is a purely political artifact.

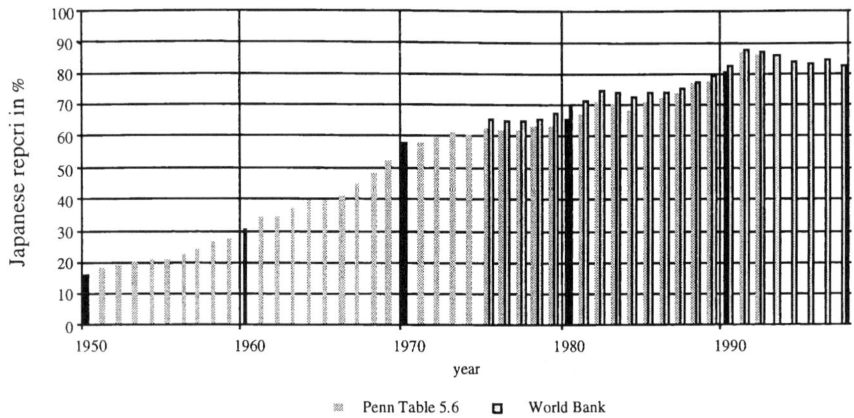

Chart A1.1.4 Are the decennial years representative?

APPENDIX 1.2 THE IMPLICATIONS OF TREND ACCELERATION

Note that (1.2.4) differs slightly from the usual formula associated with the Gompertz type of the logistic curve and adopted by economists like Mansfield.[40] The reason that we choose this form is that the growth rate of the repcri has the analytic expression of d logv/dt and not dv/dt. The Gompertz formula implies:

$$d \log v/dt = \Gamma (1 - v), \text{ for some constant } \Gamma > 0.$$

This implies the growth rate of the latecomer declines throughout time. But that contradicts the phenomenon of 'trend acceleration,' observed first for Japan by Ohkawa[41] and then for all the four NIEs (See Lucas, 1988).

(1.2.4) is equivalent to:

$$dv/dt = v\,[\Gamma v\,(1 - v) - c].$$

By partial fraction expansion and the interchange of dependent and independent variables, this form is said to be 'solvable by quadrature,' though without a closed form for v in terms of t. Choosing the unit for time, we simplify by equating Γ to unity, hence suppressing it, and get:

$$dt = -\,dv/[v(v - \underline{v})(v - v^*)] \qquad \text{(cf. Figure 1.2.1)}$$

$$= \{[A/v] + [B/(v - \underline{v})] + [C/(v^* - v)]\}\,dv$$

---

[40] See for example, Mansfield et al. (1977).

[41] In Ohkawa and Rosovsky (1973).

$$= A \text{ dlog } v + B \text{ dlog } (v - \underline{v}) - C \text{ dlog } (v^* - v)$$

$$= \text{dlog } [\, v^A (v - \underline{v})^B (v^* - v)^{-C} \,]$$

$$= d\Psi(v)$$

where by *completing squares,*

$\underline{v} = (1/2) - m$ and $v^* = (1/2) + m$ are the roots for: $(v)(v-1) + c = 0$, with $m = [(1/4) - c]^{1/2}$.

By partial fraction expansion,

$A/v + B/(v - \underline{v}) + C/(v^* - v) = -1/v(v - \underline{v})(v - v^*)$.

Clearing the fraction and setting in turn, $v = 0$, $\underline{v}$, and v^*, then *the method of undetermined coefficients* yields,

$A = -1/c$, $B = 1/m(1 - 2m) > 0$, $C = 1/m(1 + 2m) > 0$
(by equating coefficients)

and,

$m = [(1/4) - c]^{1/2}$, $0 < m < 1/2$.

For concreteness, consider the following:

A Numerical Example.

If each *decade,* American real income grows at $c = 9/100$, we have:

$m = 2/5$, $\underline{v} = 1/10$, $v^* = 9/10$, $A = -100/9$, $B = 25/2$, $C = 25/18$.

so that,

$$\Psi(v) = -(100/9) \log v + (25/2) \log [v - (1/10)] - (25/18) \log [(9/10) - v].$$

Thus, if in 2000, the real per capita income of Cyprus was 45% ($v = .45$) of the United States, and one would like to know how long it would take from then for the value of relative per capita income to rise to 60% ($v = .6$), then the above formula yields:

$$T - 2000 = 10[\Psi(.6) - \Psi(.45)],$$

or, $T = 2000 + 10[1.36 - 0.57] \approx 2008$, or, $v(2008) \approx .60$.

We next plot the $\Psi(v)$ function below (Figure A1.2.1) as indicative of the time requirement for a particular degree of catching up, measured in terms of v.

Two items of qualitative information are present. First, by itself, the catching up process tends to be incomplete. Insofar as this example is concerned, at no time in the future can the value of v reach a level of .92, say, beyond the vertical asymptote at $v = v^* = .9$ (not drawn). Second, trend acceleration characterizes the early phase of the catching up process. Until the final slowing down of growth, less and less time will be needed to raise the value of v for each additional 10%.

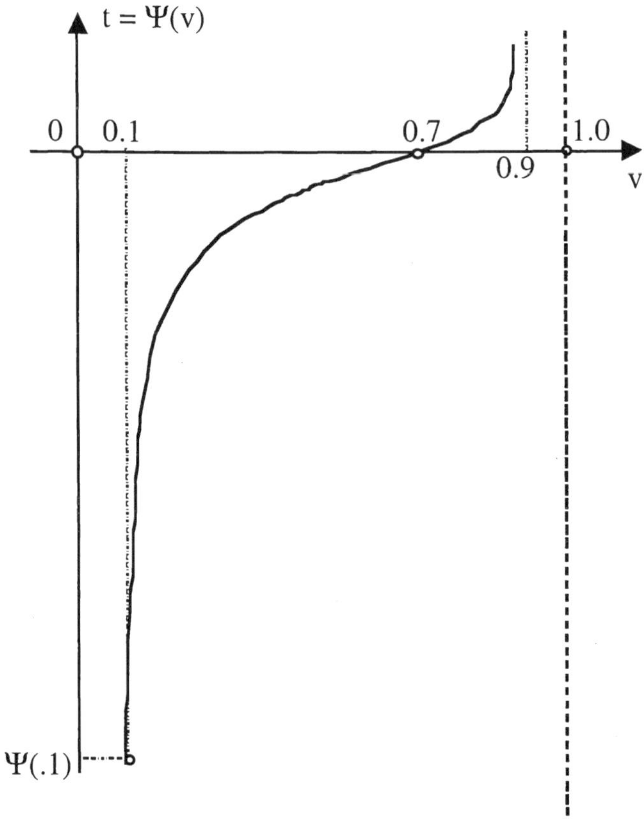

Figure A1.2.1 The numerical solution of Ψ

We next transpose and rotate the graph in Figure A1.2.1 to obtain, in Figure A1.2.2, the theoretical time path for the repcri of a latecomer economy, such as Japan.

How close do these properties correspond to reality?

In PennTable 6.0, the value of repcri is given as the y series. Taking the Japanese data for 1950-1998, and computing the growth rate for repcri, we obtain a scatter diagram, together with a quadratic trend, as shown in Chart A1.2.1. There is much noise to be sure, showing that the growth rate of Japan over half a century is actually influenced by many more factors than the catching up mechanism alone. However, three qualitative facts stand out.

First, initially, as the value of repcri increases, so does its growth rate until it reaches a peak. This is the phenomenon of 'trend acceleration.' Next, growth of repcri tapers off. Finally it reaches a steady state, falling short of a fully catching up. The quadratic trend is concave, bearing resemblance to Figure 1.2.1.

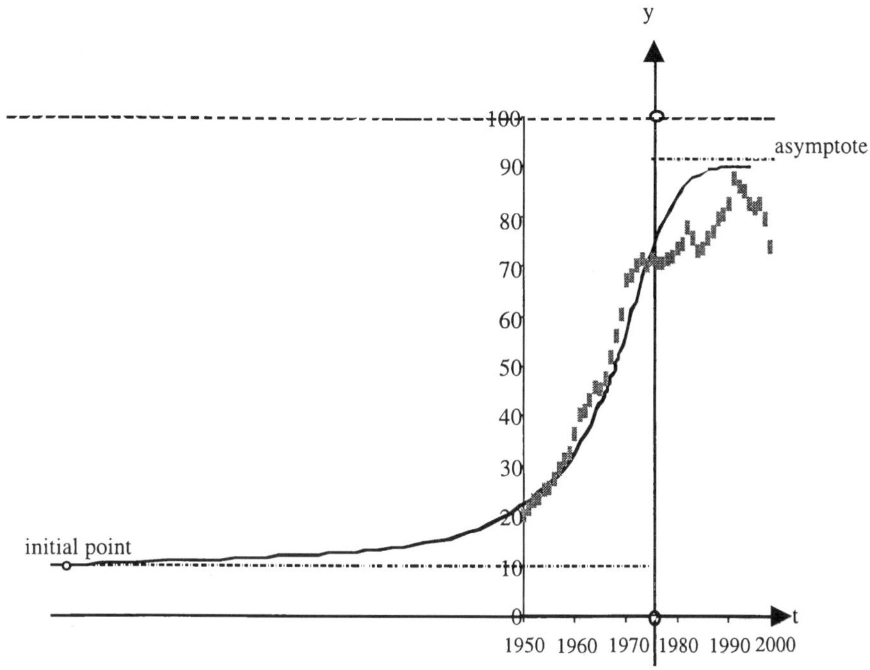

Figure A1.2.2 Repcri of a latecomer economy (Japanese data super-imposed)

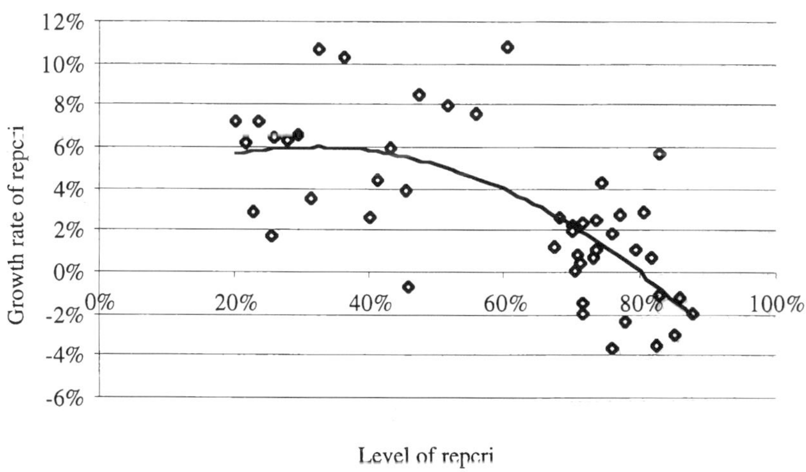

Chart A1.2.1 Scatter diagram for Japan

Our data does not cover the pre-World War II period. In view of the fact that the overall annual rate of Japanese growth since the Meiji Restoration was about 3% (See Saito, 2000, for example), there would be a better fit if such data were included.

Two reasons may explain why the fit is often imperfect. In the first place, the lead of the technological leader may vary over time. Apparently, the micro-electronic revolution has improved the U.S. lead during the last decade, and has also accelerated the catching up process of those economies serving as major suppliers for the U.S. electronics industry, such as the four Newly Industrialized Economies, namely, Hong Kong, Korea, Singapore and Taiwan – especially the latter three.

In the second place, it is well known that inside a national economy, urban regions often enjoy higher income than rural regions. See Barro and Sala-i-Martin (1995). A small economy undergoing rapid urbanization would grow faster for that reason, and may reach a steady state with a 'negative gap' from a technological leader, like the U.S,, that happens to be less urbanized.

CHAPTER SUMMARY

- ♦ Two major contemporary trends:
  - The continuous advance in transportation and communication
  - The accelerated introduction of new goods and services
- ♦ Some important characteristics of the current international political economy:
  - The present technological leader is the U.S.
  - A sizable portion of the American public benefits from low cost imports
  - Colonial powers no longer control natural resources
  - There is considerable competition in the world market
- ♦ Two mega-events in the 20th century:
  - The rise and then fall of planned economies
  - The acceleration and then deceleration of East Asian growth
- ♦ The unique promise at the turn of the millennium:
  - The East Asian events suggest that for all developing economies, an unprecedented pace of growth is possible; the 'fully developed' status is within reach
- ♦ The benchmark path for growth implies:
  - Initially, a phase of growth acceleration,
  - Followed by a period of sustained rapid growth,
  - Continued with a phase of growth deceleration,
  - Ending in a partial catching up with the leader.
- ♦ The role of international interactions through trade and investment is:
  - To acquire technology and information for production
  - To allow for the upgrading of the product-mix as skill accumulates
- ♦ The role of capital formation and the changed labor input per capita is:
  - To allow for the catching up process to go on smoothly
- ♦ The role of state policy is:
  - To provide the indispensable environment for growth

QUESTIONS AND EXERCISES

1. The manufactured exports of developing economies find easy acceptance in the U.S., but much less so in Europe and Japan. It is suggested that this may have something to do with both American party politics and American family structure. Discuss.

2. In the aftermath of the first oil crisis, the oil-producing economies quickly accumulated wealth. Yet, today, on the average, their level of per capita income has been overtaken by the East Asian NIEs. The latter economies have no natural resources of any significance, and their initial comparative advantage was in the industrial products of their cheap labor. Is there any lesson in this episode?

3. Enumerate the various ways trade may enhance growth. Now suppose that, in those economies enjoying sustained rapid growth, rates of growth are mainly influenced by trade. The fact that *their phase of 'trend acceleration' is invariably followed by a phase of 'trend deceleration'* seems to suggest that some effects of trade may be more important than others. Explain.

4. During the 1950s both Korea and Taiwan have received some foreign aid from the U.S. Both eventually became showcases of development. Although the dollar amounts involved were quite modest by today's standards, to some observers, such assistance was of decisive importance to the subsequent prosperity of these two economies. Their critics would dispute such claims and point out that for other economies – like the Philippines – the effect is none too dramatic. Comment on the merits of these opposing views by means of Figure 1.2.1, the phase diagram of the catching up model.

5. Lau and Wan (1994) have considered the general specification:

   $$dv/dt = G\, v^h (1 - v)$$

   which includes both (1.2.4) and the original Mansfield formula as special cases (specifically, for h = 2 and 1 respectively). Find the range of values for h that is consistent with the phenomenon of 'trend acceleration.'

6. Overheard: "(1.2.4) fails to explain the overtaking of the U.K. by the U.S. What is missing in (1.2.4) is the factor of 'Yankee ingenuity.'" Discuss.

7. Before the devaluation of the Singapore dollar during Crisis 1997, the 'relative per capita real income' exceeded unity. With the recovery from Crisis 1997, Singapore is likely to join Kuwait (say, in 1980) in having

levels of per capita real income higher than the U.S. Would you regard such events as a change of 'technological leadership'? Why?

8. Although both the changes in capital per worker and the demographic factor are absent in the catching up formula, the latter seems to have considerable predictive power with regard to Japan and other East Asian economies, including the PRC. Explain.
9. Strictly speaking, the catching up formula (or any one-good model) can at most explain the stagnation of the Soviet bloc but not its 'absolute economic decline' [in terms of (the value of) national output]. Do you agree?
10. Overheard: "If it has predictive power, then equation (1.2.4) suggests *predestination*, with no room left for the *free will* of any policy maker." Comment.

Chapter 2

REPLICABLE CASES?

East Asian Evidence

With the 'benchmark model' introduced in the previous chapter, we argued that, under outward orientation, *many* developing economies could catch up with the advanced economies. The remaining chapters of Part 1 provide detailed explanations of the mechanisms involved in the catching-up process. Empirical record from East Asia serves as the principal evidence presented in Part 2.

In economics, as in all sciences, internal logical consistency vouchsafes for the models, assumptions, and proofs used. However, because economics is a non-experimental science, its theories are generally only validated through the lack of refutation by observed evidence.[1] Our evidence will be meaningless if the sustained rapid growth in East Asia is solely due to the region's unique culture, tradition, and heritage, and is thus not relevant elsewhere. The present chapter examines this question. We believe the East Asian experience is relevant for two reasons. Section 1 of this chapter argues that in performance, East Asia is no oddity, but in fact resembles West Europe, with differences between the two regions being largely a matter of degree. Sections 2-4 examine the impact of culture, tradition, and heritage on East Asia's economic performance. These factors matter, but East Asia enjoys neither an unmixed blessing in this regard, nor an

[1] This is a line emphasized by Samuelson (1948).

advantage so unique and decisive as to place its experience beyond replication. Those who need no reassurance on this point may skip this chapter in the first reading.

1. EAST ASIAN ECONOMIES IN THE TRADING WORLD

Consider now some facts about East Asia in the trading world. Although at the midpoint of the 20th century, no East Asian economy was more developed than such Latin American economies as Argentina, several became fully developed over the next fifty years. Lessons may be learned when one latecomer passes another in industrialization. For an in-depth understanding of this process, we proceed in a sequence of steps.

For motivation, we revisit the Argentina-Japan comparison in more detail. Next, we show that the Japanese performance is quite typical in East Asia. To gain perspective, the performance of selected West European economies is surveyed. We conclude that after World War II, East Asian growth resembled that of West Europe, albeit at a somewhat faster pace. The latter fact leads to further study, after a brief recapitulation.

For the present purpose, we rely on the data from Penn World Table, version 6.0. For our purpose, this series has two advantages in comparison with the World Bank data: it extends back to 1950 rather than to 1975, and it includes data from the Taiwanese economy, one of the four NIEs from which we draw lessons. There are some differences between the Penn Table data and the World Bank series, but in general, the divergence is relatively minor.

The Argentina-Japan Comparison

Chart 2.1.1 presents the real gross domestic product per capita, on the basis of Purchasing Power Parity (by the Heston-Summers method) for Japan and Argentina, computed by the chain index method, for the period 1950-1998.

Argentina enjoyed higher per capita GDP than Japan before 1967, but from 1968 on, Japan took the lead. The crossover provides a useful point of reference, and is illustrated in Chart 2.1.1. Over the five decades 1950-1998, real per capita income increased eleven-fold for Japan, but it had less of a clear trend for Argentina. Per capita real income grew over 1950-1980, then it slid back over the period 1980-1990; growth recovered in the 1990s, but never doubled once. The recent crisis further exemplifies the unsteady pace of Argentina's development.

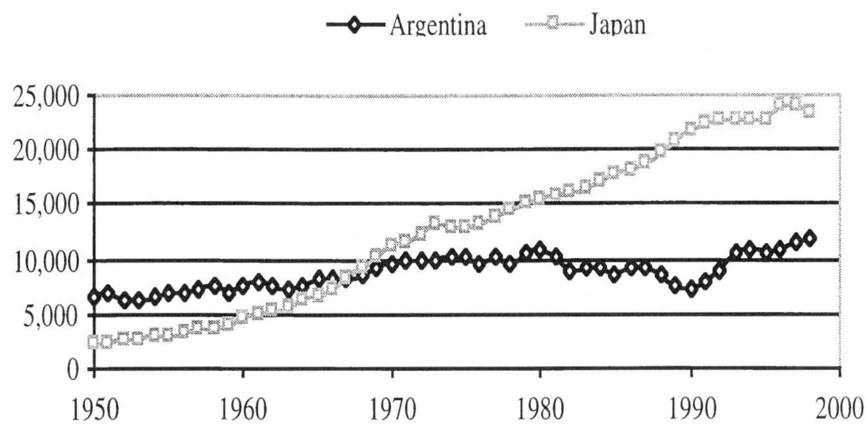

Chart 2.1.1 Japan vs. Argentina: real per capita GDP Source: PennTable 6.0

The situation of Argentina is by no means that unique. For example, the levels of income do vary across various large Latin American economies, from Brazil, to Chile, to Columbia to Mexico. In general, these economies are less affluent than Argentina, the country once predicted to be the next one to be a major industrial power in the world a century ago. Yet, there exists a great similarity among these economies. Thus, as an example of one latecomer taking over another in industrialization, the comparison between Japan and Argentina may well be substituted with Korea and Chile.

Compared to Japan, Argentina both enjoys a much richer agricultural resource base per capita and has a closer cultural affinity to the Western world. Any intrinsic advantage Japan may have had over Argentina during the period in question is not obvious.

One might attribute the high growth of Japan to the high savings rate in the country. Yet the direction of causality between growth and saving is not clear-cut. The mechanism whereby high savings rates can stimulate high growth calls for little comment. On the other hand, the reverse causal link is also quite straightforward. Following the life-cycle hypothesis, people save for their own consumption in old age. With diminishing marginal utility in spending, individuals attempt consumption-smoothing, seeking to avoid a life of feast-then-famine. For a society whose per capita real income has increased eleven times in fifty years, most individuals would feel that they had not saved enough in their poorer past for their coming old age. Thus, a high saving/income ratio can be expected for economies enjoying rapid growth. See Lau and Wan (1991).

Additional insight can be obtained by focusing on the *relative* per capita real gross domestic product of Japan and Argentina, as displayed in Chart

2.1.2. The Japanese score has climbed, closing the gap against the United States with little interruption, but Argentina has fallen back relative to the U.S. This comparison relative to the U.S. (rather than any other economy, say, Finland or Brazil) here is not spurious. Since the United States is the current technological leader, the increase or decrease of the repcri indicates the rate at which an economy is catching up with or falling behind *the times*.

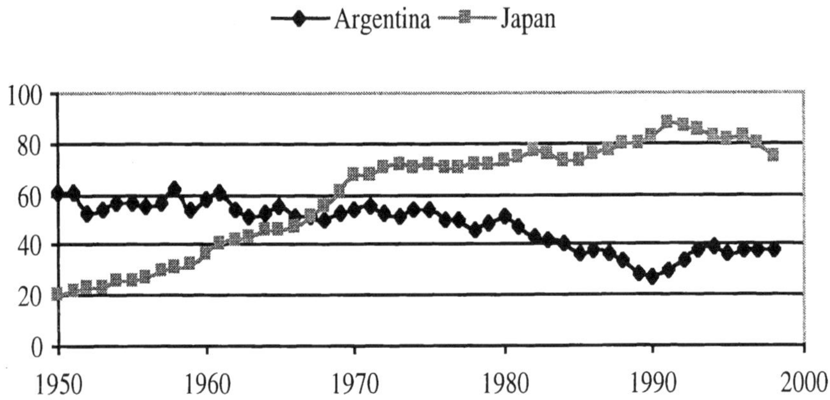

Chart 2.1.2 Japan vs. Argentina: repcri Source: PennTable 6.0

The reason that the growth performance of these two countries is so different is suggested by Chart 2.1.3, which displays the index of 'openness,' that is, (export + import)/GDP, supplied from the Penn Table 6.0.

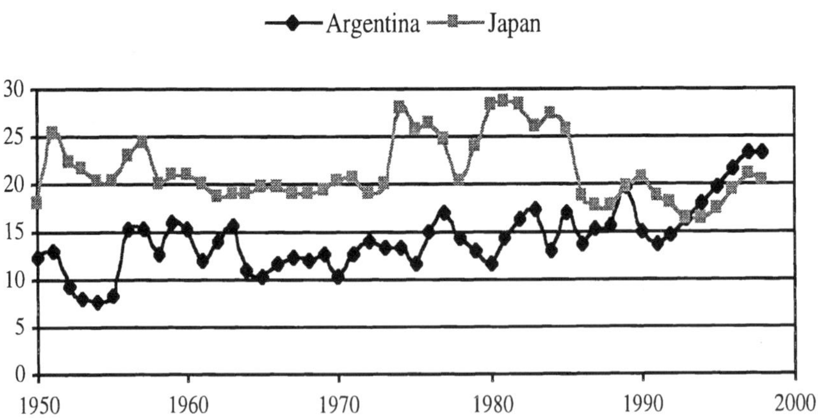

Chart 2.1.3 Japan vs. Argentina: 'openness' Source: Penn Table 6.0

In a world of rapid technological advances, re-inventing the wheel is of little value to an economy at the early stage of development. Significantly, the Japanese economy was 'more open' than the Argentinean until the middle 1990s, after Japan had acquired a formidable industrial base of its own.

It is true that both Japan and Argentina pursued trade policies with some protectionist bent. But there were some major differences between them. Whether for reasons of politics or socialist ideology, the Argentinean government protected any sector that could not compete, in order to save jobs. The Japanese industrial policy, on the other hand, has been characterized by Krugman (1987) as a 'narrow moving band' in a world with many traded goods. At any time, it only protects a few industries that can improve productivity with a sheltered home market, but cannot make better progress otherwise. No effort is wasted on the hopeless.

As data from the World Trade Organization indicate in Chart 2.1.4, we face an ever more integrated world. Total trade has outpaced total output in growth over all sub-periods in the last half century. Furthermore, in production technology, the 20th century is 'the American century.'

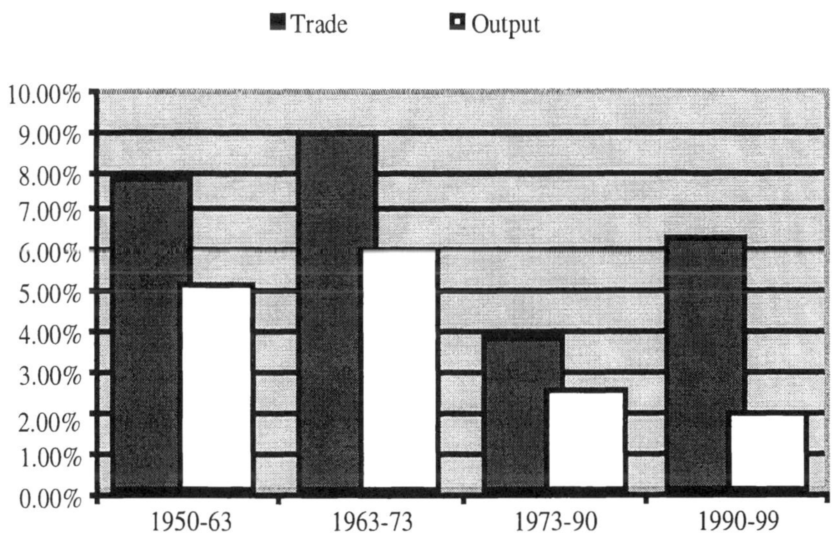

Chart 2.1.4 World trade outgrows world output Source: World Trade Organization

Systematically, Japan's policy only promotes infant industries where there is a potential to improve a technology that is still immature. In this environment, resources are always focused on the most promising sector of the time. This allows the economy to approach steadily the 'best practice' of the U.S., improve upon the latter here and there, and capture a much larger world export share than before. Japan often competed against U.S. producers, and at other times, adapted American technology innovatively to create its own comparative advantage.[2] In this same half century, Argentina – and in fact, most Latin American economies –catered to vested interests in its trade policy. Static comparative advantage was eschewed, but dynamic gain was not strategically pursued. Thus, Argentina let a gap continuously widen between its own practice and the best practice. The result has been that, over time, the importance of Latin America as a whole has declined in the world market. This again can be illustrated with data from the World Trade Organization in Chart 2.1.5. From 1948 to 1999, the Japanese share of world exports went from 1/30 of Latin America's to more than 140% of the latter. Japan's share in world trade has surged, while the share of Latin America has declined.

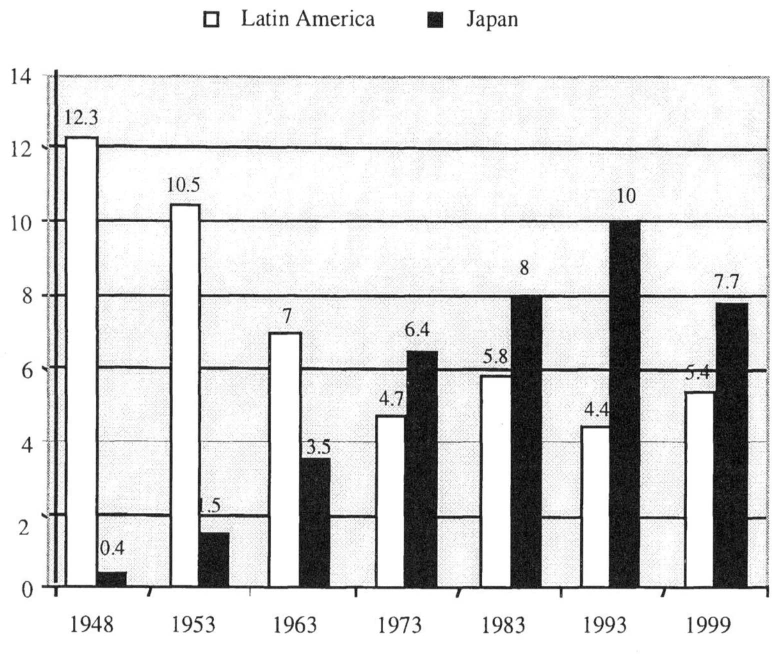

Chart 2.1.5 World export shares, selected years Source: World Trade Organization

Precisely because of its wealth in natural resources, Argentina had no urgent need to improve the quality and composition of its agricultural exports to earn foreign exchange. For Japan, competing in the world market for manufactured exports was the only way to afford such essential imports as fuel.

---

[2] In both camera and machine tools, for instance, the utilization of micro-electronic components has made Japanese products very competitive against the older, European technology.

East Asian Economies – A Group Portrait

What holds true for Japan appears to be also valid for the East Asian economies of Korea,[3] Hong Kong, Taiwan and Singapore, as revealed by their levels of real per capita GDP relative to the U.S. as presented in Chart 2.1.6.

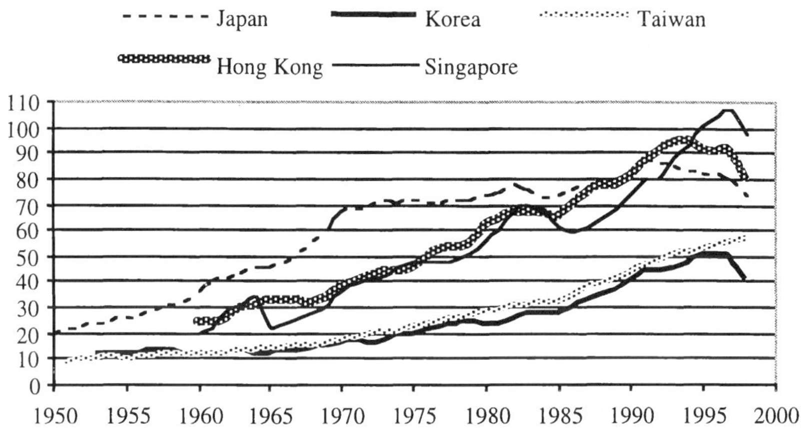

Chart 2.1.6 East Asian 5: repcri Source: PennTable 6.0

Although impressive in itself, the Japanese economy by no means exhibited either the fastest growth, or the highest level of real per capita GDP by the 1990s. Hong Kong surpassed Japan around the early 1990s, and using extended data sources, one can conclude that Singapore surpassed both Japan and Hong Kong toward the end of the decade.[4] All of these economies have narrowed their per capita income gap versus the U.S. After a phase of trend acceleration, there is some sign of growth tapering off.

The interested reader may also verify that the pattern of Argentina is also shared by economies such as Australia, Brazil, Sri Lanka, Ivory Coast, Morocco and Zambia. None of these countries specialize in export manufactures in the international division of labor.

---

[3] Unless otherwise stated, the Republic of Korea will be referred to simply as Korea.

[4] According to the recently revised World Bank data, Japan still has a slightly higher figure than Hong Kong.

East Asia and West Europe

Are East Asian economies exceptional? We do not think so. Chart 2.1.7 shows that five selected West European economies have also demonstrated their general pattern of convergence toward the United States, with the latecomers converging at somewhat higher relative speed.

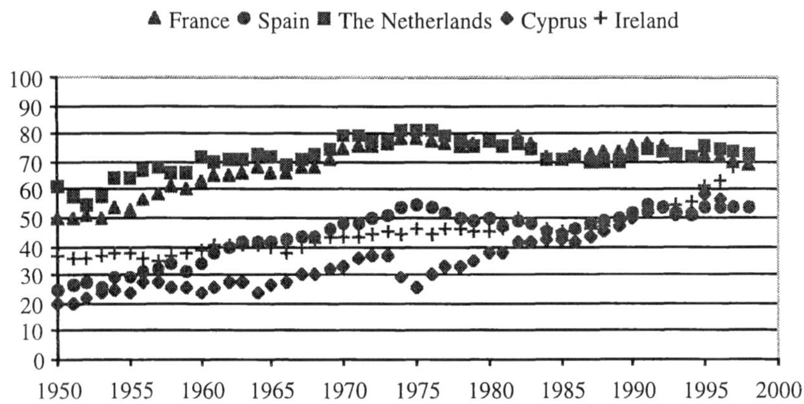

Chart 2.1.7 The European 5: repcri Source: PennTable 6.0

Note these five economies include two large (France and Spain) and three small (The Netherlands, Ireland and Cyprus) economies, also two (France and The Netherlands) with high income, two (Spain and Cyprus) with 'mid-income', while Ireland has moved rapidly from the latter group to the former group. The interested reader may consider other West European economies. Our experimentation persuades us that these five represent some broad characteristics shared with East Asia. In particular, (a) each catches up with the U.S. (b) without surpassing the U.S., and (c) the progress of each economy seems to be faster when the per capita GDP relative to the U.S. is in the range of 25% to 65%, and slower outside that range.

To reinforce the Asia-Europe comparison, in Chart 2.1.8 we superimpose Chart 2.1.6 (for East Asia) in lines on top of Chart 2.1.7 (for West Europe) in markers.

Among East Asians, the upper three (Japan, Hong Kong and Singapore) overtook France and the Netherlands, the upper two West Europeans, and the lower two (Korea and Taiwan) approached or crossed two lower West Europeans: Cyprus and Spain. Only Ireland from West Europe grew at the East Asian pace. Of course 'repcri' is only one performance measure, reflecting neither all qualities of life nor resilience under shocks.

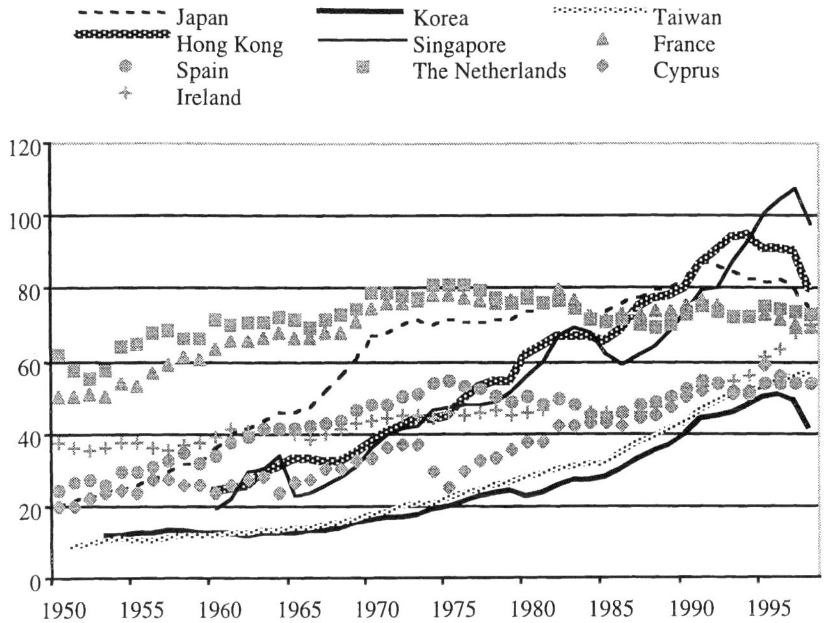

Chart 2.1.8 East Asia and West Europe: repcri

Chart 2.1.9 is a scatter diagram of the values of repcri for these ten economies in 1960 and 1996. All these ten are represented by points above the 45-degree line, showing convergence. The broken line parallels the 45-degree line and has a vertical intercept of 35%. It divides the East Asian Five from the West European Five. This shows the differential pace for convergence. Over these 36 years, the least gain among the East Asian Five was 38% for Korea and the most gain among the West European Five was 32% for Cyprus.

In summary:

East Asia basically resembles West Europe, though it grows faster.

Over all, our broad conclusion drawn from examination of the data is that the benchmark model presented in Chapter 1 is consistent with observed developments after World War II. American technological leadership has endured throughout this half century. Economies closely interacting with the United States partially closed the income gap, first in an accelerated pace, then settling into a period of synchronized development. Economies that trade little (such as the former Soviet Union and East Europe), or that supply primary goods only (including most economies in Latin America and the Middle East), or that have a very low initial income (many African economies) tend to fall back, unable to keep up with the current furious pace of technological progress.

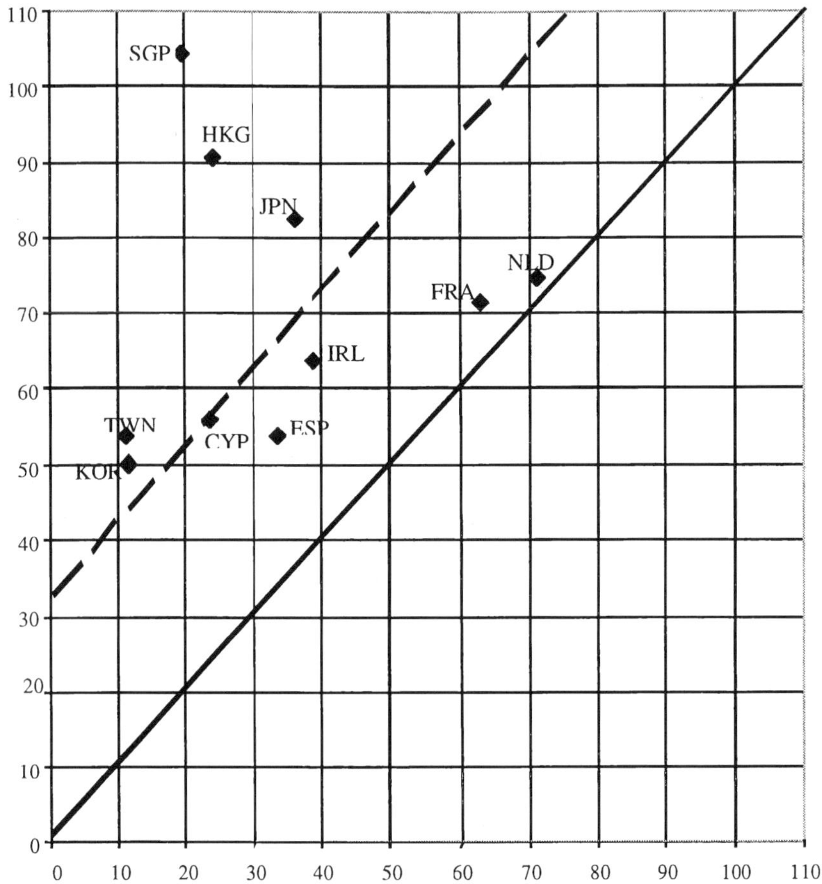

Chart 2.1.9 repcri in %, 1960 and 1996, 10 economies

We hasten to point out some limitations of the benchmark model. It predicts the trend but not one-time shocks,[5] the level but not the rate of change,[6] the average for an economy but not the dispersion,[7] and finally, the direction of convergence, but not the limit path.[8] Yet the theory does isolate

[5] For example, why growth slackens for Singapore during the mid-1980s.

[6] For example, why the growth rate of Hong Kong decreases and then increases several times in the last 25 years.

[7] For example, it does not stress that Hong Kong and Singapore might have overtaken the average income of Japan as an economy, but not that of Tokyo, as a metropolitan area.

[8] For example, why is it that the average income of Britain stays below that of Germany?

the effects of given conditions and policy from trend.[9]

More *specifically*, one is now left with the puzzle, why should the East Asian 5 progress at a pace apparently faster than that of West Europe? At the risk of over-reaching, we offer some tentative answers. The differential pace may be due to either initial conditions or to factors related to culture, tradition and heritage. By initial conditions, we mean the severe dollar shortage in East Asia after World War II, as well as the unwillingness of the people to accept the life style and living standards imposed by Pyongyang and Beijing. This made most East Asian economies eager to export to the United States, *and to undertake all means necessary to do so.* For example, to preserve export competitiveness, these societies, as a whole, were ready to acquiesce for decades in suppressed wage levels, lax environmental standards and authoritarian rule, and they adopted the designs and technology suitable to the 'American century.' Such East Asian eagerness probably exceeded what was possible, in socio-political terms, in West Europe at the same time. The factors of culture, tradition and heritage are examined in the next three sections.

Returning to the discussion of this topic in chapter 1, we can take two alternative views. When each was facing the same technology gap (or 'potential to learn'), East Asians were more eager (or 'hungry') to learn than were the Western Europeans. Or alternatively, given the same achieved pace of learning, East Asians faced a wider technology gap than the Western Europeans. That difference in technology gap was called 'artificial ignorance' in Chapter 1. The rate of growth is the product of the pace of learning and the technology gap.

Culture as a Factor for Economic Development

At least since Morishima (1982), culture has been invoked to explain East Asia's economic success. At that time, Japan had far outdistanced all its neighbors in per capita income, and Morishima focused on the 'Nipponized' aspects of Confucianism. Since then, sustained rapid growth has pervaded most of East Asia, and all varieties of Confucianism have now been rated a plus. This is in contrast to the reservations expressed by Max Weber with regard to 'Oriental traditions' at the beginning of the 20th century.

Actually, the old and new views are not necessarily mutually exclusive. In principle, it is entirely possible that the East Asian culture is conducive to emulation but not innovation. Hence, to assess the weakness or strength of

---

[9] Thus, it does not support Ross Perot's view that a changed policy will make the United States grow like Korea.

the East Asian economies, we must be ready to take culture and tradition seriously (See Wan, 1995), without necessarily agreeing with Morishima on every point (See Wan, 1988).

At the outset, it is essential to make clear that this is a study of economic issues, written by an economist for economists. It is not our purpose to inquire whether economic development ennobles the human soul, or debases the capacity to appreciate nature or art. Nor shall we discuss the economic consequences of history and philosophy, and avoid the notions and terms customary to economists. If we deem history and philosophy (or weather) to be relevant to the level and rate of growth of per capita income, it is obligatory to trace this influence through such *economic* concepts as preferences and production capability, benefits and costs, and so on. Thus, tropic heat can be detrimental to economic development, through such mechanisms as the rapid leaching of nutrients from the soil (a matter of *technology*), or the heightened individual desire for leisure relative to work and income (a matter of *preference*). As *economists*, we can never rest our case after simply stating 'obviously, the average temperature here is so many degrees centigrade in the shade ...'.

Today, development economists agree upon two points about East Asia. First, the region's per capita natural resource base and initial wealth are meager; and second, the region's recent growth is meteoric. In economist's terms, such a record means that 'human capital' is likely to be the key factor in the East Asian success story.[10] The rest of this chapter relates the notion of human capital to such human factors as culture, tradition and heritage in East Asia. The context is the question of the *replicability* of the East Asian experience elsewhere.

Usually, discussions about culture, tradition and heritage emphasize the particularistic, and suggest the non-replicability of development patterns. In contrast, the 'human capital' approach of economists stresses the operation of some general mechanism.[11] Thus, once the role of the initial conditions is understood, there can be the hope of improving 'destiny' through effort.

The next section provides a bird's eye view of the culture and traditions common to East Asian economies. Following that are two sections on the economic consequences both of Confucianism and the influence of Japan over the last century and a half.

---

[10] Should preference for saving be the *only* reason, then the per capita wealth of some Asian societies must have been unusually high already, as an initial condition. There is no evidence of that.

[11] Thus the general term 'human capital' may need refinement. It may concern individual skill, or group aptitude for coordination, or the valuable, collective reputation of reliability to outsiders, which motivates the society to maintain reliability, through peer pressure.

2. THE SHARED INITIAL CONDITIONS

In describing how the electric equipment industry was initially introduced into Japan in the late 19th century, Uchida (1991) emphasized that, although Japan lagged behind the United States and Germany by less than a decade, the initial process of catching up was particularly difficult for Japan. Two points are emphasized:

(a) Unlike textiles and machinery, the electric equipment industry is related closely to science;

(b) Unlike other European countries and the U.S., Japan suffered a double handicap, since:

   1. it had never had a local tradition of scientific inquiry,[12]
   2. it had little chance of attracting enough foreign scientific and technological personnel with a European cultural background.[13]

In economic terms, there was a scarcity of industry-specific human capital for the electric equipment industry in Japan, and this scarcity could not be surmounted quickly through immigration.

The double handicap that faced the Japanese electric equipment sector is still relevant to other East Asian economies now, in various high tech industries from electronics, to biotechnology, to advanced material science. By and large, such disadvantages can be ameliorated. But, even under correct government policies, the situation can only improve gradually, when current workers have acquired experience and a newly educated labor force takes the field. For Japan, foreign joint venture was the key to human capital development. The diagnosis is the beginning of the cure.

What we can deduce from history are: *what* initial handicaps faced East Asia – situations shared by many other developing regions today – and *how* they were surmounted over time in East Asia, in one case after another. Next, we shall discuss *which* common features of East Asia may account for East Asia's successful economic performance.

The society of almost all East Asian economies is remarkably homogeneous, and has been so at least for hundreds if not thousands of years. Proportionately speaking, there is no *numerically or economically significant* group which is regarded a minority, by reason of race, language, creed, or inherited social strata. The only exception may be Vietnam, where ethnic Chinese merchants played a significant role in the not too distant past.

The following pairwise comparisons highlight the above point on East Asian homogeneity. In numerical proportions, society is far more pluralistic

---

[12] More on this is in the next section.

[13] In contrast, the United States and Belgium drew British talent in metallurgy and engineering for industrialization.

in India than in Japan. In economic terms, minority communities play more prominent roles in Malaysia than in Singapore.

By and large, in the process of catching up, a multi-communal society poses more challenges to human capital formation than does a homogeneous society. Here, the Singapore-Malaysia comparison is quite instructive. In Singapore, under the notion of 'meritocracy,' educational attainment and examinations are relied upon as criteria for social advancement. At least in the catching-up phase, these criteria can be met by an average member of the majority community as easily as by a member of the minority community. Thus, the system operates without significant resistance. Even at the *pre-school* stage (and from that phase on), families and children feel obliged to devote time, effort and finance to preparations for competitive examinations, not only to get admitted to school, but to gain entrance to schools with the most prestigious reputations.[14] School ties matter greatly in the society for career (and matrimony!) prospects. In such a society, a government of any ideology, be it the current Peoples' Action Party or its predecessors, must support the system – as indeed occurs in Japan, Korea, Taiwan, Hong Kong and many areas in mainland China today. The system is conducive to the formation of human capital (at least, of a certain sort). It also promotes vertical social mobility.[15]

In Malaysia, historical forces have molded a country with a rural majority community of Malays and urban minority communities of Indians and Chinese. In the short run, development along the Singaporean line will tend to accentuate the income polarity between the majority of the rural poor and the minorities of the urban rich. As Mahathir (1970) argued forcefully in *The Malay Dilemma*, in order to head off recurrent inter-communal bloodshed, the Malaysian government had to take affirmative actions of sorts, to balance the goal of human capital formation against the need for socio-political stability.

Social homogeneity has other advantages as well. For two reasons, both rooted in game theory, human cooperation tends to be easier *within* a particular community than *across* communities.

(a) Because of *common knowledge*, the transaction cost for co-ordination is lower among individuals.
(b) By the *logic of repeated games*, an individual is less ready to engage in opportunistic behavior, lest the aggrieved party retaliate, at least by complaining widely within the same community.

---

[14] Private tutors and cram sessions are endemic throughout East Asia.

[15] This is strictly a *positive* analysis of economic consequences, not a defense of any system in terms of its effects on the minority communities, the healthy development of the child, or the nurture of creativity.

Social cohesion reaches an apex in some areas in Japan. A person can place an order for a delivery of rice at home, leave cash payment under the rice container, and go to work, leaving the house with the doors unlocked. Such behavior often impresses casual observers from other East Asian lands, such as China. Again an explanation in terms of *repeated games* suggests itself. In a crowded, close-knit environment, people know totally and implicitly the living habits of all their neighbors, and no one is likely to be able to get away with enjoying misbegotten wealth. Moreover, people are so dependent upon the esteem and goodwill of one another that life would be unbearable under the ostracism of one's peers.

In economic terms, such social cohesion can be translated into corporate practices and organizational behavior, from *lifetime tenure* to the *quality control circle*. In general terms, it reduces transaction costs and simplifies the task of monitoring. More specifically, in product development, the organizational behavior of group effort can be counted upon to improve product quality and process technology, through the process of incremental improvement. Astute Japanese firms have capitalized on such social traits to build up a comparative advantage that foreign rivals find hard to match.[16]

In economic terms, the labor market of a homogeneous society is less likely to be segmented. Other things being equal, such an economy can mobilize its resources more effectively in response to market signals.[17] In turn, a faster response of the output mix to price changes means a higher elasticity of output substitution along the production frontier. One consequence is that, with a production possibility frontier having little curvature, there is less chance of suffering from poor growth and less cause to be concerned with export pessimism.

Summing up, the Industrial Revolution occurred in England, and all European and Europeanized countries (such as the United States and New Zealand) enjoyed its initial benefit. The handicaps faced by East Asia are common to other non-European societies. The lack of certain types of human capital (science and technology capability, as well as other market-related information and institutions) is the key. Such disadvantages take time to be overcome through human capital formation. In some important

[16] Large Japanese corporations rely on promotion from inside, wage progression curves are steep, and the bonuses awarded in profitable firms are sizable. The peer pressure of employees for high performance forms a pressure cooker atmosphere. In spite of the nominal institution of lifetime tenure, Morishima (1982) reported that 47% of white collar workers and 27% of blue collar workers who started in large firms ended elsewhere. See also Wan (1988).

[17] Such discussion may appear unfamiliar in the context of conventional microeconomics (including the theory of international trade), where 'technology' (or, production sets) is taken as given. Here we are dealing with forces that determine how the comparative advantages of various economies become what we observe in real life.

aspects, the higher degree of homogeneity is a strength of the East Asian economies *both* for the pace of human capital formation *and* for its deployment.

Of course, the advantages of a homogeneous society are only relative. For a fully developed economy, such as Switzerland, the diversified cultural texture can be both an aesthetic asset and economic strength. In contrast, human fault lines can develop to sunder an apparently homogeneous nation such as Somalia.

After discussing these generic factors about East Asia, we shall consider next the specific factors of Confucianism and the Japanese example.

3. THE ECONOMIC CONSEQUENCES OF CONFUCIANISM

To many people, Confucianism is synonymous with East Asian culture. Thus, any cultural influence on East Asian growth is associated with Confucianism. Since Confucian thought has little impact outside East Asia, this argument then concludes, the replicability of East Asian performance elsewhere is therefore in doubt.

Confucianism as a Moral Philosophy

This volume is prepared under the premise that the above view is over-simplistic. Confucianism is a moral philosophy with certain specific characteristics. These particular aspects of Confucianism are not necessarily relevant or conducive to growth. So one possible benefit of Confucianism to East Asians is merely that it gives them a moral philosophy of some sort. Since many developing economies also have moral philosophies of other non-Confucian types, the replicability of East Asian experience remains intact.

To pursue this line of reasoning, we must review first the effect of moral philosophy in general, and then the particular characteristics of Confucianism.

Most religions are associated with their own moral philosophy. As an exception, Confucianism is a moral philosophy but not a religion. In the current context, we maintain these moral philosophies share four elements:

(a) The cultivation of self-discipline;
(b) The codification of behavior norms;
(c) The promotion of study and scholarship;
(d) The discounting of secular (including economic) success as the purpose of life.

Historically, most moral philosophies undergo three stages of evolution:

1) the quintessence stage, when effects (a) through (d) are strong;
2) the sublimation stage, when the effects of (a) through (c) are strong, but (d) begins to weaken; and
3) the dissipation stage, when all four effects taper off.

It is clear that effects (a) and (b) enhance the effectiveness of a labor force, and effect (c) improves the potential for both innovation and emulation. But counteracting these three is effect (d), which steers the best brains away from worldly success toward lofty, spiritual ideals.

Certainly, the Confucian *Analects* is replete with exhortations for leading a simple, righteous, and *disciplined* life.[18] The central tenet of Confucianism is *li*, a body of traditional rituals and practices of ancient China that have evolved and been refined over the millennia. This acts to regulate individual *conduct* toward others, between family members as well as between the superior and the subordinate, all based upon a system of mutual responsibilities. The Confucian doctrine was further developed under Mencius (371–289 B.C.). Through the concept of the *heavenly mandate*, the sovereign is obligated toward d*estiny*, which is supposed to be benevolently disposed toward the common people. The failure of the sovereign is to be rectified through either the deposing of the ruler by the chief minister, or the replacement of the entire dynasty by popular revolt. The high cost of such drastic remedies is the weakness of the Confucian political agenda, relative to representative democracy.

A sense of moral responsibility permeates East Asian societies, and is not limited only to the literate. It appears in folklore, drama and music, and is transmitted from the old to the young. Through the presence of behavior norms, the Confucian ethos clearly has left its imprint on both the collective behavior of the labor force and on inter-firm behavior. In formal, economics terms, the aggregate production set of an economy is influenced in two ways: the efficiency of the labor force acts upon the individual production set, and the interactions of firms act upon transaction costs.

For East Asian economies, the Confucian ethos influences both static efficiency through individual *discipline* and the code of *conduct*, and dynamic efficiency through emphasis on *study* and *education*. Characteristically, the very first sentence of the Confucian *Analects* is the proclamation,

> *Is it not enjoyable to study, and to refresh one's learning time and time again!*

In country after country, sovereign after sovereign, from Manchu China to Meiji Japan, East Asian courts upheld the supreme importance of

---

[18] An interested reader may consult *The Analects of Confucius*, translation and notes by Leys (1997).

education through edicts disseminated throughout their realms.[19] In China, in addition to the emphasis on literacy by both the sage and the sovereign, there is also the folk religion, according to which the invention of the Chinese characters moved Heaven to rain grain and ogres to cry at night (presumably out of frustration). According to such belief, any written Chinese word is sacred and should be free from desecration (like the Torah in Judaism).

Under all these influences, it is understandable that East Asian parents, however poor and disadvantaged they themselves may be, would struggle to give their children a chance in life through education. The rationing of education opportunities through test scores gives such drives a further Darwinian twist. Under the constant and intense popular pressure for educational opportunities, East Asian political leaders do not have to be visionaries to allocate resources accordingly. From the economic point of view, all this would facilitate human capital formation, *provided the conditions are right.*

The last proviso is important. Just like religions elsewhere that focus upon spirituality and discount the importance of worldly success, Confucius would focus on the study of the code of conduct as well as statecraft (naturally, his followers would add to these, *the correct* interpretation of Confucius), and discount the importance of handicraft, technology and commerce. During the quintessence of Confucianism, the formation of human capital of a pragmatic type is not likely to blossom. Exhibit A of this fact is the Chinese imperial examination. Future prime ministers were chosen among those most successful in such nation-wide triennial examinations. These were essay contests written in fine calligraphy, according to pre-set style, and relating obscure Confucian themes to issues chosen at the presiding officer's pleasure.

Parallels of a fashion can also be found from other societies. The explosive contributions of scientists of Jewish descent came only when Talmudic scholarship was no longer the exclusive preoccupation of Jewish intellectuals. The flourishing of Western European capitalism under the Protestant Ethic was possible when doctrinal issues did not pre-empt the best minds in those societies. Yankee mercantile success occurred only in generations when the lifetime ambition of North American immigrants went beyond the founding of a Puritanical paradise on Earth. Missionary families in Hawaii brought up children who emerged to be millionaire entrepreneurs. So there is nothing all that exceptional in the fact that the 'sublimation stage' of Confucianism coincides with the sustained rapid growth of East Asia. It is interesting to speculate that, in the fullness of time, similar development may come to South Asia subcontinent, or to the entire Middle East.

---

[19] Such as the Imperial Rescript of 1890 in Meiji Japan.

The Particulars of Confucianism

We must next study the particulars of Confucianism, as a moral philosophy. Confucius was an intensely humane thinker, deeply appalled by the violence and atrocities around him, as law and order of the Zhou Dynasty broke down. To stave off human carnage, he was prepared to do *whatever* was necessary. He refrained from speculating about an afterlife. He viewed with opprobrium his own disciple who enjoyed commercial success.[20] He caused his students to be chastised for their sedentary life and ignorance about farming. He emphasized tradition, etiquette and protocols so that the force of conventions would constrain human greed and ambition and promote stability. To discourage political assassination, he doctored the historical record *with pride*[21] to cast down the fame of assassins into everlasting obscurity.

As power was centralized under the Han Dynasty, Confucianism – the school for order and stability – was elevated to be the *imperial philosophy* in 136 B. C., 343 years after the passing of Confucius (and 461 years before the Council of Nicaea), to the exclusion of all other philosophies. The latter include the pacifist Mohism, the school of philosopher-engineers. They studied fortification to volunteer and defend against *all* aggressors in the Era of Warring States, and could have been China's answer to Archimedes.

Imperial philosophy was a perilous subject. Mirroring the schisms over the Nature of Christ, blood flowed in both Chinese and Korean courts when Confucian principles were invoked in annual ancestral offerings, and over such arcane issues as whether the royal birth mother deserved precedence over the First Consort of the previous sovereign.

Of more lasting consequence was the separation of scholars from artisan-inventors. Even in recent decades, engineers from Chinese societies are relatively reluctant to dirty their hands in laboratories, though their Japanese counterparts have no such aversion. In ancient China, this heritage stunted science and retarded technology. In contrast to Europe and the Mediterranean world, where academies flourished in the Age of the Pythagorean Brotherhood, down to the Era of the Alexandrines, there was little systematic Chinese attempt to improve understanding of the physical

---

[20] He went on, "to be rich is not to be benevolent; to be benevolent is not to be rich." In contrast, Theravada Buddhists mention their followers in business. Islam notes that The Prophet was once a businessman.

[21] To the applause of generations of his followers. To him, the importance of truth pales before that of human life and social stability.

world, for the lack of institutional support.[22] Many inventions by isolated (and often illiterate) artisans became lost. The cumulative effect was devastating (See Appendix).

At a more general level (at the least in Chinese societies), the high regard for education can be easily distorted from *substance* to *form*. Diplomas and college degrees take precedence over the pragmatic content of training. Colleges avoid offering technical or scientific courses because they are expensive. Students flock instead to study English literature for no other reason than it is the best route for a college degree, of *any* sort.

At a deeper level, the East Asian educational system emphasizes rote learning. There is nothing equivalent to the Judaic tradition of rabbinical debate. As the potential for research and innovation become more crucial aspects of human capital than are discipline and specialized information, East Asian educators today are scrambling to reform their education systems and promote originality and initiative.

In many ways, Japan, Korea, and Vietnam were all influenced by Confucian thought. Until the Industrial Revolution, none of these societies had made advances in science (and technology) comparable to those of the Islamic world.

Of course, an Industrial Revolution is a process requiring a complex of pre-conditions. Although the Islamic world served as the indispensable bridge for Europe between the Hellenistic Age and Renaissance, the Industrial Revolution came only to 18th century Britain. Only after the liberation of academic inquiry (from an environment that muffled Galileo), could West Europe make lasting progress in research. Ultimately, it further took the affirmation of intellectual property rights (by the Statute of Monopolies of 1624) for inventors such as James Watt to flourish in Britain. Over all, it is the success of Britain, rather than the failure of East Asia (along with South Asia and the Middle East), that is the exception.

Leaving larger issues to be discussed elsewhere (see Wan, 1995), what is important for economic development is that Confucianism provides both advantages and disadvantages to East Asia. The advantages are shared by other moral philosophies of various major religions: a disciplined life, a code of interpersonal conduct, together with a keen respect for scholarship. The disadvantages are specific aspects of the East Asian heritage, namely, the lack of interest in scientific inquiry and the separation of the *literati* from the *artisan*. The Japanese only managed to overcome these disadvantages in the Meiji era.

---

[22] In Europe, beside the futile search for the Philosopher's Stone (which also had a parallel in Chinese alchemy), there always had been more systematic attempts to study physical laws and put them to practical use in levers, ballistics, etc.

In short, insofar as the initial condition is concerned, Confucianism does not seem to provide any non-replicable net advantage to East Asia.

4. THE EXAMPLE OF JAPAN: ACHIEVEMENTS AND IMPACT

Japan as a First-Mover for Industrialization

Japan was the first non-Western economy to become fully developed. It is also the second largest economy in today's world. When Japan started to industrialize, more than a century ago, the world was quite different from the world now, both in *technology* and in *international politics*. The history of Japan's economic catching up is inseparable from the sequence of unique events between World War I and the Korean War. Over this period, Japan achieved world-class industrial competence. It also fought on and off for 15 years (1931-45), lost the world's first nuclear war, and recovered in the Korean War by serving as the supply base for the United States.

For the developing economies today, the experience of Japan is less *replicable* than that of the Newly Industrialized Economies (NIEs). Therefore, notwithstanding its size, we allocate fewer pages to the Japanese economy than to the NIEs. Much of the study of the Japanese economy is for context, or with emphasis upon its impact on the NIEs.

The impact of Japan results mainly from the fact that in all Asia (in fact all non-Western societies), it industrialized first.[23] This singular achievement deserves our attention. In 1842, when China lost the First Opium War, all three Northeast Asian countries, Korea, Japan and China, were isolated by choice. Japan encountered Commodore Perry only in 1854. In contrast, Emperor Gialong had already unified Vietnam, with French support, back in 1802. Japan's early start in industrialization was not any historical fluke. That achievement is both a *tour de force*, in itself, and also part of the historical pattern of Japan's adaptability.

Geography made Japan. Like the cell membrane, the seas around Japan admit incoming information and technology, but rarely military invasion and conquest. The Home Islands support a population which is both too large to fall easy prey to aggressors, but also too small to allow complacency in times of change. In a fine balance, there is the timely awareness of threats and challenges, but also the confidence to adapt and reform and come out of the contest all the stronger.

[23] Rather than because of its size, or historical importance.

History fertilizes what geography spawns. From the dawn of history until 1945, Japan was never occupied by foreign aggressors. The circumstances of the Cold War then made the U.S. occupation far from harsh. Continuity nurtures growth. Like the forging of the Samurai sword, repeated challenges reinforce the capacity to respond, by seizing the strength of the adversary to fortify oneself, or by using a crisis for self-discovery (See Table 2.4.1). Neither Vietnam nor Korea nor China (nor India, for that matter) had such luck.

Time	Challenges	Adaptation by Reform
660s	Lost the fleet to Tang China	Adoption of Chinese technology / institutions
1174-81	The Mongolian invasions	Reawakening of national identity
1543	The coming of Portuguese	Replication of the Tanegashima muskets
1853-4	Arrival of Perry's 'Black Ships'	Reform after Meiji Restoration
1945	Lost WWII	Reform to become a fully developed economy

Table 2.4.1 The perils facing Japan

Japan as a Catalyst for Change among Nearby Societies

Success breeds emulation. The example of Japan has been closely observed and utilized throughout the developing world. But for reasons enumerated below, emulation goes further among the Korean and Chinese societies.

First, in dim pre-history, all three Northeast Asian peoples were somehow related. DNA evidence suggests the affinity of Yayoi Japanese to Koreans. The tale of Tang'un, legendary founder of Korea[24] was first displayed in the Chinese tomb of Wu-liang T'zu.[25]

Next, at least until World War II, written Chinese characters were extensively used in both Korea and Japan, along with a heavy dose of borrowed words in the spoken languages. Wave after wave of cultural influence came to Japan from all points west, passing through China and

[24] By tradition, the next two dynasties after Tang'un were founded by Kija and Wiman, both refugees from China. See Han (1970).

[25] In *Analects*, Confucius exclaimed, "If [my] precepts are not accepted, [I] will ride a raft and float over the sea..." Certainly he did not have in mind ending his earthly existence, but going somewhere he knew: Korea and Jomon Japan were the only possibilities (Hawaii would be a stretch).

Korea, and adding new ingredients along the way.[26] The motif of the lotus came from the Egyptian pyramids. The art style of Gandhara had its roots in Greece and Persia.[27] Various South Asian heritages arrived with Buddhism. Diverse Korean and Chinese traditions were also carried over with Confucianism.

In time, this historical nexus facilitated an important reverse flow, which is at the core of our interest. It made it much easier for Chinese (as well as Korean) officials and students to visit Japan rather than Europe or America during the late Manchu period and the Republican period. They quickly gained knowledge about the Western world by assimilating Japanese translations and surveys. A massive body of terms used in Chinese today, such as economics, democracy, railroad, and radio are all direct borrowings from Japanese. The same goes for various customs and institutions.

In economic terms, the transaction cost for emulation is far lower when other East Asians heed the Japanese – rather than the American or the European – example.

Third, in reducing the emulation cost, past history is often reinforced by (economic) geography. All three peoples in Northeastern Asia live on densely populated land. Scarce resources and relatively abundant labor mark the shared initial conditions. Technology adapted to one location tends to be applicable to another. Moreover, the same sea route linking the Persian Gulf and Southeast Asia to the American Pacific Coast skirts the West Pacific Rim, where Japan, the four Asian NIEs and many ports in Mainland China and Vietnam are located. Shipping lines serving one area can easily accommodate another port of call. The supply base from a developed location can be easily shifted to a less developed one, to lower labor costs, using similar technology.

In economics, forward-looking agents take actions to face a risky environment based on their probabilistic beliefs. The Japanese success within a *similar* environment gives other East Asians the confidence to experiment. Once they make trials, they have the opportunity to correct initial errors. The fact that the Japanese had been satisfactory suppliers of certain products encouraged their U.S. or European clients to try out nearby sources with lower wages, offering information when needed.

Emulation extends beyond the activities of the private sector. Public institutions and policies are also fertile grounds for adopting and adapting the successful practices of neighbors. Here the Japanese model has been

---

[26] Although all these three peoples have benefited from cultural contacts from outside, each has shown innovative power of their own, such as the invention of the Tatara process of steel-making in Japan, the moving metal type in Korea, as well as the first use of silk, paper and the compass in China.

[27] See for instance Malraux (1953).

followed more in Korea and less in the other NIEs. However, even in Korea, emulation is not simple imitation, since a hundred per cent copying is impractical, in many cases. A few examples illustrate the point.

Broadly speaking, in promoting national industry champions, protecting the home market and supporting heavy industries, Korea followed in the Japanese steps. But in other aspects, many differences emerge.

After MacArthur purged the owners of the Japanese *zaibatsu*, corporate governance passed into the hands of professional management, under the aegis of the Japanese Ministry of International Trade and Industry (MITI).[28] In contrast, the present Korean *chaebols* were once headed by the newly released defendants under the Act against Illicit Wealth.

Again, in launching new industries, Japan controlled the sequential entry of oligopolist firms to internalize the informational externalities from the first-mover, but avoid the dead-weight loss of monopoly. Korea tended to allow business groups to compete against one another right from the beginning. The inter-firm co-operation in the Japanese VLSI project also seems not to have been attempted in Korea.

Next, the history of intra-East Asian interaction was also complex. Neighboring lands do not always enjoy *neighborly* relationships. Faced with the encircling Western colonial powers, survival instinct urged the nineteenth century Japanese to organize a countervailing force. In the view of the Japanese, because they were the first East Asian society to answer the wake-up call, they ought to take the leadership, with all the rights, privileges and advantages[29] going with it. Resistance of other East Asians to this Japanese agenda must be overcome with force. The more the resistance, the more force is called for to secure compliance. But to the Koreans and Chinese, the former messengers who brought Japan culture and technology, this Japanese agenda was utterly unacceptable. For seven decades, 1876 to 1945, the conflict went on, East Asians against East Asians. Taiwan, Korea and the Manchurian part of China passed under Japanese rule for decades.

Meanwhile, Korea and Taiwan were molded into bases for Japanese expansion: infrastructure was laid, and modern agriculture and certain industries were introduced. In schools segregated from Japanese settlers, local youth were given practical training to serve the Japanese cause. This aroused resentment more intense from the Koreans than from the Taiwanese.[30]

---

[28] The complex process is described by Miyajima in Miyajima et al. (1999).

[29] Due a colonial master.

[30] Perhaps partly due to their less than satisfactory experience under the rule of both the Manchus, before, and the Republican Chinese, afterward.

The impact of Japan in economic development was far more pervasive than the Japanese Rule, which only lasted for a few wartime years in Hong Kong and Singapore. For Korea and Taiwan, the Japanese Period did raise both the living standard, then, and the potential for growth, later. However, the benefits of the Japanese rule can be easily overstated. In Hong Kong and Singapore, both formerly ruled by Britain rather than Japan, the ethnic Chinese have achieved even higher income per capita than in Taiwan. For North Korea, Japanese Rule alone has done little good.

Finally, in real life, the emulation of Japan by other East Asians is frequently not an unaided act. For economic self-interest, rising Japanese wages after World War II encouraged the Japanese to supply their foreign clients from new bases abroad, through trade (by subcontract arrangement) if possible, with investment if necessary. The mechanism of these will be discussed in detail later. The point is, according to Kojima (1978) and Ozawa (1979), the Japanese turned to Taiwan and Korea first to minimize transaction costs.[31]

To sum up, the fact that Japan achieved industrialization early has benefited the development of other East Asian societies in several ways. We now come to the crux of the matter. Granted that this is the case, the question to be addressed is, does it make the East Asian experience non-replicable elsewhere? Facts suggest that a resounding "no" is the answer to this question.

Evidence shows that historical connections and cultural affinity certainly matter. Yet they are neither sufficient nor necessary for the trade and investment flows that carry along technology. They are clearly insufficient: before their respective economic reforms, Mainland China and Vietnam attracted few investors. They are also obviously unnecessary: Hong Kong invested in Mauritius; Korea invested in Bangladesh; Singapore participated in the software development of India; Taiwan supplied personal computers to Russia from Finland and to Latin America from Paraguay. In fact, Japan was never the sole source of investment and export orders for the Asian NIEs in the first place. Fields (1995) showed that European and American procurement agents also played important roles.

In this world, few things are unmixed blessings. As labor costs rose, on the one hand, neighboring economies industrialized when Japanese firms relied on them to supply their former clients. On the other hand, out of self-interest, Japanese firms made arrangements in such a fashion that they not only sought profit from such operations but also that they prolonged

---

[31] In contrast, a vivid example was given by Smith (1983), that when a Japanese manager commented on the work of a shop floor worker in Malaysia, it touched off a labor incident, since communication out of the normal channel was against the Malay standard of propriety.

Japanese control over such trade as long as possible. Technology transfer is calibrated at a pace that will not dilute Japanese influence too fast. Sources for subcontracts are diversified to retain bargaining advantage. Joint venture agreements are designed so as to exercise hegemony through the monopoly of indispensable components and technology. Product specification is so structured that buyers of equipment can switch to new sources only at high cost. Supplies of parts are manipulated so that users of Japanese inputs cannot easily compete against the final products of allied Japanese firms. As downstream production is shifted abroad to regions with lower wage, the Japanese suppliers of strategic components[32] improved product quality to forestall competition.

For many years, the intra-East Asian division of labor has been *vertical*, with Japan always securely on top. The same environment that made it easier for the NIEs to industrialize also made it much harder for them to become fully developed. This situation drives Korean firms to specialize in industries with scale economy,[33] and the government to back giant firms with directed credit. It also drives the small and medium high tech firms of Taiwan to ally themselves closely with U.S. firms as a countermeasure. Eventually, everyone has succeeded, though not without cost. Japanese firms won precious time for adjustment with their rearguard action. The Koreans competed directly against the Japanese; the Taiwanese indirectly by assisting Japan's U.S. rivals.

Thus, a nuanced picture emerges. Given that Japan was the first non-Western economy to become fully industrialized, historical connections and cultural affinity probably did help the rest of East Asia industrialize subsequently. Connections with Japan, however, were not sufficient for industrialization, nor did they determine the rate of industrialization.

As a conclusion to this chapter, the sum and total of evidence indicates that, for the development of the NIEs, social homogeneity, Confucian ethos and their relationship with Japan were all important, but none of these factors was decisive. Their influence is mostly positive, but was also blended with some negative aspects. The experience of East Asia appears to be relevant to all, *mutatis mutandis*. The *modus operandi* of these economies toward development is not so idiosyncratic as to preclude other economies from traveling a similar path.

Later, in Part 2, we shall draw evidence from an economy outside East Asia, namely Mauritius, to buttress our case. As in planetary science, facts from exo-solar stars shed insight about the general mechanism of stellar

---

[32] Like Shimano for the derailleurs of bicycles and Fanuc for controllers of machine tools.

[33] Such as steel and ships, cars and memory chips.

evolution, a process first studied only from observing our own solar system. Additional insight can be drawn also from the less than happy record of the self-sufficiency experiments, from the former Soviet economies, to the present situation in North Korea and Myanmar. Apparently, there is no viable alternative to outward orientation. As Chile, PRC and India have illustrated, once an outward-oriented reform has been launched, even changes in political leadership do not turn the clock back, whatever the ruling political form.

APPENDIX 2.1 A MODEL FOR THE DYNAMICS OF HUMAN CAPITAL IN ANCIENT TIMES

Let x be the stock of knowledge (on some subject like engineering), f(x) be the gross addition to such knowledge and δ be the proportional rate of loss of such knowledge, due to the death of the inventor, civil disturbance or war, etc. In the spirit of current endogenous growth theory, we assume that,

f(x) is positively valued, increasing, convex as well as smooth.

Example.

$$f(x) = [x - a + (1 + x)^{-1}],\ 0 < a < 1,$$

where we assume,

$\forall x,\ f(x) > 0,\ f(0) = 1 - a,$

$\forall x,\ f'(x) \geq 0,\ f'(0) = 0,$

$\forall x,\ f''(x) > 0.$

The net rate of knowledge accumulation is thus,

$$dx/dt = f(x) - \delta x.$$

Let b be the slope of the tangent of f through the origin, so that:

$$b = f(x^*)/x^* = f'(x^*) > 0,$$

where in the example,

$$x^* = \theta + (\theta + \theta^2)^{1/2}, \qquad \theta = a^{-1} - 1 > 0.$$

We assume that initially the value of x is near 0.

Two cases are of interest:

Case 1 (*The Chinese Case*). $\delta \geq b$.

A stable *equilibrium of stagnation* will be approached as x approaches $x_1 \leq x^*$, where the ray from the origin δ x first cuts f(x).

Case 2 (*The European - Mediterranean Case*). $\delta < b$.

The value of x will grow forever.

It is the separation of the *literati* from the *artisan* that causes a quick dissipation of the fruits of the illiterate artisan-inventors (that is, a large value of δ in Case 1). In the case where the inventors are literate (as was true in the Hellenistic world), the value of δ is much reduced, and ultimately the critical mass of knowledge accumulates to yield an Industrial Revolution. See Figure A2.1.1.

An interested reader may compare our view with that of Landes (1994).

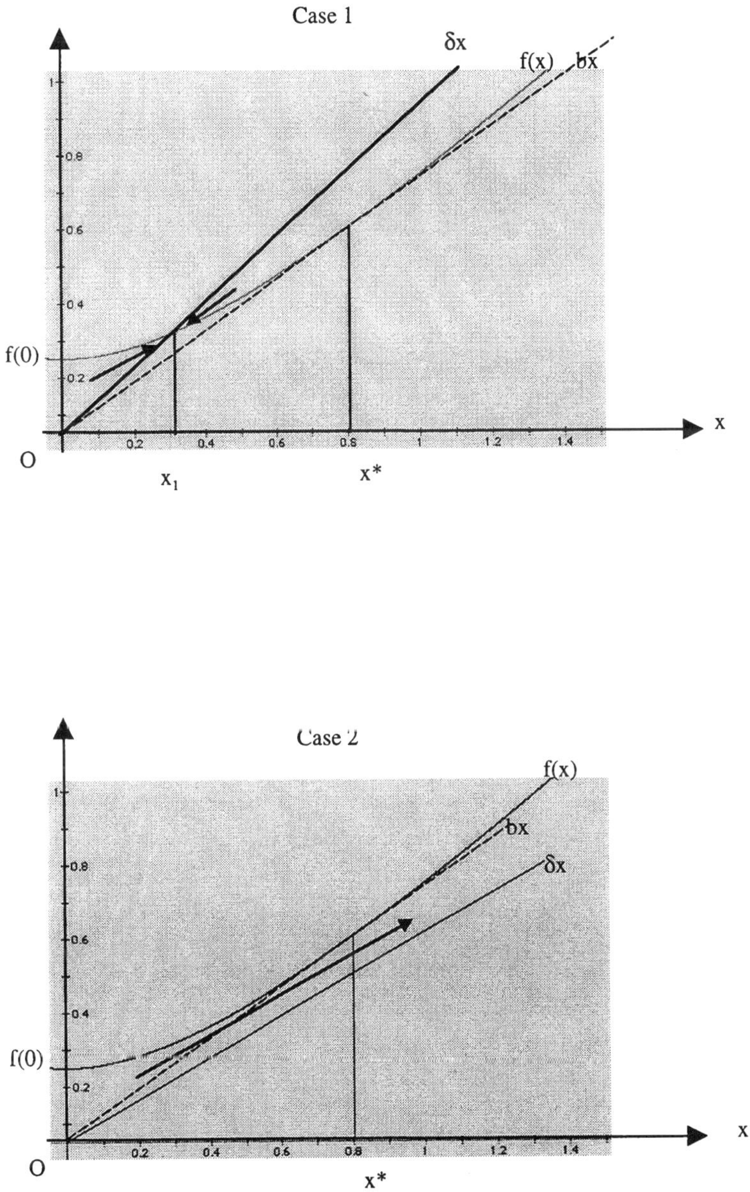

Figure A2.1.1 Knowledge dynamics

CHAPTER SUMMARY

- *Culture* has been cited as the cause for Japanese and East Asian growth:
  - Such influence must be explained through aspects of human capital, its level and growth.
- Today, each East Asian society is highly *homogeneous:*
  - Homogeneity benefits interaction among individuals and human capital formation;
  - Homogeneity is neither necessary nor sufficient in itself for growth.
- *Confucianism* is a moral philosophy that promotes discipline, harmony and learning:
  - A moral philosophy is a strength for economic growth in its 'sublimation' stage;
  - As a moral philosophy, Confucianism has specific aspects not helpful to growth.
- Japan has geographic and historical circumstances favoring its early industrialization:
  - *Their relationship with Japan* helped other Asian economies in early industrialization;
  - This relationship later complicates the task of gaining full development by limiting their ability to compete against Japan.
- Overall, the East Asian experience is not that atypical, and its replication in other areas is not ruled out.

QUESTIONS AND EXERCISES

1. Culture may affect the saving behavior, which does not affect human capital. Why is human capital likely to be part of a cultural explanation of East Asian advantage?
2. Are there factors other than Confucian ethos that may form a cultural explanation for an East Asian advantage?
3. Discuss with examples the pros and cons of the East Asian attitude toward education.
4. 'The high literacy rate of the current East Asian economies is due to the visionary leadership of their political leaders.' Comment.
5. 'Japan started industrialization early in East Asia because it had close contact with Westerners earlier than its neighbors.' Comment.
6. Does having Japan as a close neighbor help in both starting industrialization and becoming fully developed? Explain your view.
7. Over all, should one regard culture as being irrelevant to East Asian development? Or should cultural differences disqualify the East Asian experience as being an applicable precedent for other developing societies?
8. Barro and Sala-i-Martin (1995) found that in Japan, the per capita income levels of the heavily urbanized Tokyo and Osaka far exceeded the Japanese average. What does this fact imply about the significance of Singapore's surpassing the U.S. in repcri over 1995-7, according to PennTable 6.0, but not World Development Index, version 2001?
9. Use Chart 2.1.9 to verify the assessment of the growth experiences by Lucas (1988), cited in the beginning of Section 2, Chapter 1. According to PennTable 6.0, the repcri for Argentina is 58.62% in 1960 and 37.23% in 1996. Add that data to modify Chart 2.1.9 and comment.
10. Before his death in 1920, Max Weber (1930, 1951) concluded that the tenets of Confucianism and Taoism of China made a society incapable of industrializing or developing capitalism. Later, Morishima (1982) stated that Japan 'succeeded' economically (his own quotation marks) due to the 'Confucian ethos' that was selectively adopted in Japan. After the rise of the NIEs, many authors in Singapore, Hong Kong, and Taiwan regard Confucianism

as the underlying explanation of their prosperity. Are all these views *post hoc, ergo propter hoc*? Or is only one of these three correct? Or, is there in fact never any conflict among these opinions? Discuss carefully.

11. [Korea I] (Study Project) Historical accident, cultural affinity, and market forces can conspire to cause unexpected consequences:
    (a) It is a historical accident that the PRC undertook its outward-oriented reform in 1978, Vietnam followed later, but after 25 years, North Korea has not yet taken a similar step.
    (b) As rising wages induce all the NIEs to move labor intensive industries abroad, Korea faces the fact: it has the least 'Chinese connection', and hence no opportunity to outsource with the minimum coordination cost (Problem 6, Chapter 3).
    (c) Thus, the re-routing of the Asia-Pacific supply chain takes more of the nature of 'trade diversion' for Korea, but 'trade creation' for the other NIEs (Problem 5, Chapter 4).
    (d) For technology acquisition, the OEM approach leads Korea to a less-than-satisfactory result, in Linsu Kim's view (Problem 3, Chapter 12).
    (e) Ex post, this vindicates the Korean option for original brands (e. g., Samsung, Hyundai) rather than further development of Masan.

Chapter 3

CONDITIONS FOR SUSTAINED GROWTH

Industrialization and Human Capital

1. REGULARITIES, EXPLANATIONS AND IMPLICATIONS

Using a one-good model, Chapter 1 describes the evolution of the globalized economy in terms of the benchmark path, with the East Asian record cited as evidence. Chapter 2 explains that, while specific conditions may have allowed East Asian economies to be the first among the non-Western societies to industrialize, these conditions are not so unique as to make the East Asian experience irrelevant elsewhere. We now relax the one-good framework, since what happens in East Asia is not so much to produce more of the same product, but to produce more value in output from the same work force. Structural transformation pervades in the trade mix, the output mix, the job mix and the skill mix.

Industrialization was the opening move in East Asia, and it was followed by a continuing metamorphosis in the industrial composition. Industries migrate across boundaries, and sometimes the labor force moves internationally as well. These issues are examined in the present section. Subsequently, we examine how the changing specialization within the economy follows the changed spectrum of labor skills, and the role that trade plays in upgrading labor skill.

Industrialization

After the human species emerged from a precarious life based on hunting and gathering, societies survived largely through agriculture – as many still do. Understandably, the economic literature on the less-developed economies is preoccupied with such issues as land tenure, sharecropping, the use of water, and farm credit. The next step in economic development is to establish trade based on the advantages provided by the land – be it weather that favors particular cash crops, or mineral deposits offering oil or metals.

One can observe the following regularities:

1) In most less-developed societies, the population is rural – in fact, agrarian.
2) In no fully developed economy is agriculture the dominant sector in terms of either jobs or output.
3) In few advanced economies is the primary sector the principal activity.
4) Industrialization is a phase of development for most developed economies.

The explanation has much to do with Engel's Law:

As income rises, the share spent on food declines.[1]

Suppose that the world is divided into regions completely specialized in producing food and other items. Even if all outputs increase at the same proportional rate, as the world economy grows, food suppliers must receive a lesser share of income, with the terms of trade turning against them. This lies at the heart of the export pessimism thesis of Prebisch (1959). In Figure 3.1.1, dotted and solid lines stand respectively for situations before and after the change. The arrow signs highlight the tangent points on the indifference curves.

For illustration, see Example 1, Appendix 3.1.

But the matter does not stop there. First, food production critically depends on land. Countries with their given *lebensraum* would find it harder to double output in food than in manufacture. Second, the farmland of food producers is likely to be geographically concentrated. Since food production depends more than does manufacture on weather, and weather conditions tend to vary from place to place, output variation imposes more risks of local harvest failure on food producers than price variation due to general harvest failures on food consumers.[2] Third, taste and technology changes are

---

[1] It is suicidal for a person 5 times richer than one's neighbor to consume 5 times as much in calories as the latter.

[2] The work of Newbery and Stiglitz (1981) is relevant here.

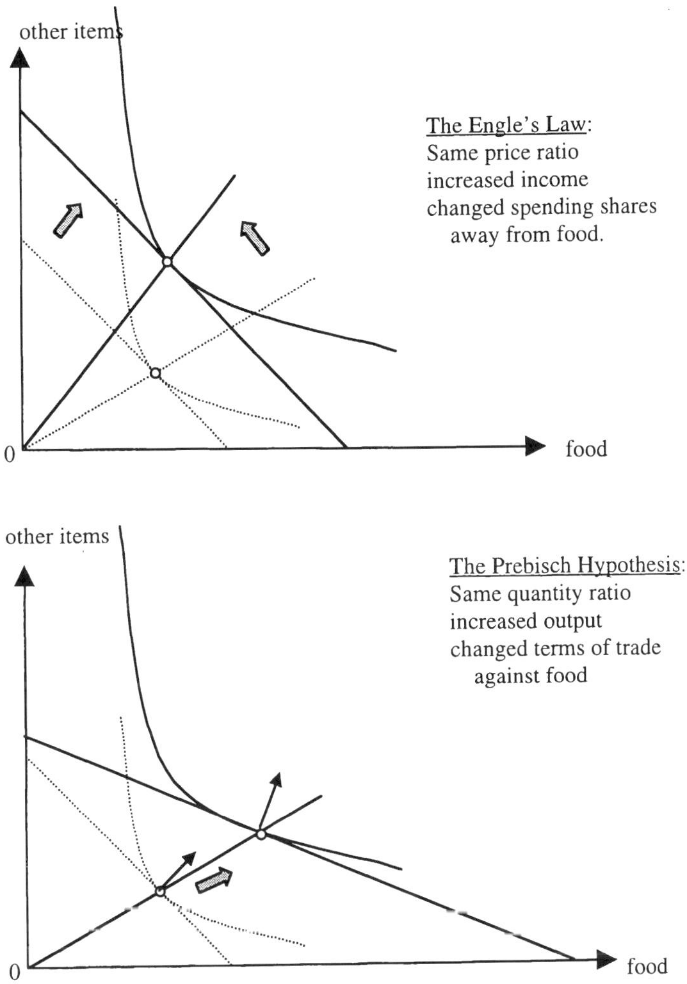

Figure 3.1.1 Food versus other items

likely to threaten food producers more than food consumers. Fourth, skill acquired in the 'land-based' technology of food production is likely to be product-specific and non-resilient in a risky world. These points about food production are often applicable to other agricultural products and other primary outputs. For primary output using an exhaustible resource, such as mineral reserves and some timber, the situation is not better. There, an increase of output per worker may only mean a trade off of current feast for future famine, even though the future may only be relevant to one's children. Finally, should the technology for food production advance by leaps and bounds, the limited availability of land and the scale economy of modern technology are likely to unload surplus labor on urban areas for non-farm jobs.

A comparison with industry is relevant here. In post-industrial societies such as the United States, manufacture seems to go the way of agriculture, although the outputs of both sectors remain important for both sustenance and the earning of export revenue to meet import needs. Historically, it would not have been possible for the U.S. or most other countries to skip the Industrial Age, going directly from agriculture to the post-industrial society. Whether New Zealand will be a country that manages to accomplish this feat remains to be seen.

This conveniently brings us to the question of whether an agricultural revolution is necessary before industrialization. It is commonly argued that there needs to be an agricultural surplus to finance development, and to supply low-wage labor for labor-intensive industries. For most economies that already have a large population on the farm, this argument sounds reasonable. However, among the Asian NIEs, both Hong Kong and Singapore did not go that route. In short, the conventional wisdom of staged growth needs careful scrutiny.[3]

Chapter 2 indicates that Japan, Korea and Cyprus have been very successful in the catching-up process, while Argentina actually has fallen back. Chart 3.1.1 displays the manufacturing share of the exports of these four economies over the period 1963-1996. This provides some indication of their comparative advantage in manufacturing. Japan and Argentina have changed relatively little, but both Cyprus and Korea have registered dramatic changes.

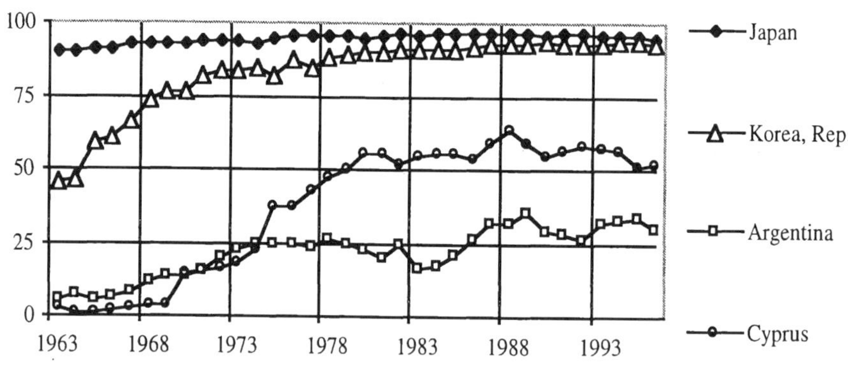

Chart 3.1.1 Manufacturing share in exports

In the catching-up process, industrialization is the opening move, but it is certainly not the last. Continuous upgrading of the economic structure is called for. For example, one may consider the changing export mix of

---

[3] The term 'industrialization' has often been associated with a model of Matsuyama (1991), which emphasizes increasing returns. Actually, the analysis is also applicable, for example, to irrigation farming, where critical mass matters.

Taiwan over the years. The percentage share of food, beverage and tobacco preparations (mainly a single crop, sugar cane) has declined from more than 80% to insignificant proportions. Textiles, etc., rose to a share of 30% until its importance was overtaken by electric machines (mainly, personal computers and peripherals). There has been continued change, but there has also been a broad tendency toward diversification. The increased shares of the 'others' categories reflects the improved resilience of the economy. Based on the Taiwan Statistical Data Book, Chart 3.1.2 offers a graphic representation of Taiwan's export mix.

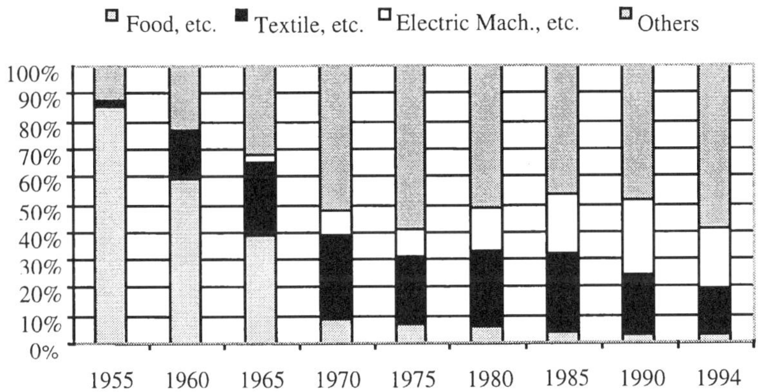

Chart 3.1.2 Taiwan's export mix

The restructuring process is always challenging; however, it is less so for an industrial society than for an economy producing primary goods. Taiwanese workers servicing machines for sugar refineries can produce machine tools later on. Hong Kong garment workers can be retrained to supply design clothing for European high fashion. It would be a different story if one tries to reassign workers tending oil palms to drilling oil wells.

In the catching-up process, industries migrate and the labor force might move across borders. This concerns the pattern of specialization of an economy.

The Pattern of Specialization

The importance of industrialization is of course well understood. In fact, that realization caused the wide adoption of import substitution policies after World War II. By themselves, however, none of the import-substitution initiatives resulted in sustained growth. Whether such policies served as a useful platform for later development in Korea and Taiwan remains debatable. Hong Kong also has enjoyed sustained rapid growth, but never practiced import substitution.

The truly important issue about East Asia is not how its industries got *started* but how its industrialization became *sustained*. In Argentina, industries blossomed during the supply disruptions of both World Wars, but the country failed to develop comparative advantages in these industries when the wars ended. These industries survived only by retreating, once and for all, behind high protective tariff barriers. In contrast, it was no surprise that after their initial large devaluations, Taiwan and Korea became competitive in labor-intensive industries. Yet these two economies managed to retain their export market as their wage rates rose. Eventually higher wages did cause these economies to exit from such industries – only to enter sectors with even higher value-added.

The Simple Case – Learning by Exporting

To understand the dynamics behind what happened, it is necessary to become familiar with the static positions at each instant. A motion picture is the aggregation of snapshots, frame by frame.

For this purpose, it is best to use a modified diagram of Dorbusch, Fischer and Samuelson (1977) in Figure 3.1.2 for the problem facing a small 'country.'

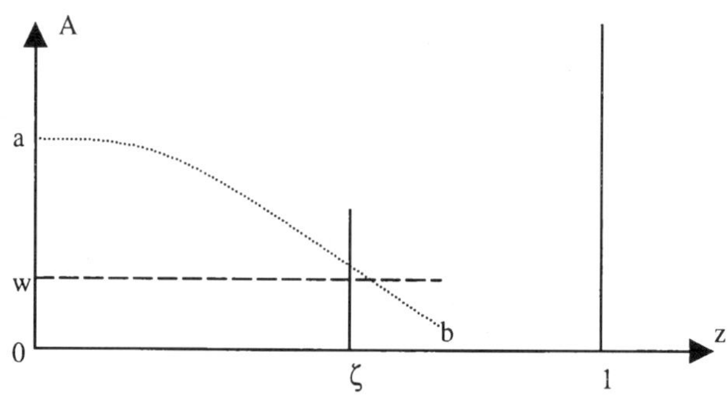

Figure 3.1.2 Spectrum of goods

Suppose there are infinitely many goods, indexed by z, $0 \leq z \leq 1$. Each good is produced by labor alone. Choose the unit of good in such a way that the unit labor cost of good z produced abroad is one unit of a hard currency, say, the U.S. dollar. Alternatively, one can think that the unit of each good z is chosen as a dollar's worth, *if the production is carried out abroad.* Assume that currently, every good z can be produced at home with domestic labor, where the unit product of labor is A(z), shown as the dotted line ab. The goods z are so arranged that A(z) is a strictly decreasing function of z. At the present, the domestic wage rate according to the current exchange rate is w in the hard currency.

Clearly, without any tariff, good ζ can be produced at home only if: $A(\zeta) \geq w$.

In other words, *if prices are based on the labor cost abroad,* the producer can make profit on ζ, since the value of the labor product exceeds the wage. (At equilibrium, price is competed to wage cost at home, and profit is zero.)

Now, in Figure 3.1.3, we consider two economies X and Y, which face the world market and initially share the same technology, as represented by the dotted curve ab. However, the wage rates are at w and ω, respectively, so that good ζ is produced by the low wage economy X, but not by the high wage economy Y. For example, if X plays host to many refugees.

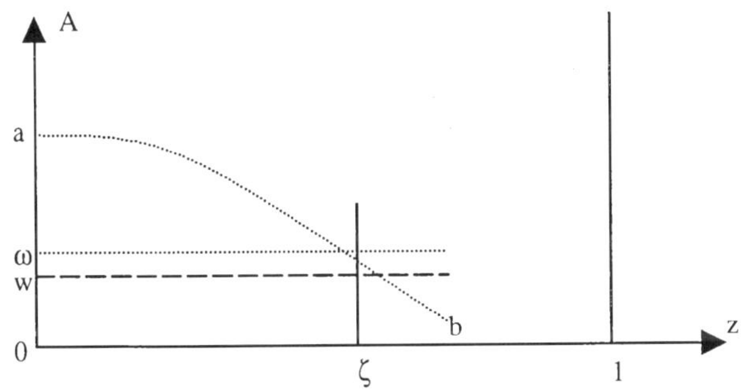

Figure 3.1.3 Specialization pattern

Subsequently, in economy X producing good ζ, it is observed that the wage rises to W. Yet against Y, the other economy, which *still* has a wage level ω < W, this economy X remains competitive in the market for ζ. The inference is, economy X (which retains the industry) must have benefited from a rise of labor productivity. This is represented in Figure 3.1.4 by the curve, aB, which lies above ab over y1. More is discussed next section.

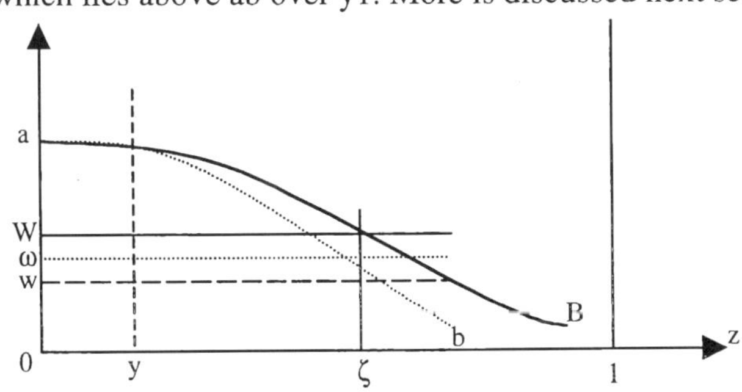

Figure 3.1.4 Under different technology

The above discussion seems to fit well the description of Morawetz (1981), who found that the textile suppliers in Colombia (Y, in the above story) were not competitive against their East Asian competitors (X, in the above story). The Colombian explanation of their difficult competitive position was that the East Asian firms enjoyed the advantage of cheap wages, a statement that probably *was* true at some time before the visit of Morawetz. Yet during his field study, Morawetz found that by then the East Asian wage was no longer very low; it was the differences in efficiency which provided the East Asians the competitive edge.

Morawetz further reported that East Asians exported to the North American market, where the requirements of tight quality control and punctual delivery must be satisfied in order to retain the clientele. In contrast, Colombian factories either catered to their domestic market or their customers inside the Andean Group, a customs union, where standards for garments were lax.

This episode implies that the process of economic development may well be 'path-dependent.' When neither economy exports to a market with demanding customers, the economy with a lower wage (say, Hong Kong with its refugee workers) would have the comparative advantage. After some time, when one economy is a seasoned supplier for the demanding markets, while the other is not, then wage differential alone may not make the difference.

A Two-Stage Example – Fragmentation and Guest Workers

We next consider a good that is producible by labor at home or abroad in two processes, U(p stream) and the D(own stream). The units of labor required are respectively A and a units at home, and A* and a* abroad. The wage rate is w at home and 1 abroad. The production may be carried out in two places with an additional coordination cost in the proportion of δ. Labor can work overseas, at a proportional extra pay, which is Δ for workers from home, and Δ^* from abroad. The interested reader can verify that the unit product cost assumes the following values according to the eight different arrangements (Table 3.1.1).

At any market equilibrium, the competitive force ensures that the unit profit is driven down to zero,[4] which means:

$w = \text{Min}\ \{C_j\text{: } 1 \leq j \leq 8\}$.

Our intention is to explore several simple cases, which provide us with insights but involve a minimum of details. In the tradition of international trade theory, we shall assume that each of the two economies in question has distinctive comparative advantages. Without losing generality, it will be assumed

[4] In real life, part of the 'labor cost' would be the return to 'entrepreneurial labor,' which is known as normal profit.

Produced at Home	No guest worker	$C_1 = w(A + a)$
	Guest worker for U process	$C_2 = (1 + \Delta^*)A^* + wa$
	Guest worker for D process	$C_3 = wA + (1 + \Delta^*)\, a^*$
Produced Abroad	No guest worker	$C_4 = A^* + a^*$
	Guest worker for U process	$C_5 = (1 + \Delta)wA + a^*$
	Guest worker for D process	$C_6 = A^* + (1 + \Delta)wa$
U process at Home; D process Abroad		$C_7 = (1 + \delta)(wA + a^*)$
D process at Home; U process Abroad		$C_8 = (1 + \delta)(A^* + wa)$

Table 3.1.1 Costs under 8 arrangements

that labor At Home (Abroad) is relatively more efficient for process D (U), or,

$$a / a^* < A / A^*$$

Case 1. Zero coordination cost ($\delta = 0$) and ∞ overseas pay ($\Delta = \infty = \Delta^*$).

Figure 3.1.5 displays the minimum unit cost envelope, which is made up sequentially of linear segments along the C_1, C_4 and C_8 lines.[5] Any efficient arrangement must be on the envelope. The alternative arrangement of carrying out the U-process at home and the D-process abroad yields a linear line C_7. One can verify that this line has a positive intercept and cuts the horizontal C_4 line to the left of the vertical line at the position of $(A^* + a^*)/(A + a)$. Hence, it lies above the Min C envelope (in heavy lines) at every value of w. If the parameter δ takes positive but small values, the C_8 line will shift upward. When the shift is far enough, then 'fragmented production' represented by C_8 cannot be efficient.

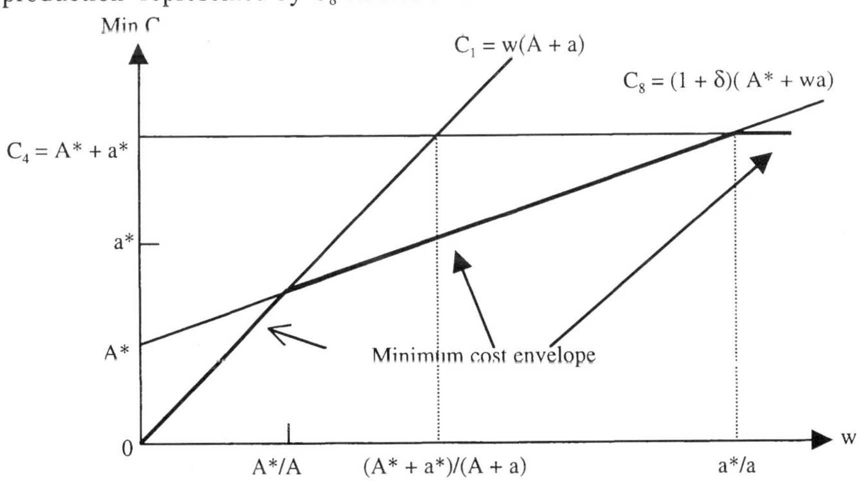

Figure 3.1.5 Unit cost envelope

---

[5] It is plotted for $A = 2/3 = a^*$ and $A^* = 1/3 = a$.

Now consider the opposite scenario, in which the coordination cost was initially too high for the product to be produced at two locations. A reduction of the transportation or communication cost will facilitate coordination. This leads to the relocation of part of the process – say from the advanced economies to the developing economies. That is precisely what happened in East Asia. Even today, the central processing units of most personal computers used around the world are produced in the U.S. Other elements are supplied from Malaysia to Taiwan and Korea and Japan.

Case 2. Infinite coordination cost ($\delta = \infty$). Finite overseas pay ($\Delta > 0$, $\Delta^* > 0$).

Assume that it is not efficient to either assign workers from Home to the U-process (say, they may be inadequately trained) or the workers Abroad to the D-process (say, they are over-qualified), so that neither C_1 nor C_4 is a realistic answer. C_3 and C_5 are similarly ruled out. In view of the prohibitive cost of coordination when the product is produced at two different locations, one must use guest workers. The question is who goes to which location. Here the values of Δ and Δ^* are often decisive. In other words, at the equilibrium wage ratio as reflected in w, does C_2 or C_6 imply a lower cost? In the real world, the low-paid workers are less 'choosy' in leaving their home, while high-paid workers can demand to stay close to their family and friends. A low w (as implied by our parenthetic statements) means a lower value of Δ as compared to Δ^*. A real life case is that when the U.S. firm General Instruments decided to produce a new product in Asia, hundreds of Thai production workers were recruited to go to Taiwan to work with the (relatively smaller number of) Taiwanese-trained production engineers. The graphic illustration is left for readers as an exercise.

The examples for two-stage production are relevant for three reasons: the decline of transportation and communication costs encourage globalized production, the 'fragmented' product cycle is an important force behind industrialization in East Asia,[6] and finally, labor migration contributes to reverse brain drain, which is important for technology spillover (to be elaborated later).

Human Capital

So far we have discussed the changing technology in the world, and how economies may restructure themselves to take advantage of it. Facing the same world, not all developing economies have benefited, let alone

---

[6] See for example, Crown and Coleman (1996) for bicycles, Hobday (1995) for electronics, Levy (1990) for shoes, and Jones and Kierzkowski (1990) for deeper issues.

benefited to the same degree. Just as a person needs a television set to gain access to a television program that is broadcast freely over the airwaves, an economy must have enough human capital to seize the opportunities presented to it.

Human capital has many forms, from the fruits of one's own R&D, to formal education, individual knowledge and information, to various mutual relationships that are relevant for production. Some are the result of cost and efforts. Others are acquired only with experience.

Charts 3.1.3 and 3.1.4 indicate where East Asia stood in the mid-1990s in both available manpower and R&D spending relative to the advanced economies.

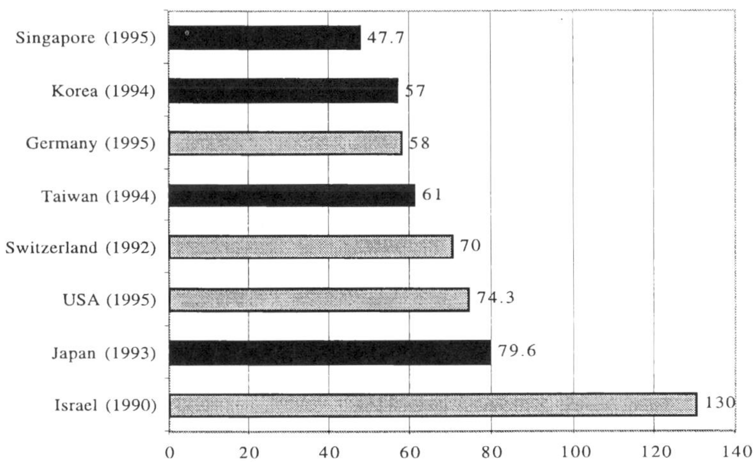

Chart 3.1.3 Research scientists and engineers/100,000 in labor force Source: Hang (1999)

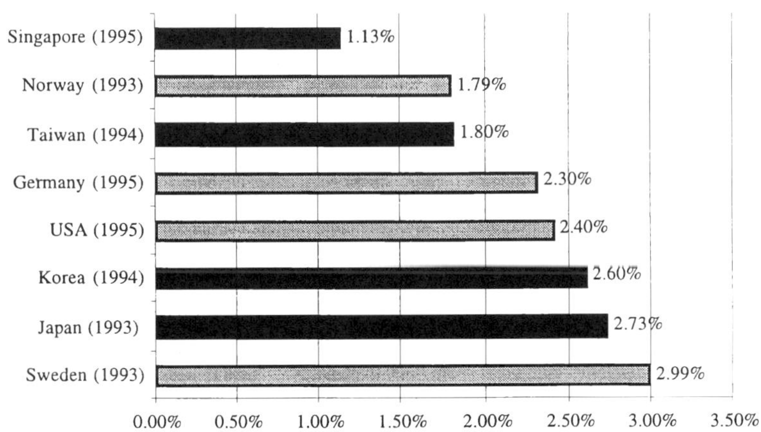

Chart 3.1.4 Gross Expenditure on R&D/GDP Source: Hang (1999)

In terms of the benchmarks for scientific and research potential, the NIEs of East Asia are comparable to the leading industrial societies. This is quite a change: 40% of the Korean labor force in 1946 and 44% of the Taiwanese population older than six years in 1950 were illiterate, while at Independence, Singapore lagged behind Sri Lanka in education and health. These facts signify both these countries' progress over time and also the fact that their modest initial conditions did not prevent their rather rapid development.

Beside education, learning-by-doing is also a very powerful factor in industrialization. This is treated carefully in the next section.

2. LEARNING-BY-DOING AND TRADE

Information for production may be gained in many ways. One can read users' manuals for new equipment, or pay engineering and management consultants. One can acquire information in the same way that one purchases fuel or raw material. One may decide to train the labor force or launch R & D projects, quite similar to the way one invests in physical assets. We now introduce the phenomenon of *practice makes perfect*, known as *learning-by-doing* in the literature. Four properties make this phenomenon important in development policies.

First, there is a wealth of potentially useful information that is specific and diffused. This is acquired from experience, not from education or R&D, and so on.[7]

Second, since current production may enhance future productivity, certain present action is justified only by this complementarity.[8]

Third, latecomers gain information from the first mover; this externality breeds inaction unless public action is taken to overcome private greed.[9]

Fourth, inasmuch as the situation is complex and changeable, detailed involvement on the part of the state can lead to corruption, bureaucratic gridlock or both.[10]

In addition, the literature on this topic deals with the advisability of 'openness,' which is close to our present interest. In our belief, all these imply that successful development calls for the informed containment of *both* market and government failures. One should not hope for perfection.

---

[7] For theory, see Auerswald, Kaufman, Lobo, and Shell (1999).

[8] For an early study about the economic effect of learning-by-doing, see Arrow (1962a).

[9] To explain how learning-by-doing justifies industrial policy, see Itoh et al. (1991).

[10] The complexity of the optimal policy under learning-by-doing is seen in Clemhout and Wan (1970).

When we discussed the path-dependence of the development process with Figure 3.1.4, the key is the shift of the A(z) curve from ab to aB due to technology gain. According to Morawetz, such a change might come from trade. But it has been argued in the literature that, under some assumptions, trade can retard or even prevent development. This deserves examination in detail.

First off, the assumption that A(z) is decreasing with z in Dornbusch, Fischer and Samuelson is not restrictive. The good index, z, can be rearranged at will. They have so arranged that (a) the relative labor efficiency of the country in question decreases as z increases. Additional assumptions can be made. (b) Goods with a higher z value also use technology that is more advanced and demanding, in some objective sense.[11] (c) Goods using more advanced technology appear later in time. (d) The earlier a good has appeared, the less room is left for further improvement.[12] (e) Earlier technologies provide fewer opportunities for acquiring knowledge that may improve technology elsewhere.

In spite of some occasional exceptions, the assumptions (b) through (e) appear generally valid. Take 'the country in question' to be a developing economy in assumption (a). Now add (f) the economy that discovers new knowledge during production gains more from it than others do. These assumptions *seem* to jointly imply that a developing economy should seek self-sufficiency, rather than trade. This was argued by Alwyn Young (1991) and concurred in by Stokey (1991).

To illustrate this argument, we adopt from Young (1993) the ingenious Principle of Bounded Learning. This means no knowledge can be gained by producing goods with a very low z index. Thus, in Figure 3.1.4, if $z \leq y$ for some y, then aB coincides with ab. To make the argument clear-cut, we reproduce this diagram as Figure 3.2.1, where the wage w for the developing economy is such that all goods produced are to the left of y. The developing economy is then 'shut out' from all production that promises learning.

Paradoxically, self-sufficiency is precisely the *tried and failed* policy of all communist economies, from the former Soviet Union throughout East Europe to North Korea and Cuba, as well as Vietnam and Mainland China before their reforms. Moreover, under different political and economic institutions in Africa, Latin America and South Asia, similar policies brought equally unsatisfactory outcomes. In contrast, in East Asia, fast growth occurs precisely when trade expands by leaps and bounds. Asian history suggests that a 'shut out' is very likely for North Korea, which practices self-sufficiency, but unlikely for South Korea, which trades extensively.

---

[11] Such as more precise process control, longer training for workers, etc.

[12] The production method is said to be more 'mature.'

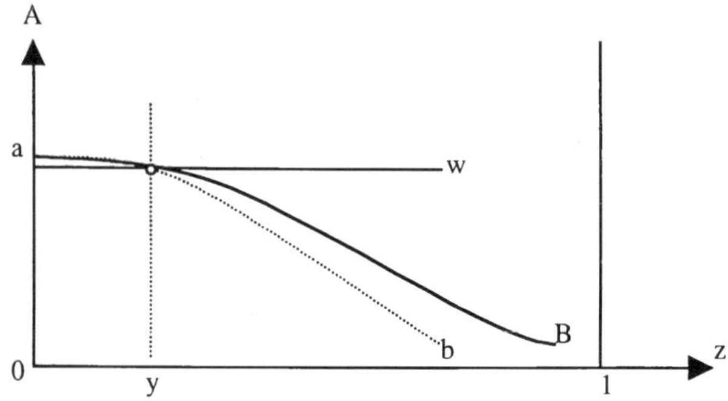

Figure 3.2.1 'Shut out'

Young explained how this happens in a model with three or more economies. A more advanced developing economy (say in East Asia) may gain at the expense of those that are even less advanced (say in Latin America). This mechanism is consistent with logic, but not necessarily reality. Percentage wise, Japan certainly gained world export share and Latin America lost. But this mainly reflects *trade creation* between Japan and everyone else, and not *trade diversion* from Latin America, and so on to Japan. With or without Japan in the trading world, it is most unlikely Latin America would have supplied what Japan exported: ships, cars, and memory computer chips.

For an explanation, the analysis of Dornbusch, Fischer and Samuelson must be adapted more fundamentally, in two steps. The conceptual discussion is presented below, with analytic notes in an appendix. The first step concerns *demand.* Assume that every product includes a pair of goods, for export and for domestic use. Packaging is needed for shipping. Due to the cost of returning defective products to factory, exported units must be better controlled for quality, through inspection or process design. In East Asia, goods for the affluent export market are often of a higher grade than goods intended for domestic consumption. It used to be that Hyundai cars sold in the U.S. came with Mitsubishi engines, while those sold at home were entirely Korean. Higher-priced garments offered in Taiwan were labeled 'export quality.' Given the need to spread the overhead cost, high quality products may lack a viable clientele at home when industrialization starts. This is due to the same income effect that underlies Engel's Law in Figure 3.1.1. If for export, one produces with quality, and in quality, one meets challenge, then the useful experience learned only in overcoming challenges can come from export operations.

The second step concerns *supply*. Here we introduce the Principle of Complementarity. Like a bar-bell set which includes a bar and two bells, goods of export quality may be viewed as made up of several different complementary components: the basic component, the 'domestic additives' (such as quality control) and *sometimes* also the 'imported additives' (such as the imported engine). Substitutability among these three is strictly limited. Without exports, the 'imported additives' cannot be afforded. For lack of material, some products simply cannot be produced. For other components, due to the Principle of Comparative Advantage (which was introduced in Figure 3.1.1), the production of goods of customary quality with 100% local input content can be very costly. Firms selling these goods at high cost are not likely to survive in a developing economy, given the high income elasticity of the demand for high quality goods.

The implications of the Principle of Complementarity for the 'domestic additives' are even more far reaching. We maintain that, through export operations, a developing economy almost always can gain useful knowledge for its future. Initially the exports may seem trivially simple. The knowledge gained may not be 'new' or 'useful' to others, especially the advanced economies.

Figure 3.2.2 displays schematically the development of an economy. Over time, the content of export evolves from sugar ξ, to textiles η, to computers ζ. Sugar is produced through the refining process, x, and supported by such satellite industries as machine shops, a, for equipment maintenance.[13] Textile η is produced by the weaving process, y, and supported by both machine shops, in fabricating spindles and shipping agency operations, b, for inspection and packaging. To produce computers ζ, one needs computer fabrication, z, supported by machine shops, a, shipping agency, b, and chip design houses, c. Sugar export may improve the skills of machine shop workers, who produce later both textile machines and the

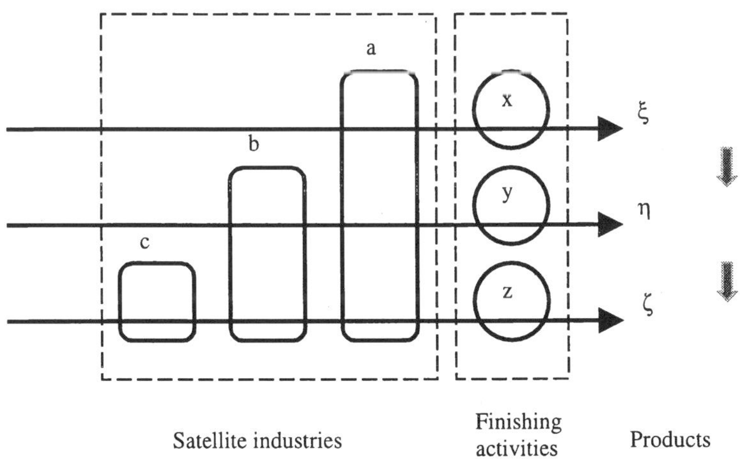

Figure 3.2.2 Changing exports

[13] Formally, such complementarity in production may be written as X = Min {x, a}, if one unit of output requires one unit of each type of activity.

mechanic parts of personal computers. The satellite industries provide generic skill more than specific products. When learning from some specific product reaches its ceiling, the competence in generic skill may continue rising. Before the technology of one wave of satellite industries becomes fully 'mature' (with no learning potential whatsoever), another wave joins with new challenges. So learning goes on. The production cost for final goods decreases as the satellite industries grow and gain competence.

Figure 3.2.2 may appear simplistic, but it is far from artificial. According to Fransman (1986), the initial labor force for the Taiwanese machine tool industry was comprised largely of former maintenance workers from sugar refineries. By the time sugar exports sank into insignificance in the economy, machine tools exports to the U.S. had reached such a point that the U.S. requested Taiwan to impose voluntary export restrictions, along with Japan, Switzerland and Germany. According to Hobday (1995: 141-2, 157-8), Singapore attracted foreigners to produce hard disk drives there, by the 'pre-electronic' skill of its workers in precision machining, such as the 4000 trained by the failed Rollei (Lee, 2000).

The 'domestic additives' should not be interpreted literally as involving only products or industries. They may pertain to individual operations, which can subsequently be provided by spin-off firms. Shieh (1992) describes in detail how a plethora of operations in garment making, such as cutting, sewing, etc. were carried out by proliferating mini-firms in Taiwan to accommodate U.S. market demand for various types of clothing. Watanabe reported on a U.S. plant in Hong Kong assembling car radios from various imported inputs.[14] A supervisor, having learned how to recruit and train workers, arrange plant layout, schedule production runs and control product quality, quit to start his own assembly shop for digital watches. All these specific case studies share the theme that learning takes place at the level of operations and activities, and in the production of various specific goods. In short, it is not likely that a developing economy facing a trading world will be 'cornered' by the force of trade into technological stagnation.

So far we have shown that the force of comparative advantage need not lead the less developed economy to a dead end, and self-sufficiency is not necessarily as promising an alternative as it may seem. Individual cases were enumerated for illumination. More sweeping conclusions have not been reached, but this is not to be expected, in any event. Models can always be built to show that trade can either retard or enhance learning, and thus development. Whether such activities yield *useful* information or otherwise all depends on the assumptions about the productive activities under the

---

[14] See Van and Wan (1999).

trade-induced specialization. In truth, the key appears to be not whether one learns anything *new*, but whether one learns the *right* new thing. After all, the rapid industrialization of East Europe after World War II did introduce new knowledge to workers there, under Stalinist methods. What is *useful* and *right* may not be known until decades later, and then only in hindsight.

We offer some schematic explanation of our own in Figure 3.2.3. At the beginning, a less developed economy L produces outputs that are both simple and not competitive. The ultimate goal is the fully developed status, marked D. Two strategies are open: either it is outward oriented, or it follows import substitution. The former approach leads to a competitive but simple technology. This is marked as position E, to signify East Asia. The latter approach yields outputs that are complex but not competitive, typically in heavy industries. This is marked as position S, which signifies the former Soviet Union. Initially, both approaches lead to success, in the technical sense. To reach the fully developed status from position E, any progress is in the context of learning-by-doing. Any R & D is largely self-financed, as in Japan. To start from position S, one has to catch up with the technology leader, the United States. By not pursuing an outward oriented strategy, it is hard to tap into the technology backlog.[15] Out of policy choice, there is little economic interaction with the outside world. This is a situation true for communist economies, but also for Brazil and India, both democracies with little ideological conflict with the U.S. Beyond the initial stage, one cannot rely upon resource mobilization to outgrow the U.S. The only way to close the gap is by fortunate technological breakthroughs. Obviously, that is not something to be relied upon in the long run. Eventually, the technology gap widens.

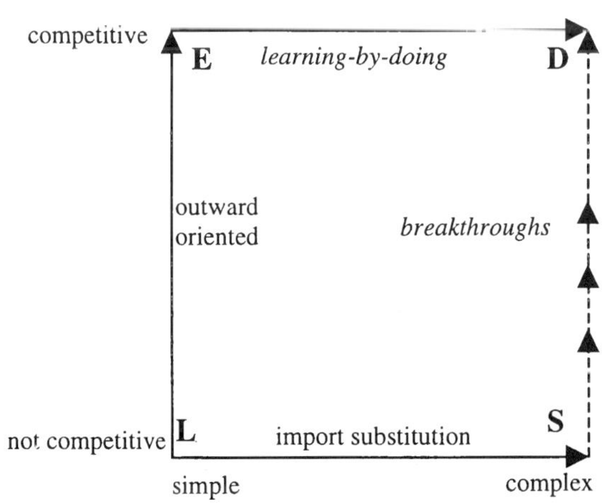

Figure 3.2.3 Alternative agendas

[15] Apparently, on that score, even espionage helped little.

Thus, to conclude, the superiority of outward orientation over self-sufficiency rests upon a fuller utilization of the technological backlog. Based on past evidence, the mechanism of learning-by-doing does not offer any tendency offsetting that superiority. By selectively protecting its domestic market, Japan has managed to partially close the gap with the U.S. at a fast pace. However, even if it does not have a domestic market large enough to protect, Singapore has succeeded equally well. Hong Kong never had an industrial policy, but in terms of (average) per capita GDP, it has not done that badly either. Apparently, under quite different policies the mechanism of learning-by-doing has done its share in making these economies successful. As Morawetz found out, it did play a role in making the East Asian economies more competitive than Latin Americans in their industrial exports. The role of learning-by-doing and international interaction will be revisited again in later chapters.

APPENDIX 3.1 EXAMPLES OF LEARNING-BY-DOING

To make our discussions precise, we present below several examples.

Example 1. A Two-Country Example

Consider a world with two countries, 'home' and 'foreign,' with the same size labor forces, $L = L^* = 1$. There are two sectors. In both countries, the learning bound has been reached for one sector, but not the other. Call the former agriculture, and the latter industry. Both produce outputs with labor only, under constant returns.

For agriculture and industry, the production levels are x and y at home, and x* and y* abroad, while the consumption levels are γ_x and γ_y at home, and $\gamma_x{}^*$ and $\gamma_y{}^*$ abroad. Their unit labor productivities are $q_x = 1$ and $q_y < 1$ at home, and $q_x{}^* = N$ and $q_y{}^* = N$ abroad. Goods require no extra treatment for export.

The representative individuals maximize the same form of felicity index, defined over consumption:

$$U = \gamma_x (\gamma_y + \Delta) \quad \text{and} \quad U^* = \gamma_x{}^* (\gamma_y{}^* + \Delta) \text{ (The Geary-Stone form)}$$

where $\Delta \geq 0$ shows an income effect, similar to what was depicted in Figure 3.1.1.

Here the implication is that industrial goods (say, cars) are not essential to subsistence. The very poor live solely on agricultural produce (say, food). Conceptually, one may follow Lancaster and consider individuals not to consume goods (food and cars) but characteristics of goods ('sustenance' and 'mobility'). Since people can get around somehow, with or without cars, they are all endowed with Δ units of the characteristic of mobility. These are non-tradable, but still substitutable with manufactured goods in consumption.

Let the agricultural good be the unit of value; the unit price of the industrial good is p or p* respectively for the two countries. In free trade, p = p*. There is neither lending nor borrowing. Thus, the value of consumption equals all income equals the value of production:

$$\gamma_x + p\,\gamma_y = I = x + py, \text{ or } \gamma_x{}^* + p^*\,\gamma_y{}^* = I^* = x^* + p^*y^*.$$

We can solve the consumption problem below.

Because of the 'virtual endowment' of industrial goods, the 'virtual income' is $I + p\Delta$ or $I^* + p^*\Delta$. By the symmetry between the characteristics, γ_x and $\gamma_y + \Delta$, or $\gamma_x{}^*$ and $\gamma_y{}^* + \Delta$, this means that, *if possible*, the 'virtual income' should be split half-and-half between the two. Thus, *ideally*, 'industrial goods' receive $(I + p\Delta)/2$ or $(I^* + p^*\Delta)/2$ in value, or, $(\Delta + I/p)/2$

or $(\Delta + I^*/p^*)/2$ in quantity. Should the *ideal* amount fall below the *virtual* endowment Δ, one *would like* to sell off the excess part of the latter, which is of course *impossible*. So, when $\Delta \geq I/p$ or $\Delta \geq I^*/p^*$, *all* income is spent on the agricultural product.

For our purpose, assume that:

$$N - 1 > \Delta \geq 0.$$

These conditions assure that at least one country (the foreign country) always consumes some industrial goods. In addition, the price ratio under free trade equals the cost ratio of the foreign country.[16]

Case 1. The policy regime of free trade.

It can be routinely verified that at the market equilibrium, the budget is balanced for each country, and all markets are cleared at the solution:

$$p = p^* = 1;$$

for $\Delta \leq 1$, (There is some trade under free trade)

$$x = 1, \qquad y = 0,$$

$$\gamma_x = (1 + \Delta)/2, \qquad \gamma_y = (1 - \Delta)/2,$$

$$x^* = (N - 1 + 2\Delta)/2, \qquad y^* = (N + 1 - 2\Delta)/2,$$

$$\gamma_x^* = (N + \Delta)/2, \qquad \gamma_y^* = (N - \Delta)/2;$$

for $\Delta > 1$ (There is no trade under free trade)

$$x = 1, \qquad y = 0.$$

$$\gamma_x = 1, \qquad \gamma_y = 0,$$

$$x^* = (N - 1 + 2\Delta)/2, \qquad y^* = (N - \Delta)/2,$$

$$\gamma_x^* = (N - 1 + 2\Delta)/2, \qquad \gamma_y^* = (N - \Delta)/2.$$

The home country is shut out, in any event.

Case 2. The policy regime of no trade.

For the foreign country, it can be verified that at the equilibrium,

$$p^* = 1,$$

---

[16] Home country is 'small.'

$$x^* = \gamma_x^* = (N + \Delta)/2,$$

$$y^* = \gamma_y^* = (N - \Delta)/2.$$

For the home country,

$$p = 1/ q_y,$$

$$x = \gamma_x = [1+(\Delta/q_y)]/2, \quad y = \gamma_y = q_y\,[1-(\Delta/q_y)]/2, \quad \text{if } q_y \geq \Delta,$$

$$x = \gamma_x = 1, \quad y = \gamma_y = 0, \quad \text{if } q_y < \Delta.$$

The home country remains shut out, if $q_y < \Delta$.

Figure A3.1.1 displays the budget line ab of the home country under free trade, where the industrial good is consumed at some positive level. However, the comparative advantage of the home economy lies in good x that is produced with mature technology.

The key issue is, would protective tariff be adequate to nurture the industrial sector? As was shown above, that depends on both (a) how much the industrial good is regarded as a luxury, and (b) how efficient is the industry at home relative to abroad. These are captured here in the two parameters Δ and q_y.

Given the value Δ (say, at 1/2), Figure A3.1.1 shows that in contrast with the budget line with a slope $-q_y$, the slope of the indifference curve through a is $-\Delta$. If the home country is relatively efficient (say, $q_y = 3/4 > \Delta$), the indifference curve at a is cut from the above by the production frontier ab'.[17] Some industrial good will be produced under sufficient protection. However, if the home country is much less efficient relative to the foreign country (say, $q_y = 1/4 < \Delta$), as when the production frontier is represented by the line ab", then the industry is not viable even with the total cessation of trade. Figure A3.1.2 shows the relationship between the parameters and the effect of protection. Thus, regarding the learning effect, protection is no panacea.

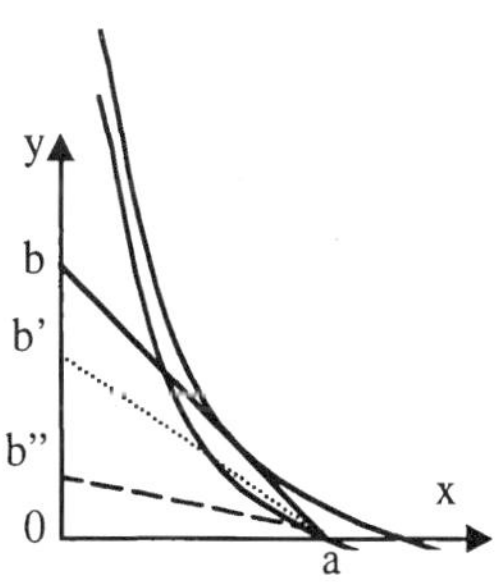

Figure A3.1.1 Learning

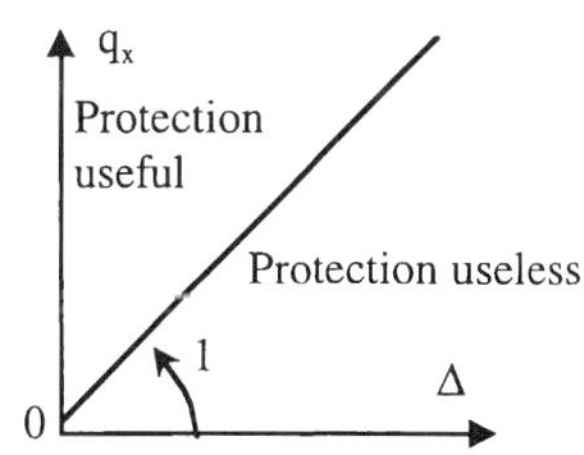

Figure A3.1.2 Parameter map

[17] In the absence of trade, the consumption point (not shown) implies some car consumption, and hence production.

By the last example, the claim that *protection aids learning* overestimates the efficacy of protection. It will be shown next that the claim that *trade retards learning* equally underestimates the possible benefit of trade.

Example 2. The Principle of Complementarity

We now modify the last example, with the focus on the home country. For simplicity, assume that the industrial good (y or y*) is assembled in fixed proportions, with one unit each of the M tradable components, θ_j, j = 1, ...M (say, M = 2). The assumption of fixed proportions is essentially true. The use of one unit each of every component is a matter of choosing the unit. Next, set q_j to be the amount of the jth component that can be produced by one unit of domestic labor (say, $q_1 = 4/15$ and $q_2 = 4$). Then:

$$q_y = 1/[(1/q_1) + \ldots + (1/q_M)]$$

which gives the labor productivity of good y in the home country, with 100% local content (say, 1/4 = 1/[(15/4) + (1/4)]). Denote the corresponding productivity of foreign labor as q_j^* (say, $q_1^* = 2N = q_2^*$) and q_y^* (say, N). Recall the discussion of the two-stage production in the last section. Under the policy of free trade for components, one may compute the sign of the 'discriminant form':

$$\text{Max}\,\{(q_j/q_j^*): j = 1, \ldots, M\}/(1+\delta) - q_x/q_x^*$$

where (1+δ) represents the factor for coordination cost (say, 3/2, with δ = 1/2). Any component (say, θ_2) with a positive discriminant (say, 1/3N = (4/2N)/(3/2) - 1/N))) is a viable export. In contrast, to require 100% self-sufficiency in components, one must compute the discriminant:

$$q_y/q_y^* - q_x/q^*_x$$

which may well be negative (say, -3/4N = (1/4)/N - 1/N < 0)). Set the 'truncated cumulative output' of θ_j at home as Θ_j (which rises with current output until a 'learning bound' is reached). They form an M-dimensional vector, Θ. Labor productivity for j is an increasing function, $q_j(\Theta)$.

In the world market, a developing country may have a comparative disadvantage in supplying an industrial good *as a whole* (with a 100% rate of local content), but not in supplying some component of that good. Since the industrial good is *new* to a developing country (even though it may be not *new* to the rest of the world), the learning bound is likely not yet reached. Thus, the production and export of its parts will impart experience of some sort to the local producers. Even if, under free trade, the component to be exported uses only mature technology, one may still be able to design an industrial policy to promote the export of a particular component which yields more valuable experience. Thus, the choice is not just free trade versus no trade, but the selection among the component export industries for promotion. The prerequisite for such industrial policy of selective export promotion is the outward orientation of Mainland China or South Korea, and not the *juiche* (self-sufficiency) of North Korea. Since different final goods (say, personal computers and mobile phones) may share many components (such as integrated circuits), learning-by-doing at the component level provides the linkage for industrial upgrading from one final good to another final good. Since the presence of coordinating costs limits the possibility of fragmented production, export of a final good based on the experience of supplying one component (say, ASIC, or application specific integrated circuit) can nurture the production of other components (such as specialized chip design) at home, and builds up experience there.

The above scenario is consistent with the East Asian evidence. In bicycles, currently Japan exports more of such key components as derailleurs, rather than complete bicycles. In the 1990s, Singapore supplied more than half of the worldwide demand for the 2.5", 3.25" and 5.25" computer disk drives (see Perry et al., 1997: 116). In 1996, the world market shares of Taiwan for palmtop scanners and motherboards were 95% and 74% respectively (see Chen and Liu, 2000).

The above example explains how an economy may gain from learning by trading intermediate goods. The economic structure gets continuously upgraded. The next example shows how such a process gets started even if all goods exported are produced with mature technology.

Example 3. Complementarity Once More

We now sketch out some details behind Figure 3.2.2. This exercise shows that, in principle, an economy may develop solely on the learning effect in the satellite industries, even if initially all the exports are made with 'mature technology' (such as the hand-made toys made early in Hong Kong's development). Their production offers nothing to learn. This exercise also may assure some readers that the ideas in Figure 3.2.2 can be formally modeled in order to check for logical consistency, and perhaps to provide numerical simulation as well. While learning deals with dynamic gain, at least for now we shall start with some comparative statics.

There are initially six productive processes, for the final goods x, y, and z and the intermediate inputs a, b, and c. Part of the final goods, namely, $x_\xi \leq x$, $y_\eta \leq y$ and $z_\zeta \leq z$ may be exported *after further processing* into exportable goods, ξ, η and ζ, during which the non-tradable outputs of the satellite industries are used. So there are nine production processes in all. What is left, $x - x_\xi$, $y - y_\eta$, and $z - z_\zeta$ are used at home. The exportable goods are processed under the following fixed coefficient production functions:

$$\xi = \text{Min}\,(x_\xi, a_\xi),\ \eta = \text{Min}\,(y_\eta, \lambda a_\eta, b_\eta) \text{ and } \zeta = \text{Min}\,(z_\zeta, \mu a_\zeta, \phi b_\zeta.\ c_\zeta).$$

The notation $r_\sigma \geq 0$ stands for the amount of input, either labor or intermediate good r = a, b, c used in an output, say, export good $\sigma = \xi, \eta, \zeta$. a is used as the sole (new) 'additive' for x, and its unit is chosen such that these two are used in the ratio 1:1. b is used as the sole new 'additive' for y, and its unit is chosen such that these two are used in the ratio 1:1. So is the unit for c chosen.

Each period, the allocation of labor and intermediate goods are subject to the following constraints:

$$\Sigma_s L_s = L,\ s = x, y, z, a, b \text{ or } c \qquad \text{(for labor)}$$

$$a_\xi + a_\eta + a_\zeta \leq a,\ b_\eta + b_\zeta \leq b,\ c_\zeta \leq c, \qquad \text{(for intermediate goods)}$$

Assume for simplicity that the labor supply is constant in all periods at the level L. The unit labor product for s is $q_s(t)$ in period t, where:

$$q_s(t) \equiv 1 \text{ for } s = x, y \text{ and } z, \text{ all } t. \qquad \text{(They are produced with mature technology.)}$$

Assume for simplicity that there is no cross-product effect of learning, so:

$$q_a(t) = Q_a[A(t\text{-}1)],\ q_b(t) = Q_b[B(t\text{-}1)],\ q_c(t) = Q_c[C(t\text{-}1)],$$

where Q_s are strictly increasing functions for s = a, b, and c, and

$$A(t\text{-}1) = \min\,[A^\circ, \Sigma_0^{\,t-1}\, a(\tau)],$$

$$B(t\text{-}1) = \min\,[B^\circ, \Sigma_0^{\,t-1}\, b(\tau)],$$

$$C(t\text{-}1) = \min\,[C^\circ, \Sigma_0^{\,t-1}\, c(\tau)],$$

are the 'truncated cumulative outputs,' with A°, B° and C° being the *learning bounds*. Figure A3.1.3 illustrates this construction.

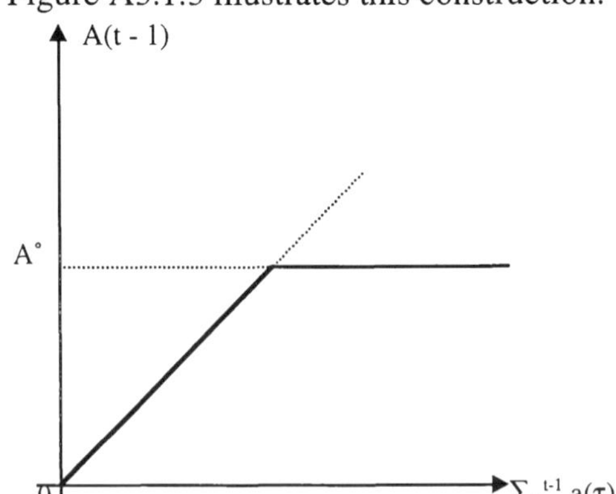

Figure A3.1.3 Bounded learning

In addition, we assume,

$$q_a(0) = 1, \text{ all s}; Q_a(A) = 1 + A, Q_b(B) = 1 + B, Q_c(C) = 1 + C.$$

Since we are dealing with the Leontief type of technology, market competition makes sure that for each unit of x exported, exactly one unit of x and one unit of a will be used: $x_\xi = a_\xi = \xi$. The total unit labor cost must be:

$$1/q_\xi = (1/q_x) + (1/q_a).$$

Let $\lambda = 1/3$. $\mu < \lambda$, and ϕ is a very small, positive number. To export η, one must have $y_\eta = a_\eta/3 = b_\eta = \eta$, or,

$$y_\eta = b_\eta = \eta, \qquad a_\eta = 3\eta.$$

Its unit cost is then,

$$1/q_\eta = (1/q_y) + (1/q_b) + (3/q_a).$$

To produce in period 1, the initial unit costs are $1/q_\xi = 2$, $1/q_\eta = 5$. The cost ratio is 2:5. Assume that the unit cost ratio abroad is 29/70 for all periods. Since 2/5 < 29/70, the home economy must specialize in good ξ in the first period, with an output: $q_\xi(1)L = L/2 = A(1)$. For the second period, the unit costs for x and y then become 1 + 1/(1+A(1)) and 2 + 3/(1+A(1)), with a ratio, (2+A)/(5+2A). Suppose $L \geq 2$, then $A(1) \geq 1$, and (2+A)/(5+2A) > 29/70, good η will supplant good ξ as the export good. If not, the exporting of good ξ continues, but the value A(t-1) also increases, postponing the cross-over to a future date. This is depicted in Figure A3.1.4.

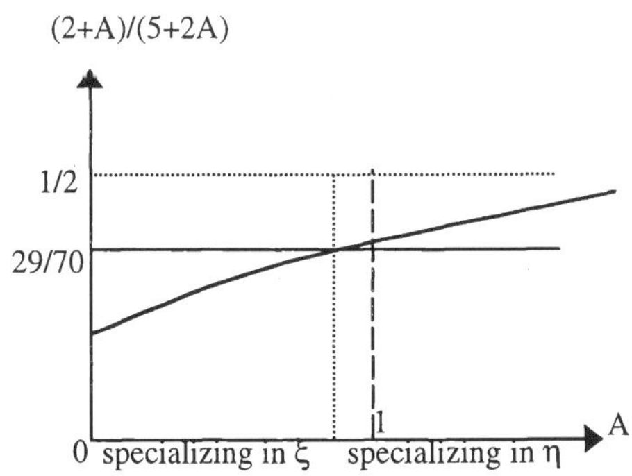

Figure A3.14 Experience in services changes the export mix

This example illustrates that even the export of such goods as wigs and toys may spearhead economic development. The final goods themselves are produced with 'mature' technology. Their life cycle as exports may be short, due to fashion change or rising domestic wage. But the economy does not stagnate. In this example all learning is export-induced, taking place only in the satellite industries for 'domestic additives.' The efficiency gain takes the form of the 'output augmenting' type. The same labor input yields more output as experience increases with accumulated output, up to some finite level of learning bound. Since the same satellite industry may serve more than one final good, the efficiency gain there may make new final goods competitive in the export market. This can increase labor demand and wages, and phase out old exports. The cost reduction of exports and the efficiency enhancement in the satellite industries goes on and on. Rapid growth is therefore sustained.

CHAPTER SUMMARY

- ♦ Advanced economies are mostly industrialized.
- ♦ Rapid growth is impossible to sustain in primary sector:
  - Engel's Law implies a tendency toward deteriorating terms of trade;
  - Limited resource base causes diminishing returns in production;
  - Experience obtained is not transferable from sub-sector to sub-sector.
- ♦ Pattern of specialization continues to change after industrialization:
  - Changes in relative wage and outputs are history-dependent;
  - Technical advances make both industries and labor force footloose;
  - Cost for fragmentation and pay for guest workers decide the pattern;
  - Policy shapes alternative evolution paths and national advantage.
- ♦ Comparative advantages evolve due to information acquisition:
  - Productivity improves with learning if technology is not mature;
  - Learning depends on production patterns, and thus trading regimes;
  - Both income effect and fragmented production matter;
  - Trade may either help or hinder developing economies in learning.
- ♦ History shows that learning aids catching up under an outward orientation:
  - Developing economies can learn by exporting some parts;
  - Even the export of simple goods helps as satellite industries improve.

QUESTIONS AND EXERCISES

1. In the literature, the effect of abundant natural resources is known as the 'Dutch disease.' Use the Japan-Argentina comparison to discuss both its static effect and dynamic implication. What should a government do when natural resources are discovered?
2. Discuss with examples how the development effort can be either hindered or helped when laborers work abroad.
3. According to the 'infant industry' argument of Hamilton and List, the policy of trade protection is supposed to help development. When England was the leading industrial power in the 19th century, both the U.S. and Germany succeeded in industrializing by this strategy, In contrast, after World War II, many Afro-Asian economies experimented with a similar strategy in vain. According to Example 1 of the Appendix, a protectionist policy is sufficient to nurture an industry only if $q_y \geq \Delta$. Try to interpret the model in the context of the experience of the historical episodes.
4. Based on its export-mix or output-mix, an industrialized economy like Taiwan may undergo very rapid transformation, from living off of sugar exports to supplying machine tools. But such rapid change may be more apparent than real. Explain by reference to Figure 3.2.2.
5. Modify Figure 3.1.5, using the same parameter values for a, a*, A and A*. Assume now the coordination cost is prohibitive, so that the processes of product design (U-process) and fabrication (D-process) cannot be split in two locations. Further, the workers from the home country demand no extra pay when working abroad, but the workers from abroad demand double pay if they are assigned to work in the home country.
6. [Korea II] Like their Hong Kong rivals, Koreans know the advantage of outsourcing to PRC, but invest in Vietnam (Applebaum and Smith, 2001: 33). To see why, let the cost to produce garments 'offshore' be the sum of:
   (a) returns to supervisors in the 'home economies', Hong Kong and Korea
   (b) returns to the workers in the 'host economies', China and Vietnam, and
   (c) a coordination cost, except between two culturally similar economies.

   If all supervisors are equally efficient, all workers are equally efficient, and the market operates as if a social planner seeks efficiency, show that: either
   (i) Koreans only invest in Vietnam where wage is lower than China, or
   (ii) Korean supervisors get returns lower than those from Hong Kong.

Chapter 4

CHANNELS FOR TECHNOLOGY ACQUISITION

Trade, Foreign Investment, Reverse Brain Drain

1. PRODUCT CYCLE AND STAGED DEVELOPMENT

We have studied individual economies and how they evolve from one stage to another. Now we focus on industries as they migrate from one country to another. *Why*, *how* and *where* an industry migrates is decided by the two economies involved: the country of origin and the destination. Patterns of trade shift as industries migrate, because industries bring technology along with them. By riding on the associated product cycles, many economies have been able to fulfill their development agenda. Chapter 2 offered East Asian examples in context, while Chapter 1 highlighted the phenomenon of catching up through emulation.

Emulation is a *game of contact*. Contact takes the form of the movement of products and factors, via trade, investment, and migration. Games are for two parties or more, and are played according to each player's capability and intention. Emulation means the transfer of technology, and may be compared to the energy transfer in solar power collection, as in Figure 4.1.1. The working fluid in a solar power collector carries energy (shown as a shaded arrow) from the collector to storage; the fluid then returns to the collector. Similarly, trade and investment carry technology (shaded arrow) from the North to the South; trade flows return to the North. Like the working fluid, the movement of goods and factors may be indispensable as a catalyst for technology transfer, but it is not our center of attention.

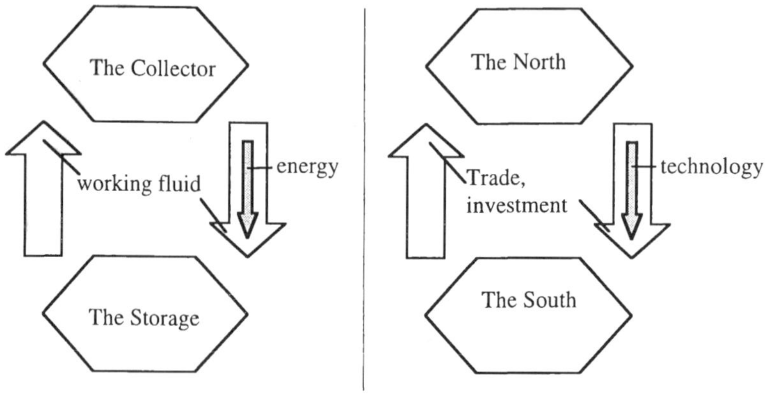

Figure 4.1.1 Circular flows

This analogy is not quite exact. Working fluid circulates according to physical laws. Trade, investment and migration are the chosen actions of sentient agents. *Why* they participate, and *what* they get out of the deal deserve careful attention. Understanding *how* the system works is a prerequisite for policy interventions and institutional designs that improve performance.

In biology, *prior conditions and circumstances cause adaptation.* Under the pressure for survival, birds, bats and pterodactyls all took to the air using their fingers and limbs. Wings took form in these animals because of their need to fly; once the process had begun, wings improved to become stronger and more efficient over time. Likewise, the refugees in Hong Kong and under-employed labor in Japan supplied export industries with inexpensive manpower. Experience then molded these workers into skilled labor able to fill niches in the world market with high value-added. For Hong Kong and Japan, the Chinese Civil War and World War II are the circumstances that shaped their respective processes of industrialization.

Economic analysis gives us the insight to replicate historical successes under different circumstances. Thus the foreign investors attracted to Hong Kong by refugee labor could be drawn to Singapore with investment incentives. The experience gained by Japanese labor in wartime industries could be equally cultivated in Korea with government-promoted export drives.

This chapter has four sections. The first two deal with North-South interaction at four different levels. In the rest of this section, we start with the evolving circa-Pacific trade flow, which is followed with an example at the economy-to-economy level – the Japan-Taiwan investment flow studied by Kojima (1978) and Ozawa (1979). We then consider subcontract relationships, which is a variation on the theme of investment at the firm-to-firm level, based on the study of Schwinn Bicycles by Crown and Coleman (1996).

The next section provides a game-theoretic analysis of the North-South interaction at the player level. Again, investment is the focus. Van and Wan (1999) show that the North-South transfer of information is an equilibrium outcome between willing players. We study *why* each party would participate, and *who* gets *what* in return. Following this, we take stock and consider North-South coalitions, as well as the reverse brain drain. The concluding section discusses the nature of 'growth slowing' and the culmination of the catching up process.

The growth of East Asia took place in an expanding world economy. Between 1950 and 1998, the world output rose by 18 times, and total exports grew by a factor of 34. The Asia-Pacific region was the heart of this drama. Figure 4.1.2 displays how the principal trade pattern evolved.

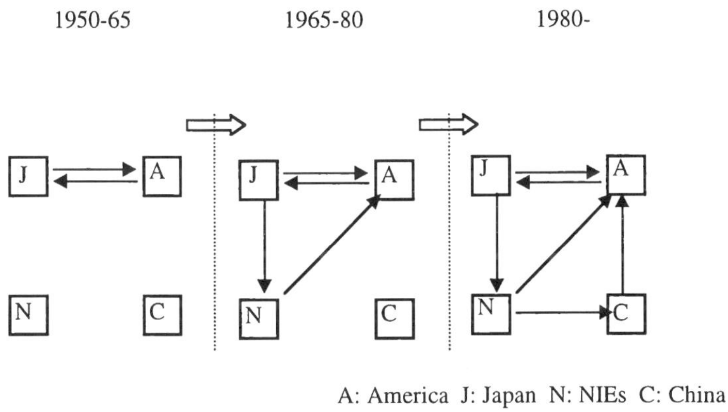

Figure 4.1.2 Trade Flows

What has been taking place is the continued rise of U.S. demand for imports. This brings prosperity and progress across the Pacific. Better equipped for this opportunity than others, Japan was the first to supply such needs, until the point at which Japanese labor could not completely satisfy the demand, and wages rose sharply. The NIEs were then brought in to join the supply chain, although the parts and components requiring higher skill were still imported from Japan. Next, the NIEs developed a labor shortage of their own, and the PRC (and some ASEAN countries) also joined the operation. Take bicycles from China for example: 30% of the components continue to be supplied by Japan, another 30% are made in Hong Kong and Taiwan, with the body produced in Mainland China, before the entire bicycle is shipped to the U.S.

Lucas (1988) noted that all the NIEs *have exported goods that were not initially produced in these economies.* These goods came to be produced there by the working of the product cycle. As was discussed in Section 3.2, such goods are produced with a technology that is not yet mature, insofar as the local workers are concerned. Hence, there is scope for learning. As

Figure 4.1.2 shows, new exports went to an East Asian economy twice in recent decades, first from Japan to the NIEs and then again from the NIEs to the PRC. The second move shows the generality of the phenomenon; the first is studied below, to see how the process works.

Case Study—Japanese Investment in Taiwan: Push and Pull

Economic forces 'pushed' Japanese firms to migrate. Kojima (1978) and Ozawa (1979) described this in detail. In the 1960s, three factors acted on the market for semi-skilled labor. On the supply side, there was both (a) a *demographic* shift, whereby the falling Japanese birth rate lowered the supply of young workers, and (b) an *income effect*, as more newly prosperous Japanese parents sent their children to further schooling, rather than to dead-end jobs. On the demand side (actually, the cause of (b)), there was factor (c): Japan prospered due to differential productivity growth, which favored the 'modern' sector (say, artificial fiber) more than the 'traditional' sector (say, garment making). In Japan, the latter technology was mature.

Given the Japanese reluctance to recruit foreign workers to live among them, many firms in the traditional sector could not survive at home. This is displayed in Figures 4.1.3–6. Figure 4.1.3 depicts the Japanese labor market before the impact of the three factors. The total supply was marked as 1. Subtracting the reservation demand of the households, we get the market supply. At the initial wage w, the traditional sector got $\alpha\beta$ units of labor and the modern sector got 0β units. At w', the 'choke wage' for the traditional sector, only the modern sector can afford the workers and survive. Figure 4.1.4 displays the supply shift due to the demographic shift. Both the vertical total labor supply and the labor market supply curve move horizontally to the left.

Figure 4.1.5 shows the rise of the reservation demand for labor by the households, since more children stayed in school for more years. This moves the market supply curve of labor further to the left.

Figure 4.1.6 indicates the rise in labor demand of the modern sector, on account of the increased labor productivity in that sector. The final result is that the traditional sector can no longer hire labor at the new equilibrium wage rate, w'.

At the same time, the technology that became mature for Japan was still sufficiently competitive abroad. It happens that the regime then in power in Japan (the Liberal Democrats) relied upon the traditional sector as its basic political constituency. So, to salvage the residual human capital in the traditional sector, the Japanese government took the initiative. It assisted these firms to invest in the NIEs, with the help of the Japanese general trading

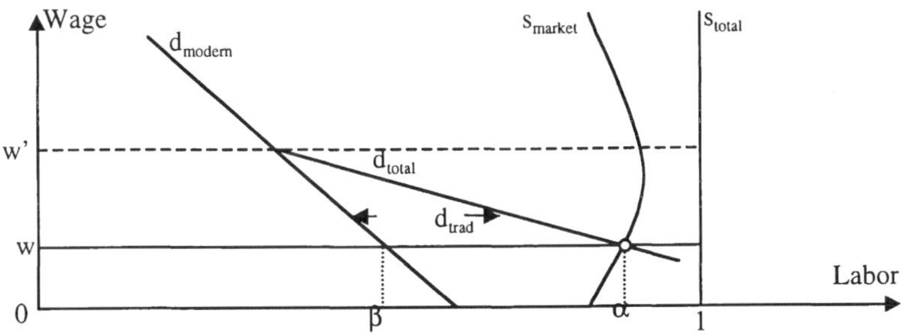

Figure 4.1.3 The Kojima–Ozawa narrative: initial condition

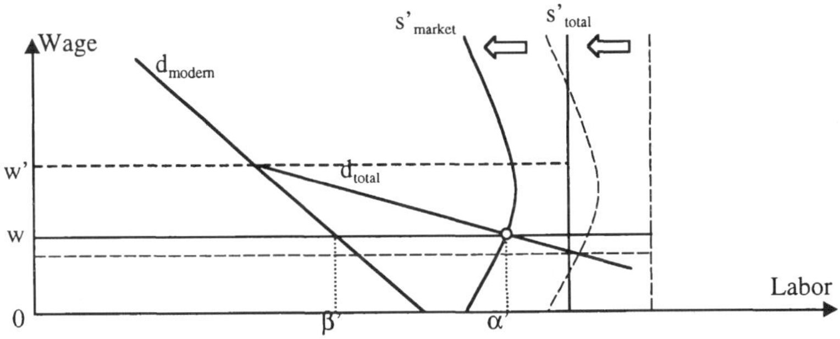

Figure 4.1.4 The Kojima–Ozawa narrative: the demographic shift

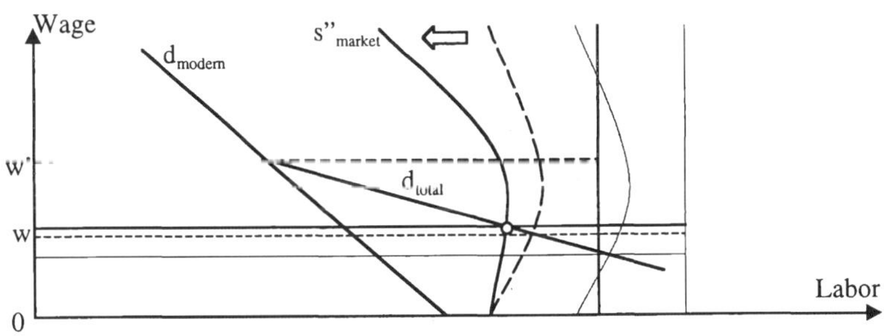

Figure 4.1.5 The Kojima–Ozawa narrative: the income shift

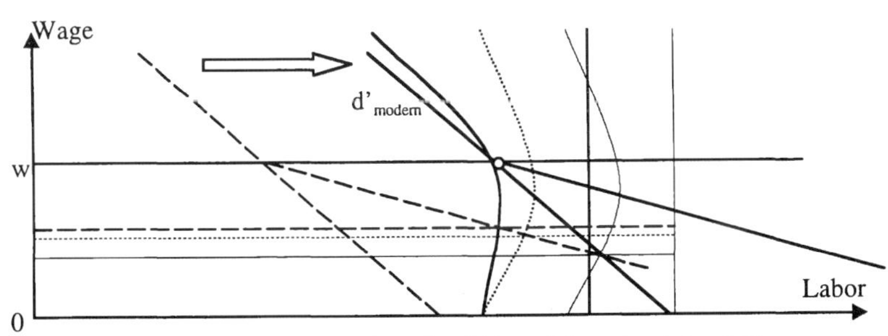

Figure 4.1.6 The Kojima–Ozawa narrative: the differential productivity shift

corporations. The latter had the expertise to intermediate on behalf of the small-medium firms in the traditional sector.

Granted that Japanese firms had to emigrate; the question of their choice of destination deserves study. What is the 'pull' factor on the Taiwanese side? According to Kojima (1978), Japanese businessmen felt Taiwan was congenial to them, since there were still technicians there who could speak Japanese well at that time. This explanation appears plausible, but more recent events suggest that culture may also be an important factor. Currently Taiwanese workers know little or no Japanese, but for the transfer of thin film transistor (TFT) technology, Japanese who went to Taiwan were able to communicate with hand signals. In Malaysia, on the other hand (as was mentioned in the last chapter), cultural differences made it difficult to implement the Japanese style of management.

An additional factor in the choice of Taiwan as a destination for Japanese traditional industries was the steps that the government in Taiwan took to attract foreign investors. We shall now see why and how. At this time U.S. aid to Taiwan was coming to its end. In the hope of covering the balance of payment deficit, the government was eager to get the foreign exchange that would accompany foreign investment. Their readiness to accept outside investment led to a rapid onrush of Japanese investment, especially to the Kaohsiung Export Processing Zone.

How were Taiwan's policy-makers so successful in attracting foreign investment? The answer seems to lie not in their long-term plans, but in their alertness to the investors' needs. The initial aim concerned only the easing of the balance of payment shortfall, rather than jobs, the income from future sales, or the acquisition of technology. But, by setting up a compact area as an industrial park,[1] they lowered the transaction cost of the investors tremendously, in several ways. Inside the enclave, a set of streamlined special laws and regulations simplified investors' lives. Land acquisition was automatic, once the investment plan was approved. Labor could be recruited with government help. The availability of utilities and transportation was part of the deal. In locating various foreign businesses in one place, the agglomerative externality was realized. In addition, one needed official approval to operate in that enclave. This last feature offered the government a chance to pick and choose among the applicants. A high proportion of top administrators were trained as engineers, so they were used to being pragmatic. On top of these advantages, the offer of tax holidays also helped.

Not all the advantages favoring Taiwan came from the government. Geography helped as well. Many workers commuted from home, bringing their own lunch, using bicycles, then company busses. The need for new

[1] Which started operation in the mid-1960s.

dormitories was reduced. Most of the jobs in garment factories and electronic assembly shops were filled by women before marriage. They worked not for subsistence (as in the Iron Law of Wage) but for dowry, and they preferred to work in factories rather than as live-in maids, the only other job option available to many young women. Working with foreign firms was considered respectable, and would in turn lead to better marriages. Taiwan's traditions were a further reason the country's labor force was attractive to Japanese investors; graduates of Taiwanese primary and secondary schools were used to highly structured student lives.

The importance of female labor force around the early 1970s is seen in Table 4.1.1.

	Textile, apparel & leather	Electric generators	Communication equipment
%	70	63	72

Table 4.1.1 Female proportions in employment – selected export industries

We now join the 'push' and 'pull' factors together in Figure 4.1.7. Panel a displays the factor price frontier of the traditional sector in Japan. Panel b depicts the value of the marginal product curve of Japanese human capital in the NIEs.

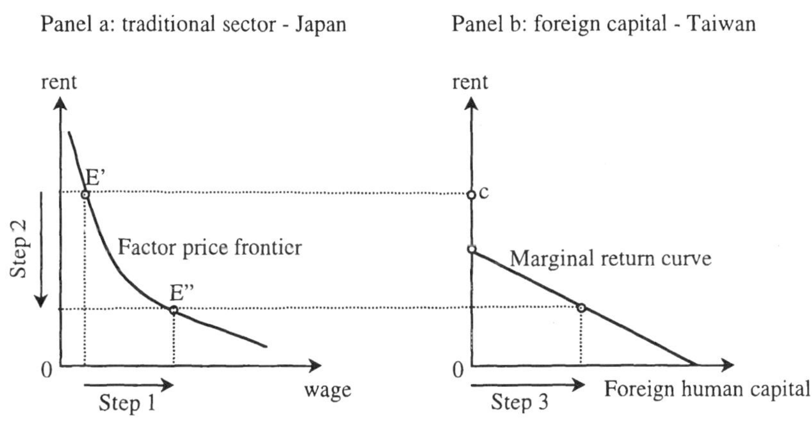

Figure 4.1.7 Return on foreign capital shapes investment flow

Panel a shows that for a particular traditional sector, the events in Japan shifted the equilibrium pair of (wage, rent) from E' to E" and reduced the rate of return of the sector-specific human capital toward zero. Panel b indicates that the highest return of such human capital in a NIE is c. Before those events in Japan, no one would have considered moving abroad. After the shift to E", there was really no choice. The assistance offered by the Japanese government for investing abroad and incentives such as 'tax holidays' offered by the host economy would shift the marginal return curve in Panel b upward somewhat, with an intercept above c (not shown in graph).

Typically, Japanese investment was made by small firms, and took the form of minority partnership in joint ventures. The investors retained much control, by virtue of their specialized expertise.

Once the production operation was shifted to the NIEs, technology transfer happened through several channels. First, there is the basic process of learning-by-doing. The indigenous workers gain proficiency over time

Second, the foreign investors can earn their return only by offering timely advice, lest the whole operation fail. Since 'knowledge' has a non-rival nature, once the advice is offered, the host economy will reap the benefit.

Finally, in such factories, the turnover rate of common workers is high. Sometimes it reaches 100% per year. Additionally, most female workers quit at the first childbirth, if not already at marriage. Yet the transfer of technology comes, either from the indigenous supervisors who stay for the long haul, or from the former workers who often help to start small-medium firms as subcontractors. High labor turnover may be a barrier to the development of corporate culture in the Japanese style. Yet it is an effective way to spread entry-level experience around in the fastest possible way.

Other Channels of Technology Acquisition

Direct foreign investment is only one of an entire range of forms for the transfer of technology. In the literature, technology transfer may be ranked according to the degree of 'bundledness,' as shown in Figure 4.1.8.

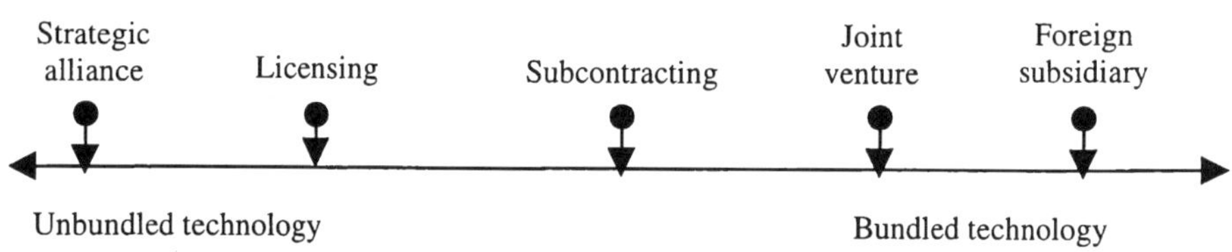

Figure 4. 1. 8 Modes of technology transfer

By bundledness we mean how much everything is arranged by the 'informed' party from the developed North for the 'uninformed' South. The more bundled is the technology, the more user-friendly it is, but also the more expensive it is. Most of the Japanese investment in Taiwan takes the form of a joint venture, not a full-fledged foreign subsidiary. In part, this is because Japanese firms, especially the small and medium sized firms, are either unable or unwilling to invest so much. In part it is also that, because of rather recent history, the government in Taiwan does not feel completely at ease with firms fully owned by Japanese or in majority ownership.

Before delving into a special case in subcontracting arrangements, we now make some general observations. First of all, because of the possibility of observing foreign firms operating among the local population, and because local employees can acquire information on the job, even if the foreign firms produce for the local market, the host economy can gain information. But more can be learned in joint ownership, or if the output must meet the standards of the export market in more affluent societies. Komiya (1972) noted how Japan benefited before World War II from Western investment in both the automobile and electric appliance industries.

Second, in the more bundled form, technology transfer often involves implicit, generic matters such as how personnel in modern firms may be motivated by stock options or how plant layout and inventory management is implemented. This knowledge is needed when the developing economy lacks general know-how. When the latecomer is much farther advanced, then in a cross-license agreement, firms can each use the fruit of the other's research, while outsiders must pay special license fees for patented processes. Again, the degree of development matters: when Japanese firms pay license fees to Western firms, sometimes they pay in addition for development reports that give them access to the laboratory notebooks on experiment data that were not actually utilized. Taiwanese firms rarely do this. This practice was held in the 1970s to be an example of the farsightedness of the Japanese, but it may actually reflect the R&D capability of the licensee.

Finally, all these channels transfer more technology than one would get through the purchase and use of specific foreign equipment and the support services that go with it. But even this last item yields benefits not available to economies that restrict imports for financial or policy reasons under an import substitution regime. This is not to say that in specific circumstances, selective protection cannot advance industrial development. However, such selective measures are as different from the mass patriotic fervor for using domestic products as is the surgeon's scalpel from a battle-axe.

Next, one can compare subcontracting arrangement with joint venture. In a joint venture, local personnel have the opportunity to observe the daily decisions of those from the advanced economy. How this helps is the subject matter of the next section. Our interest here is whether the party from the developed North would enter into a deal which benefits firms from the uninformed South. Under subcontracting arrangements, specific instructions and advice pass along with certain implicit information (such as the size, frequency and variability of the market demand and the tolerance requirements in products) that comes with the orders. This information raises the general competence of the trade partner. It also opens the door for the latter to become competitors, using forward or backward linkages (a quite frequent development). As the saying goes, there is no free lunch. The issues from the point of view of the informed party are: (a) why do they provide the information, and (b) what decides the *quid pro quo* they get out of the action.

The answer to the former question is simply: 'operational necessity.' Firms operate under competition. 'Competition is war' and 'war is hell,' as the sayings go. To survive *today*, one cuts costs. Competent suppliers become costly. One then trains cheaper suppliers to improve their competence. That may increase competition *tomorrow*. But tomorrow is another day.

The answer to the second question then follows naturally, in a competitive market. The market again decides how much one pays the supplier whom one trains – how cheaply can one get by. More generally, one gains advantage either by paying less today, or in anticipation of future favors in return. The latter is an implicit and incomplete contract, enforced by tit-for-tat in a repeated game. It also carries the risk that the opposite player may find itself so strong in the future that it no longer has to play.

What happens if the market is not competitive? If it is a situation of bilateral monopoly, between an informed party from the North facing an uninformed party in the South, one would think that the former would capture the entire 'surplus value' (or gains from trade). This turns out to be not the case, if there is information asymmetry. Suffice it to say here that following the principal-agent model, the Northern firm typically does not have the ability to monitor the production process. To maximize the expected return to itself, it can do no better than a performance contract, which must reward the Southern firm to counter its urge to shirk.

Case Study—Schwinn, Giant, and so forth: Subcontracting

Here comes a special case. The Crown and Coleman (1996) story about Schwinn Bicycles speaks volumes. This leading American producer imported the first complete bicycle from Japan in 1972[2] with a sticker, 'Schwinn approved,' to finesse its 'made in America' tradition. Bridgestone and Matsushita were the two Japanese suppliers. Yoshi Shimano from the bicycle component supplier served as the translator, partly to learn the sales and production forecasts of Schwinn. The following year, the Taiwanese firm, Giant Manufacturing, tried to get orders from Schwinn to boost its image, but was rebuffed because it lacked both plant capacity and quality (Giant was then doing welding on hand-held parts). About 1972, the average monthly wage for skilled labor was $72 in Taiwan against $272 in Japan,

---

[2] When the product image of Japanese bicycles in the U.S. was not high.

and the Taiwanese efficiency was just below that of Japan and the U.S. By the mid 1970s, rising Japanese costs allowed Giant to undersell the Japanese by 25-30%. Sometimes at the urging of Schwinn, Giant upgraded its equipment and process, making improvements such as using a bit rather than tightening spokes by hand, and enhanced its plant layout. Giant got its first order from Schwinn in 1977. It displaced Bridgestone, though not the high-end products from Matsushita. An order of 100,000 units then doubled its output and helped it against its Taiwanese rival, Merida Industry Company. During the 1980 strike at Schwinn, Giant got large orders, impressed Schwinn with quality, delivery and service, and expanded its factory. To ensure high product quality, Schwinn engineers shared details and equipment drawings just as they had provided their Japanese suppliers with blueprints in the early 1970s. Mutual visits helped to troubleshoot production problems and to engineer new design (Crown and Coleman, 1996).

Schwinn used to be self-sufficient in parts, and then imported some parts from Europe, until Shimano, a Japanese company producing bicycle parts including derailleurs, demonstrated that it was more adaptable to Schwinn's needs than was the French supplier for Schwinn. Shimano had started in the 1920s researching metallurgy and the use of heat treatment to improve its product. In the early 1970s, it offered Schwinn one-year exclusives with the label 'Schwinn approved.' By continuing product innovation through such means as collecting gravel samples from American and European roads and sending teams to monitor American sport bicycle events, Shimano became 'the Intel of the bicycle industry' and standardized its parts supply. By requiring the purchase of entire sets of its products and making its name count to bicycle buyers, it gained great leverage and higher profit. In leveling the playing field for all of its customers, it made established bicycle firms such as Schwinn lose distinctiveness and advantage. Although Schwinn and many other bicycle producers tried to back Shimano's rival, Sun Tour United, to re-establish a balance of power in the bicycle parts market, their efforts were to no avail, and Shimano now enjoys a 60% world market share. Together with Sun Tour United of Japan, Sachs of Germany and Campagnole of Italy, they hold 800 patents which discourage new entrants. (It took until 1996 for ITRI, a Taiwanese government institute, to file their first six patents for bicycle parts in 1996).

What weakened Schwinn was partly the shift of power from bicycle makers to parts makers, and the rise of Shimano as a world leader in bicycle parts production, beating out Sun Tour, its Japanese rival, and forcing the Europeans into their own merger under Sachs of Germany. Schwinn had expected better deals from Shimano due to their former connections. One of its employees said, "Our attitude was that Shimano should have helped Schwinn. Helped us because we helped them. They were getting so popular, they didn't have to play the game" (Crown and Coleman, 1996).

By 1984, Giant supplied 500,000 units to Schwinn, accounting for 2/3 of its sales. Losing the buyer's leverage, Schwinn then proposed to buy an equity share in Giant in 1984. By this time, Giant had no real interest and made a counterproposal of cross stockholding with Schwinn, which was swiftly rejected. Giant then launched its own brand in Taiwan and Europe. It also proposed joint distribution with Schwinn in the U.S. but the negotiation got nowhere.

Behind the back of Giant, Schwinn then bought a 1/3 interest in China Bicycles Company, a joint venture between Hong Kong business and the government of the PRC, and shifted part of its orders from Giant, so that China Bicycles would become the leading supplier. At the same time, Schwinn also invested in the Csepel Works in Hungary and set up a shop in Mississippi. But neither Csepel nor the Mississippi plant performed well at all. Feeling wronged, Giant then entered the U.S. market as a competitor to Schwinn, hired former Schwinn employees, set up a similar dealer chain with a better profit margin, and advertised that Giant was still the supplier for Schwinn (Crown and Coleman, 1996). It also became less accommodating to Schwinn in price and service. In four years its U.S. sales amounted to more than half of Schwinn's. Although labor in China was much cheaper than in Taiwan, labor cost had shrunk by then to 6% of the cost of a bicycle. China Bicycle was not ready then in quality or capacity to take the place of Giant. The paint on its bicycles peeled, and its delivery was not fast. Schwinn had to ask Giant to help out in filling orders. Moreover, against the initial agreement, China Bicycles took orders from Western States, an American rival of Schwinn, while it delayed its delivery of products Schwinn ordered. Eventually, the Hong Kong partner of Schwinn in China Bicycles bought Western States. The conflict of interest got worse.

Ultimately, Schwinn went into bankruptcy in 1992 and Giant sustained a bad debt of U.S. $9 million. About the benefit received by its Asian suppliers from their tangled association, Tanzer (1992) quoted:

(a) Anthony Lo of Giant, "Without Schwinn, we would never grown to where we are today. We learned many basic things from them: quality, value, service."

(b) Sze of Chinese Bicycle, "Schwinn helped to promote our products in the U.S."

Tanzer also confirmed some other points of interest. First, Giant improved upon the technology of Schwinn, so its emulation went further than mere copying. Second, selling to tough foreign markets also helped U.S. firms. Paul Brodek, the Director of Trek, Japan, which is a wholly owned subsidiary of Trek, U.S.A. said the following. "We've learned things in Germany and Japan, the most demanding markets, that have improved the quality of our bikes in the U.S." Third, Giant's Lo and China Bicycles' Sze believe that China, and not the West, would be their best growth market.

Eventually, under new management, a re-emerged Schwinn and Trek gained market share at the expense of Giant and The Specialized, another American firm, in the U.S. market. Trek and the new Schwinn now rely upon Giant and its Taiwanese rival, Merida, respectively as subcontractors (Crown and Coleman, 1996).

The story of Schwinn is like a Rorschach test. Each reader may find in it confirmation of his or her cherished views regarding economic development. We believe the facts of the Schwinn case indicate that:

First, a cheap wage only gives a limited advantage. Schwinn's premature shift from Taiwan to China did no good. Matsushita and Shimano had no need to fear the lower wages in Taiwan and China.

Second, it was the inability to adapt to the times rather than reliance on Asian subcontractors that did Schwinn in. Trek has thrived by using the same Taiwanese firm (Giant) as a subcontractor while simultaneously dominating it in the U.S. market. As Schwinn's experience with China Bicycles and Giant show, its different investment strategies made little difference to the equally unsatisfactory outcome: to become dependent on suppliers, with or without paying out investment funds in addition.

Third, the strength of Shimano, the Japanese firm, depends on neither 'Japan Inc.' nor the size of the protected Japanese home market, nor the mutual support of the *keiretsu* relationship. It was a small firm that rose to a world power through its own creativity in product design and marketing strategy.

Fourth, the successful firms from the NIEs, such as Giant, are not copycats (Tanzer credits Giant with having improved on the technology of Schwinn). But nor can they succeed for long in the U.S. as a major force under their own brand name. Giant wisely cashed in on its ability to export to the U.S. to impress Chinese consumers and to increase its war chest.[3] What will become of its lofty ambition in electric motorcycles remains highly uncertain.

Fifth, their dealings with U.S. firms allow Asian firms to gain technology with their eyes wide open. Such transfer of technology is similar to what happens under joint ventures, or the hiring of indigenous workers in direct foreign investments.

Sixth, as a channel through which to gain technology, the subcontracting arrangement (as well as direct foreign investment) is similar to learning-by-doing for developing economies in two senses. It is a byproduct of current operations, and it also takes time to get results. Of course, unlike learning-by-doing, interaction with foreign firms is always part of the operation.

---

[3] With its plant in China, Giant produced three million bicycles in 1995. Giant remains innovative in bicycle design. By 2002, it had become the first Asian producer with products being used (by the Spanish team) in the Tour de France.

Seventh, international reputation has been repeatedly cited as a factor in the success of NIE firms. Reputation is a revenue-enhancing asset just like equipment or results from R&D. Obviously, it can be acquired only in conjunction with satisfactory performance in the world market.

Finally, the development process means a constant shift in comparative advantage. Yet everything has its time. Schwinn was correct to foresee that, with its lower wage and accumulating experience, China probably would replace Taiwan as the best location to produce bicycles at some future time. But for an individual business, jumping the gun only penalizes one's self.

2. THE GAME OF TECHNOLOGY TRANSFER[4]

Motivation

So far we have followed the literature, discussing such concepts as information, technology, production function, learning, technology transfer and so on in terms that are surrogates for reality. It is important to make sure that nothing essential is missed when we proceed to conduct policy analysis and institution design. At least for this once, we shall delve into the microeconomic foundation of all these concepts and rethink all the related issues from scratch. We now come to face to face with a host of questions that have rarely been posed: Why are certain matters in production not taught in formal schools and training programs? Why cannot professional consultant services provide certain knowledge? Why, as a result, in the search for such information, must a developing economy allow foreigners to set up factories in their midst and make huge profits in the bargain? Why do such learning processes take time? How can such knowledge be acquired and transmitted, once the foreign investment has taken place? What type of information is likely to be acquired in this manner? If the information is so precious, why should foreign investors allow it to be acquired by the host economy? Why would not the knowledgeable party get all the gain when they agree to share the information?

All these matters are important for policy analysis and institution design. To clear up such questions and ambiguities, we formulate a Bayesian model,[5] consider situations described in engineering manuals, and recast the theory of production to fit the framework of a multi-stage game. Our understanding comes from studies of experimental psychology and expert systems, as applied to welding and machining operations.

---

[4] This section is based on Van and Wan (1999).

[5] Our approach is based on the work of Nermuth (1982)

Our exercise serves three specific purposes. First, we show how direct foreign investment transfers technology, at the most basic level of microeconomic foundations. Hopefully, in future policy debates for or against foreign investment, the issue can be joined at such an operational level. Second, as a by-product of this exercise, we have to rethink *what* is production technology and *how* contact transmits *which* kind of information. This should help institutional design when developing economies attempt to attract foreign investment. The clear identification of mutual interest should lead to mutually beneficial improvements for all concerned. Finally, technology transfer is viewed as an *equilibrium outcome* from interactions among forward-looking individuals. Policies and institutions should be designed to work when everyone knows what to expect, and not when someone becomes outwitted.

Some Facts of Life

We start with two citations from engineering about the production processes:

On the daily decisions facing the producer, Tonkay and Knott (1988: 647-8) wrote about welding:

> Of interest are the effects of current, voltage and travel speed on the quality of the weld. Because of the extremely large number of materials, electrodes, shielding gases, and other variables, an experimental design to determine the interaction effects is prohibitively large. . . . Experienced welding engineers have encountered many of the interaction effects of these variables throughout their careers. They use this knowledge whenever they estimate the values for the welding situation they have not previously encountered. This knowledge, in the form of experience, was coupled with the knowledge of the steps they use to solve the problem.

On the actual methods and the nature of knowledge, Wright and Bourne (1988: 19) made two points in relation to the operation of machining:

> Many decisions may be arrived at, seemingly, by 'gut feeling.' For instance, a machinist may be able to tell when a cutting tool is dull simply by looking at . . . the general shape of wear scars on the top surface, corner and flank surface of the tool, and in addition . . . relate these features to events in the last machine pass. Changes in chip color, vibrations of the machine tool, and the surface finish obtained on the component are the first signs that the tool is becoming worn and should be checked at the end of the machine pass.
>
> It takes many years for a person to acquire enough information to be called an expert. It usually takes a long time . . . to get the information out of the expert person . . . but hopefully not as long as it took the expert to acquire the information in the first place.

A Formal Model

In contrast to the 'sanitized version' of the production process we usually use, real life presents a repeated sequence of problem-solving exercises. Producers face random events and receive imperfect observations (or signals). Actions are taken based on knowledge and beliefs. The pattern of actions in response to signals is referred to as the 'contingent plan' or 'decision rule.' This is updated when better knowledge becomes available. In the current context, better knowledge is acquired by observing the behavior of the better informed. In the scheme of Nermuth (1982), seven concepts are essential to production: the state (of nature), the prior belief, the signal, the information, the action, the pay-off, and the decision rule. We illustrate these with a simple example, motivated by the machining process in Wright and Bourne (1988).

Example

State $e \in E = \{0, 1\}$, where:

$e = 0 \Leftrightarrow$ the machine tool is *fine*,

$e = 1 \Leftrightarrow$ the machine tool is *dull*.

Prior $H = [h(e)]$, where:

$h(e)$ is the probability that the state is e.

It is *common knowledge*, that after each machine pass, the chance that the tool is worn out is $h(1) = .2$. The chance that it is good for another run is $h(0) = .8$.

Signal $s \in S = \{(s_1, s_2, s_3, s_4): s_i \in \{0, 1\}, i = 1, 2, 3, 4.\}$, where:

$s_1 = 0 \Leftrightarrow$ the chip color is *normal*, $s_1 = 1 \Leftrightarrow$ the chip is *discolored*;

$s_2 = 0 \Leftrightarrow$ the machine is quiet, $s_2 = 1 \Leftrightarrow$ the machine vibrates;

$s_3 = 0 \Leftrightarrow$ the component is *smooth*, $s_3 = 1 \Leftrightarrow$ the component is *scratchy*,

$s_4 = 0 \Leftrightarrow$ the wear scar is *shallow*, $s_4 = 1 \Leftrightarrow$ the wear scar is *deep*.

S is partitioned into a *filter*, or a class of subsets $\Sigma = \{\sigma_1, \sigma_2, \ldots\}$, where any s in S belongs to one and only one σ in Σ. Perfect information means a 'fine filter': for each s in S, $\{s\}$ is an element of Σ. Different persons may have different filters. One person is better informed than another if one has a finer filter.

Because this concept is important, some digression is necessary. The signal space S in this example has $2^4 = 16$ elements, and may be represented as the vertices of a 4-dimensional hypercube. The operational signal s_1, s_2 and s_3 are represented in the directions of left-right, up-down, and front-back. The inspection signal s_4 is represented with the outside-inside dichotomy. An individual who can benefit from inspection has the fine partition Σ_0. This has all the 16 singletons in S as subsets. An individual who cannot tell on inspection whether the wear scar is shallow or deep has a coarser partition. Associate each vertex on the outside cube with the corresponding vertex in the inside cube to form a two-element subset of S. These eight subsets form a partition, Σ_1. In plain language, any person who cannot tell which type of wear scar is the most likely, given the true state, gets no benefit from s_4.

Figure 4.2.1 and Figure 4.2.2 display two information filters. The fine partition Σ_0 is associated with the perfectly informed individual. The coarser filter Σ represents a less informed individual. Figure 4.2.1 displays a hypercube that is just an ordered pair of cubes, one inside the other. The elements of the signal space are the 16 vertices located on either cube. Those on the outside cube are associated with $s_4 = 0$. Those associated with the inside cube are those vectors with $s_4 = 1$. The elements (1, 1, 0, 0) and (1, 1, 0, 1) are at the two ends of the thick linear segment, denoted as μ. Each vertex is a member of the fine filter, Σ_0. Figure 4.2.2 depicts the coarser filter, Σ_1, which has only eight 'elements.' Each element is a subset joining two corresponding vertices located one on each cube. These are joined with thick line for easy identification. One example is μ, which is the collection of the two circled vertices (1, 1, 0, 0) and (1, 1, 0, 1).

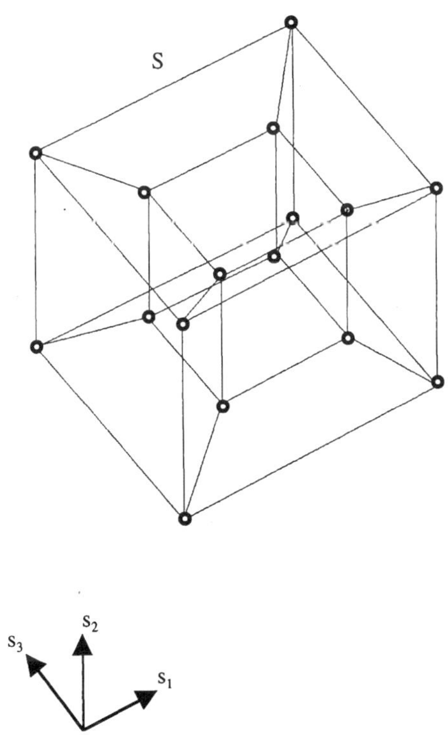

Figure 4.2.1 Signal space

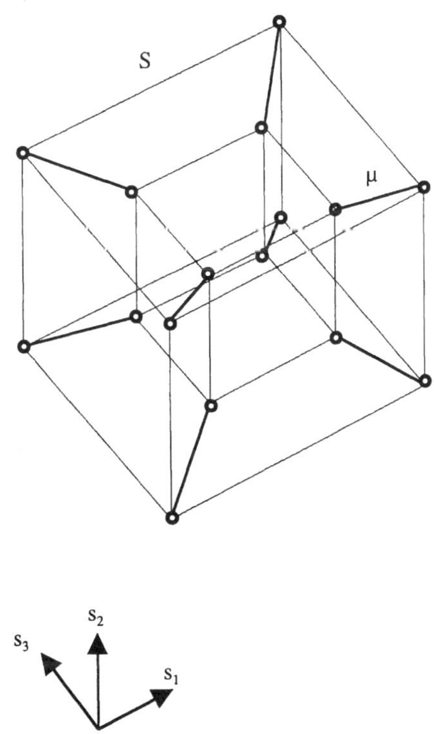

Figure 4.2.2 Information filter

Information $Q = [q(\sigma, e)]$, where:

$q(\sigma, e) \geq 0$ is the probability of σ, a subset of signals, given the state e;

$\Sigma_\sigma q(\sigma, e) = 1, \forall e.$

Assume $q((1,1,1,1), 0) = .025$ and $q((1,1,1,1), 1) = .9$. This means if the tool is fine there is only a 2.5% chance to observe s = (1,1,1,1), that is, the discolored chip, the vibrating machine, the scratchy component and the deep wear scar. If the tool is dull, there is a 90% chance to get this signal. By Bayesian inference, when s = (1,1,1,1), the chance that the tool is dull is,

$$(.2)(.9)/[(.2)(.9) + (.8)(.025)] = .18/.20 = 90\%.$$

Action $a \in A = \{(a_1, a_2): a_i \in \{0, 1\}, i = 1, 2.\}$ where:

$a_1 = 0 \Leftrightarrow$ do not inspect the tool, $a_1 = 1 \Leftrightarrow$ inspect the tool,

$a_2 = 0 \Leftrightarrow$ do not replace the tool, $a_2 = 1 \Leftrightarrow$ replace the tool.

Thus, for example, $a = (a_1, a_2) = (0, 1)$ means 'replace the tool; no inspection.' The action space can be represented as the vertices of a square. See Figure 4.2.5 below.

Payoff $U = [u(a, e)]$, where:

$u(a, e)$ is the expected payoff of taking action a when the state is e.

To be concrete, assume that a machine pass with a dull tool causes waste material and a loss of -100. An unnecessary replacement of the tool costs 40 and an inspection causes a delay, which reduces profit by 5.

Decision (rule) $D = [d(a, s)]$, where:

$d(a, s) \geq 0$ is the probability of adopting a if the observed signal is s;

$\Sigma_s q(a, s) = 1, \forall s.$

Since no signal s gives any sure prediction of any state e, Bayesian inference must be used to make decisions. By observing a better-informed decision-maker at work, individuals can update their information estimate. Geometrically, if the signal space and the action space are linear segments, the decision rule may be represented as a curve, as in Figure 4.2.3.

Now model each machine pass as a two-stage process. Observe the 'operational signals,' $s' = (s_1, s_2, s_3)$ at the end of the last pass, and decide to inspect or not. Then, observe any 'inspection signal' s_4, and decide whether to replace the tool. Figure 4.2.4 depicts the two-stage decision process.

To visualize how a decision is made, assume now the operational signal at the end of the last run is, say,

$$s' = (1, 1, 0) = \mu.$$

This means discolored chips and a vibrating machine, but with smooth components. One may decide to inspect the tool, (action $a_1 = 1$). The controlling question is what is the value of that choice in cost reduction. Suppose that

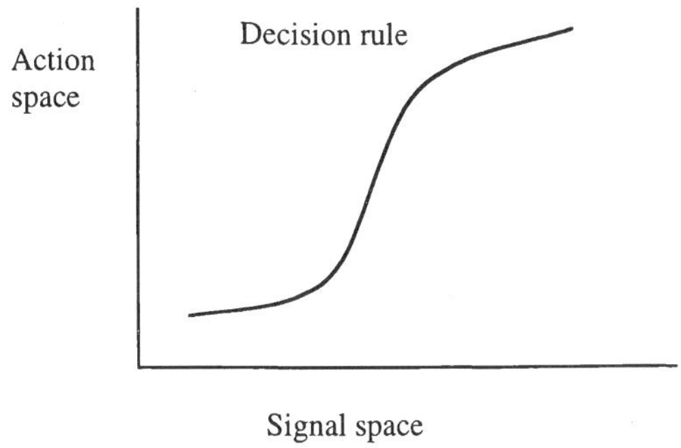

Figure 4.2.3 Signal space, action space and decision rule

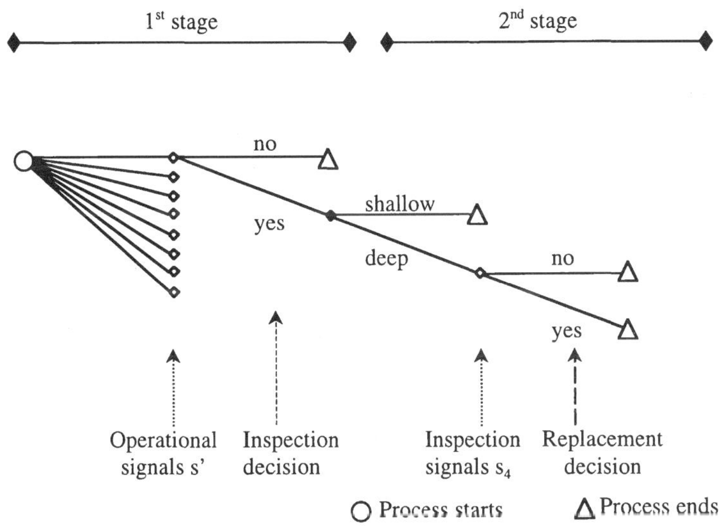

Figure 4.2.4 A two-stage decision process

after a signal μ, the expected result of inspection is half and half: 50% of the time the wear scar is shallow ($s_4 = 0$), and the rest of the time, the wear scar is deep, ($s_4 = 1$). Unlike the operational signals, the inspection signal does not come free. The cost of delay is 5. The question is then what is the significance of the result. Table 4.2.1 gives the probabilities of what the state of the tool is likely to be when a particular inspection result obtains.

	Chance of s_4	e = 0 tool fine	e = 1 tool dull
$s_4 = 0$ (shallow scar)	50%	90%	10%
$s_4 = 1$ (deep scar)	50%	10%	90%
Chance of e		50%	50%

Table 4.2.1 Conditional probabilities

One considers the possible consequence before any decision. So the choice to be made can be tabulated below (Table 4.2.2):

Expected cost	To replace	Not to replace	Minimum Value	Choice
Not knowing s_4	40	50	40	Replace
Knowing $s_4 = 0$	40	10	10	Not to replace
Knowing $s_4 = 1$	40	90	40	Replace

Table 4.2.2 Expected cost and decision

Therefore, given the 50:50 chance of the result of inspection and what consequence the inspection result is going to lead to, the value of knowing it reduces the expected cost from 40 to (50%)(10) + (50%)(40) = 25: a gross cost reduction of 15, against which the cost of delay of 5 must be deducted. Therefore inspection is the choice after the signal s' = μ is received, provided that one has the information to deduce the probabilities about the state (of the tool) from inspection.

To repeat, for the well-informed decision-maker the response to signal μ is to inspect ($a_1 = 1$), and then replace the tool if and only if the wear scar is deep. This is represented formally in Figure 4.2.5 as a pair of responses, in broken arrows. The answer to the scenario

$$(\mu, 1) = (1, 1, 0, 1)$$

is $(a_1, a_2) = (1, 1)$ (or, 'inspect and replace') in the action space. The answer to the scenario

$$(\mu, 0) = (1, 1, 0, 0)$$

is $(a_1, a_2) = (1, 0)$ (or, 'inspect but not replace').

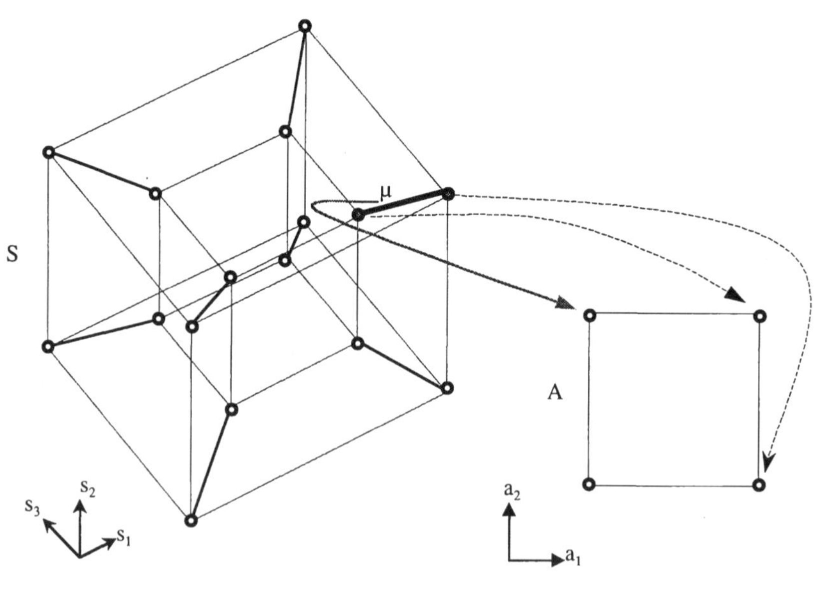

Figure 4.2.5 Signal space, action space and information filter

In contrast, for an imperfectly informed decision-maker who cannot decode signal s_4, one is forced to operate with the coarser filter, Σ_1. This latter contains μ as a legitimate member. Starting from there the solid arrow points to the vector of actions, (0, 1), 'replace but not inspect.' Here the moral is, if the inspection signal cannot be utilized, there is no point to engage in the costly inspection, so just replace the tool in any case.

We have now solved a fragment of the decision rules under the alternative assumptions on information. The choice for the best decision rule (say, under full information) is not trivial. To appreciate the scope of the problem, consider the class of all possible *decision rules*. For the first stage, there are $2^3 = 8$ possible vectors of operational signal, s'. To each s', there are two values of a_1 as possible responses, namely, to inspect or not. That yields $2^8 = 256$ possible patterns. Again, in the second stage, there are two possible values, 0 and 1, for the inspection signal, s_4. In principle, each possible s_4 value may be responded with two values of a_2, to replace the tool or not to, which makes $2^2 = 4$ different responses. Therefore, the number of all decision rules is 1,024. It is not a trivial task for one person to discover the entire decision rule of another person, (say, an expert) by observation. The reason is, not all the contingencies are likely to be encountered in real life. Even to discover a meaningful portion of it will take long association.

It is not realistic to specify in detail how the players from the less informed South acquire information from the individuals of the better-informed North, since that takes time. Yet, one can formulate a three 'period' game as in Table 4.2.3.

	Period 1: Negotiation	Period 2: Cooperation	Period 3: Separation
Northern Player	Informed	Informed	Informed
Southern Player	Not informed	?	Informed

Table 4.2.3 A three-period game

By informed, we mean with regard to matters of production. The fact that the Southern player is less informed during the period of cooperation is not important, since the party from the informed North will make the critical decisions. During the negotiation, both parties foresee that technology will be transferred from the North to the South, and account for it to settle for the terms over the cooperation phase. Actually, the negotiation is subject to some 'participation constraint,' in that each player has other alternatives.

In a nutshell, it is South-South competition that keeps the South-North wage gap from closing. It is North-North competition that keeps the engine of product cycle going. It is North-South cooperation that facilitates the diffusion of technology.

So what is technology diffusion? Identify technology as the ordered pair of a collection of probability estimates and a decision rule. In diffusion, it is not those estimates getting more accurate about anything in particular; rather they become increasingly detailed. It is not that the information allows producers to do more of the same, *ad infinitum*, but to do things smarter – faster, better, cheaper. This kind of information cannot be purchased or transferred in the same way that one acquires inputs. Since the information is in many ways highly dispersed, the subject matter cannot really be taught in any formal manner or acquired efficiently from consultants. Rather, through long-term association, the informed can transform the technology of the less informed by making it smarter. Even if foreign investors try to hide some of their industrial techniques, the less informed could still gain. What is gained can be a 'threat' to the investor, but, in any case, it will be only one of the threats that constantly come from all directions all the time.

3. BRAIN DRAIN AND REVERSE BRAIN DRAIN

We have studied a model of joint venture. In common with learning-by-doing, it involves complementarity between some economic activity now, and improved productivity in the future. Like learning in the process of trading, it is not something for the self-sufficient, but involves an interaction between two economies. Here the less-informed Southern partner learns from the better-informed Northerner. The parties need not be partners; they might be in an employer-employee relationship. The context does not have to be direct foreign investment in the host economy; it could also involve guest workers in the developed economy.

The insight obtained points out that the effectiveness of the deal for technology diffusion depends upon the nature of the work, the position held by the less-informed party, and the incentive to learn. Learning is likely to be easier in mechanical or electronic processes than in chemical processes, which are less readily observable. When labor takes jobs abroad, the job of a chief engineer offers a much better chance of observing something valuable than does manual employment building roads. As an inducement to learn in the present, the future likelihood of applying what is learned in a start-up firm at home is different from the prospect of serving bureaucratic superiors in the state sector or large business. When employees are rotated to work in a joint venture with foreigners, how they are viewed among their colleagues after that period makes a great difference. Will these staff be entrusted to apply their experience after their return in supervisory posts, or will they be reassigned to desk jobs with no connection to their previous employment?

In contact with the better informed, *how* much the developing economy gains depends on *how* institutions are designed and in *what* environment. Similar institutions can perform differently for subtle reasons. Taiwan succeeded to induce the Singer Corporation to invest and train local firms to supply the parts it uses. This strengthened the entire sewing machine industry for export (Schive, 1990, 55-66). By 1999, Singer has left all fabrication for local firms (Amsden and Chu, 2003). But if either the training is too costly, or it is believed that dangerous local rivals may develop, the *local content requirement* might deter all investors. A plant scientist will not be surprised that too much fertilizer is as bad as too little. There is no reason to expect that in planning economic development, we economists should find that the relevant measures (say protection) meet the 'monotonic property' of either *the more the better* or *the less the better*.

The workers taking jobs abroad may be the better trained or the more experienced among those in the home economy, so there is the issue of brain drain to be considered. Does such development help or harm an economy? To a great extent, the answer depends on *what* these workers do and *where* they go. Are they going to become more productive, and if so, will they eventually come back (reverse brain drain)? In *what proportions* are they heading back and *how valuable* will they be in that case? *How long* will they stay away, and hence *how much* remaining working life will be left? Moreover, the matter of complementarity enters into the picture once more. *Whether* and *how many* of those leaving today will return and in *what manner* they can be valuable on their return depend on *what type* of an economy one will have in the future. How does one compare an engineering undergraduate going abroad and a trained nurse taking foreign employment? Is 10 technicians leaving and one coming back as an expert 20 years later a good deal? A larger proportion of scientists trained abroad have returned to Taiwan than to the PRC so far. Is timing the main difference?

Matters like this are similar to playing chess. A poisoned pawn is a brilliant move only when played by someone who can exploit the openings that follow from the opponent's taking it. It is not likely that things like this can be perfectly planned. Common sense and judgment are needed in formulating a policy. One may think that there is no unifying principle, that all we are offering is hominy and platitudes. We shall argue this is not quite so.

Perhaps it is useful to stand back and take a long view. Ultimately, the success of an economy in catching up with the advanced societies depends upon the continuous upgrading of its labor force. There is little chance that one can skip any major step. The labor force has a distribution of skill levels. The reliance on immigrant workers can be a stopgap device but not a permanent solution. The more skilled is the person the less is the likelihood such a person can be hired from abroad at affordable cost for business firms. Without family ties and friends, the 'hired guns' are ready to go for the highest offer, next day. Without a permanent supply of key personnel, industries with high value added cannot be maintained. Shortage of necessary skill is often the bottleneck for industry upgrading.

Not all such persons can be trained entirely at home. Moreover, to have advanced training abroad, a candidate must have some sound training at home. Consequently, qualified candidates trained at home must be allowed to be further educated abroad. This opens the door to permanently losing such people abroad, and their human capital with them. For a low-income economy, the chance of loss is greatest exactly when such loss seems to be hardest to bear. But for most developing economies, the changes in domestic need cannot be synchronized with the pace of training of local talent. It is inevitable that a portion of domestically trained persons will spend part of their lives abroad after further education. Not all of these will eventually return.

Moreover, those who become further trained and experienced abroad can only be attracted back home with rewards commensurate with their current qualification. This will be quite jarring when compared against the remuneration for those who have stayed and toiled at home. Worse, whether the high qualifications earned abroad can be deployed advantageously can never be foretold. Experience shows that a person highly valuable in a fully developed economy may or may not be able to adapt to a less developed industrial environment After attracting such individuals home, their employment within the public sector, or in state enterprises can easily demoralize those who had stayed behind. A demoralized workforce certainly cannot engage in good teamwork, which is needed to survive in a competitive world market. The only solution must be baptism by competitive fire: if a person can make it in a start-up firm, criticism will be silenced. Therefore, the only way to use such returned talent is within a freewheeling private enterprise system operating under the rule of law (rather than a rule of man).

In other words, to tap into the reservoir of high quality labor force stored abroad, one must provide an environment without undue institutional rigidities or bureaucratic gridlock. Unless the capable and hard working can achieve career objectives by their effort and ability as easily as in their positions abroad, the experienced and highly trained cannot be attracted home. By Fei and Chu (1999), at the late stage of development, socio-institutional reform is needed for further progress. One might cite *Herr Eugen Duhring's Revolution in Science* by Engels (1934), which argues that an enduring institution must allow for the advance of productivity.

The alternative will be a long term, debilitating shortage of key personnel for industries promising high value added. This is not to say one should do nothing against brain drain. Some balance and proportion are always called for.

4. CULMINATION OF THE CATCHING UP PROCESS

It is time to discuss what one can reasonably expect far down the road of the catching-up process. Two issues deserve consideration. First, why is it that overtaking the leader is not something one can reasonably predict? Second, what precautions should one take to assure that growth can be secured with stability?

On the first issue, we shall revisit the ideas in Wan (1993). Consider a world of a finite number of economies but with an uncountably large number of goods. Each of these is produced by labor alone under constant returns. Next, set a_{kit} as the unit product of labor in country k for good i during period t, a_{0it} as the maximum of these items over all k (for the same i and t), and finally, $b_{kit} = a_{0it} - a_{kit}$ as the *technological gap* for country k in good i at time t.

Postulate that the periodic improvement of a_{kit} is due to two influences called imitation and innovation. The former reduces the technological gap by some fraction. The latter depends positively upon the past history of productivity of the same country. It is in fact a particular type of positively weighted average of the past productivity. One may introduce indices for the effectiveness of imitation and innovation. The former equals the proportional reduction of the gap each period. The latter equals the sum of those weights for past productivity.

Under an assumption that requires the 'imitation force' to be sufficiently strong relative to the 'innovation force,' then the current practice of every country will catch up with the best practice. In other words, mutual convergence of productivity obtains. That is to say, irrespective of the initial array of productivity, the difference in productivity between any pair of countries and for every good i will grow smaller than any finite positive number, given a sufficiently long time.

Now the 'force of imitation' and 'the force of innovation' may differ from country to country. Between two countries, where one is more advanced than another in the sense that the former is stronger than or equal to the latter by either index, then irrespective of the initial productivity, the latter cannot overtake the former in the long term.

Next we note that as an economy becomes more and more advanced, there is some tendency to develop specialized expertise within some particular cluster of industries. This is true for Finland, which concentrated in wood and wood products in the past, and telecommunication in the present. Or for Singapore, which specialized in computer hard drives. This specialization makes the country vulnerable, so this tendency should be counteracted, when possible, by diversification. The six-year deep recession for Finland (with 20% unemployment) in the early 1990s is an example. See Wan (1998).

This serious and perplexing issue will be discussed at somewhat greater length in our last chapter. Suffice it to say, the situation is less debilitating for larger economies like Britain, with its deindustrialized North, than for a small economy, say, Norway, with its communities isolated around the remote fjords, once the shipbuilding industry lost its comparative advantage. It is a type of problem without perfect solutions,[6] but it is perhaps more amenable to amelioration through international, collective measures (sort of a 'mutual insurance scheme') than through efforts of individual states.

[6] It reminds us of the depressing movie, 'God's Little Acre.'

CHAPTER SUMMARY

- ♦ For the developing South, the key to growth is to acquire technology from the developed North; the major channels through which to acquire technology are trade, direct foreign investment and migration.
- ♦ Like the working fluid in energy transfer, the circular commodity flow of trade allows for the unidirectional transmission of information from the North to the South.
- ♦ After World War II, the growth of world trade outpaced the growth of world output; the ever-growing supply chain from Japan to the United States included the NIEs, Southeast Asia, and the PRC.
- ♦ Different economies joined the trading world due to different triggers, and under policies specific to each economy. However, the processes are similar, and much of their experience is replicable.
- ♦ At the economy level, the Japanese investments in Taiwan illustrate both the product cycle and staged growth: rising wages and falling birth rates caused the Japanese firms to supply labor-intensive goods from Taiwan to the U.S. market, with government blessings from Japan and Taiwan.
- ♦ At the firm level, the interaction between Schwinn, of the U.S., and Giant, in Taiwan, illustrates how some kinds of technology get transferred more readily than others: Giant acquired expertise in production from Schwinn, and Schwinn went bankrupt under failed management; but Giant lacked sufficient design and market know-how to compete successfully against the reorganized Schwinn under new management.
- ♦ At the level of the individual decision maker, the engineering literature makes it clear that production technology involves far more than operation manuals and blueprints. Foreign direct investment allows individuals in the host country to observe how actual decisions are made and acquire *crucial* but *imperfect* knowledge.
- ♦ North-North competition justifies the urge of Northern firms to seek lower labor costs; South-South competition keeps the North-South wage gap wide; North-South cooperation permits technology spillover and eventual catching up.
- ♦ Brain drain may cause the South to lose the more gifted members of the labor force; reverse brain drain occurs when some of these eventually return with their experience.
- ♦ The likelihood of a complete catching up depends upon a tug-of-war between the 'force of innovation' and the 'force of imitation.' For a complete catching up, any economy in the South must innovate. Innovative success depends on existing technology and the industrial base. A complete catching up is logically possible, but not very easy.

QUESTIONS AND EXERCISES

1. To reduce its labor cost, Schwinn subcontracted Giant, and later, went bankrupt. Had it erred? How did the reorganized Schwinn beat back Giant?

2. Europe uses guest workers for services; Japan moves its labor-intensive industries abroad. How such policies affect economies nearby?

3. Overheard: "International relations being a zero-sum game; foreign investment is against national interest. Those beneficial to the host country would never come; those who come must be predatory." Comment.

4. Study Project: Read Rasiah (1999); compare the interactions: between Eng Hardware and Intel, Malaysia versus between Giant and Schwinn.

5. [Korea III] Problem 3, Chapter 12 (p. 352) suggests that the 1978 reform of PRC caused different rearrangements of the Asia-Pacific supply chain:
   (a)'Trade creation' for Hong Kong and Taiwan, by outsourcing, but
   (b) Trade diversion' for Korea, by market switching.
   In Table 4.Q.1, let A, C, H, J, K and T stand for America, PRC, Hong Kong, Japan, Korea and Taiwan; solid and dashed arrows stand for material flow and sales order. If technology follows sales orders, and exports to America yield more information than exports to PRC, explain the impact of PRC's reform on Hong Kong, Taiwan and Korea.

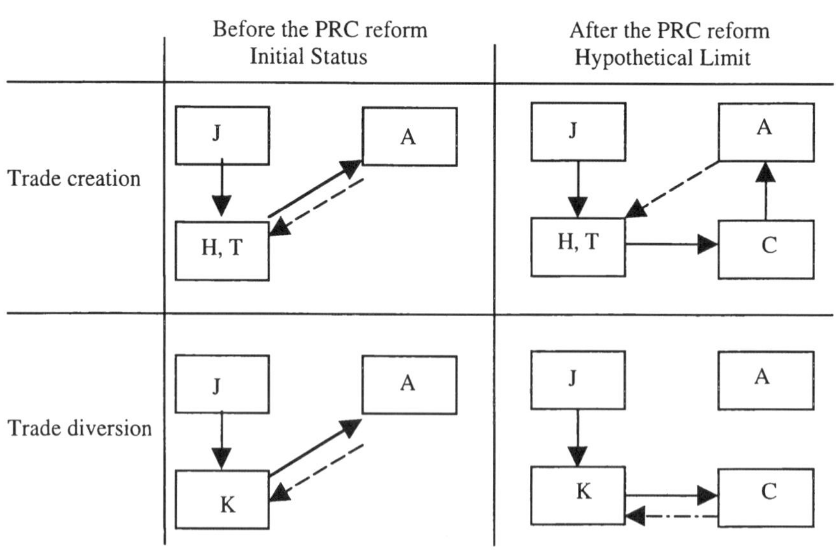

Table 4.Q.1 Re-routing

Chapter 5

MAJOR DEBATES IN ECONOMIC DEVELOPMENT

The Role of the State and the Role of Trade

1. INDUSTRIAL POLICY FOR A DEVELOPMENT STATE

So far we have focused on our own theme. This chapter covers some alternative points of view, and the associated policy implications.

Much of the study of economics today traces its roots to Adam Smith's *The Wealth of Nations* (1776). Smith's doctrine of *laissez faire* limits the role of the government to providing for law and order, national defense, public works and so forth. Trade, both domestic and foreign, is not to be restricted by either the government or a monopolist. Recent debates in development policy cluster around three issues:

(a) *How* active should the government be in a developing economy?

(b) *Whether* giant firms are essential to development, and thus deserving of support?

(c) What role has trade played in East Asian growth?

Related to (c), there are further controversies concerning:

(d) *Why* should or should not one draw particular conclusions from the statistics on total factor productivity?

Dynamism, Decentralization, and Selective Pressure as Sources of Market Efficiency

We start with the case for *laissez faire*. Unlike Smith and his immediate followers, most discussions in the literature are presented in analytical terms, under simplified assumptions.

The *case against monopoly* (or cartel), and hence against giant firms, has been made both in partial equilibrium terms with deadweight loss, and in general equilibrium terms with the Fundamental Theorems of Welfare Economics. Such proofs are established under highly abstract assumptions such as fully rational individuals, no increasing returns, and a timeless world. Yet to many observers, the efficiency of the institution of market competition also has a *dynamic* and more basic source: by *Arrow's Law*, freer entry (and less support of *giant firms*) allows for more innovations.

The *case against state intervention* requires more discussion. If we conduct our analytical discourse within the usual models, then, in principle, a wise and selfless social planner can duplicate whatever the market can do; the market system cannot be shown to be superior to a planning system that imitates the market.

In fact, the real world is far too *complex* and *dynamic*. In the former Soviet economy (which was far simpler than the economy of the West), there were 24 million types of different goods, where many pairs of different types lack mutual interchangeability (Ericson, 1991). In the PRC before the reform, to formulate the annual state economic plan, the center and the subordinate units could exchange messages at most 3 or 4 times (see Wan, 1992). For resource allocation, no economic planner can ever match the *information efficiency* of the market, where decision-making is *decentralized by price*. There is little hope that central planning can ever be efficient even in any approximate sense.

Moreover, shortcomings of central planning arise not only from 'the theory of teams,' where individuals have fully shared goals though not fully shared information, but also 'the theory of games' where bureaucrats operate under their personal agendas. Attempting to contain the malaise of corruption by *bureaucrats*, one ushers in a system of suffocating *bureaucracy*: an imperfect cure often worse than the ailment. Before the Indian reform, to complete a single transaction, it often takes hundreds of forms and the approval by dozens of officious officials (Roy, 1998). As proposed by Alchian (1950), and underlying the evolutionary games today: market efficiency is self-enforced by Darwinian selection. The inefficient does not survive. Thus, the case for market competition can also be made on the incentive ground of *market discipline*.

The State as Guarantor against Monopoly

Yet, here is a paradox. Prices are taken as given only when rivals are many. Thus the institution of 'perfect competition' has a tendency toward its own destruction. The causes for market concentration are not limited to luck, increasing returns, differences in ability, or manipulation of rules. In contrast to the standard, atemporal economic models, dynamic studies like Bewley (1982) show that, when agents with different time preferences meet in a perfect capital market, the most patient tends to inherit the Earth, due to self-selection. Even as everyone knows what one wants and pays for what one gets, evolution by the rule of market competition *may* leave a single class (or only one) as surviving firms. It is natural for the surviving few to 'corner the market' for profit, as monopolists do. Efficiency is then lost. Thus the State must always be there, with the necessary anti-trust power.

The State as the Provider of Public Goods

There also exists a defense for state intervention in the teaching of Adam Smith. Smith was no anarchist. To him, the State must not only act when *laissez faire* threatens to degrade by its own operation, but also provide what private firms are ill suited to supply: defense, law and order, and public works, to cite a few.

Extending the above list, economists have since developed the theory of public good (which can be shown as equivalent to externalities). If one can enjoy *freely* what others pay for, like the fragrance of the rose, there is no reason for that person to pay much for that good. When free riders cannot be excluded, too little of that good will be provided by the market.

The argument that holds true for perishable goods also applies to inputs used in future production, like R. & D. (Thus, promoters for *giant firms* would argue their indispensable role for R. & D.) This gives rise to both the endogenous growth theory, first studied by Shell (1966), and the theory of industrial policy (Itoh et al., 1991), including the case for infant industry protection (say, with tariffs or quotas). By the criterion of Kemp (1960), government must intervene only if firms hesitate to expand their production to what is socially desirable, for learning-by-doing. See illustration below.

A Simple Example

Our example comes in four cases: (a) an isolated individual (Friday or Crusoe) making decision for one period, (b) the same individual facing two periods, (c) two similar and interacting individuals (Friday and Crusoe) facing two periods without co-ordination, and (d) the same two persons acting in coordination. Each case builds upon the previous one.

Consider an island economy: each period the, each agent i has 1 unit of labor time L, either for leisure or to make coconut meal q for consumption.

(5.1.1) $q_{it} = a_t (L_{it} - L_{it}^2/2)$,

where a_t, the labor productivity at t, increases with current experience, Q_t:

(5.1.2) $a_t = \alpha(Q_t) = 2+Q_t$,

say, and experience is simply the total past labor input on the island:

(5.1.3) $Q_t=\Sigma_i \Sigma_{s<t} L_{is}$.

Each individual has the payoff:

(5.1.4) $U_i = \Sigma_t u_{it}$ (time preference is omitted here for simplicity)

with the periodic utility equal to consumption plus leisure:

(5.1.5) $u_{it} = q_{it} + (1 - L_{it})$.

These individuals arrived by shipwreck and are sure of an early rescue.

We now analyze the four cases in turn:

Case a. An isolated individual facing the last period on the island

By substitution,

(5.1.6)
$$\begin{aligned} U &= \alpha(Q_t) (L - L^2/2) + (1\text{-}L) \\ &= 1 + [\alpha(Q_t)\text{-}1]L - \alpha(Q_t)L^2/2 \\ &= 1 + L - L^2. \end{aligned}$$

which reaches a maximum of

(5.1.7) $1 + [\alpha(Q_t) -1]^2/2\alpha(Q_t) = 5/4$

at,

(5.1.8) $L = [\alpha(Q_t) -1]/\alpha(Q_t) = 1/2$.

Here work may yield product - specific experience that raises future productivity. But in the last period on the island, the 'future productivity' in *preparing coconut meals* has no economic value for Crusoe. Thus, only the current marginal labor productivity is matched against the disutility of work.

Case b. Isolated individual, penultimate period on the island

Here, using (5.1.6), one obtains,

(5.1.9)
$$\begin{aligned} U &= u_1 + u_2 \\ &= \{1 + [\alpha(Q_1)\text{-}1]L_1 - \alpha(Q_1)L_1^2/2\}+\{1 + [\alpha(Q_2)\text{-}1]L_2 - \alpha(Q_2)L_2^2/2\} \\ &= \{1 + L_1 - L_1^2\} + \{1 + [\alpha(Q_2) -1]^2/2\alpha(Q_2)\} \\ &= 1 + L_1 - L_1^2 + [1+(1+ L_1)^2/2(2+L_1)]. \end{aligned}$$

In contrast to (5.1.6), the last expression of (5.1.9) has the bracketed terms with a learning-by-doing effect. Pitted against leisure, first period work now yields both output and the useful experience that raises future productivity.

We turn to graphic analysis in Figure 5.1.1, and start from the right-hand side panel. This depicts the leisure-work choice for an individual in the last period on that island. The marginal product of labor (identical to the marginal utility of output in this example) is matched against its opportunity cost in leisure (which is unity here).

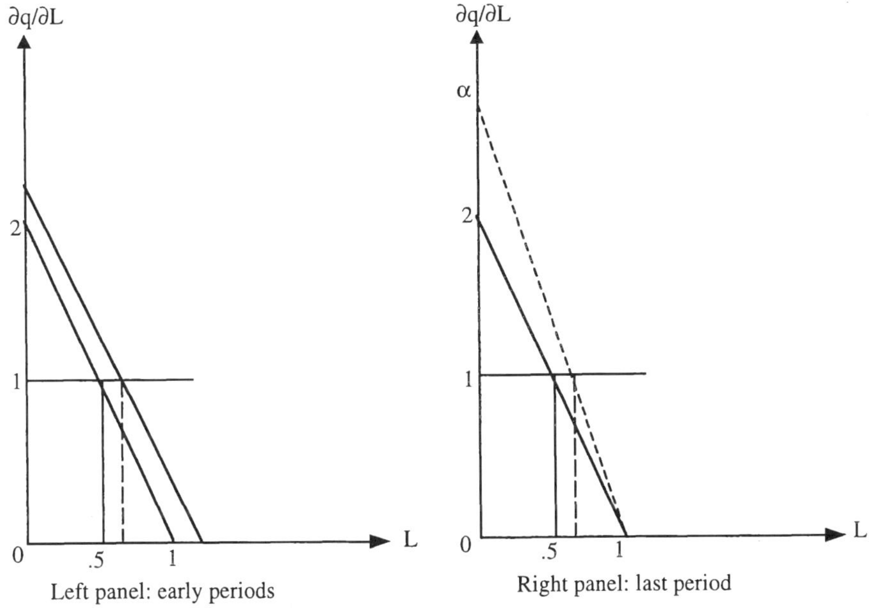

Figure 5.1.1 Work–leisure choice when learning may be possible

For case (a), the last period is also the first period. By assumption, $\alpha = 2$, and optimal work is $L = 1/2$. For case (b), workers have some experience last period, so $\alpha > 2$. More important, such experience depends on the first period choice. The dotted line depicts a more skillful work force with a higher marginal product schedule, and hence a higher level of work, $1\text{-}1/\alpha$.

Now in the left panel, the marginal labor product in *output* is augmented with the marginal labor product in *experience*, both measured by their contribution to the payoff. By numerical methods, we find the optimal choice for work exceeds the level 1/2 (and equals to $0.606 = L^*$, say).

Remark.

When current work makes valuable contributions to future productivity, it must be reflected in the leisure – work choice. But rational individuals can be expected to make the right choice, without government intervention. This point was noted by Kemp (1960).

We can now consider the truly interesting case, when both Friday and Crusoe are on the island, aware of each others' presence and, more important, learn from the work of each other. Here is a scenario where a social compact, in the form of a government, may be valuable.

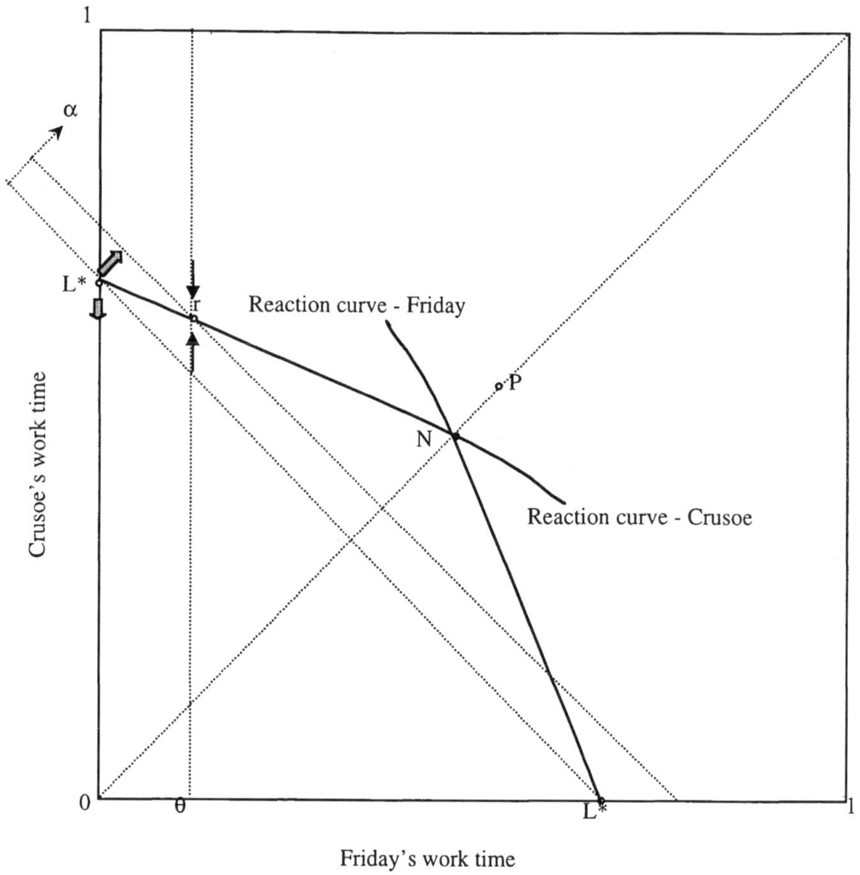

Figure 5.1.2 Uncoordinated and coordinated interactions

Case c. Crusoe and Friday in uncoordinated interaction

With a time horizon of two periods, the above analysis shows that all interesting facts about individual behavior are decided in the first period. The second period only gives motivation to decision-making in the first period. Further more, the only relevant variable is how much each individual work. As Case b hinted that even with a single individual, the two goods (*food* versus *leisure*), two periods (*now* versus *later*) model is sufficiently complex to require numerical methods. When two individuals interact with each other, our analysis can become intractable sooner than one realizes.

Fortunately, with graphic demonstration as well as logical deduction, we can obtain all relevant results.

To begin with,

1) In every situation, we focus on the labor time chosen by these two individuals during the first period.

2) We look for a 'Nash equilibrium' where neither of these two individuals has any motive to act differently, *alone*.
3) In addition, we look for symmetry so that these two perfectly symmetric players will act in a symmetric manner.

Because of 1), each such pair is represented as a point in Figure 5.1.2. Because of 2), once Friday has decided his labor time in the first period, say θ, Crusoe must choose his best response on the vertical line through θ in the square, say, at r, which is better for him than any other point on that line. The collection of all such best responses forms his 'reaction curve'. A similar statement can be made for Friday, and the equilibrium point is where such two curves intersect. Because of 3), we are interested only in such intersections on the 45 degree line that bisects the square.

We now focus first, on the reaction curve of one individual, say, Crusoe. Before meeting Friday, his optimal labor time in the first period is L*. By our assumption, his second period productivity will be raised to 2+L*. The arrival of Friday and thus the opportunity of watching the latter's experimentation is a windfall, like the receipt of free gift.

Since L* > 1/2, Crusoe's extra effort reflects a desire for future productivity. Suppose Friday's labor time amounts to θ in the first period. According to (5.1.3), for raising future productivity, this can substitute for Crusoe's own labor, one for one. Should Crusoe reduce his own labor time? Or should he set a higher goal for next period productivity, boosting it beyond $\alpha = 2 + L^*$? Due to the principle of diminishing marginal returns, he would split the difference: both reducing the current labor time and boosting future productivity. In Figure 5.1.2, the movement from L* to r, along Crusoe's reaction curve, has been decomposed into two components in shaded block arrows: a reduction in L* as well as an increase in α.

The reaction curve of Friday can be derived in exactly the same manner, with both curves crossing each other at point N, the Nash equilibrium point. In moving along the contract curve, away from the point marked L* on the axis, one observes the value of α increases monotonically. This implies at N, the curve for Friday must be steeper than the curve for Crusoe.

Remark.

Although uncoordinated as these two individuals are, there is some effect of increasing returns in the accumulation of 'human capital', as it has been noted all along in the literature of endogenous growth.

Case d. Crusoe and Friday in coordinated interaction

Thus, under coordination failure, each person takes the other's effort for granted, in deciding one's own work-leisure choice. While enjoying benefits from the effort of the other, each would not make one's full effort to account for its benefit to the other person, in raising the latter's productivity.

A social compact, usually enforced by a government, can be beneficial. In this example, it can work like the device of a 'matching grant'. Both

Crusoe and Friday would jointly select work schedules of a common length. Thus, they can internalize the externalities of learning, equate the marginal social product and marginal private cost of efforts, and reach the Pareto optimum point, P. Compared with N, under coordination failure, this means a longer labor effort, also higher than future productivity as well as payoff.
Remark.

This case meets the Kemp Criterion.

The Clemhout-Wan Results

Clemhout and Wan (1970) studies an economy with two industries, say, x, elephant taming and y, sword making. Both promise valuable learning. The result of that study can be illustrated here in simple terms. For each period t, the economy is endowed with a constant supply of labor, L (t) = 1. Leisure provides no utility. Labor is allocated to the two industries in amounts, $L_x(t)$ and $L_y(t)$,

$$L_x(t) + L_y(t) = 1.$$

Outputs x(t) (tamed elephants) and y(t) (swords) are both produced by Cobb-Douglas production functions, each with labor and fixed supplies of sector-specific factors, forests $Q_x \equiv 1$ and iron ore $Q_y \equiv 1$:

$$x(t) = [a_x\, L_x(t)]^{1/2}\, Q_x^{\ 1/2} = a_x^{\ 1/2}\, L_x(t)^{1/2}$$

$$y(t) = [a_y\, L_y(t)]^{1/2}\, Q_y^{\ 1/2} = a_y^{\ 1/2}\, L_y(t)^{1/2}$$

where $a_x > 0$ and $a_y > 0$ are input-augmenting indices. By substitution, the periodic production frontier has the form of a quarter ellipse. Suppress time t,

$$x^2/a_x + y^2/a_y = 1,$$

or, parametrically,

$$x = a_x^{\ 1/2}\, L_x^{\ 1/2}, \qquad y = a_y^{\ 1/2}\, (1 - L_x)^{1/2}.$$

Treat sword y as the medium of exchange,[1] so its unit price is always unity. Assume this economy faces given world market prices that stay constant and choose units for the two goods, we denote the price of elephant at time t as p(t) at home and $p^* \equiv 1$, abroad. At any equilibrium, market force causes the maximization of the (domestic) value of the national output,

$$z = px + y = p\, a_x^{\ 1/2}\, L_x^{\ 1/2} + a_y^{\ 1/2}\, (1 - L_x)^{1/2}.$$

[1] Archaeologists find bronze money in the shape of swords, but not elephants. This suggests the historic use of swords as currency. Elephants, tamed or otherwise, tend to make money matters more weighty than they are.

The first order necessary condition gives,

$$p\ (a_x/\ a_y) = x/y.$$

Therefore, other things being equal, the government can steer the output ratio by changing the domestic price in proportion. The domestic price exceeds (or lags behind) the world price by T, the amount of tariff (or subsidy):

$$p - p^* = p - 1 = T,$$

or

$$p = 1 + T.$$

Given the values of a_x and a_y, by routine calculation one can solve both x and y in terms of the single parameter, p = 1 + T:

$$x(t) = x[p(t);\ a_x(t),\ a_y(t)] = pa_x/[p^2\ a_x + a_y]^{1/2};$$

$$y(t) = y[p(t);\ a_x(t),\ a_y(t)] = a_y/[p^2\ a_x + a_y]^{1/2}.$$

The same is true for z and the value of the national output in world prices:

$$z^* = p^*x + y = x + y.$$

Next, the learning effect means the labor-augmenting efficiency indices, a_x and a_y are increasing functions of the cumulated outputs prior to t:

$$X(t) = \Sigma_{s<t}\ x(s) \quad \text{and} \qquad Y(t) = \Sigma_{s<t}\ y(s),$$

namely,

$$a_x = \alpha_x\ (X),\ \alpha_x' > 0; \qquad \text{and} \qquad a_y = \alpha_y\ (Y), \qquad \alpha_y' > 0.$$

Adopt now two more simplifying assumptions to get to the essential insight and avoid technical complexities. First, there is no time preference. Second, the experience has economic value only over a finite time horizon. The social objective now becomes the world market value of the cumulated outputs over the horizon, or just the sum of cumulated outputs (since $p^* \equiv 1$).

The cumulated output pair is of course just the sum of a sequence of periodic output pairs, each within a conditional periodic production set. Each set is conditioned upon past experience. The slope of any conditional production set at the periodic output pair gives precisely the domestic terms of trade making the latter the equilibrium output pair. To steer the private firms to produce the desired outputs, that price ratio must prevail with protection. For a two period case, these are depicted in Figure 5.1.3.

Panel a shows how tariff T raises p, the domestic price of y, above the world price. The reciprocal of p is the slope of the tangent line for the production frontier. Panel b shows this imposition of tariff shifts the current output point along the current production frontier.

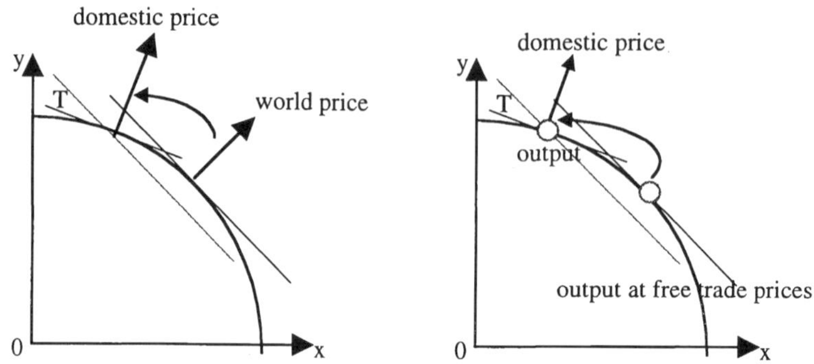

panel a
To each tax, a unique domestic price

panel b
To each domestic price, an output pair

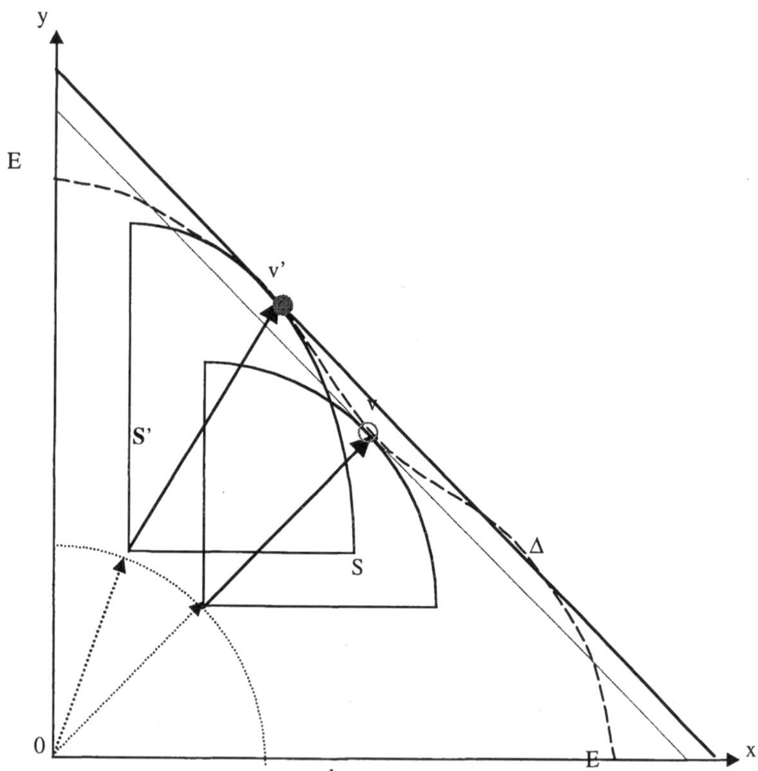

panel c

To each output pair, an experience, a future potential, an output sequence, and thus, a value for the cumulated output over the entire horizon

Figure 5.1.3 With learning, each policy causes a chain of outcomes

Next, one studies the learning effect in panel c. If *laissez faire* prevails in the first period, output would accumulate and labor efficiency would increase, yielding a production set, S, expanded in a somewhat balanced fashion. In contrast, the production of more tamed elephants makes the elephant tamers so experienced that the production set S' will expand more vertically, favoring the output of tamed elephants rather than swords. The two output sequences leading to v and v' are displayed. The cumulated output vectors at the end of the second period are the sums of their corresponding parts. The solid and dotted linear contours of equal international value demonstrate that tariff protection raises the value of cumulated national output. One can further construct an envelope EE, in broken line, to represent any realizable cumulated output pairs under any domestic price sequence. For the sake of argument, the highest value of national output is reached at the point marked Δ. So in fact, for the international value of the cumulated output, the tariff-ridden path we considered gives a local, and not a global maximum.

As shown in Clemhout and Wan (1970), tariff is inefficient. It distorts the prices facing both the producers and the consumers. The former distortion is necessary but the latter is pointless. However, in principle, the substitute for tariff is subsidy, which has to be financed out of taxes of other types. The administrative costs of such taxes and subsidies can be prohibitive.

Next, we shall revisit a result in Clemhout and Wan (1970) and classify the optimal policies for three period models. In each of the three periods, the optimal policy specifies a value $T = p - p^*$. So the triplet of T-values captures the nature of the policy. Figure 5.1.4 displays the four different cases.

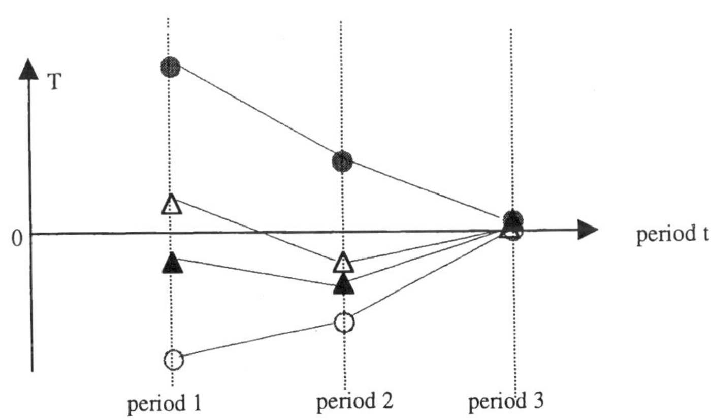

Figure 5.1.4 Alternative T sequences

Like in our earlier example, the value of T must be 0 in the last period for all the four sequences. Yet, for minor differences in the learning functions $\alpha_x(.)$, $\alpha_y(.)$, and the initial values of the cumulated outputs, a sequence can be monotonically decreasing or increasing toward 0, or first decrease and then increase, or even change in sign. In the last case, represented by hollow triangles, the optimal policy should be to protect good y first and then good x. If this can happen for a two-good model with the simplest production structure, then these results suggest that complexities exist in real life. It will be difficult for a government to come up with the *optimal* type of intervention, regarding *which* industry to protect, to *what* extent and for *how long*.

For two reasons one may argue that, for the policy maker, the above model may be unreasonably tough. In a world with exactly *two* goods, protecting one is penalizing the other. When both goods present opportunities for valuable learning, the worst option is to protect nothing at all. So if one hesitates because one does not know exactly which is the best, *the best can be the enemy of the good.* On the other hand, with an indefinite future horizon, one must forecast how long the information related to a particular technology, say, the internal combustion engine, is going to last. That is not easy either.

The policy-relevant implications of this study come in three parts. (a) Protect an industry that clearly shows a strong learning effect in comparison with all the rest. (b) Protect any industry in a class that shows very strong learning effects, since action is better than inaction. In the above example, missing the point Δ may mean missing the 'optimal sequence' by a long shot, yet in terms of the social objective we assumed, it is not something one should lose sleep about. Figure 5.1.5 emphasizes this by rotating Figure 5.1.3, panel c, to emphasize the value of the social objective. (c) Refrain from protecting industries showing marginal benefits of learning, since rent-seekers may exploit the opportunity of government intervention. They always

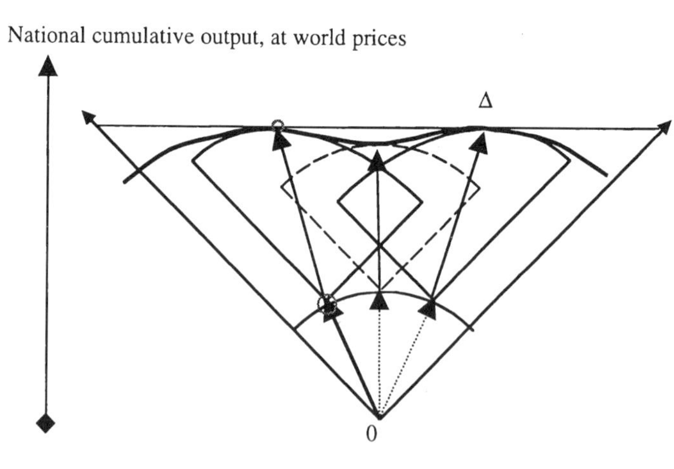

Figure 5.1.5 Social objective

argue for protection, justified or otherwise. Attempts to prevent rent seeking may introduce further inefficiency through bureaucratic practices.

History shows it is not helpful for a government to protect industries over the long haul. It creates vested interests and a chronic dependence on the government.

For some readers who prefer to have a complete, numerical example, we return to the two period model and consider a symmetric case where,

$$\alpha_x(X) = 1 + 25X^3, \qquad \alpha_y(X) = 1 + 25Y^3.$$

Thus,

$$X(1) = 0 = Y(1),$$

$$a_x(1) = \alpha_x(0) = 1 = \alpha_y(0) = a_y(1),$$

$$X(2) = x(1) = p(1)/[1 + p^2(1)]^{1/2} \; Y(2) = y(1) = 1/[1 + p^2(1)]^{1/2}$$

$$a_x(2) = 1 + 25p^3(1)/[1 + p^2(1)]^{3/2} \; a_y(2) = 1 + 25/[1 + p^2(1)]^{3/2}$$

Now for the second and hence the last period of a two period model,

$$p(2) = p^* = 1.$$

Therefore,

$$z^*(1) + z^*(2) = [(1+p)/(1 + p^2)^{1/2}]+[a_x(2)+ a_y(2)]/[a_x(2)+a_y(2)]^{1/2}$$

$$= [(1+p)/(1 + p^2)^{1/2}]+[a_x(2)+a_y(2)]^{1/2}$$

$$= (1+p)/(1 + p^2)^{1/2} + [2 + 25(1 + p^3)/(1 + p^2)^{3/2}]^{1/2}.$$

By graphic analysis, one finds there are two global maxima at:

$$p = 0.13956 \text{ and } 7.163.$$

Note in this symmetric case, shown logarithmically in Figure 5.1.6, no local maximum is not a global maximum.

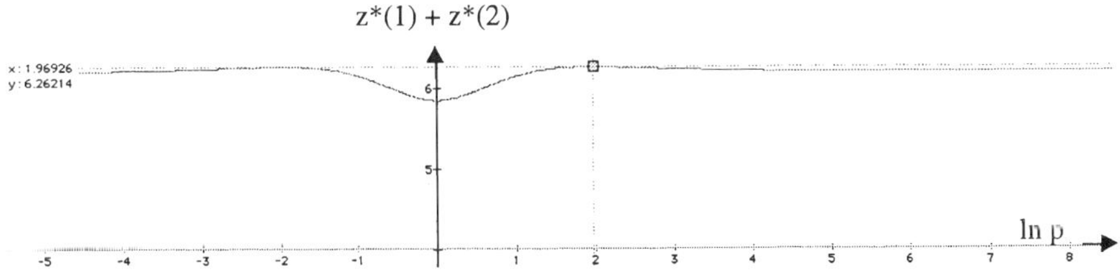

Figure 5.1.6 Two global maxima

Case Study—Japan Launched the Synthetic Fiber Industry

The argument by Japanese economists about launching a new industry is based upon the Industry Promotion campaigns of Japan in the period of the 1950s and 1960s. The basis of the argument is externality. The latecomer can free ride on the experience of the first-mover, so no one would do anything unless the State grants temporary monopoly to the first-mover. The argument can be cast in the framework of learning-by-doing, but there are important differences. One would not like to duplicate the effort of having a single first mover. Also, in terms of the bounded learning model of Alwyn Young, as long as a single entry is effected, the bound is reached. It is a very interesting case. The State can do its job without creating the 'moral hazard' of dependency. Apparently, different governments can achieve the same purpose through alternative means. Japan, Singapore, Korea and Taiwan all have had some success, each using a different approach.

The particularly interesting features of the Japanese case for launching industry are exemplified by the steps taken to promote the artificial fiber industry, according to Suzuki (1991). These include:

a) Selecting artificial fiber as a product that Japan could produce for export.
b) Setting up a government-business forum to exchange information, choose technology and decide on steps for development.
c) Agreeing upon the principle that since latecomers benefit from the experience of the first-mover, who bears the cost and risks, the State must act.
d) Since the State cannot afford the required subsidy, it should allow the first-mover to survive on monopoly profit from the large domestic market by excluding both imports and domestic entry.
e) Subsequent entry can be granted to limit the disadvantage of having a monopolist.
f) The firm with the best technological potential should enter the industry first. Ultimately, the industry price should not be too low to constitute barrier to entry.
g) After the above principles have been agreed upon, then comes the selection of the first mover. When the choice is met with some contest by the second best claim, the latter is selected as the next entrant, with a relatively short delay.
h) Ultimately the entrenched firm was requested to charge a price higher than the 'stay-out' price, so some marginal firms would be able to survive.

The approach used here cannot be easily reduced to models and equations. It acts on an oligopolistic industry that approached a competitive industry over time. It is a rather sophisticated policy in containing both market failure and government failures. Although the government is involved, it is not quite in a position to be corrupt. The only tricky decision is the selection of the first-mover. But one can balance the risk against the expected monopolistic profit according to terms agreed upon in advance. This approximates the game of 'fair division,' in which the one who cuts the cake into nearly even shares is to take the last cut. So, in principle, no one should be ready to pay much of a bribe.

Eventually, according to Suzuki, to protect downstream small and medium-sized Japanese firms in garment making, the Ministry of International Trade and Industry (MITI) restricted Japanese producers of synthetic fiber from expanding facilities to export the products to foreign garment makers. So Southeast Asian firms expanded their outputs in a startling manner. By 1989, the output of Taiwan surpassed that of Japan.

Japanese Industrial Policy in Practice

Although this monograph does not focus on Japan, it is reasonable to sketch briefly the experience of Japan in certain aspects, because of its intrinsic interest and its influence on other East Asian economies. After Japan's long recession in the 1990s, Japanese economists took stock of the Japanese industrial policy practiced in the early post-World War II days. No consensus has been reached. However, certain conclusions can be drawn from their research.

(1) The Japanese government, through the actions of the MITI, the Ministry of Finance and so on had much impact in many areas. These include the industry mix, technology acquisition, corporate governance, the size distribution of firms, and trade frictions.

(2) There has never been a single-mindedness of purpose, overall long-term planning, or an irresistible dominance over the private sector. Policy objectives have been thwarted by the private sector (like the crowding of the auto-making sector). Forecasts have been proven wrong by events (like the delayed approval for Sony to buy transistor technology). Planned actions have been found ineffective (like the futile attempt to limit entry into petrochemicals by setting a particular minimum capacity size for entrants). There are also policies that are clearly the result of compromises toward entrenched interest (as Suzuki stated about the restriction of synthetic fiber exports).

(3) There have been repeated gatherings of experts, business representatives and government officials to consider in which direction the economy should go, what policy to implement, and so forth. The exchange of information and the coordination of plans, and the implicit deterrence of opportunistic behavior among all parties have been highly valuable.

(4) One particular instrument of policy in Japan is 'administrative guidance.' This dates probably to the days of World War II, when under the influence of the Third Reich, the wartime State would intervene in the internal decisions of various private firms for prosecuting the war. In early post-war years the government had extensive control over the economy, and could promulgate administrative regulations affecting the firms. Therefore what the official wished could not be lightly dismissed.

(5) The abundance of science and engineering manpower relative to other Asian economies, the size of the home market, the social cohesion, the willingness of the people to plan thoroughly and the shock of defeat in World War II all played roles in Japan's early success.

(6) Internal democratization, external restrictions resulting from Japan's entry to GATT, and repeated strong pressure from the U.S. have continuously narrowed the scope of Japanese government to carry out industrial policy.

Kikkawa and Hikino (1999) wrote, "If rapid economic growth is the product of a well-organized and articulate industrial policy, led by a competent bureaucracy, that is the experience of South Korea and Taiwan (and possibly China), not Japan." We shall see that certainly the industrial policies of Korea and Taiwan are no better than those of Japan. What they said correctly is that Japanese firms are more competent technically than Korean and Taiwanese ones, so that the Japanese bureaucrats play more of the role of a coordinator. They care for the efficiency and competitiveness of Japanese industries, rather than any particular firms. They support these firms competing fairly against each other, but not rent-seeking.

Kikkawa and Hikino (1999) argued convincingly that industry targeting was much easier for Japan in the 1950s than for the U.S. in the beginning of this century. Japan enjoyed a high growth period between the Korean War and the oil shock. This coincided with the quintessence of its type of industrial policy. The Japanese growth rate tapered off since then, and for the last decade Japan has been in recession. When discussing industrial policy, it is appropriate to offer some comment about the current Japanese economy.

In comparison with the other OECD members, the record of Japan is far superior, recession or not, in terms of avoiding inflation and unemployment. Whatever debt crisis Japan has pertains to domestic debt, and Japan remains a country with the largest foreign reserve assets. The real per capita income of Japan is still one of the very highest in the world. The strong yen reflects international competitiveness. There is no reason to expect that the Japanese economy will fall backwards. Thus, it is hard to criticize Japanese industrial policy on account of its current macroeconomics.

On the other hand, one cannot say that the economy of Hong Kong performs badly either. In inflation and unemployment, Hong Kong may not be quite comparable to Japan, but the difference is minute. High average per capita income and no debt burden are again the characteristics of the economy. There may be hardly any manufacturing industry left in Hong Kong – but that is almost as objectionable as the fact that the U.S. today has few farm jobs. Hong Kong has an economy regarded as atypical. We shall consider that later. What is important is that there has never been any industrial policy for Hong Kong. So how much the Japanese population gained from its industrial policy is not clear, either.

2. LIBERALISM AND REVISIONISM

We have argued that, in theory, it is highly likely that the *best* policy calls for government intervention. In principle, if the *laissez faire* doctrine of Adam Smith leaves the government to provide law and order, then it cannot be diametrically opposed to a government enhancing knowledge capital formation, using a concept from endogenous growth theory. This involves the creation of competitive assets, adopting the terms of Alice Amsden. Such interventions include policy measures related to the launching of industries. If, on paper, 'the social planner' is frequently used in dynamic economic theory, why should one object to a social planner in flesh and blood? Figure 5.2.1 presents a case motivated by Figure 5.1.5, and depicts how, under a 'big push' led by the government, the economy can gain a great deal. The 'quantity' axis represents some change of parameters, such as re-

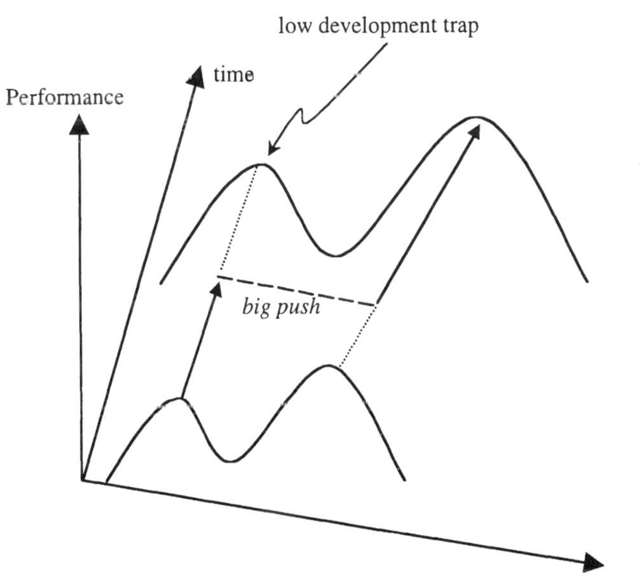

Figure 5.2.1 'Big Push'

source allocation that accompanies the launch of a new industry. Because the information uncovered by the first mover is a public good, government initiative may be needed to make the new industry a reality.

Thus, the best case for market force should always be the impersonal nature of its selection, for efficiency, and its economy of information, in decentralized decision-making. After all, any argument in terms of distortions has been made moot by the theory of second best. The most serious drawback against intervention is government failure, due to corruption or bureaucratic red tape. The universal failure of the centrally planned economies in the late 20th century should give us pause. If bureaucrats cannot plan and carry out production well by themselves, *why* and *how* should industrial policy be entrusted to them *as individuals*, once removed from production? If all they offer is their 'good office' to internalize externalities, their basis for choice must be straightforward.

We have discussed the theoretic roles of the State and industrial policy, now we review the highlights of the literature, before conducting a quick survey of some empirical studies.

As shown in Table 5.2.1, on the role of the State and the role of trade, different views rose and gained popularity at different points in time.

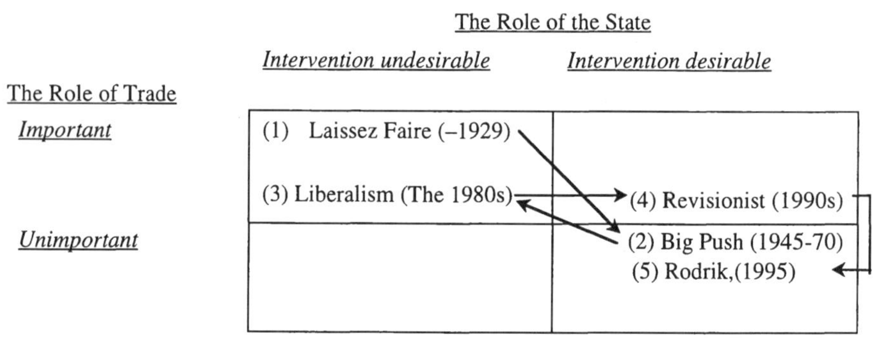

Table 5.2.1 Alternative views

(1) The *laissez faire* view prevailed before the Great Depression. Tariff protection was suspect because of possible rent-seeking.
    During the Great Depression and World War II, development concerns took the backseat.
(2) The Big Push view dominated the period of 1945-70. Keynesian revolution and wartime experience convinced most economists that the State could work wonders independent of the market. The export pessimism view of Prebisch was also in vogue; trade was seen as a threat to nascent Latin American industries that emerged duringWWII.
(3) The Liberalism revival. The rise of the Japanese and the four NIEs as well as the Latin American debt crisis discredited the import substitution view. The World Bank and the IMF, backed by the U.S., developed the

Washington Consensus. Rescue was often conditioned on the dismantling of borrowing countries' protectionist barriers

(4) The Revisionist School. Amsden (1989) and Wade (1990) studied Korea and Taiwan and found that these governments had active State with complex law and regulations. They believed that the success of these economies and Japan was mainly due to the 'governing of market'. They still perceived that under government policy, trade can help.

(5) Dani Rodrik (1995) supported both the revisionist argument for the importance of state-led development but also some of the anti-orthodox opinions (see next Section) and disputed the importance of trade.

3. PITFALLS IN MEASURING PRODUCTIVITY GAIN

Ever since the early 1980s, the NIEs have been held as model economies for development. Economists who differ on macroeconomics (like Lucas and Stiglitz) or development policy (like Amsden and Bhagwati) are united in their view on these four economies: technical progress and trade are main factors for their sustained, rapid growth.

Such conventional wisdom met a severe challenge in almost every aspect by the early 1990s. Table 5.3.1 summarizes six anti-orthodox positions.

Six 'anti-orthodox' positions	Researchers		
	Kim and Lau	Young	Krugman
(1) The NIEs have negligible efficiency gain	√	√	√
(1') EPBC* gain the most in efficiency		√	
(2) The NIEs gained largely from accumulation	√	√	√
(2') The NIEs gained also from long working hours		√	
(3) Trade has at most an one-shot benefit		√	
(4) The NIEs will fail like the Soviet economy			√

*Botswana, Congo, Egypt and Pakistan

Table 5.3.1 The 'anti-orthodoxy' on the NIEs

Underpinning the anti-orthodoxy are the studies of Kim and Lau (1994) as well as Young (1994, 1995). Although the data source (say, on capital input) is never perfect, these authors applied standard econometric procedures with methodical care and drew inferences by tight reasoning. Coming from respected researchers, their results received the support of Krugman (1994: 70-1), in words deserving quotation:

> Consider, in particular, the case of Singapore. Between 1966 and 1990, the Singaporean economy grew a remarkable 8.5 per cent per annum, three times as fast as the United States; per capita income grew at a 6.6

percent rate, roughly doubling every decade. The achievement seems to be a kind of economic miracle. But the miracle turns out to have been based on perspiration rather than inspiration: Singapore grew through a mobilization that would have done Stalin proud. . . .

Krugman predicts that the NIEs will fail like the Soviet economy. Such views are reported with approval in leading textbooks on development (Ray, 1998) and growth (Aghion and Howitt, 1998). However, among economists like Amsden, Bhagwati, Lucas and Stiglitz, none has joined this anti-orthodox bandwagon. Thus, the profession remains sharply divided on the performance of the NIEs, and the merits of their strategy.

This is a matter of central importance to all developing economies where more than two thirds of the world population reside. Thus one need to assess those anti-orthodox positions with the utmost care.

In particular, one must go beyond the usual practice, which only asks whether the best technique of an approach, or the most reliable data on the topic has been used. One must question, that given the limitations of both methods and observations, whether the line of evidence pursued is decisive in view of the evidence from all other sources. The ultimate conceptual goal must be the construction of a 'theory', that is consistent with all available information. This is, after all, the same evidential standard for both science-based issues like global warming and court proceedings in forensic inquest.

Next, from a range of angles, we present seven preliminary assessments on the six anti-orthodox positions. These should all figure in the final analysis. We then go over to methodological issues, to place the study of the NIEs in the context of similar empirical investigations on all economies.

Seven Preliminary Assessments about the Anti-Orthodoxy

As evidence, *four* qualitative and *three* quantitative points may be raised in relation to the six tabulated positions.

Qualitative issues. Here one questions whether an anti-orthodox position is in agreement with intuition, or consistent with economic reasoning.

The intuitive aspects:

A. In position (4), Krugman predicts that the Singaporean economy will fail, the Soviet way. Now Soviet income suffered an absolute decline, and not just the loss of momentum for growth. This distinction is important. What happened was essentially an isolated economy fallen victim to creative destruction in the hands of a technically more dynamic West. Quantitative output decline came later, only after the implosion of the State. In contrast, Singapore is a 'most – connected' export platform, for multinational corporations from America, Europe and Japan to produce outputs with high value-added. Foreign firms are responsible for major portions of jobs, output and export. Technological obsolescence is unlikely.

B. On position (3), that trade offers NIEs only the initial one-shot benefit, one may compare it with the keen observations of Komiya (1990: 101), that without international trade, Japanese growth will stop. For the NIEs, one would expect even stronger trade-dependence. Case after documented case indicates that export to America provides valuable information for firms in the NIEs (e.g., Stern et al, 1995 about Hyundai Motors, Korea; Crown and Coleman, 1996 about Giant Manufacturing, Taiwan; Morawetz, 1981 about various garment firms in various NIEs).

The aspects related to basic economic reasoning

C. In relation to position (3), one may consider the intertemporal angle. If the *international capital* market is absent, then by Ramsey (1928), capital accumulation is influenced by the rate of return on capital, which is usually higher with trade than without it. If that market is present, trade liberalization should attract international investors, especially, for such active traders like the NIEs. Basic economic theory predicts that opening to trade will lift an economy to a higher growth path, and not just provide a one - time gain.

D. Regarding both positions (2') and (3), Shieh (1992) reports that, American subcontract orders have attracted Austronesian – speaking tribesmen from their off-shore island abode to Taiwan's booming garment trade. Trade provided fuller labor - utilization today (the one-shot gain), as well as the experience for later opportunities.

Quantitative issues. Here one must check whether the empirical foundation for the anti-orthodoxy is as solid as it appears, whether alternative data set may provide quite different results, and whether the computed Total Factor Productivity (TFP) growth provides the conceptual advantages as promised.

E. Krugman drew confidence from the parallel studies by Kim and Lau and by Young: supposedly similar findings (the NIEs have low TFP growth) from independent research. The fact is: Kim and Lau concluded that their OECD economies had uniformly higher TFP growth than the NIEs – thus Japan outperformed Korea; Young tabulated a set of his estimates, where Korea outperformed Japan.

F. Usually, the record of the past we studied is for predicting the future we care for. The reliability of this inference depends on the stability of the pattern measured over time. Liang and Jorgenson (1999) studied Taiwan by sub-periods. Their estimated TFP growth is similar to Young's, over the sub-period covered by Young, but takes much higher value afterward. What this reveals is *not only* the measured pattern lacks stability over time, *but also* the pattern of variation may reflect *systematic bias* of the method, not *random noise*. In that case, the question is no longer one *may* err, *any* time, but one *will* err, *each* time. This is discussed below.

G. Leave the one-economy (Taiwan) clues for now, we go for the rationale for using TFP growth. We all care for (a) the *future* values of income per capita, and not (b) the *future* value of TFP, itself. Kim and Lau (also Young) focus on (c) the *current* growth of TFP but not (d) the *current* growth of income per capita, because the growth of income per capita is the result of (e) the growth of capital per capita and (f) the growth of TFP. (e) converges to zero in neoclassical (*but* not endogenous, or 'new') growth theory. Then, an *implicitly assumed* constancy of (f) implies that (c) predicts (b): higher *current* growth of TFP means higher *future* growth of per capita output. Young found *then* that Egypt, Pakistan, Botswana, and Congo (EPBC) had the highest TFP growth. 18 years passed after his period of study. Today, there is no sign of any 'EPBC' miracle. Knowing now what Young could not, that TFP growth is a *tried-and-false* guide to pick winners among the nations, we must never use it to show NIEs' performance as satisfactory *or* otherwise.

Methodology of TFP Computation; the Nature of the NIEs

From the above discussions, understandably many economists continue to regard the growth record of the NIEs as exemplary. At the same time, proponents of the anti-orthodoxy will emphasize that theirs is the verdict of empirical evidence, dictated by well accepted methods. In fact, position 2' comes directly from data. Positions (1), (1') and (2) are derived by standard econometric procedures. Claiming that trade can yield either static gains from trade or technology transfers (cf., however, Points C and D above), Young then maintains position (3): if the NIEs have no appreciable technical progress, they can only enjoy from trade the once for all gains. Position (4) of Krugman is an extension from (1) and (2).

To locate the source of the anti-orthodox findings, one must explain that in computing the TFP growth, not only (a) how the standard methods got wrong for the NIEs, but also (b) why the same methods performed reasonably well in other applications.

In broad outline, we maintain that the *special assumptions* underlying the standard methods will introduce systematic bias when applied to those NIEs, with their *special features*.

Three assumptions in the standard methods for computing TFP growth

There are three common assumptions adopted to compute TFP growth:

1. (*Aggregation*) There exists an *aggregate production function.*
2. (*Simultaneity*) Production uses inputs of *the same (or last) period,*

3. (*Substitutability*) Various *factors substitute freely for each other.*

Although these assumptions appear harmless in usual applications, Solow, who founded 'growth accounting' in Solow (1957) is fully aware of their limitations, and advises caution:

(a) His views on the aggregate production function in Solow (1966) is reproduced below:

> I have never thought of macroeconomic production function as a rigorously justifiable concept... It is either an illuminating parable, or a mere device for handling data, to be used as long as it gives good results, and to be abandoned as soon as it doesn't or as soon as something better comes along.

(b) He himself has steered clear of development economics, stating that the specific institutional and cultural context is too important there, making a purely analytic treatment difficult (Solow, 2000).

The challenge is to decide whether a method has caused serious bias.

Three features in the nature of the NIEs

Unlike economies in a steady state of stagnancy, an economy in the phase of early industrialization, has distinct features at three different levels:

(a) At the *firm level*, management commits to long term projects, with phased investments at specific levels, to enter desired markets. For example, Hyundai Motors, Korea, started expansion under President Park, sought exhaust control technology, and prepared for an initial loss of $1000, per car, and only entered the American market after a decade – long campaign (Stern et al., 1995).

(b) At the *industry level*, pioneer firms launch new industry by trial and error, often with government support, and latecomers free ride on their costly experience. For example, Taiwan's semiconductor sector was spearheaded by two firms spin-off from a government lab. Private business groups joined several years later (Tung, 2001).

(c) At the *national level*, with the accumulation of human capital by education and experience, and the completion of infrastructure, the economy gains comparative advantage in sectors which promise high value-added, use complex technology, and deploy expensive equipment. For example, in Singapore, workers experienced in precision machining attracted the investment of Seagate and made the city state the principal supplier for computer hard drives worldwide (Hobday, 1995); the supertanker terminals had transformed Singapore into the 'swing supplier' for refined fuel between the Middle East and California (Perry et al., 1997; Tonzon, 2002). Thus, labor shortage 'crowded out' the garment industry.

All these three features imply either initial capital spending bringing benefits after long time lags, or structural changes where technical progress is inseparable from 'capital-deepening'.

For advanced industrialized economies, either the costly transition is a matter of the past, or, proportionately, enough projects reaping the benefit are balanced against those projects (or industries) incurring the initial spending. Thus the system becomes *ergodic*: the cross - project distribution of the capital-labor proportions of a period approximate the cross - period capital - labor proportions for a project..

To recapitulate, our argument can be conveniently summarized in Table 5.3.2.

Nature of an NIE	Characteristics	Features of the standard methods		
		aggregation	simultaneity	substitution
Economy wide	Structural shift	Causing bias		
Industry level	Appearance of pioneers		Causing bias	
Firm level	Long run commitment		Causing bias	Causing bias

Table 5.3.2 Sources of systematic bias

In particular, the traditional aggregate production function has the form:

$$Q(t) = A(t)\,F[K(t), L(t)]$$

where Q(t), A(t), K(t) and L(t) stand respectively for the aggregate output, technological index, aggregate capital input and aggregate labor input in period t, where each of the explanatory variables, A, K and L can vary independently. For simplicity, capital here represents rents on leased equipment, being a *flow* rather than a *stock*. For further simplicity, we shall assume the labor force is constant, and L(t) is normalized to 1, and suppressed from now on. We then set f(K) = F(K, 1).

For the NIEs in the process of either launching a new industry or making special investment for a new project, capital spending is divided into two parts: the regular component, $K_r(t)$ and the special component $K_s(t)$:

$$K(t) = K_r(t) + K_s(t).$$

Example 1. The technological index only takes two values:

$$A(t) = 1, \text{ or } 1 + B,\ B > 0.$$

The benefit B may be attained, once for all, by making at least a special capital spending of level m, for n periods.

Thus the choices facing the developing economy are:

I. Staying with the original technology:

Q = f(K) for all periods. (Shown graphically as OA below)

II. Making the necessary investment to attain B:

Q = f(K – m), first n periods, (Shown graphically as O'A' below)

Q = (1 + B)f(K), all later periods. (Shown graphically as OA" below)

This situation is depicted in Figure 5.3.1.

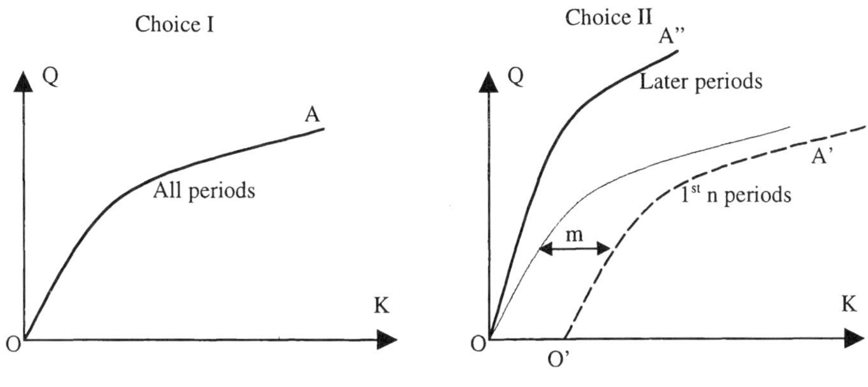

Figure 5.3.1 Initiating long term projects or launching industries

'Inspiration'-today and 'perspiration'-yesterday are not substitutes but complements, here. In ignoring the time-separation between the cost and benefit of industrialization, the standard methods would both (a) understate the efficiency of the NIEs in early years (as in anti-orthodox positions (1) and (1')) and (b) under-predict their later performance (as revealed by Liang and Jorgenson).

To represent the implications of the structural shift of the NIEs, we shall illustrate with:

Example 2. The economy has three sectors, Sector 1 (garments), Sector 2 (machines), and Sector 3 (semi-conductors), with increasing capital/labor ratios, when facing the same factor prices in the economy. Specifically, the production function for sector j is loglnear:

$$\ln Q_j = \ln A_j + \alpha_j \ln K_j + (1-\alpha_j) \ln L_j , \quad \alpha_1 < \alpha_2 < \alpha_3 .$$

Except for the sector subscript, the meaning of the symbols Q, A, K and L are similar to the Example 1. A plausible hypothesis is that,

$$A_j = g_j(s), \qquad \text{for all j},$$

where g_j is an increasing function of s, the latter being some skill indicator for the economy, and s itself usually increases with time, t.

The productivities of different sectors have different relationships with s. For example, the productivity of Sector 2 (machines) responds most with the skill improvement when the skill index s is at some medium range, but less so at lower or higher ranges. The maximum response is at $s = s^*_j$, for sector j. To be specific, one may consider,

$$g_j(s) = h_j/[1 + \exp(-s + s^*_j)], \text{ where } h_j > 0 \text{ is a scaler parameter.}$$

It is intuitive to assume that $s^*_1 < s^*_2 < s^*_3$, so that the productivity in the garment (machine, or semi-conductor industry) is more related to the primary school (high school, or college) education. Thus, the set $\{s^*_j\}$ is a strictly increasing transform of the set $\{\alpha_j\}$ (maybe, $s^*_j = \alpha_j$). Assume the h_js are all unity by choosing the units for the goods, we can display the functions $g_j(s)$ below in Figure 5.3.2. Note that skill acquisition affects the relative industrial efficiencies most for the NIEs.

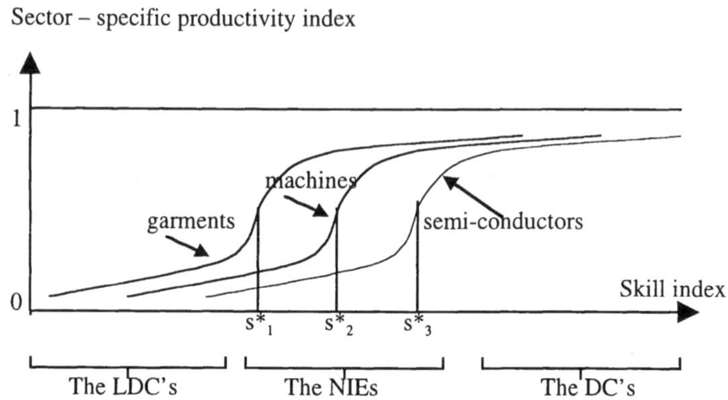

Figure 5.3.2 Sector-specific productivity and economy-wide skill

Next, by assuming world prices as given, we can first construct the sector-specific unit-value isoquant, depicting the minimum capital-labor pairs that can produce one unit of value in each sector. Construct the envelope for these sector-specific isoquants, and one obtains the unit - value contour for the economy.

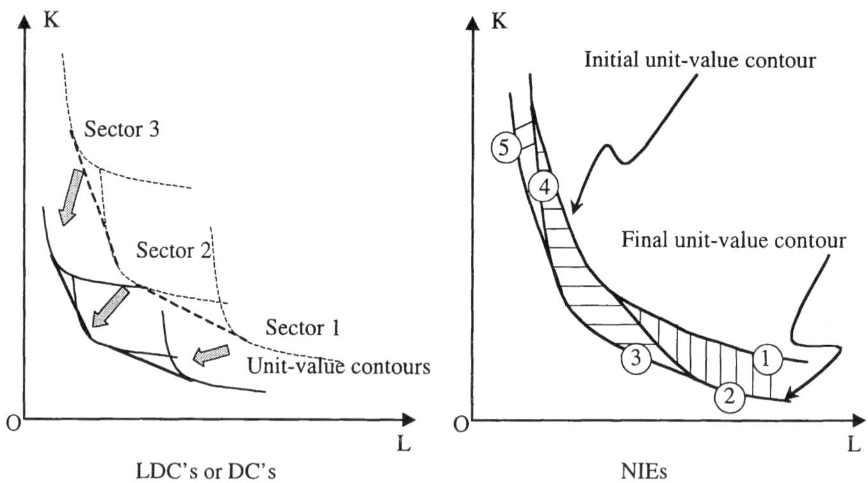

Figure 5.3.3 Unit-value isoquants and unit-value contours

As skills accumulate, other things being equal, it takes less inputs to produce the same value of output. Therefore, we can conclude (a) both the sector - specific unit-value isoquants and the unit-value contour will shift toward the origin. Since the productivity indices shift at speeds which are different from sector to sector, it follows that (b) instead of moving toward the origin proportionately (as the sector-specific isoquants do), the unit-value contour will 'change shape'. In addition, we can conclude that (c) such changes in shape will be quite pronounced for the NIEs but hardly perceptible for the developed countries (DC's) or the less developed countries (LDC's). These facts are shown in Figure 5.3.3.

The story for the DC's or LDC's is a series of gradual, balanced gain in productivity. This can be studed by the standard methods, via the aggregate production function. The story for the NIEs presents an entirely different situation. A hypothetical scenario with five successive equilibria (each shown as a circle in Figure 5.3.3) is tabulated below.

Equilibrium position	Remarks	Efficiiency gain in	Output
1	On the initial unit-value contour		1
2	Productivity gain in sector 1	Sector 1 (garments)	1
3	Productivity gain in sector 2	Sector 2 (machines)	1, 2
4	A change in input ratio	-	2, 3
5	On the final unit-value contour	Sector 3 (semiconductors)	3

Table 5.3.3 A hypothetic scenario as human capital accumulates

Each time, a gain in sector-specific productivity allows the economy to produce a unit value of output with new input pairs, each requiring reduced usage than before. In Figure 5.3.3, such pairs form areas marked with horizontal, vertical, or diagonal parallel lines. Such productivity gain, although genuine, cannot be represented with TFP.

When presented only with information in terms of the time series of aggregate input requirements per unit of output, at the historical sequence of equilibrium positions, econometricians using standard methods would detect no clear sign of techncal progress, but only a strong tendancy of rising capital/labor ratio. The five numbered circles in Figure 5.3.3 may come from a single contour, given some random shocks. No wonder Krugman would conclude that: "the miracle turns out to have been based on perspiration rather than inspiration."

We have now explained why, in studying the NIEs, standard methods have caused the artifacts underlying the anti-orthodoxy.

In fact, independent from the above discussions, there are some reasonable concerns about the tempo of future growth for the NIEs, due to the impact of worldwide trade patterns on technology upgrading. That will be considered in Chapter 12.

CHAPTER SUMMARY

- There is much debate regarding industrial policy:
  - conceptually, on the roles of the State, the large firms, and trade,
  - statistically, on how meaningful is total factor productivity growth.
- *Laissez faire* is not *anarchy*. Since the time of Adam Smith the State has almost universally been accepted as having some role to play in the economy, for reasons of equity and efficiency, such as supplying public goods – the analytical equivalent to externalities. Actually, the debate is never *whether* the state should intervene, but *where* and *how much*.
- An all-controlling State has proven to be undesirable; the market has its advantages in terms of preventing possible *government failures* due to corruption or bureaucracy. The advantages of the market lie not so much in terms of the marginal tradeoff, but in terms of its informational efficiency, and its powerful but imperfect pressure for 'Darwinian selection.'
- Market competition may self-destruct and the State may be needed to limit monopoly. The market also may be unable to internalize the benefits of learning, which resembles public goods.
- Learning-by-doing is a form of dynamic externality. Government protection may improve welfare in principle, but the complexity of the economy and the lack of information available to the State make intervention hard in practice.
- As the case of Japan indicates, intervention may be justified when industries are initially being launched. Successful intervention becomes more difficult as the catching-up process becomes more advanced.
- Korea, Taiwan and Singapore have all intervened in their development, sometimes usefully, some times ineffectively, and sometimes causing harm: sweeping conclusions are not valid. The Korean strategy of promoting large business groups is costly and not economically crucial to development for all economies.
- The measurement of total factor productivity growth is systematically biased against economies in the early stages of catching up, for various reasons. For example, much capital spending at that stage has long-term benefit and cannot be treated routinely to measure productivity residual.
- In consequence, arguments based on productivity residuals – which have suggested such problems as excessive accumulation, low efficiency gain, the irrelevance of trade to growth and the impending collapse of East Asian economies – must be discounted.

QUESTIONS AND EXERCISES

1. How did Japan promote the synthetic fiber industry by generating beneficial externalities and limiting the undesirable effects of monopoly? Explain.
2. What does the history of Hyundai Motor's entry into the U.S. market show about (a) the roles of trade and learning in Korean development; (b) the validity of using the computed total factor productivity growth to draw conclusions both about the Korean efficiency gain and the role of capital accumulation in Korean growth?
3. Consider an example of learning-by-doing, in which both of the industries learn in a two-sector economy. What can be said about the program of 'protection of all sectors all the time'? How likely is the achievement of dynamic efficiency under *laissez faire*? How likely is it that a government would be able to plan perfectly for a program of industry-specific protection?
4. (Arrow's law) Arrow (1962b) points out that firms with profitable products may choose not to launch a new good at the socially desirable time.
   Opinion A: "This observation is of little interest. Apparently, over that profitable good, this firm already earns monopoly profit, which should always be prevented by the State with anti-monopoly legislation, anyway."
   Opinion B: "To promote innovation, a developmental State should not be concerned with the presence of monopoly. Witness how did the Japanese MITI carry out industrial policy against coordination failure. Thus, Arrow's Law misses the point for a developing economy."
   Opinion C: "Arrow's Law is of central importance for the current reform programs of both Japan and Korea."
   Comment on these three views.
5. In Figure 5.1.2, show that at N the slope of the reaction curve is steeper for Friday than for Crusoe. (Hint: Draw the iso-α locus through N; note that one's contract curve meets higher α values, if the other person works more).
6. Based upon the discussion of Section 3, this chapter, comment on Prescott (1998).

Chapter 6

CRISIS AMIDST GROWTH

Lessons to Learn from Crisis 1997

1. GENERAL REMARKS

Crisis 1997 was the last of the three financial shocks of the 1990s. Three characteristics contributed to the shock value of this episode: its abrupt onset, its virulence against apparently healthy economies, and its widespread reach. It is useful to identify these characteristics both in order to diagnose the problem and to prescribe a remedy. One needs a thorough understanding of the menace in order to prevent its recurrence; no stone must be left unturned. Our attention here focuses on the three aspects mentioned above.

In some ways, the crisis can be related to the catching-up process in East Asia. We shall present the case that the rise of East Asian economies might have made the world economy more volatile. Further, the maturing of the once rapidly growing East Asian economies might have helped to induce over-investment. Finally, considerations of political economy in some Asian economies might have caused the sharp reverses and widespread impact when the crisis occurred. However, more evidence is needed to make a definite statement.

Before going further, three issues call for clarification. First of all, for East Asia as a whole,[1] Crisis 1997 was neither inevitable in its occurrence,

[1] Should East Asia include Indonesia, or exclude Singapore? These are subjective decisions. Usually, China, Japan, the 4 NIEs, Macao, Vietnam and North Korea are regarded as East Asia.

nor universal in its impact, nor irreversible in its consequences. Not all of East Asia was troubled by debt; not all troubles were international in scope. Beijing, Hong Kong, Taipei and Singapore were not under siege; Japanese banks owed much to fellow Japanese, but owned hundreds of billion dollars in foreign assets, including U.S. treasury bills. Taiwan and Singapore only slowed down their growth. Hong Kong kept its fixed exchange rate intact, although it sustained a sharp but short recession. In East Asia, Korea suffered most. The rapid expansion in the region resumed quickly, even though internal restructuring remains slow and difficult.

Second, it is generally agreed by now that Crisis 1997 does not repudiate 'openness' as a sound development strategy. At the most, one needs more safeguards in the process of globalization. As an analogy, automobile accidents bring calls for safer car design, better drivers' training and stricter traffic laws – not calls to give up motorized fire trucks or ambulances.

Third, although Crisis 1997 was not purely a debt crisis,[2] it was the foreign debt of several afflicted economies that made the crisis important worldwide. Foreign debt is as central to Crisis 1997 as the Danish Prince is to *Hamlet*.

It has to be said that for lending and borrowing that occur in real life, current economic theory offers valuable parables, but it does not provide a full-fledged analysis that is anchored in its microeconomic foundations. Real life loans are specified in detail with regard to the borrower, the amount, the duration and the purpose of the borrowing, the type of assets mortgaged and the precedence of claim on assets in bankruptcy, besides the rate of interest. One may argue that this is similar to ice cream in 64 flavors. However, the market for ice cream can be usefully idealized with the Walrasian parable of centralized exchange and a market-clearing price. But here the central issue is bankruptcy. Regardless of the amount of the loan, the claim of the creditor is capped by the debtor's ability to pay in bankruptcy. The information, the belief and the control of the lender are crucial. There is just no easy way to approximate the situation in terms of such concepts as a single market-clearing interest rate, as it is done in the literature.

For now, what we can do is to construct some parables that are relevant to the issues at hand. The crux of the matter is to analyze the change of market volatility that depends partly on 'fundamentals' (the total as well as the distribution of outputs and so forth) but also partly on the beliefs of individuals. It is neither realistic nor useful in the present context to assume that the equilibrium terms of trade must *always* be unique under rational

[2] For example, the problem facing Hong Kong was unrelated to foreign debt.

expectations, nor that there is *always* an infinity of equilibrium terms of trade. If institutional reform is aimed at volatility, then the task is unnecessary in the former case and hopeless in the latter case.

To simplify analysis, we take a leaf from the 'real theory' of international trade. In that literature, an economy is a 'small country' if any possible actions in that country cannot affect the terms of trade for the rest of world. Here we assume that in any situation to be analyzed, the aggregate loan transaction is 'small' relative to the aggregate equilibrium pattern.[3] The terms of trade are unaffected by the presence or absence of such transactions. A partial justification of this assumption is the empirical work of Feldstein and Horioka (1980).

The next section studies the volatility of the world economy. Following that is a discussion of how the industrial policy of some economies may translate the volatility of the world economy into the debt crisis for an economy. Finally, the spread of the crisis is explained in terms of the lack of transparency in the current financial market. To reduce the burden of a surfeit of symbols and notations, we shall analyze each aspect with a separate model, instead of a single integrated model for all the three aspects. Nonetheless, the connection between these three separate parts should be clear.

2. THE VOLATILITY OF THE TERMS OF TRADE – A SIMPLE EXAMPLE

We now focus on default; that is, when the assets of a borrower have fallen short of a loan at maturity. This never happens in a deterministic world, when both the lender and the borrower have full information. It is well known, however, that default can happen in a risky environment when individuals act under rational expectations. In an uncertain world, there is no objective probability with regard to the possible class of outcomes, so an individual must act according to subjective belief. Default again may happen. Under either a risky or an uncertain environment, there are conditions that cause every individual to make sure that all loans will always be repaid. This is true when a borrower suffers a utility of negative infinity *if and only if* default of any magnitude happens. Here the worst can always be avoided by not borrowing. Thus, conceptually, assuming away objective probability offers us no novelty. By the same token, ruling out uncertainty yields no analytic simplicity either. On the other hand, once risk is removed,

[3] Thus, the aggregate volume of international loans does not have to be infinitesimal in size.

uncertainty becomes a necessary condition for default. When uncertainty is traceable to the state of system evolution, one can readily determine when the system is free from default, and debt crisis. That will be a case of least volatility.

Uncertainty obviously happens when there exist multiple terms of trade that clear the market. In this situation, the system is more crisis-prone. Thus, we can meaningfully ask whether the world tends to become more volatile. The analysis below is a variation of the model of Uchupalanun (1999), in which two results may be established:

(A) It is possible to have multiple equilibrium terms of trade, and

(B) The likelihood of multiplicity may increase, as the poor catches up with the rich.

To provide some general notion of our discussion, we present a two-country model, where the home country is catching up with the best practice, which is assumed to be fixed. After the opening of trade, its index of efficiency x rises over time, as shown in Figure 6.2.1.

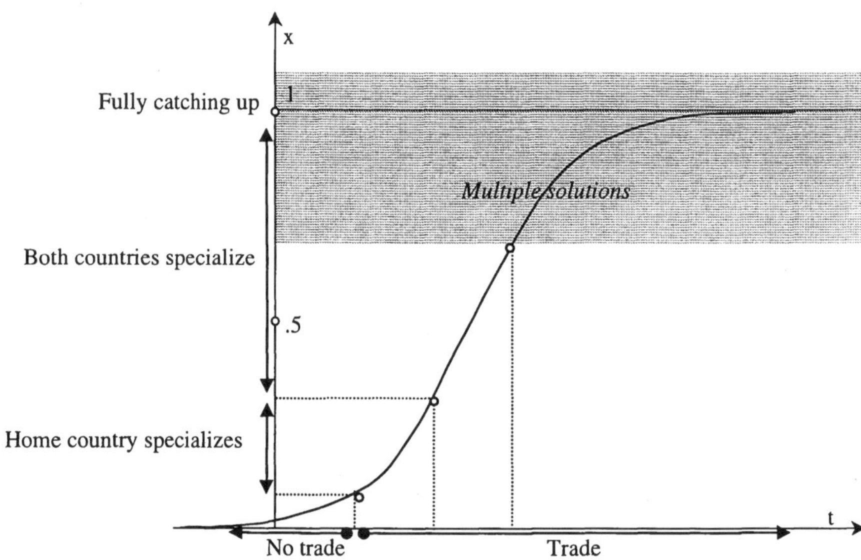

Figure 6.2.1 The evolving world

To track down the source of multiple solutions for market clearance, we illustrate with:

A Simplified Example

In a four-good Ricardian world there are two symmetric economies. In each country, the representative individual has a fixed labor endowment of 1 unit, and a homothetic preference that can be represented as a constant elasticity of substitution function over three goods, two traded goods and a local good that is non-traded, say, housing.[4] Between any pair of goods consumed the substitution elasticity is $\sigma \in (0, 1/2)$. Everyone treats both traded goods equally. Identical amounts will be consumed if the price ratio between them is one to one. Due to environmental differences, each economy enjoys symmetric comparative advantage in one particular traded good. Against the other, the values of unit labor product are 1 and $m \in (0, 1)$. With the cost ratio being always one-to-one between housing and the natural export good, one may assume the spending ratio between housing and the exportable good is always A - 1 to 1, where A > 1. Identify the degree of effectiveness in utilizing labor (e. g., training, organization, etc.) as human capital, say, x and $x^* = 1$, respectively for the home and the foreign country. Human capital operates like a labor-augmenting index.

The Situation of Symmetry—Domestic Labor Fully Efficient

We shall start with the subclass of cases where the catching-up process is complete. Thus, in both economies, labor efficiency is at its maximal attainable level, which is set at unity: $x = 1 = x^*$. An entire family of examples can be parameterized by the pair of parameters, (A, σ). Each economy always exports one traded good and imports the other. Thus, *complete specialization* obtains. One might choose a unit for the natural export of a country such that the unit labor productivity for it is one. It is harmless to set the unit labor productivity as zero rather than m for the substitute for import. By selecting units, the labor productivity for local housing will be normalized as unity also.

The Excess Demand Function

In this model, any real exchange rate is identical to the wage ratio, or the double factorial terms of trade. Let the domestic labor be the numeraire, so that the domestic wage is $w \equiv 1 \equiv p$, the unit price of the natural export and housing for the home country. Income wL is also 1. Attention may be focused on the foreign wage rate, $w^* \equiv p^*$, the unit price for both the natural export and housing for the foreign country. Complete specialization requires

---

[4] More generally, one may assume a two-level utility index. In the lower level, the consumed exportable product and the home good serve as arguments for a sub-utility index that is homogeneous of the first degree. This sub-utility and the imports are arguments in a constant elasticity of substitution utility index.

that $m < p^* < 1/m$. Under our assumption of symmetry, there is always a *benchmark equilibrium*: $w^* = 1 = w^*L^*$. The latter is foreign income. Denote h, t and τ respectively as housing, tradable product consumed and tradable product exported for the home country and h^*, t^* and τ^* for the corresponding magnitudes of the foreign country, then all these six magnitudes are functions of the single variable w^*.

The *full employment conditions* for home labor L and foreign labor, L^* are:

$$h + t + \tau - 1 = 0 = h^* + t^* + \tau^* - 1.$$

The balance of trade calls for:

$$b = \tau^* - \tau/w^* = 0.$$

At the benchmark equilibrium, clearly,

$$h = (A-1)/(A+1) = h^*, \qquad t = \tau^* = 1/(A+1) = t^* = \tau.$$

Also, the consumption ratios by factor content are:

$$(h + t)/\tau^* = A = (h^* + t^*)/\tau.$$

Now by the definition of a constant elasticity of substitution function, one can integrate between the benchmark value and any alternative value of w^* to obtain,

$$\log[(h + t)/\tau^*] - \log A = \sigma(\log w^* - \log 1) = \log A - \log[(h^* + t^*)/\tau],$$

or, equivalently,

$$(h + t)/A\tau^* = (w^*)^\sigma = A\tau/(h^* + t^*).$$

Using the *full employment* condition to eliminate h and t as well as h^* and t^*:

$$(1 - \tau)/A\tau^* = (w^*)^\sigma = A\tau/(1 - \tau^*),$$

or, after rearrangement,

$$\tau + A\,(w^*)^\sigma\,\tau^* = 1$$

$$A\tau + (w^*)^\sigma\,\tau^* = (w^*)^\sigma.$$

These are two equations to solve for τ and τ^* in terms of w^*. By Kramer's Rule,

$$\tau = [1 - A\,(w^*)^\sigma]\,(w^*)^\sigma/\,\Delta,\quad \tau^* = [(w^*)^\sigma - A]\,/\Delta,\quad \Delta = (1 - A^2)\,(w^*)^\sigma.$$

With these, the *balance of trade* means a zero value for the excess demand of the foreign balance. That can be written as:

$$0 = b(w^*) = \{[(w^*)^\sigma - A] - [1 - A\,(w^*)^\sigma]\,(w^*)^{\sigma-1}\}\,/\,(1 - A^2)\,(w^*)^\sigma.$$

Or, equivalently,

$$A\,(w^*)^{2\sigma-1} - (w^*)^{\sigma-1} = A - (w^*)^\sigma$$

Under our assumption of symmetry, the above equation is always satisfied for w* = 1, at the *benchmark equilibrium*. If there exist multiple solutions, there must be another solution, w* ≠ 1. By symmetry, 1/w* ≠ 1 must be a solution as well. So there must be at least three solutions. Now under Ricardian technology, no import substitution operation can make positive profit in any country. In short, if there are multiple equilibria, every one of these terms of trade must be within the range, [m, 1/m].

At any equilibrium w* ≠ 1,

$$A = [(w^*)^\sigma - (w^*)^{\sigma-1}]/[1 - (w^*)^{2\sigma-1}]$$

$$= \sinh[\omega/2]/\sinh[(1 - 2\sigma)\omega/2]$$

where $\omega = \log w^*$, and $\sinh z = (e^z - e^{-z})/2$. The right hand side expression gives a family of smooth, positive, and convex curves symmetric to the vertical axis, each corresponding to a specific value of $\sigma \in (0, 1/2)$. Figure 6.2.2 displays such a curve.

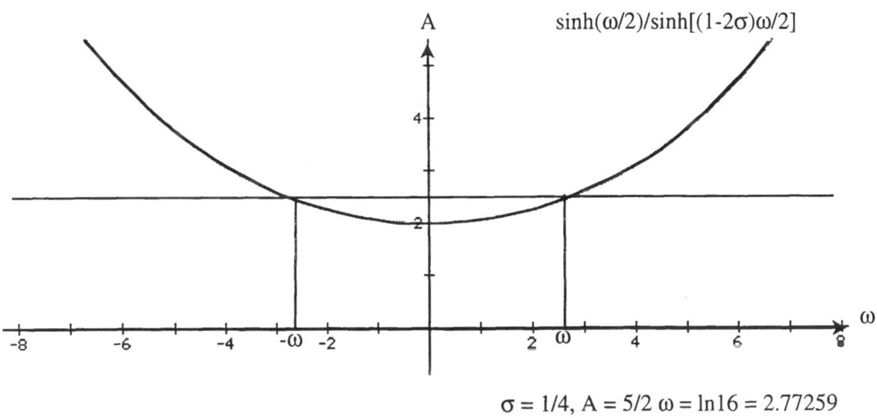

Figure 6.2.2 Multiple solutions

It is clear that given the value of σ = 1/4, there can be multiple solutions only when A is larger than 1/(1 - 2σ) = 2. To have multiple solutions when the two economies are symmetrical, the minimal value of A, the parameter for 'home good bias,' increases with σ, the elasticity of substitution. This is captured by the condition:

$$A = 1/(1 - 2\sigma).$$

Actually, for A = 5/2, σ = 1/4, the (excess) demand function for foreign exchange, b(w*) has three roots 1/16, 1 and 16. This is shown as Figure 6.2.3.

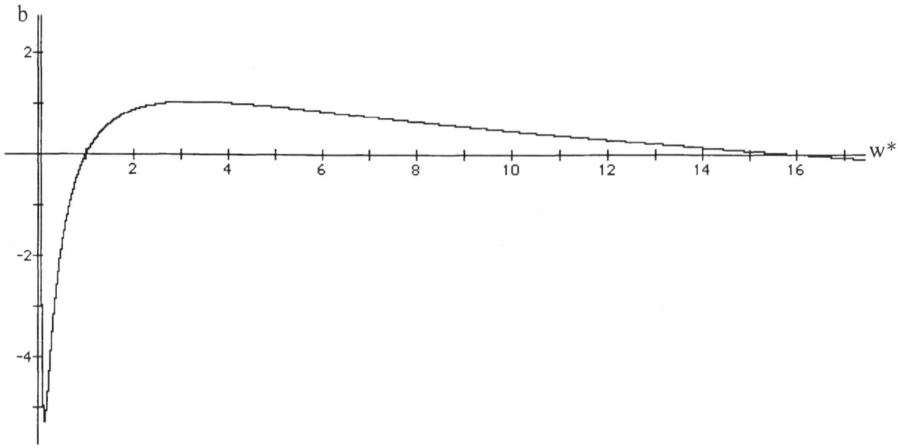

Figure 6.2.3 Excess demand schedule (scale modified)

The Situation of Asymmetry — Domestic Labor Not Fully Efficient

We next consider the case when x_0, the initial value of x, is very low. The equilibrium conditions must be modified accordingly. In particular, the foreign country may be incompletely specialized, and producing υ units of import substitute, with υ/m units of labor.

The *full employment conditions* for home labor L and foreign labor, L* are:

$$h + t + \tau - x = 0 = h^* + t^* + \tau^* + \upsilon/m - 1.$$

The balance of trade calls for:

$$b = \tau^* - \tau/w^* = 0.$$

At the *benchmark equilibrium*, the consumption ratios by factor content are:

$$(h + t)/\tau^* = A = (h^* + t^*)/(\tau + \upsilon) .$$

Now by the definition of a constant elasticity of substitution function, one can integrate between the benchmark value and any alternative value of w*, including m, to obtain,

$$\log[(h + t)/\tau^*] - \log A = \sigma(\log m - \log 1) = \log A - \log[(h^* + t^*)/(\tau+\upsilon)],$$

or, equivalently,

$$(h + t)/A\tau^* = m^\sigma = A(\tau + \upsilon)/(h^* + t^*).$$

Using the *full employment* condition to eliminate h and t as well as h* and t*:

$$(x - \tau)/A\tau^* = m^\sigma = A(\tau+\upsilon)/(1 - \tau^* - \upsilon/m),$$

or, after rearrangement,

$$\tau + A\, m^{\sigma}\tau^{*} = x$$

$$A\tau + m^{\sigma}\tau^{*} = m^{\sigma}(1 - \upsilon/m) - A\upsilon.$$

Use balance of trade to rid of τ^{*},

$$\tau(1 + Am^{\sigma-1}) = x$$

$$\tau(A + m^{\sigma-1}) = m^{\sigma} - (A + m^{\sigma-1})\,\upsilon.$$

Solve τ from the first equation and substitute that value into the second equation, one finally obtains the expression for the import substitute produced by the foreign country:

$$\upsilon = [m^{\sigma} - x(A + m^{\sigma-1})/(1 + Am^{\sigma-1})]/(A + m^{\sigma-1}).$$

Clearly as the labor efficiency of the home country rises, υ eventually falls to zero, and both countries become completely specialized. That is, when,

$$x = (m^{\sigma} + Am^{2\sigma-1})/(A + m^{\sigma-1}).$$

For any larger value of x, we have $w^{*} = p^{*} > m$. Eventually, when x grows even larger, multiple market clearing prices obtain. For $A = 5/2$, $\sigma = 1/4$, a value of $x \geq 28/30$ would lead to multiple equilibria. This is displayed in Figure 6.2.4 for the relationship of x and w*, with $b\,(w^{*}; x) = 0$.

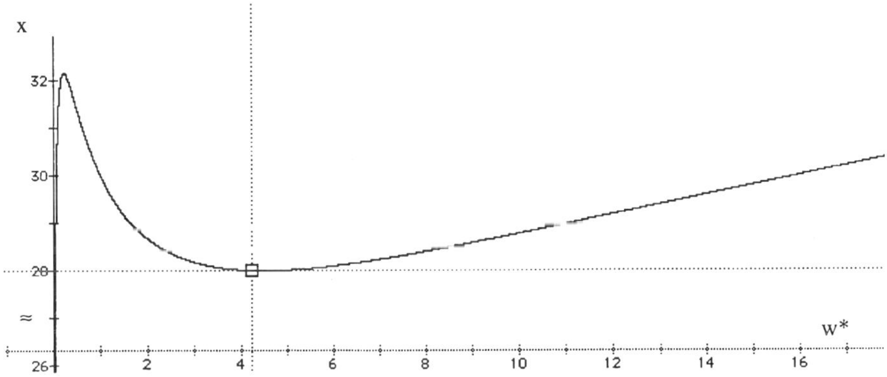

Figure 6.2.4 Growing into multiplicity

To be complete, denote the value of x at period n as x_n, one may consider a logistic law of motion:

$x_{n+1} = x_n + c\, x_n\,(1 - x_n)$, where c is a suitable small positive number, which implies the tapering off of the growth rate $(x_{n+1} - x_n)/x_n$.

Interpretation

We can now gather the earlier results for the following interpretation. In our model, initially, the home country is relatively inefficient. By joining the trading world, efficiency rises asymptotically toward the best practice. In the earlier phase, the latecomer completely specializes where it has comparative advantage, yet the export does not entirely satisfy the needs of the advanced economy. The world becomes completely specialized only later. As the latecomer gains efficiency and therefore relative income, a stage will be reached where multiple equilibria exist. That is to say, a rise of the home wage leads to more favorable terms of trade (caused by a cost-push), which means more home income and a corresponding increase toward the non-traded good at home, like a housing boom. This justifies higher demand for home labor and the rise of wage to begin with. Since the market selection among the multiple market-clearing terms of trade depends on psychology only, the world becomes more volatile. Therefore, the catching-up process has the tendency to bring the real terms of trade into a 'turbulence zone.'

This story bears some resemblance to reality. The fluctuation of the value of the dollar against the yen may well represent the fluctuations described above. Real estate prices certainly have been quite volatile in the East Asian economies. The fact that East Asia has become the major supplier of a range of products from garments to sport shoes and from ships to memory chips make our assumption of complete specialization not farfetched.

It is important to emphasize that both the element of 'fundamentals' and the concept of multiple equilibria are not new in the literature. The differences are three: (a) the 'fundamentals' we consider pertain to the interaction of the trading world, and not to the performance of an individual economy in isolation; (b) the multiplicity of solutions arises from the 'real sector,' and not due to monetary matters; (c) the shifting relative income between the two trading countries makes a difference. We by no means take issue with the existing analyses in the literature. However, if our concerns are not groundless, then a careful diagnosis is important to prevent the recurrence of the crisis. The fact that some aspect (that we focus on) has not been studied before surely should not mean it is therefore not a possible source of crisis. This is particularly relevant if our approach implies that once and for all, the world may have entered into a 'turbulence zone.'

3. THE POLITICAL ECONOMY OF DEBT CRISIS

We have seen that the 'fundamentals' of an evolving world economy may cause volatility in the terms of trade, also known as the real exchange rate, in international finance. Now consider a world with two countries, say the United States and Thailand, both using paper currencies and neither having price level changes at a double-digit rate per year. The terms of trade oscillation we previously discussed must manifest itself in sharp swings of the nominal exchange rate. The Thai borrower of dollar-denominated debt will find the repayment to be an unbearable burden when the baht suddenly loses half of its value against the dollar. The U.S. lender expecting the Thai borrower to face extreme difficulty in repaying the debt would hesitate to make such loans in the first place. Major financial crisis arises only when loans of substantial sum are involved. International financiers are cautious by nature. They usually hesitate to make loans to the developing world, and especially to private businesses in such economies.

In that light, the debt problem in the Crisis 1997 appears atypical, as Table 6.3.1 shows.

	Nature of Debt	
	Public sector	Private sector
Indebted country		
Developed		Central European banks (1930s)
Developing	Latin American governments (1980s)	Asian businesses (1997)

Table 6.3.1 Major financial crises

Thus, such loans would not be made, unless it is perceived that the resources of the state are ready to back such loans. For that matter, not all states may qualify. On one level, Crisis 1997 appears unexpectedly virulent because the victims were supposedly economies with 'sound fundamentals,' such as low inflation, little public budget deficit, and so on. Rapid growth or bountiful natural resources were the typical profile of those economies. At another level, if such a major crisis were to happen at all, those private debtors must be from healthy economies, backed by the State.

Why the State lends backing to private borrowing is then a matter of 'political economy.' To analyze the root cause of such government behavior, it is not particularly useful to attribute the issue to 'cronyism.' First of all, favoritism of government officials toward certain business interests is quite universal. It exists in the U.S. as well as in Japan and France, even though debt crisis does not. There is no evidence at all that economies that suffered a debt crisis (like Korea under Kim Young Sam) were distinctively more corrupt than ones that did not (like Taiwan under the KMT). Second, it is foreign debt and not domestic debt that can lead to an acute crisis. When such acute crises develop, those in the government are most likely to lose power. Indonesia, Thailand and Korea are the clear examples. Should those in government be interested in providing advantages to groups they favor, there are safer channels than abetting them to engage in foreign borrowing.

It seems that debt crisis is neither universal nor inevitable, even before one has achieved the lofty goal of wiping out all favoritism in politics. The crux of the matter is how would the policy maker act when private business requests support in borrowing from abroad. This is studied below with the simplest decision-theoretic model.

Consider the goal of the policy maker to be the survival of the current government. There is the strategic outcome function, F, and two government choices: c_1, to support the private business in borrowing from abroad; and c_2, not to support. There are also two alternative states of Nature, s_1, there will be no adverse turn of the terms of trade, and s_2, there will be. There are four possible outcomes, $\Omega_1 = F(c_1, s_1)$, high growth at g %, $\Omega_2 = F(c_2, s_1)$, low but positive growth, say, at $(g - \Delta)\%$, $\Omega_3 = F(c_1, s_2)$, a debt crisis and $\Omega_4 = F(c_2, s_2)$, no growth (0%). Assume that if there is an external shock, the population will reject the government if its wrong policy caused a crisis but otherwise rally around the government in the face of adversity. Thus the associated survival probabilities for the government with Ω_3 and Ω_4 are respectively: $\pi_3 = 0$, $\pi_4 = 1$. On the other hand, the survival probabilities for the government with respect to high and low growth is a matter of *vox populi*. For simplicity, assume these take the values of $(1/2) + X$ and $(1/2) - X$, respectively, $X \in (0, 1/2)$. We further hypothesize that the actual value of $X = X(y, z)$ is a function of two explanatory variables: y, the legitimacy of the government and z, the performance expectation of the population. $\partial X/\partial y < 0 < \partial X/\partial z$. In other words, the less legitimate is the government, and the better the economic performance demanded by the population, then the higher is the premium for growth. For any given subjective probability q that one attaches to the chance of a sudden shift of the terms of trade, the government's choice is then between:

$(1 - q)(1/2 + X)$ for supporting foreign borrowing

and $(1 - q)(1/2 - X) + q$ for not supporting.

The situation is recapitulated in Table 6.3.2.

	Nature	
	s_1, there is no shift (subjective probability, 1 - q)	s_2, there is a shift (subjective probability, q)
Government attitude toward borrowing		
c_1, to support	π(high growth) = (1/2) + X	π(debt crisis) = 0
c_2, not to support	π(low growth) = (1/2) - X	π(no growth) = 1

Table 6.3.2 Decision problem for the government

It is reasonable to argue that the process of development is path-dependent. For Taiwan, the KMT regime had hyperinflation in the early 1950s. Thus, the government advocated stability rather than mere growth, to dampen z, the growth expectations of the population. With X low, the policy choice is 'safety first.' For Korea, since President Park came to power through a coup against the parliamentary Second Republic, he had to emphasize high growth for self-legitimization. Once z, the growth expectations, had been built up, the government of Kim Young Sam had to maintain growth whenever possible. Private borrowing had to be backed, lest the appearance of performance might suffer. Ironically, again it was all done against the competition of Kim Dae-Jung.

Figure 6.3.1 presents a parametric map, showing what combinations of q and X will induce the government to support foreign borrowing. Two governments sharing the same subjective probability estimate for a sudden shift of the real exchange rate, say, q = 1/5, may act differently. One with high value of X (represented with a solid square) will support foreign borrowing while the other with lower value of X (represented with a hollow box) would not.

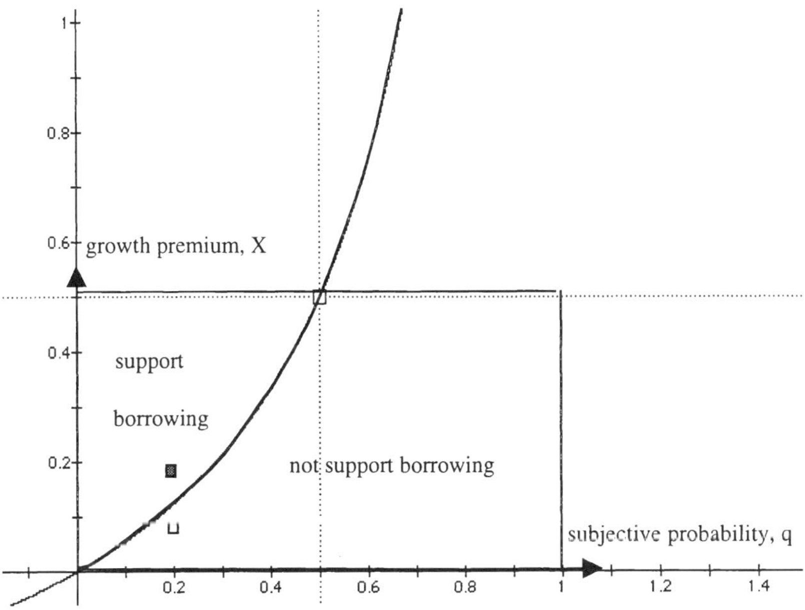

Figure 6.3.1 The parameter map

Thus, the civil aircraft industry appealed to Indonesia under Suharto, presumably because it was a market the Japanese hesitated to enter. To keep the per capita GDP above the magic figure of US $10,000, Kim Young Sam's Korea approved short-term foreign borrowing rather than a devaluation;[5] to raise national pride, Mahathir built the Petronas towers,[6] bought Britain's Lotus Engineering to launch high-performance cars and constructed the world's largest flag. Even behind Thailand's futile attempt to defend the baht and the successful but costly decision to peg the Hong

[5] Chang (1998: 227).

[6] These are the highest buildings in the world.

Kong dollar to the U.S. dollar rather than a currency basket of trading partners, political considerations were involved.

If, in a search for rapid growth, one invokes the State against market failure, the economy may be prone to government failure in a time of financial crisis. If the power to rule can be won through economic nationalism, then inevitable market shocks will be resisted vainly, to the last extremities, making the adjustment costly and very abrupt. In the final analysis, when bread and circuses were sufficient to purchase allegiance, the Roman public only got the governments they deserved. *Caveat emptor*!

The point here is that, rather than moralizing about the sins of 'cronyism,' which is neither easy to eradicate, nor has much of a strong causal linkage to the debt crisis, economists can do something that is much more feasible and effective. By explaining the inevitable growth slowing down when the catching-up process is near its triumphant culmination, they can cool down the popular passion for unattainable high growth expectations. It is the latter that goads both private business and the government to lure foreign lenders into a lose-lose-lose game.

4. CONNECTEDNESS OVER DISJOINT SUBSYSTEMS

Crisis 1997 affected many economies. The major victims of the financial storm came in the following chronological order: The Czechlands, Thailand, Malaysia, Indonesia, Korea, Brazil, and Russia. This is often explained by a theory of contagion,[7] in which, by logic, any pair of afflicted entities must be connected by at least one 'path of contagion' made up exclusively of afflicted entities, within some financing (or trading) network. For institutional reform, the implication is, future crises can best be contained by 'firewalls' that compartmentalize risk.

However, how this explanation can fit Crisis 1997 is less than clear. The time path is highly peripatetic. Any chain of transactions linking some pair of victims – say, Brazil and Russia – is likely to pass through some advanced economies – say, the U.S., Japan or some European economies – none of which were ever seriously affected in the Crisis.

As an alternative, the 'inductance hypothesis' may be illustrated below (Wan and Wong, 2001). Consider a world of two disjoint 'credit chains.' The 'Latin' (or respectively, the 'Greek') chain consists of a debtor d (or respectively, δ) borrowing funds from a creditor c (or respectively, γ), who in turn owes loans from a banker b (or respectively, β), while one of the bankers also has an additional investment in A. Who has invested in A is

---

[7] See for example, Allen and Gale (2000).

known to A and the bankers, but not necessarily to others. All the loans are short-term, but are used to finance some long-term projects, so that periodic extensions are relied upon to keep the systems afloat. Concurrent applications for extension of all loans are presently under simultaneous review. To save one's own position, any banker suffering a loss in investment must reject credit extension to the creditor, any creditor who approves a credit extension to the debtor but gets rejected by his own banker will then become insolvent. A debtor goes bankrupt if the creditor denies the loan extension. Denoting a real (conjectured) relation with double lines, (single line), Table 6.4.1 shows that when A defaults, the equilibrium outcome is a subsystem crisis under complete information, but is possibly a 'world-wide crisis' under incomplete information.

Information Structure	Complete Information					Incomplete Information				
Additional Investment			A					A		
		//					//		\	
Banker	b				β	b				β
	‖				‖	‖				‖
Creditor	c				γ	c				γ
	‖				‖	‖				‖
Debtor (italicized if bankrupt)	d				δ	d				δ

Table 6.4.1 The non-transparent system

The implication of this exercise is that 'system transparency' is desirable. If it is common knowledge that a particular bank is not affected by any failure in its investment, then those borrowing from it have no cause to tighten their credit and cause the crisis to decimate the particular local system.

Crisis 1997 can be compared to a wildfire: it ignites with lightning; it spreads by wind; yet it happens only to forests that are tinder-dry. The state-backed private foreign debt supplies the spark. The lack of financial transparency facilitates the panic. As we have explained above, the international economic situation was already crisis-prone.

5. CONCLUDING REMARKS

There are many different aspects one can explore about Crisis 1997. The present literature already contains a rich collection of important results. Yet, in view of the importance of the issues involved, one cannot misuse Occam's razor in this connection. Specifically, in nineteenth century medicine, a patient's complaint was often diagnosed as 'fever.' Over time we have learned that the patient's temperature may rise due to many reasons. Knowing a single cause or a class of causes for fever is not a sufficient reason to stop medical research. That is our justification for focusing on aspects not yet quite adequately addressed in the literature. In Section 2, we emphasize the importance of 'global fundamentals' rather than 'country-specific fundamentals' and the 'real' rather than 'monetary' source of unpredictable shifts in the exchange rate. In Section 3, we highlight the political economy of the debt crisis, where popular expectations may induce political leaders to gamble the fate of their own regime as well as the fortune of domestic borrowers and foreign lenders in unsound policy measures. In Section 4, we further propose the inductance theory as an alternative to the contagion theory to explain the spread of Crisis 1997. Clearly much follow-up research should be conducted. The last word is certainly not yet written. At the present, regarding policy concerns, the words of caution in Bhagwati (1998) deserve as much attention as we can devote to them.

In 'The Capital Myth' (Foreign Affaires 77:3, pp. 7-8), Bhagwati wrote: "Until the Asian Crisis. . .many assumed that free capital mobility. . .[is] exactly like free trade in. . .goods and services, a mutual gain phenomenon. Hence restricted capital mobility, just like protectionism, was seen to be harmful to economic performance in each country, whether rich or poor." For justification of this opinion, he invoked the observation of Kindleberger that capital flows are characterized by panics and mania.

We now offer an analytic interpretation to this view. In real life, the future is uncertain, and there are many non-insurable risks, but no objective probability regarding relevant economic events such as those regarding the future demographic structure. Yet these have profound effects on future asset prices. As a result, 'the market is incomplete,' especially when future claims are concerned. Moreover, there is always a fundamental asymmetry between the lender and the borrower. For the borrower, the gain increases with the scale of borrowing, but the loss is subject to the same limit in bankruptcy. This is why in real life, the price-taking model is a much less satisfactory approximation for the behavior of lenders and borrowers of capital than it is for the sellers and buyers of goods and services. That is also why the familiar arguments about gains in the trade of goods and services do not carry over to the gains in capital movement.

For example, in loan negotiations, risk assessment is based upon the market value of the security, and the business operations the loan is supposed to finance. The accuracy of assessment is a matter of experience and available information. The honest representation of facts and the scrupulousness in adhering to promised plans depend upon the enforcement of contracts and rules in a society. The playing field is never level between a developed economy and another in the development process, insofar as international capital flow is concerned. For elaboration, see Appendix 6.1.

APPENDIX 6.1: DEBT CRISIS AND RESCUE — A THEORETIC PERSPECTIVE

Economic Theory and Market Liberalization

Economics resembles medicine: desperate decision-making is routine before *all* facts can be known with their full ramifications. However, medical decisions are the concerns of individual physicians and patients; economic policy is shaped by opinions of political leaders, interested parties and the public. Yet what appears as exotic to the laymen may be critical in public issues. For lack of relevant data, formal economic theory leaves many questions unanswered. The challenge is to apply one's intuition to options involving the unknown. A frank reappraisal of the toolkit must be the pre-requisite for the practitioner of economic analysis.

The classical example of markets is the spot market for a perishable good. Equilibrium is reached when a rising supply curve meets a falling demand curve: an efficient and stable outcome emerges when matters are left to the market force. But from this to reality, six points merit recognition.

(1) The spot market for durable goods, like housing, presents difficulties. Asset value should equal the discounted sum of future rent, which may extend to successive generations, even some unborn. Current asset price reflects the expectations of the present generation. Thus, the real estate market can be turbulent, and constitute a possible source of 'asset bubbles'.

(2) Borrowing and lending (as well as futures market) involve claims, rather than physical assets. Future enforcement is the additional complication.

(3) Additionally, bankruptcy marks the limit of debtor's risk, and invites heavier borrowing for larger potential gain. Hence, a creditor often imposes a ceiling for borrowing. The textbook behavior of price-taking is not always a close approximation to the financial market.

(4) In real life, instead of a detached grand auctioneer quoting all prices, individuals – like stock brokers – conduct a sequence of decentralized exchanges at their own risk. The performance of a market depends upon the experience of the individual participants.

(5) Market is incomplete: individuals often cannot trade across periods or states. Capital market may be absent for agents to satisfy mutually reciprocating wants; there exists non-insurable risks. Partly, this is because there may be no objective probability over some (non-repeated) events. Partly, some market may be so 'thin', making the situation a one-on-one bilateral monopoly, where the terms of settlement defy useful prediction. There may exist no competitive equilibrium, or there may be many, and Pareto-ranked, so that 'The First Fundamental Theorem' no longer holds.

(6) Both the existence of alternative market clearing terms of trade and the constant turnover of individual market participants make it logically unlikely that agents can form rational (or perfect) expectations.

Not all is lost for the application of theory to policy. First, much of the efficacy of market competition rests on the selection of the fittest, not the conditions of marginal equalities. Second, for developing economies at least, the benefit of 'openness' rests not so much on the traditional gains from trade, but on the spill-over of technology[8] and the freedom to upgrade the product mix to fit the rising skill mix.[9] Third, the real life economy is approximately separable, in that piece-meal welfare economic analysis remains valid. For example, consider a two sector, small open economy producing both consumption and investment goods. Although the level of domestic investment may be debatable, two goals remain desirable: (a) to eliminate factor distortion, and produce on the production frontier, and (b) to choose that output mix which maximizes the value of national product.

At the same time, our 'six point proviso' helps to draw the following conclusions, regarding Crisis 1997 and international finance, in general:

(a) Points (1), (2) and (3) provide a theoretic corroboration to the distinction drawn by Bhagwati (1998), the liberalization of capital market is not to be promoted in analogy to the liberalization of the goods market.

(b) Point (4) supports the view that financial liberalization must proceed gradually so that individuals can acquire adequate experience, and institutions and regulations may be set up to enhance market stability.[10]

(c) Point (5) implies 'free trade' itself is not always the best. Consequently, the Malaysian approach of temporarily suspending convertibility and imposing capital control[11] is not all that 'heretic', when viewed from a microeconomic foundation.

(d) Point (6) corresponds to our analysis in Section 2. In addition, together with Point (1), concerning real estates, it can explain how the Thai crisis developed, namely borrowing dollar loans through the Bangkok International Banking Facility for the Thai real estate market.[12]

---

[8] See Coe, Helpman and Hoffmaister (1997).

[9] See Lucas (1993).

[10] Compare Stiglitz (2002). By extension, 'shock therapy' is of dubious merit for the transition economies. See Wan (1992).

[11] See Mahathir (1999).

[12] See Lauridsen (1998).

The IMF Rescue Programs

There has been much debate about the appropriateness of the IMF approach in resolving the 1997 financial crisis.[13] The issue is complex. Malaysia chose self-help and Thailand cooperated fully with the IMF. Both had reasonably quick recovery. Not all economies can follow the Malaysian approach, since much of the capital inflow to Malaysia was in the form of direct foreign investments, not loans. If an economy must depend on outside help, then the 'political economy' of the rescue operation must be recognized.

The affected Asian economies in Crisis 1997 differ greatly from the Latin American economies in stress, yet the IMF programs imposed similar conditions of budget–cutting, tight money, etc. Critics hold such apparent contradictions as the proof of the irrationality of the IMF. The reality is slightly more complex.

The IMF usually assembles an *ad hoc* consortium to finance *any* rescue program, in which its own contribution is relatively modest. The conditions imposed by the IMF are generally anti-inflationary in nature, causing a recession to the local economy, but promising to generate a surplus in the balance of payments. Such a policy is reassuring to the partners of the IMF in the consortium. The need to placate consortium partners probably explains the similarity of IMF's conditions in all rescue operations.

Given the limited resources available to the IMF itself, and the wide-spread nature of Crisis 1997, it is unlikely that the IMF could pull off all those rescue missions alone. Whether the IMF programs can be less punishing depends largely upon the balance of power in the international political economy and not the decisions of the leadership at the IMF. So, either the IMF should practice triage and not help everyone in crisis, or else it had to defer to its consortium partners, and impose painful programs of retrenchment.

For an economy in the process of catching up, history shows there are three options. First, there is the approach of Japan, Taiwan, Hong Kong and Singapore: foreign exchange reserve is kept high and foreign debt is negligible. They all have achieved rapid catching up at a pace not dominated by any other economy, and none had looked to the IMF for potential succor.[14] Second, the Malaysian option is self-help under financial crisis. It is after all, qualitatively similar to the formation of the Sterling block by Britain during the Great Depression. Finally, the Thai solution is to cooperate fully with the conditions of the IMF-led consortium.

---

[13] See for instance, the criticism of both Mahathir, ibid, and Stiglitz, ibid.

[14] Unlike the case of Hong Kong, for Taiwan, current political reality rules out any possible assistance from the IMF or the World Bank, for the Taiwanese economy.

CHAPTER SUMMARY

- Crisis 1997 was a severe shock: its onset was sudden; its widespread reach was unexpected; its virulence against some showcase economies was such to cast doubt about the validity of outward-oriented strategy.
- Truth becomes clear in due course: the sustained rapid growth in East Asia remains a marvel; the crisis was neither universal, nor irreversible, nor inevitable.
- Today the nature of the crisis remains not generally well understood; understanding its nature is essential to prevent its recurrence.
- Crisis 1997 was in substance a debt crisis superimposed upon growth-induced volatility.
- Volatility is caused by the presence of multiple prices that clear the world market: which among these will prevail is neither certain, nor predictable with objective probability.
- In such a world, each economy may have 'sound fundamentals,' yet the terms of trade remain utterly volatile, even without monetary factors involved.
- Examples demonstrate that multiple equilibria exist when three conditions are met: (a) the presence of a 'home good bias,' (b) the absence of high substitutability among the goods, and (c) the existence of two economies not too disparate in size: a condition that might be met in 'catching up.'
- Given the volatile terms of trade, a debt crisis develops when a debtor gets caught between a debt denominated in foreign currency and a foreign exchange rate that shifts suddenly.
- The debt crisis of 1997 arose out of private debt with public endorsement; what the government endorsed was often projects meeting voters' enthusiasm.
- The debt crisis of 1997 spread because of the lack of transparency on the lenders' part, and because short-term loans were repeatedly rolled over for long-term needs. Lenders who suffered loss refused to roll over credits. As debtors failed, the lenders that were involved remained unknown; the resulting speculation translated local distress into systemic crisis.

QUESTIONS AND EXERCISES

1. The catching up of the Japanese economy with the U.S. economy has been accompanied by rapid and unpredictable changes in the Yen/dollar exchange rate. No debt crisis ever happened. Is this consistent with the thesis in this chapter? Explain.
2. The catching up of the Korean economy with the U.S. economy has been accompanied by rapid and unpredictable changes in the Won/dollar exchange rate. Debt crisis happened for Korea, not for the United States. Is this consistent with the thesis in this chapter? Explain.
3. If no borrower had ever taken out a sequence of short loans for long term purposes, how would that have affected the course of Crisis 1997? Explain.
4. For Singapore, to be a regional financial center is just like to be a tourist destination: more service exports and well paid jobs. For this, international confidence was built through accumulating foreign reserves, regulating against speculation and keeping an interest rate near or below the international level. There was little foreign borrowing (Lee, 2000). For Thailand, after pegging the baht to the dollar for years, financial liberalization and the setting up of the Bangkok International Banking Facility in 1993 allowed the Thai financial sector to borrow from abroad and invest in local real estates. The July 1997 crisis came when export glut and trade deficit forced a devaluation. The exchange rate fell from 26 baht to 1 dollar before the crisis, to 50 to 1 in six months (Lauridsen, 1998). Discuss with the analysis of this chapter.

PART 2
ECONOMY-SPECIFIC EVIDENCE

Introduction to Part 2

We offer Part 2 to substantiate the catching up process in Part 1. The four interlocking chapters, 7 to 10 form its core. The structured comparisons between the four NIEs sharpen the competing merits of policy options, in both the short and the long term.

The shared theme of Chapters 7-10 is the benefit of outward-orientation. Chapter 11 buttresses this conclusion with the relevant experience of three more economies: Malaysia, the Mainland Chinese economy and Mauritius, each resembling the NIEs in performance, but differing from them in size, ethnicity, and location.

Chapter 12 rounds off other relevant issues to the catching up process: externally, what are the impacts from outside shocks and effects on other economies and internally, how does growth affect distributions inside the economy.

The four chapters on the NIEs have some independent interest to those studying Recent Economic History. These four economies form a 'way-station' for *industry wandering* from Japan to PRC. Their importance is more than proportional to their size.

Appendices to Chapters 11 and 12 concern respectively the Chinese economy, and the inequality measures. They present a non-traditional viewpoint.

Chapter 7

THE REPUBLIC OF KOREA

1. GENERAL OBSERVATIONS

In the second section of this volume we study the four Asian NIEs, both for their own sake, and because of the relevance of their experience for developing economies elsewhere. Of the four, (South) Korea is by far the largest in population as well as in total GDP. We present Chart 7.1.1 in three panels for context. In GDP and in population, the percentage weights of each economy in the four-economy total are displayed in the middle panel. In total GDP and population, we take the 4 NIEs as a whole to compare with a European country, namely, France. The results are shown in the top and bottom panels. The four NIEs together are not quite a United States or Japan in size. Still, they are comparable to a typical major country in Europe. Although they are a bit poorer now, their per capita growth rates are 2 or 3 percentage points higher than that of France or indeed of any other large European economy for the last 30 years, meaning that they will soon 'grow into size.'

Chart 7.1.2 displays the per capita GDP for each of the four Asian NIEs and their average value. The French figure is inserted in the lineup. Two among the four have lower figures than that of France. The other two are higher. So in strictly economic terms, these economies are not all that different from the West Europeans.

There are similarities and differences between Korea and the other three. They are all market economies, with outward orientation, a Confucian cultural

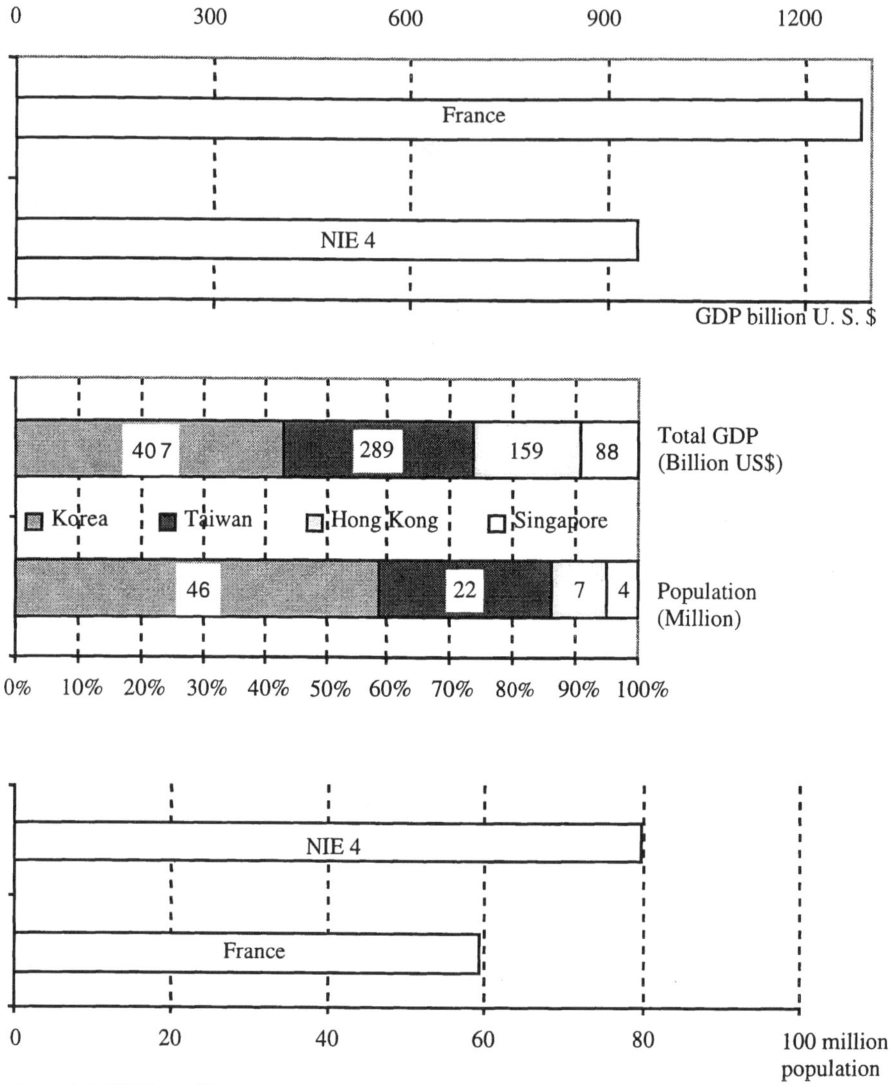

Chart 7.1.1 NIEs and France, Total GDP and Population, 1999

Source: World Development Index; Taiwan Statistics Data Book

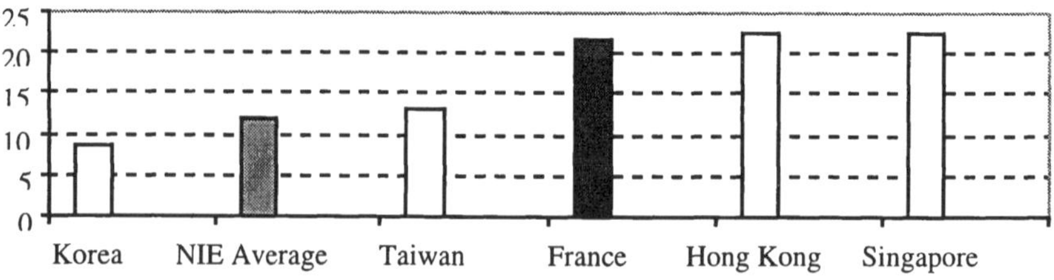

Chart 7.1.2 Per capita GDP in 1999 ($ 000)

Source: World Development Index; Taiwan Statistics Data Book

heritage and a record of sustained rapid growth over one third of a century. Differences exist in market size, the date of industrialization, the length of their history as an independent state and whether there is a Chinese majority. All these are relevant for the evolution of the economy. A large economy is an advantage if one relies on the domestic market to nurture infant industries. But it poses challenges in 'command and control' for an economic planner who relies on top-down policy coordination. A long independent history means that one can count upon nationalism to mobilize public effort. In few economies beside Korea will citizens donate gold and jewelry in a debt crisis, as they did in 1997.[1] It can also tempt both the ruler and the ruled to adopt ambitious policies, for glory and grandeur. The lateness of Korea's industrialization may explain the persistent Taiwan-Korean difference in per capita GDP. For Korea, a looser 'China connection' than Hong Kong and Taiwan had made it harder to profit from the 'China trade.'

The Koreans are a people with great technological precocity, and little territorial ambition. Metal movable types were in use before 1234 and ironclad soon after 1592. Unlike the Khitan, Juchen, Mongol, Manchu and Japanese peoples, never once did Koreans take Chinese land when China was weak. Although several Korean kingdoms had long histories,[2] their relatively late unification in 668[3] and small population often made Korea vulnerable against Japan and China, as well as against more warlike, nomad neighbors in ancient times. Korea under the Yi Dynasty (1392-1910) was long on stability, but short on dynamism. Isolated and dominated by the hereditary *yangban* ('twin echelons') of civil and military elites, Korea could not offer effective resistance against the Japanese annexation in 1910, which lasted 36 years.

This traumatic past presumably gives rise to the *han* psyche, discussed in Kim (1997), where *han*, a deep sense of regret, if not grudge, motivates the people to work hard and battle on with decisiveness and determination. Its economic consequences will be discussed later.

In education, vocation, and residence, both Koreans and Taiwanese were second-class citizens under the Japanese. For instance, no Taiwanese could adopt a Japanese name without official approval; no Korean could refuse to adopt a Japanese name. As cited in the popular work of Amsden (1989: 29-35), some Western economists, like Amsden (ibid., 32), claim that these 36 years left Korea with valuable initial conditions: a reasonably good physical infrastructure, certain basic and technical educational levels, a

---

[1] The French did the same after 1871, but that was to get the Prussians to leave Paris.

[2] For competing views about the origin of those kingdoms, see Barnes (1990).

[3] For comparison, that is three decades after the death of Dagobert I in 639.

society made classless by its shared fate, and the experience of living in an industrialized state.

To give some idea what such initial conditions actually amounted to, some figures for 1945 (when the Japanese period ended) speak for themselves: a 78% illiteracy rate and 2% of the population 14 and older having finished secondary school (Kim, 1997). As an example, for lack of know-how, four small steel ships left unfinished in 1945 were untouched for almost a decade. By then they had to be scrapped because of rust. The 'Korea Miracle' was mostly self-made and occurred independently of the Japanese annexation.

The post World War II history of Korea may be divided into three broad periods: the era before Park, 1945-1961, the 18 years under Park, and finally, the two decades after Park.

The first period can be sketched in brief. The Korean War laid waste to much of the country. The $6 billion of post-war U.S. aid kept people alive but supported little development. The unrealizable priorities of President Rhee, a long-time exile, were re-unification and similar political agendas. Corruption was rampant under import substitution. A student demonstration brought to power the democratic but ineffective government of John Chang. In May 1961, a desperate population acquiesced to the coup by President Park. Over the next 18 years, his rule launched a period of spectacular development that lasted for 35 years, but also led to some persisting negative effects.

The 18 years under Park contain two sub-periods: the first for export promotion and the second for the Heavy Chemical Industry (HCI) drive. In the first sub-period, export targets were set by each firm, commodity, and market, with the government overseeing the process.[4] In the second sub-period, targeted heavy and chemical industries such as steel, shipbuilding and automobiles were assigned high priority.

After the end of the HCI drive, the second oil shock posed a greater challenge than did the first oil shock six years earlier. Labor strife was followed by political repression, the assassination of Park, more stabilization efforts, two coups, and renewed repression under President Chun. At the end of Chun's term, massive demonstrations swept out the military dominance. Democratic labor unions also emerged tumultuously with democratic elections. Gradually, the wage demands of labor unions mellowed, but their power and militancy did not. Unions remain a challenge for subsequent reforms. Further democratization continued under Presidents Roh and Kim

---

[4] According to Amsden, bureau chiefs in government ministries would phone business executives to '*lecture* them on *appropriate behavior* [italics ours]' such as to buy local inputs, to introduce specific foreign technology, to invest or not, to diversify export market, to improve product quality and so on.

Young Sam. Yet with highly leveraged firms in highly concentrated industries, all that was not enough to spare Korea its most serious financial crisis in the fall of 1997.[5] President Kim Dae Jung was elected. The IMF program brought recovery under unpopular conditions. Although the IMF loan was repaid in August 2001, the financial restructuring is still going on, posing complications even today. The recovery was as yet incomplete before the U.S. recession in 2001 blanketed all of East Asia with new challenges.

Our own interpretation of Korean development focuses on five topics, each discussed in a section below:

(a) The satisfaction of the necessary and sufficient conditions of industrialization.
(b) The governing of the market in Park's style.
(c) The heavy-chemical industry drive.
(d) The long-term economic consequences of Park.
(e) A comparison of Korea with Japan and the other Newly Industrialized Economies.

A discussion of replicability follows.

Facts persuade us that the Korean overall achievement is a showcase for all developing economies in the world. Yet for inherent reasons, not all countries can expect the same gain following similar policies. The experience does illustrate certain general principles, such as the importance of human capital formation and the benefit of an outward-oriented strategy – lessons that are useful for all. The policies implemented by President Park were effective in certain aspects, but they have left long-term complications for subsequent policy makers. Many of Park's measures were not isolated moves, but were more like chess combinations that achieved certain short and intermediate-term objectives for Park's personal agenda. They were neither the only option Korea had to prosper, nor something to be emulated by any other economy, for many reasons. Yet both the successes and setbacks of Korea should be understood by all development economists.

2. THE NECESSARY AND SUFFICIENT CONDITIONS

Korea industrialized under President Park because certain necessary and sufficient conditions were then met. Among the necessary conditions, the consistent education program undertaken under every Korean president was indispensable for the catching-up process. The ultimate credit for the

---

[5] What triggered Korea's crisis in 1997 was that, when the government relaxed bans against foreign borrowing, business groups took the opportunity to raise foreign loans that were extended on the expectation of the government's ultimate support.

educational attainment of the population is due to the attitude of the society. See Chart 7. 2.1.

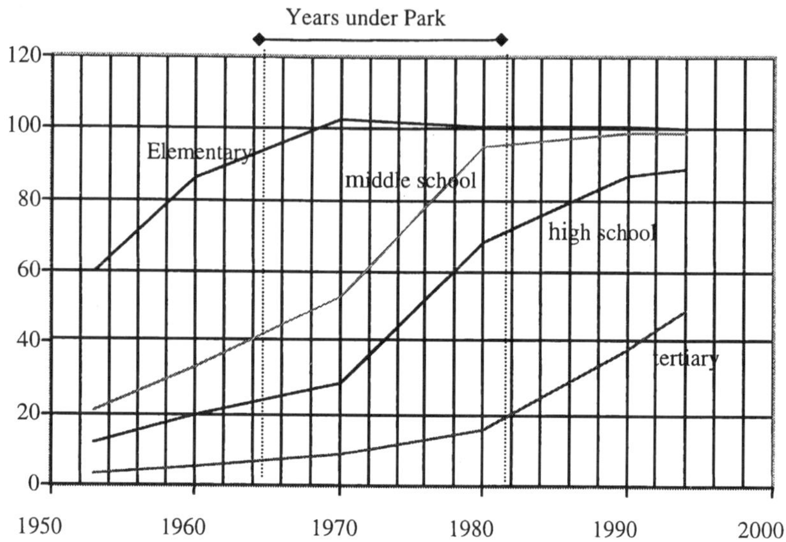

Chart 7.2.1 Korean educational attainment for population of corresponding age
Source: Kim (1997)

As Lall (1996) noted, Korea now has the highest university enrolment in the developing world, and turns out more engineers per year than does India.

But education alone is not sufficient, and that is clear when one compares the 8 years under President Rhee after the Korean War and the 18-year period under President Park. Both were dedicated to national construction. Both were autocratic. The difference between stagnation over the first period and the spectacular advance under the second owes much to the institutional factors that retard or allow interactions with the advanced world. The study of Jones and Sakong (1980) pointed to two facts:

(a) There were many policy measures taken by President Park that contributed to Korean development. They differed greatly from those in use in Hong Kong, for example. Both economies succeeded in industrialization in the same era.

(b) The difference between the periods of Rhee and Park is that entrepreneurs could gain rapid profit through lobbying more easily under Rhee than under Park. Jones and Sakong (1980) documented that in the latter period, Yi Pyong-chol, the founder of Samsung, excelled in managing his business group, while in the earlier period he merely amassed wealth through lobbying. The focus of lobbying under Rhee was the application for foreign exchange. When Korea had to earn export revenue from tungsten, ginseng roots and other primary products with limited elasticity, it was rational for the government to extract surplus from exporters through the use of multiple exchange rates. Yet that system invites lobbying for access to a more favorable rate. But when the Japanese wage rose, interaction with Japan could promote rapid development (as it did in Taiwan). The devaluation under John Chang paved the way. Under the pragmatism of Park, rather than the anti-Japanese dogmatism of Rhee, economic relations were normalized with Japan. This allowed a 'realistic,' unified exchange rate to render lobbying unimportant and in turn opened the gate for export opportunities. This turned the efforts of entrepreneurs from lobbying to managing.

What sets this thesis of Jones and Sakong apart from other explanations is that the documented evidence from Korea corroborates well with the experience of Hong Kong and Taiwan. There the government policies differed greatly from those of Korea. Nonetheless, all these economies thrived under an outward-oriented policy. For those with a trained labor force, the rapidly rising Japanese wage allowed the product cycle to work in their favor. The mechanism of learning-by-doing then led these economies from success to success.

Here the gain from an outward-orientation is to facilitate catching up, and not just to prevent distortion. The gain from limiting lobbying is to reduce distraction from learning and not merely to save the resources wasted in rent seeking. See Wan (2003).[6]

3. GOVERNING THE MARKET, PARK'S STYLE

Park was a soldier trained in Japan, with a plan for action, an iron will for implementation and a political agenda. His plan was to control banks in order to allocate directed credit. With that, mammoth businesses were created and then governed for the sake of economic construction. Public ownership and police power were not his tools of first choice. His agenda was to win legitimacy through growth.[7] Park (1962, pp. 39-40) noted ". . .[P]eople in Asia today fear starvation and poverty more than . . .totalitarianism. . . . [D]emocracy is meaningless to people suffering from starvation and despair."

---

[6] The point is also made by Chang (1994) that it is not rent or corruption itself but the act of rent seeking that is damaging.

[7] See Stern, et al. (1995: 91).

The Twin Pillars of Park's System

According to Jones and Sakong (1980), 13 business leaders were arrested after the coup under the Law against Accumulating Illicit Wealth. On their promise to cooperate, they were released with their properties restored, minus their control over banks. They were then brought under the tight rein of 'directed credit.' These business leaders were granted short term 'policy loans,' at interest rates below the inflation rate,[8] to set up a sequence of corporations with limited liability. This masterstroke fulfilled multiple goals:

(a) To preserve continuity, major firms were kept intact and their leaders were left in place.

(b) To prevent the 'domino effect' of business failures, business groups ('chaebuls') were established with compartmentalized units, each facing limited liability.

(c) To facilitate business groups' rapid growth, but under state control, loans were offered at negative real interest rates, with short duration.

(d) To keep firms on a tight leash, the government-controlled banks were ready to bankrupt any firm, should the need arise.

(e) To micro-manage the entire economy, the government-controlled banks dominated a small number of heavily leveraged business groups. Each business group maintained a far-reaching empire.

Park's methods were not isolated moves, but chess combinations in his game. While effective for immediate goals, they were not without costs or risks.

As described by Rhee et al. (1984), Park held monthly National Export Promotion Meetings with his top economic bureaucracy and invited business leaders. Jones and Sakong (1980) cited examples of his personalized control:

- When the Shinjin business group failed to manage automobile production well, he ordered its factory to be sold to the Daewoo group.
- When the Hyundai group hesitated to go into shipbuilding, Park brought its founder Chung Ju Yong to heel by hinting that further recalcitrance might lose '*government's favor.*'

There was never any Latin American type of hyperinflation, yet double-digit inflation was common when the government-controlled banks monetized public bonds to finance development. When the interest rate was raised to increase domestic saving, the Korean Development Bank (KDB)

---

[8] The largest short-term loans were to support export, and were supposed to be open to all who met the volume standard. Because of their size, business groups could meet the condition easier.

guaranteed loans from abroad to business groups at low interest rates.[9] On one hand, this tapped foreign funds to accelerate development. On the other hand, business groups owed their ability to benefit from foreign borrowings at negative real interest rates to the guarantee of the government-controlled KDB. The rates were made negative only because of inflation. So under Park, inflation was part of the toolkit for command and control. The drawback became evident when inflation caused devaluation, and the State had to bail out firms facing the inflated foreign debt.

While *directed credit* steered the economy toward the targeted industries, what ensured that these industries were sufficiently financed was the additional mechanism of *cross-subsidization* (see Chart 7.3.1). This took the following four forms:

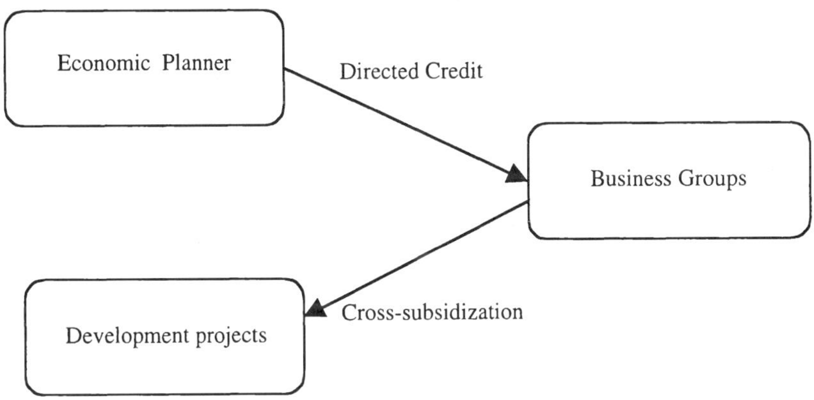

Chart 7.3.1 Architecture of the Korean Policy

(a) Service export subsidized commodity export. Again under government guarantee, business groups received profitable Mideast contracts to construct harbors and roads with Korean workers. As *quid pro quo*, these business groups invested at home in industries chosen by the government.
(b) Light industries subsidized heavy industries. The government taxed light industries such as textiles to finance the loans used for investing in heavy-chemical industries at negative real interest rates.
(c) Domestic sales subsidized export sales. Korean buyers would pay three times the price of Americans to purchase the Hyundai car, even though cars sold at home carried Korean engines while exported cars carried Mitsubishi engines made in Japan.
(d) Employees subsidized the employer. According to Kim (1997), government agents were appointed to unions to keep wages low from within.

---

9 According to Choi (1993), the difference was up to 20% per year.

Under a perfect 'social planner,' Park's methods form a powerful means to remedy market failure and improve future productivity. Yet as we shall see, with real-life policy makers, the plot thickens.

The Two Sub-periods under Park

As noted above, the period under Park contains two sub-periods: the first for export promotion and the second for the Heavy Chemical Industry drive. In the first sub-period, the State indulged in micro-managing the economy to a greater degree than in other countries, in order to promote export industries. Yet all sectors and firms were treated more or less on similar footing. In the second sub-period, targeted heavy and chemical industries (HCI) such as steel, shipbuilding and automobiles were assigned high priority. Discretionary command focused the economy on specific projects and industries.

Consider a period in which Korean business groups borrowed from abroad at favorable terms, under government guarantee. They incurred high debt-worth ratios in their expansion. Over-heated expansion led to inflation. Inflation bred trade imbalance. Trade deficit forced the declaration of devaluation. The instantly inflated foreign debt became an unsupportable burden to the heavily leveraged firms. Efforts for stabilization followed conditions imposed by the International Monetary Fund.[10] The incumbent regime lost much popular support. This scenario describes Korea in 1997. But it also describes Korea in 1971,[11] at the end of the first sub-period under Park, when he nearly lost an election to Kim Dae-Jung. Park did not learn the 1971 lesson about over-expansion. The next crisis caused labor strife, a split in the regime and Park's assassination.[12] Again, those succeeding Park failed to heed the lessons of 1971 and 1979 with regard to foreign debt. The next crisis in 1997 caused the toppling of major business groups such as Daewoo. Why the lessons were not learned may be explained by the political economy of policy making, as reflected in the nature of industry targeting. We shall argue later that what we have just described were actually three major boom-bust cycles, with important causal links in between.

---

[10] According to Amsden (1989: 64), to avoid exclusive U.S. influence Park appealed to the IMF, which gave advice in 1971 based on its stand-by agreement. In 1997, the IMF conditions caused Koreans to call the entire episode, 'the IMF Crisis.' (Let all rescuers beware.)

[11] For details see Choi (1993).

[12] According to Rhee (1994), the brutal treatment ordered against female workers in the Y. H. Strike alienated the security force.

4. THE HEAVY CHEMICAL INDUSTRY DRIVE (HCI) AND GENERAL TRADING COMPANY (GTC)

In development economics today, the vortex of debate is on the merit of industry targeting.[13] The paradigm case is Korea, where industry targeting was practiced mostly during the 75 months of the HCI drive.[14]

We focus on five aspects of this second sub-period under Park:

(1) The *reasons behind* the launch and abandonment of the HCI drive. According to Stern et al. (1995), the HCI drive started in January 1973 and ended with the stabilization plan of April 1979. It occupied 30% - 40% of the daily attention of Park. In their view, the HCI drive was launched due to the anticipated U.S. disengagement, from Vietnam in particular and from Asia in general. With the Korean army having only ammunition for three days' fighting,[15] all defense-related industries warranted building up. The switch to the stabilization plan was due to the macroeconomic stress caused by the HCI drive. By then, the latter had turned from a gain into a political burden. According to Rhee (1994), Fields (1995) and evidence in Choi (1993: 35),[16] the start of the HCI drive was also politically motivated, in defense of the Yushin Constitution of Park.

(2) The *planning* of the HCI Drive. Unlike in the period of export promotion, a secretariat was set up inside the Blue House (the presidential palace) to plan the HCI initiative, bypassing the Ministry of Finance. The rest of the government was left to implement what was already decided.[17]

(3) The *criteria* for industry targeting. Stern et al. (1995) named four considerations applied in project selection: (a) that the skill requirement matches what Korea could supply; (b) that the project has *economy of scale*; (c) that the project involves *vertical integration*, in which Korea already had some experience and advantage by then; (d) that the project is inside the *heavy-chemical industry* category.

(4) The *instruments* for industrial policy. The government also used entry permits beside the usual tax incentives and directed credit mentioned earlier. For example, for consumer electronics, the domestic market was

---

[13] For example, see Amsden (1999).

[14] Both Stern et al. (1995) and Chang (1998) agree that industry targeting stopped after 1979.

[15] See Stern et al. (1995: 21-22).

[16] According to Park's statement in the news conference, January 1973.

[17] Lest we oversimplify, we should note that business groups might also initiate specific proposals not originally chosen by the government, but they were in the spirit of the government drive.

reserved for the Lucky-Gold Star (LG) business group but not for Samsung until later.[18] Eventually, duplication of effort occurred.

(5) The *mode of operation* was to place subordinates under high pressure. Later, Korean firms presumably became molded in Park's practice. According to a survey by Kim (1997: 155-7 and 255-6), the dynamic Korean firms share certain characteristics. Among these, Kim noted approvingly the practice of 'crisis construction.' To extract heroic efforts, the top management assigns subordinates such goals as a policy, to construct a 'mission-impossible' atmosphere.[19]

The assessment of the HCI drive differs from economist to economist. We consider the Korean views first. From his empirical study, Lee (1996) claimed that government promotion was inimical to efficiency. Sakong (1993) mentioned achievements but also documented the immediate costs to financial institutions and the long-run effect on industrial concentration. Through a comparison with Taiwan, Yoo (1990) argued that without the HCI drive, Korea's heavy industry as a whole need not have had a lower relative weight, but probably would have had a different composition, with a lower capital-labor ratio. Before the crisis, Kim (1997) wrote with satisfaction that in 1997, Korea was second-ranked in the world both in shipbuilding and consumer electronics, third-ranked in semi-conductor production, and within the top five or six in the production of automobiles and steel. Equally important in Korea were several chemical products. Such achievements are not separable from the foundations Park laid down. Yet, Kim also viewed with reservation the development of the '*militaristic*' business groups. Chang (1994, 1998) is the most positive about the HCI Drive and attributes the debacle of 1997 to the regime of Kim Young Sam.[20]

Non-Korean observers are in general more laudatory about the HCI drive, at least before 1997. In Amsden (1989), Rodrik (1995) and Lall (1996), one finds no reservation at all. Kikawa and Hikino (1999: 34) wrote: "If rapid economic growth is the product of a well-organized and articulate

---

[18] As noted by Rhee (1994: 9), "The instruments for constraint provided coercive enforcement for business firms' non-compliance: economic penalties (suspending new loans, withdrawing old loans, and tax investigation) and political revenge. The instruments for inducement offered financial incentives to reward firms' compliance: preferential interest rates, tax reduction and exemption, direct and indirect government subsidies, privileged access to policy loans, and mono-oligopolized rights of production and sale."

[19] An example is the challenging target imposed by the government on the automobile industry and by Hyundai on its workers. Kim noted this is more useful in imitation than innovation.

[20] He wrote, "There has been a rise of neo-liberal ideology throughout the world since the 1980s, and it became difficult for a country like Korea, with a weak intellectual tradition of its own, to resist such global intellectual trends."

industrial policy, led by a competent bureaucracy, that is the experience of South Korea and Taiwan (and possibly China), not Japan." However, Bhagwati (1999) is far from impressed. He believes that government interventions might initially lift an economy out of some rut, but would not have other systematic benefit. The HCI Drive is an error to Krueger (1998).

In connection with the HCI drive under Park, the often asked questions are: (a) What motivated the HCI Drive? (b) How did the motivation affect the way of implementation and the industry mix? (c) In which way did these affect the Korean economy, both then and later – during Crisis 1997 and even today? We find it useful to study these once more from another angle.

Given the presence of long-term effects, we must first discuss the period between the end of the HCI drive and the present. During this period, a less-discussed event is the introduction of the General Trading Companies (GTCs) in 1975. Prior to that, much Korean foreign trade was conducted through Japanese trading companies such as Mitsui, Mitsubishi, etc. It was perceived that, to take back such businesses from the Japanese, Korea must have large trading companies that enjoyed the economy of scale. The government then set up certain minimum volumes of transaction, so that firms that exceeded such thresholds would be designated as GTCs and eligible for policy loans, generally at rates lower than the rate of inflation. Those that qualified as GTCs were all linked with business groups. To make sure that the 'volume of transaction' criterion would be met, business groups had incentives to either take over small and medium-sized firms or reduce them to the status of economic dependence. This caused a further concentration of market power in the Korean economy.

5. KOREA AFTER PARK AND A REAPPRAISAL

Motivation of the HCI Drive

Chart 7.5.1 gives a bird's eye view of the Korean economy under Park.

The seriousness of the 1965-72 boom-bust cycle not only cost Park his popularity in the 1971 election, but also forced him to proclaim the unprecedented Emergency Decree of August 1972. This granted a debt moratorium to *every* firm from *all* private borrowing. Martial Law was declared in October 1972. The Yushin Constitution was introduced in January 1993, to replace the parliament and allow Park to be re-elected consecutively for an unlimited number of times. To justify the constitutional change, Park announced ambitious plans for both export and per capita income, to be realized via the HCI drive.

So, it is reasonable to speculate that the HCI drive was at least partly a plan to consolidate power. The defense justification of the HCI drive is not

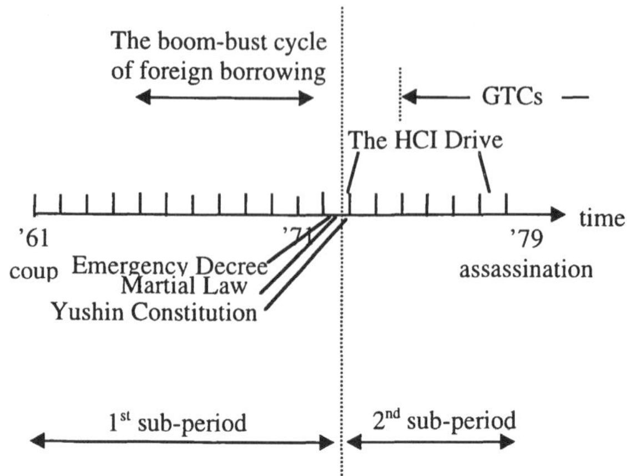

Chart 7.5.1 Korea under Park

entirely credible. Without trade, Korea could never have compensated for the lack of iron ore with basic steel mills. With trade, the Israeli Defense Force has been equipped without anything like a POSCO. The *scale* and *pace* of Park's HCI drive did not reflect the immediate needs of the Korean army.

The Planning and Implementation of the HCI Drive

The secretariat for HCI was inside the Presidential Office, headed by Oh Won Chol, an engineer, and was not subject to the usual checks and balances of the cabinet. According to Stern et al. (1995), when the economic scale of the chosen industry exceeded the domestic demand, the extra output was planned for export. Apparently, there was little concern about whether foreign buyers were ready to take Korean goods produced with an as yet untried technology. Nor did there seem to be much worry about whether a successful export industry required too long a lead-time. On the contrary, the presence of both economy of scale (which meant that the likelihood of excess capacity was high) and vertical integration (which meant that flexibility was low) were regarded as desirable attributes for industry targeting. The reliance on 'crisis construction' also suggests that not much margin for error was planned in advance.

The emphasis on Heavy and Chemical Industries clearly emulates the Japanese industrial policy. But according to careful study of Komiya (1988: 7-8), industrial targeting by the Japanese Ministry of International Trade and Industry (MITI) was also influenced by politics, and was not all that relevant to the Japanese success. He found "The government promoted exactly those industries that most Japanese felt the country had to have. . . . [T]hose involve an element of national prestige. . . . First. . .they had to be. . . symbolic of national might. . .with. . .greater or less. . .protection and promotion. Second, these. . .had to have 'news value.'" He also cited a long list of successes by emerging Japanese small and medium enterprises that owed nothing to government help.

However, there are some subtle differences between Japan and Park's Korea. Bureaucrats in the Japanese MITI had no reason to press their HCI promotion to the point of risking macroeconomic balance. Nor could they indulge in such excesses, since their power was always counterbalanced by the views of the Ministry of Finance and the Japanese Development Bank.[21]

This was not the case for Korea. Plans for the HCI drive were made inside the presidential office, backed by the autocratic Park and carried out by business groups in feverish haste. The usual bureaucratic checks and balances were bypassed, with devastating macroeconomic effects.

Consequences

We can list the consequences, from the near term to those with lasting effect.

(a) According to Kim (1991: xiii), the HCI drive siphoned off investment funds from light industries, which were then the main export industries of Korea. This worsened the trade balance.

(b) According to Sakong (1993), in order to finance the HCI drive, banks accumulated many non-performing loans, which were detrimental to their subsequent operations.

(c) Under the HCI drive, the policy loans not only gave huge advantage to the business groups, but it was done in such a *manner* and to such an *extent* that it had consequences in many more ways than one. This requires study in detail. Chart 7.5.2 shows the inflation rate (the GDP deflator) is clearly above the interest rate for export loans (given to GTCs), lower than the rate for curb loans and hovers around the rate of the general bank loans.

First, the business groups with their associated GTCs were so favored as to worsen income distribution and alienate the public.

Second, the business groups had both the motive and the means to crowd out the SMEs from export, and they did so. This occurred because the SMEs took out 'curb loans' at a positive real interest. Also, the GTCs in business groups had to meet minimum export conditions to enjoy negative real interest. Chart 7.5.3 shows the GTCs' dominance was concentrated in the export side.

Once excluded from directly exporting to advanced countries, the Korean small and medium enterprises became technically weak because of their lack of access to relevant information.

---

[21] According to Kikkawa and Hikino (1999: 25-6), until the mid 1960s, the Ministry of Finance moderated Japanese growth under the 'ceiling of international balance of payment.'

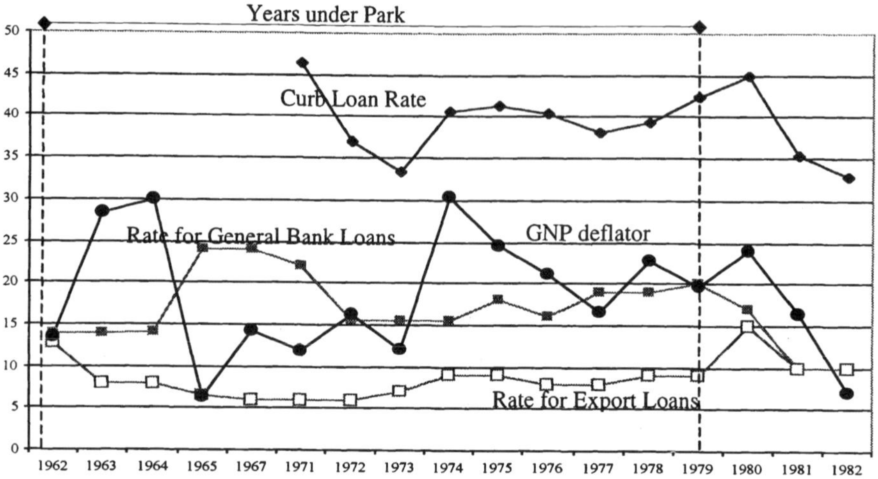

Chart 7.5.2 Inflation rate and various interest rates Source: Fields (1995), Amsden (1989)

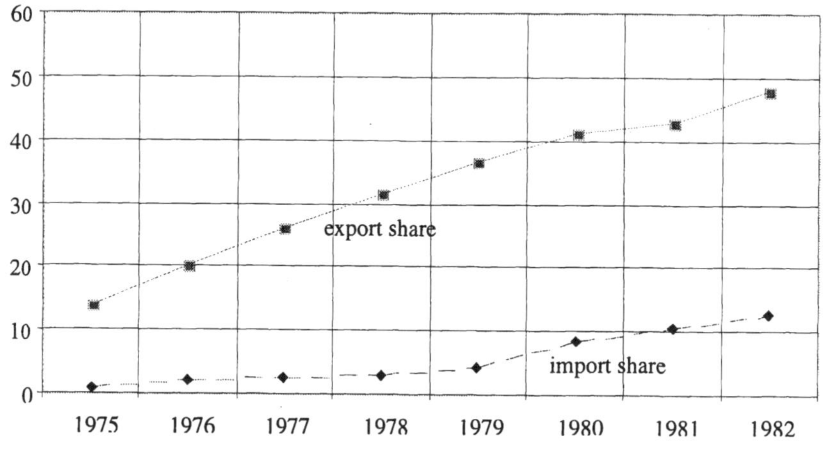

Chart 7.5.3 Market share of GTCs Source: Fields (1995)

Third, although the rising importance of the business groups began during the HCI drive of Park, the end of industry targeting under Chun did nothing to reverse that tendency. Chart 7.5.4 displays the ratio of the sales of the top five business groups to the GDP. This ratio doubled from 12% to 24% during the HCI drive, it redoubled again in the next five years to 52% and remained around 50% in 1991. This is how the Korean government banks lost credible threat against these business groups.

Finally, once the business groups got out from under government control, they competed against each other out of dynastic pride, not for efficiency or profit, mirroring the view of the behavioral school of firm behavior.[22] They

[22] Cyert and March (1963). The surrealistic behavior of Korean business groups with regard to car production, even under the shadow of Crisis 1997, is given in Kirk (ch. 8, 2000).

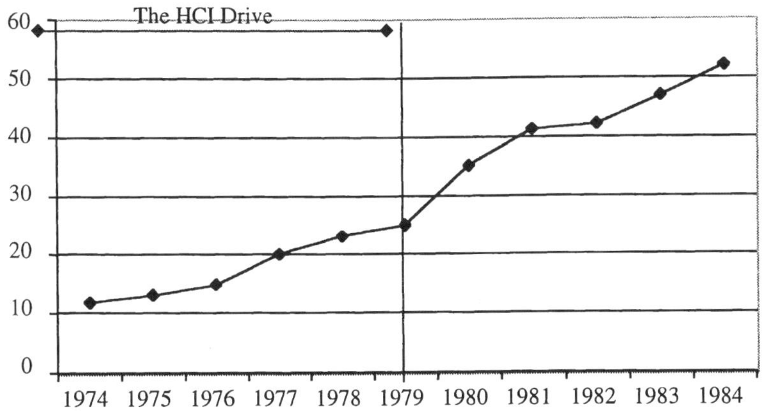

Chart 7.5.4 The ratio of the sales of top 5 business groups to GDP Source: Amsden (1989)

were 'militaristic' toward their employees and at times duplicated their own investments inside the same business group (see Wan and Thorbecke, 1999).

Thus, industrial concentration compromised both pillars of Korean development under Park. *Directed credit* was used by the government-controlled banks to harness highly leveraged business groups. Eventually, it was used to bail out firms 'too big to fail.' *Cross-subsidization* was used by business groups to finance promising new ventures under state guidance. Once business groups became no longer answerable to the State, they practiced cross-subsidization to favor their unprofitable branches and resist the painful reforms called for by both Chun, to focus on core competence, and Kim Dae Jung under the 'big deal.'

(d) One might further conjecture that President Park launched the HCI drive only partly to meet the country's defense needs, but also as part of an attempt to recapture his former popularity. The latter motive made it necessary to plan on an ambitious scale and at a blinding pace. In its scale and pace, the HCI drive might have impressed the Korean public and restored Park's prestige for a while. But its wasteful duplication and haste fueled cost inflation. When the export shortfall was worsened in the second Oil Crisis, unemployment and intense labor strife splintered the army and the security force, and resulted in the assassination of Park.

In due time, although the financial situation was stabilized, Korea was left with a mixed heritage. Beyond the rapid growth and such structural transformation that Korea shared with the other three NIEs, there remained a vision and taste of achievement that provided Koreans with a self-confidence and sense of purpose that is hard to achieve in peacetime pursuits. However, Korea was also left with a microeconomic structure that created significant challenges for later policy makers.

First of all, although the state repression has stopped, the militancy of the unions remains, the result of a backlash against the oppression under

Park and Chun. Against the unions' resistance to layoffs, industrial reform becomes exceedingly painful.

Second, the nature of the Korean industrial mix makes the economy susceptible to turbulent fluctuations. This is the heavy industry trap, which is discussed in more depth below.

The Heavy Industry Trap

Targeting heavy industries is a common practice in many developing countries. These industries share the following properties:

(a) They are highly capital intensive (like shipbuilding), so that foreign saving must be used for finance. Given that governments are generally reluctant to invite foreign ownership in such sectors, foreign borrowing is often the consequence.

(b) They exhibit strong economy of scale (often requiring heavy fixed equipment). Therefore the insufficiency of domestic demand leads to export dependence.

(c) They produce durable goods. Thus, much of the product demand is for replacement and is discretionary in terms of buyers' timing. This makes the demand highly income elastic and pro-cyclical. Consumers and investors buying such goods would postpone purchases in recessions.

(d) They involve proportionally large fixed costs. As a consequence, the supply is highly inelastic in the world market. Suppliers easily suffer losses in recession. But facilities of even the bankrupted establishments would keep on producing under new management, in view of the relative unimportance of the out-of-pocket costs. This implies a potentially sharp drop in prices in recession and very slow reduction of worldwide overcapacity in a depressed industry, like automobiles and again like shipbuilding.

(e) They emphasize vertical integration. As a result, the units running the component operations are not positioned to hunt for alternative outlets in times of market slump.

The problem is further exacerbated if the national industry produces goods only based on technical competence and not science-based expertise that can support niche demands even in lean times.

The Korean HCIs share (a) through (e) and, due to selection, are limited to those that do not require the technically most demanding operations (a trait can keep away competitors in recession). Therefore the threat of debt crisis is keener for Korea than either Japan or any other three NIEs

To appraise the legacy of Korea's initial industrialization under Park, we need the full perspective of what has happened in the two decades after 1979. Table 7.5.1 displays such aspects in six major dimensions.

	Before Park	Under Park	1978–1997
Education	Modest	Improving	Widespread
Openness	Limited	High	High
Labor	Repressed	Repressed	Free
Industry	Light	Heavy	Heavy
Market	Normal	Concentrated	Concentrated
Finance	Normal	Highly indebted	Highly indebted

Table 7.5.1 Legacy of President Park

Leaving aside the continuation of human capital formation, the results of the profound changes under President Park are both the once-and-for-all opening up of the Korean economy to export opportunities and the long lasting side effects. For some analysts, the initial benefits of Park's strategy turned unexpectedly into harmful effects, a phenomenon dubbed the 'Icarus Paradox' by Kim (1997). The same wax wings that enabled Icarus to fly so high also caused his eventual fall. This is re-examined below, in the Korea-Japan comparison.

6. A COMPARISON WITH JAPAN AND OTHER NIES

A deeper understanding of both the Korean economy and the process of economic development may be gained by comparing the experiences of Korea and Japan. It is often maintained that the industrialization of Korea is a close parallel to the earlier industrialization of Japan. This appears true in several aspects: (a) the government adopted an active industrial policy; (b) large firms played important roles; (c) heavy industry was emphasized in the program; (d) export markets were essential for such industries, from ships to computer chips; (e) firms relied heavily on debt financing; (f) there was little direct foreign investment. In fact, Korean policy makers had closely studied how the Japanese economy was developed.[23]

However, Japan developed without ever relying on foreign debt. For a long period now, it has always had a trade surplus and ample foreign reserves. If Korea had followed that pattern, it would not have had repeated debt crises. Such difference in macro-economic behavior suggests there are significant differences in the growth patterns of Japan and Korea.

A closer look reveals some of these important differences. Consider first the initial conditions. To begin with, Japan was more industrialized in 1910,

---

[23] Stern et al. (1995: 20) put it succinctly: "Most of the decision makers in the 1960s had spent their formative years under Japanese occupation, and in Japanese language schools and had been heavily influenced by the Japanese development model... however negatively they felt about Japanese colonial rule itself."

and in the 36 years until the end of World War II, there was more human capital formation per capita in Japan than in Korea. The Korean War devastated Korea, but gave Japanese industries the opportunity to revive. From cars and ships, to consumer electronics and computer chips, Japan still enjoys the comparative advantage in those industries Korea chooses to enter.

The industrialization of Korea differs from the Japanese model in at least six ways. We tabulate these in Table 7.6.1 before discussing them.

	Korea	**Japan**
1. Who controls the government?	An autocratic leader, most of the time	A political oligarchy
2. Who controls the large firms?	Founders and their families	The salaried class of the 'main banks.'[24]
3. What is the role of economic planning?	To reward and penalize large firms	To coordinate efforts (indicative planning)
4. What role do banks play?	As tools of the State out of *chaebols'* control	As the core of a *keiretsu*
5. What role do SMEs play?	Dominated by business groups they deal with	Often partially owned by the 'main parent'[25]
6. What is the source of competitive strength?	Scale economy	Scale economy backed by 'improvement engineering'

Table 7.6.1 A comparison between the Japanese and Korean economies

Now industrial policy reflects the choices of the policy maker. Korea industrialized under President Park, a hands-on autocrat. According to Stern et al. (1995: 17), during the Heavy Chemical Industry drive Park spent 30% to 40% of his time on the project. At the same time, Kim Dae Jung was kidnapped from Japan, martial law was declared, and the Yushing Constitution was proclaimed with no term limit for the president. Thus we believe that, in scale and pace, Park's decisions were influenced by his political agenda.[26] Likewise, Fields (1995) claims that his push for General Trading Companies was politically motivated.

The consequences were: (a) Korea resorted to inflationary finance and private foreign borrowing under government guarantees, but Japan could stay away from such risky options. (b) With loans at negative real interest rates, the *chaebol*-linked GTCs could out-compete and exploit the Korean

[24] Thus, the final say in Nissan used to belong to its main bank (Halberstam, 1986).

[25] The 'main client' in terms used by the Japanese economists.

[26] Symmetrically, a defender of Park might interpret his *libido dominani* as being rooted in his devotion to his economic vision, and his commitment to implement it *by all means* An interested reader may compare our view with that of Landes (1994).

small and medium enterprises.[27] With the latter weakened under exploitation, Korean suppliers of end products have to rely on Japanese firms for specialty parts and components. As a result, Korean products cannot match the Japanese in price, quality, or innovative design (see Hobday, 1995: 90ff; also Kim, 1997: 214.[28])

By 2002, Samsung of Korea has displaced Toshiba of Japan as the world's largest supplier of memory chips. But according to Ernst (2001), making costly investment to acquire such more or less standardized (rather than 'core') technology is not economically justifiable. It is such expansion that has caused the worldwide capacity of the automobile industry to exceed its demand by 50%, and the worldwide steel industry to stay in long term recession. Should the other developing countries (e. g., India, PRC) emulate the Korean emphasis of heavy industry exports, the consequence will be even more astounding.

From the macroeconomic viewpoint, it is most precarious for a developing economy to produce durable goods for export. Such industries are noted for their economy of scale. To finance the massive investment needed, a developing economy tends to tap foreign savings. To avoid foreign dominance, precedence is often given to foreign borrowing rather than direct foreign investment. This means the negotiation of foreign debt, denominated in foreign currency. In order to utilize foreign resources, the net trade balance ought to be negative. Any overheating of the local economy in the investment boom tends to ignite inflation, raising export costs and enlarging the trade deficit. As we mentioned, inflation is also one aspect of the use of 'directed credit.' To lure business groups on board, a negative real interest rate is far more irresistible than any interest rate concessions. But in order to encourage domestic savers, nominal interest rates certainly will stay positive. Thus with the market for durable goods being highly income sensitive and volatile, the trade deficit might easily reach a point that requires an exchange devaluation. That in turn will raise the debt burden to crisis proportions.

The Japanese economy developed after World War II through evolution due to the interactions between the state and businesses. The occupation force dissolved the former business groups and purged the management. The stock ownership was distributed among small stockholders. Corporations charged little depreciation but distributed heavy dividends. During the 1950s, the government adopted industrial promotion policies, under which

---

27 According to Kim (1995: 215), this takes the forms of "deferred payments and the wide practice of offering financial kickbacks."

28 Kim found that the *chaebuls* form an asset to Korea, on balance. Yet he found their 'militaristic' organization very hard to change.

tax laws permitted heavy depreciation and banks invested in and made loans to selected, promising firms that they could monitor. This became the 'main bank system.' To support prices in the stock market crash of the early 1960s, the government bought stocks and sold them to 'stable' stockholders like banks and institutions, and arranged firms sharing the same main bank (a '*keiretsu*') to cross-hold stocks of each other. This prevented the feared taking over by U.S. interests (Miyajima, 1999, chapter 2), but also allowed the salaried managers in Japanese businesses to 'hijack' their firms by supporting each other (Morishima, 2000: 79-80). Serving fixed terms, these latter do not share the 'dynastic urge' of the chaebuls' founders in Korea.[29]

The industrial promotion program in Japan was formulated through a consultative type of decision making, in which experts, bureaucrats, and businessmen participated (see for example, Suzuki, 1999, on the synthetic fiber industry). Economic plans were formulated to coordinate efforts, and not to set targets to be met (see Komiya, 1990).

In Japan, large firms often invest in those small and medium enterprises that serve as their suppliers. The large firms offer technical support. The small and medium enterprises also make improvements in quality and production costs. Thus the competitive position of the large firms may be strengthened. Such large firms are called 'main parent firms' in Itoh and Urata (1994). As a consequence, scale economy is not the exclusive source of their comparative advantage. This may explain why Japan has never borrowed foreign funds for its development.

A comparison with the other Asian NIEs may provide further light on the differences between Korea and Japan.

In that regard, Hong Kong and Taiwan industrialized without tapping into foreign savings. Singapore relied on foreign savings through direct foreign investment, but not foreign loans. Over three decades, Korea created and preserved a heavy industry under exclusive domestic ownership. That is why a debt crisis can happen in Korea, but not in Japan or any other NIEs. After Crisis 1997, Korea made a policy reversal. Workers of Daewoo had to be laid off to make the enterprise appealing to foreign buyers. So after all the pains, Korea could not sustain its initial wish to avoid foreign owners.

On the positive side, whatever the form of ownership, in production processes involving scale and vertical integration, workers in Korean firms are technically as proficient as their counterparts elsewhere in East Asia, apart from Japan, in industries from shipbuilding and steel-making to the production of advanced memory chips.[30] This gives a degree of resilience to the economy. The devaluation during Crisis 1997 was able to raise the

---

[29] Thus, presidents of Marubeni serve six-year terms (Chang, Y. F., 1999).

[30] Enos and Park (1988) presents in detail their success stories.

export/GDP ratio from 30% in 1996 to 45% in 2000. This turned the trade balance from deficit to surplus, replenished the foreign exchange reserves and staged a recovery in production faster than any other economy affected by the crisis. (See Problem 5, p. 218, for more on details.)

7. REPLICABILITY AND OTHER LESSONS

By any standard, Korean development is an impressive achievement. The rapidity of output growth and the pace of industrial transformation are unprecedented. It is an inspiring saga of what a people can attain through ingenuity, dedication and persistence, as well as an impressive sense of proportion. To wit, after democratic unions won their voice in 1987, observers wondered whether the rising wage demand would interrupt Korean development. Yet when world recession came in the early 1990s, labor unions moderated their wage demands. The concern about the export market has persuaded the society to rein in any special interest, including that of the working class.

This being said, the Korean performance is unlikely to be able to be duplicated by other economies. Industries like steel, shipbuilding and automobiles are loaded with excess capacity already. These are precisely what both Japan and Korea had focused on in their heavy and chemical industry programs. In addition, the approach to industrialization of President Park would not be feasible today under the game rules of the WTO. At any rate, that type of development program can be carried out only if the economy is of a certain suitable size, and the political leader has a certain political outlook. The system of micro-management through personalized control would be infeasible if an economy is too large, and hence too complex, as in India or China. The instrument of cross-subsidization would be inapplicable if the size of the domestic market is too small, as in Singapore. The political leader must also have an affinity with the details of economic planning. It worked with Park but not Chun.

More importantly, with its ingenuity and hardiness, as well as its vigor in human capital formation, Korea would have done no worse economically if the economy had developed as in Singapore or Taiwan. The country would have been spared the repeated crises and emergencies, but would not have suffered much slower growth. There would have been less industrial concentration, much lower foreign debt, if any, and somewhat less emphasis on heavy industry that requires a high capital/labor ratio. The Korean experience in heavy industries is an inspiring episode demonstrating what is technically possible, even though it may not be economically optimal.

APPENDIX 7.1: WHY DOES THE PHILIPPINES LAG BEHIND KOREA?

Korea has been studied in this chapter for its own sake, but more importantly, as a model for emulation. The presence of another economy, like Korea in some aspects but far less successful than Korea in growth is of particular interest. Regarding policy, *why* that economy fell back suggests *what* Korea did right. Regarding theory, it highlights the question, beside those factors for which these two economies are alike, *which* other factors make the real difference. In 'Making a Miracle,' Lucas (1993) stated that in 1960, the Philippines resembled Korea in income per capita, education achievement, openness to world trade and the export mix. But over time, the Philippines lagged behind all NIEs, also the ASEAN-3. The plot thickens.

Based on PennTable 6.0, Chart A7.1.1 offers some tentative clues. In Panel a for the repcri's, the line with no marker shows Korea's lead. But Philippines led Korea in 1953, even increased its lead until 1963. The margin narrowed, then disappeared by 1970. Since then, the lead of Korea increased steadily to a sizable magnitude. Why this sequence of events happens may be seen by the two repcri series themselves. Over the 45 years (1953-98 inclusive), Korea made tremendous progress in catching up with America, while the Philippines could not keep up. Since America is the current technological leader, the differential ability of assimilating foreign technology seems to lie at the bottom of the differences in growth performance over this phase of development.

Oftentimes, the Philippines' lack of progress has been attributed to cultural factors, and thus arose the epithet, 'a Latin American country in Asia'. Yet over the decade 1953-1962, the two repcri curves in panel a cast doubt that Koreans are inherently any better equipped for rapid growth.

Panel b presents two curves: (a) an ascending curve showing the ratio of populations, the Philippines over Korea, rises steadily, or, the relative demographic pressure looms gradually higher on the former, and (b) a generally falling zigzag curve depicts the quotient of investment/GDP ratios, the Philipines over Korea, or, increasingly, Koreans invest more intensively than the Filipinos. Both of these overall trends favor a faster growth for Korea. Yet over the decade 1953-62, Koreans enjoyed no advantage, and the outlook did not favor Korea either.

Panel c shows that if openness is measured by the sum of export and import, divided by the GDP, then Korea is more open than the Philippines only over the 22-year period of 1968-89 (with 1970 as the exception).

In short, any growth advantage of Korea over the Philippines was sealed only in the early 1960s, which was reflected by the greater openness of the former from late 1960s on.

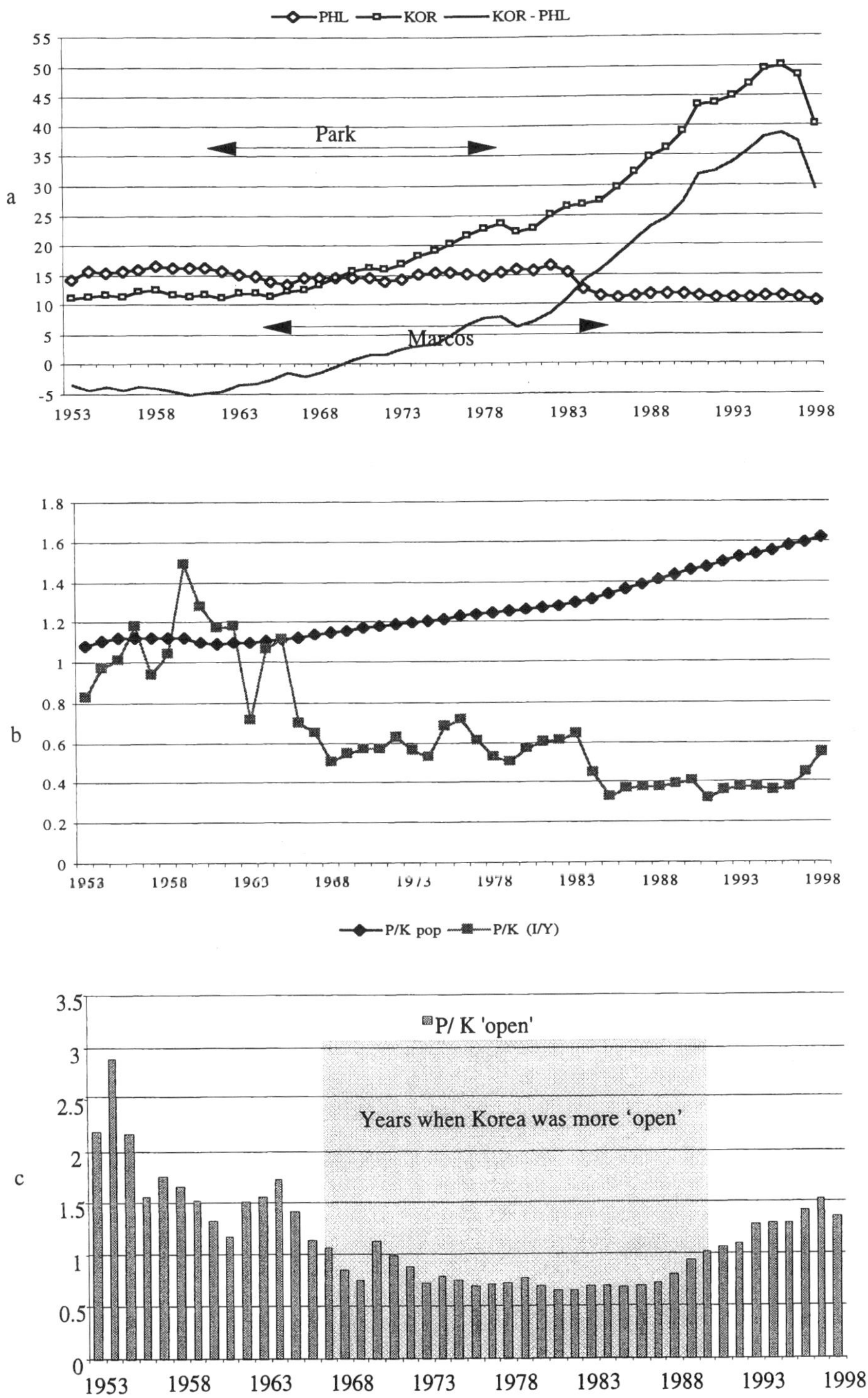

Chart A7.1.1 The Korea – Philippines comparison Source: PennTable 6.0

Some may argue that the historical link between Japan and Korea and the rising Japanese wage over its high growth period would favor Korea.

This view seems a simplification. Hong Kong and Singapore also succeeded to industrialize during this same period. Unlike Korea and Taiwan, these two were under brief Japanese occupation during World War II, just like the Philippines. Thus, the lack of growth of the Filipino economy lies elsewhere.

A quick perusal of Chart A7.1.1 panel a appears to present a further paradox. In spite of the disparity of economic performance between the Philippines and Korea from the early 1960s, both countries faced autocratic political rule: the 22 years of Marcos from 1964 to 1986 for the Philippines and the 18 years of Park from 1961 to 1979. The end of both autocratic rules was accompanied by economic decline, followed by stagnation in the Philippines but a resumed growth in Korea. The upshot is this, although not a necessary condition (in view of Hong Kong), autocracy may be sufficient to bring law-and-order. But as the case of the Philippines indicates, law-and-order, in itself, is insufficient to bring rapid growth.

What sets the Philippines (under both the autocratic Marcos and his democratic successors) apart from the four NIEs (including both Hong Kong and the more autocratic regimes in the other three) is as follows.

1) Hong Kong never had an import substitution policy regime.
2) Singapore, Taiwan and Korea adopted import substitution, then abandoned it.
3) The Philippines never gives up entirely import substitution. For details, see for instance, Antonio (1997).

As we mentioned in section 2, what makes the import substitution regime inefficient is due to over-regulation and rent-seeking, and not the resource misallocation due to distortion.

CHAPTER SUMMARY

- Korea is the newest member of OECD. The fact that its population is of non-Chinese ethnicity (unlike the other NIEs) suggests that Chinese ethnicity was not central to the success of the NIEs. Other common features should be considered as having a better claim to providing explanations for the NIEs' success.
- Korea has a long history and a homogeneous population noted for its talents and determination. Sustained, massive educational effort has always been part of Korean life. Industrialization came during the 18-year rule of President Park, when remarkable potential got unleashed by reform.
- The foreign exchange reform of Park redirected entrepreneurs from lobbying to the search for new markets; the dramatic results parallel those in Taiwan, under different government policies.
- What distinguished Korea was Park's personal rule in micro-managing the economy: state-controlled banks granted short-term loans at negative interest rates to those business groups that implemented government plans effectively and with audacity.
- Tariffs, quotas, government guarantees and wage containment were deployed to assist export expansion under private management: without sectoral distinction in early years and focused on heavy and chemical industries after 1973.
- Twice under Park, dramatic expansion ended in severe financial crises. In response to the first, Park proclaimed a moratorium for all Korean borrowers of private loans; in response to the second, he ended his Heavy Chemical Industry drive and suppressed striking labor. He nearly lost election in the first crisis and lost his life to assassination in the second.
- In laying the foundations to make Korea a leading producer in steel, ships, automobiles and computer chips, Korea ended with strained labor relations, an over-concentrated industrial structure, heavily-leveraged business firms, banks with many non-performing loans and a balance of payment frequently burdened with deficits.
- To the credit of the Korean society, the explosive strikes in the late 1980s were eventually settled with sustainable wage demands, and the deep crisis of 1997 and massive devaluation were followed with trade surplus and rising foreign exchange reserves. Factories from bankrupted business groups, like Kia, turned out competitive export products, even though massive financial and business restructuring remain incomplete.
- It is often claimed that the Korean industrialization under Park followed closely the strategy of the Japanese MITI. Careful comparison would show differences, which allowed Koreans a quicker pace in industrialization but resulted in a weaker financial structure before 1997.

QUESTIONS AND EXERCISES

1. In comparison with Japan, what are the similarities and differences in Korea's industrialization efforts under Park, and how do those differences get reflected in macro-economic performance before 1997 – in trade balance, foreign exchange reserves as well as foreign debt?
2. If Question 1 shows Japan in a more favorable light, why do Japanese economists like Kikkawa and Hikino show much admiration for Korea's industrial policy?
3. The introduction of GTCs in 1975 may be said to have been an important move, with impressive success. What is its possible cost in terms of the balance of power between the business groups and the small and medium firms, and hence the technical capabilities of the latter? What is its possible consequence for the financial position of Korean banks?
4. President Park offered Korean business groups short-term loans at negative real interest rates; thus the latter can be bankrupted at will, if necessary. Why is it that, before 1997, the business groups became even deeper leveraged, yet the Korean banks lost control over them? Explain in game-theoretic terms, if you can.
5. Data about Korea reveals:
   (a) Real GDP growth rate was -6.6%, 10.8%, and 9.2% in 1998, 1999, 2000.
   (b) The exchange rate, Korean Won for US dollar (1995 = 100), was about 85 for 1997, 60 for 1998 and 70 for 2000.
   (c) The cost of government bail-out over 1999-2000 equals 22% of GDP.
   (d) The debt/worth ratio of private firms was 400% in 1997, 135% in 2002.
   (e) Foreigners owned 17% of public stocks, in early 1998; 37%, end of 2001.
   (f) Public debt plus guaranteed debt was 17% of GDP in 1997, 40% in 2000.
   (g) Many experts are concerned about the future of the government pension fund and the medical insurance account.

   Opinion A: Crisis 1997 had little impact on Korean productive capacity, or long term growth, but made the financial structure stronger and the economy more integrated into the world market.

   Opinion B: Crisis 1997 incurred serious real cost to the households and the burden has future impact as well.

   Compare Hong (2002). Discuss.

Chapter 8

TAIWAN

1. INTRODUCTORY REMARKS

Among the four Newly Industrialized Economies, only Taiwan has its statistics excluded from the publications of international organizations. Because nature abhors a vacuum, scholars have produced many and varied views about the state of the Taiwanese economy. To some, Taiwan is essentially like Korea. For instance, according to Amsden (1999), Rodrik (1995), and Wade (1990), government intervention is the key to Taiwan's success. According to Amsden (1991), large firms are important to the story.[1] Others argue that there are distinctions between these two economies, and that Korea has followed the better approach. For example, Mody (1990), argued that Korea soon would leave Taiwan behind in electronics. Still others believe that it is important to pay attention to Taiwan's economy, however wrong or right its path. We subscribe to the last view.

First of all, the record of Taiwan reassures us that the overall experience of Korea is no fluke. We present below a lengthy list of similarities between Korea and Taiwan:

1. Like Japan, both economies have:
   a) a high population density;
   b) a culturally homogeneous population;

[1] The difference is that in contrast to Korea, Taiwan has most of its large firms in the public sector.

   c) a Confucian background;
   d) a shortage of natural resources such as coal and iron ores;
   e) an educated workforce with continued human capital formation;
   f) decades of peace after wartime destruction;
   g) a long period of deregulation and expanding international trade;
   h) a predominant segment of the economy under private ownership.
2. Both economies:
   a) were part of the Japanese empire until 1945;
   b) were industrialized later than Japan, after World War II;
   c) were under an anti-communist authoritarian regime;
   d) joined the U.S. and Japan in a triangular trade after industrialization;
   e) expanded export faster than output; and
   f) expanded manufactured export faster than total export.
3. Both economies have a government that:
   a) received U.S. aid during the acute dollar shortage of the 1950s;
   b) practiced exchange and import controls in that early period;
   c) undertook exchange rate reform before industrialization took off;
   d) adopted programs to promote export;
   e) met the reluctance of private firms to enter 'strategic industries.'

All these are matters of record. There are two key issues here, in Korea as well as in Taiwan: (a) what the government did in the face of the reluctance of private firms and (b) how effective that was.

There is as yet no consensus on these questions, and they deserve further study. Suppose the Taiwanese policy is both different from and not worse than the Korean approach, then for those economies that cannot or would not replicate the Korean program, Taiwan may serve as a possible case for emulation.

A natural agenda for inquiry suggests itself. *First*, one ascertains how the economies of Korea and Taiwan have performed, both in absolute terms and in relation to each other. If Taiwan makes the cut in performance on both scores, one goes then for the *second* topic, determining whether there are significant differences setting the structures of the two economies apart. If the answer is again yes, the *third* set of issues concerns the Taiwanese policy. What accounts for the Taiwanese policy stance, and how is that policy formulated and implemented? After that is the *fourth* question about the possibility of replication by other economies. Each of these is presented in a separate section below.

2. ECONOMIC PERFORMANCE

To evaluate both the absolute and relative performance of the Taiwanese economy, we can adopt a two-step procedure. First, we return to Korea and examine its performance in the absolute sense, and then compare Taiwan with Korea. The first step can be short. In the depth of Crisis 1997, Furman and Stiglitz (1998) considered the question of 'crisis versus miracle' in East Asia. They concluded that *the miracle was real.* Over the three decades from 1966 to 1996, Korea enjoyed a high average growth rate of 7.7% in per capita income. Only one year had negative growth of real income. This fast and sustained growth led to a rapid drop of poverty and an increase in life expectancy.

We now focus on the Taiwan-Korea comparison. Should Taiwan's performance be broadly comparable to the performance of Korea, then in one stroke, we have affirmed Taiwan's economic success in both the absolute and the relative senses. To be conclusive, we make the comparison in five aspects.

A road map is in order. Naturally, we first go for the overall picture. The comparison of average growth of per capita real income is followed by a comparison of the stability of that growth path. Since the single measure of income may not tell the entire story, one naturally looks at the Human Development Index. Since no such information is available for Taiwan, one may either approximate its value, as is done by Ranis (1999), or consider a battery of socio-economic indices, as we do. The average income comparison is next augmented by a comparison of income distribution, since one cares for the poor no less than for the rich. Macroeconomic indicators come next, since one must guard against any economy that lives beyond its means, or mortgages its birthright. Comparisons are meant to be relevant for the near future as well as the days that have passed. An assessment is then made both of the high tech sector and some measure of innovativeness. Since innovativeness is interesting here only if it accords with the bottom line, the comparative advantage of an economy should also be assessed.

Our work thus encompasses all the following:

(a) The aggregate measure, as reflected in the growth and stability of per capita real income.
(b) Various socio-economic indicators.
(c) The macro-economic indicators
(d) The technological strength that foretells future growth.
(e) The comparative advantage profile in trade that suggests the resilience of an economy.

These are considered in turn.

The aggregate measure

Chart 8.2.1 is in semilog scale. With data from the Penn Table, it displays the per capita real GDP of Japan, Taiwan and Korea, by the chain index basis.

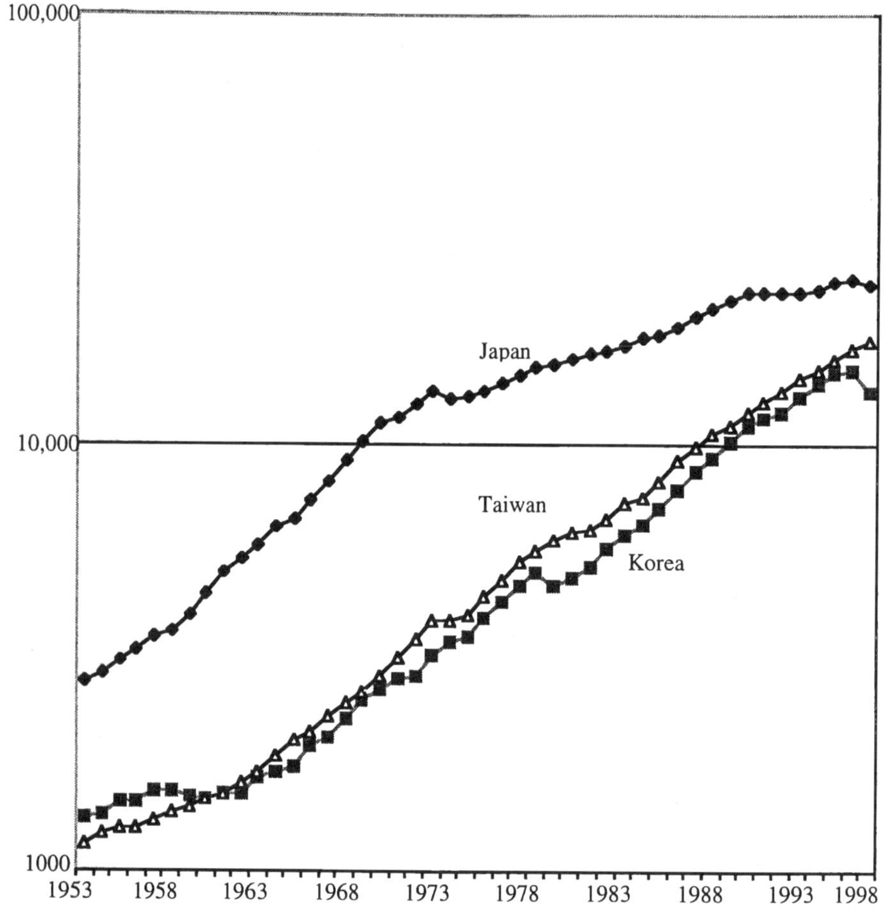

Chart 8.2.1 Log real income per capita (chain index) — Northeast Asia 3 Source: pwt 6.0

It shows that all three economies have been growing over these four and half decades: with Japan at relatively higher rates in early years, Korea and Taiwan at relatively higher rates later on. The initial trend acceleration has been observed for all these three. Japan, at least, has now reached the phase of slowing down.

Next, Chart 8.2.2 depicts how Korea and Taiwan have performed in catching up with Japan. First, starting from 1953 (about the end of the Korean War), both Korea and Taiwan faced a widening gap against Japan during its high growth period. They regained their 1953 positions relative to Japan much later: about 1982 for Taiwan and 1990 for Korea. Next, in comparison with each other, measuring in real per capita income for Japan, Korea had an 8% *lead* over Taiwan in 1953, but a 21% *lag* in 1998: the crossing over being 1961, at the time of coup by President Park.

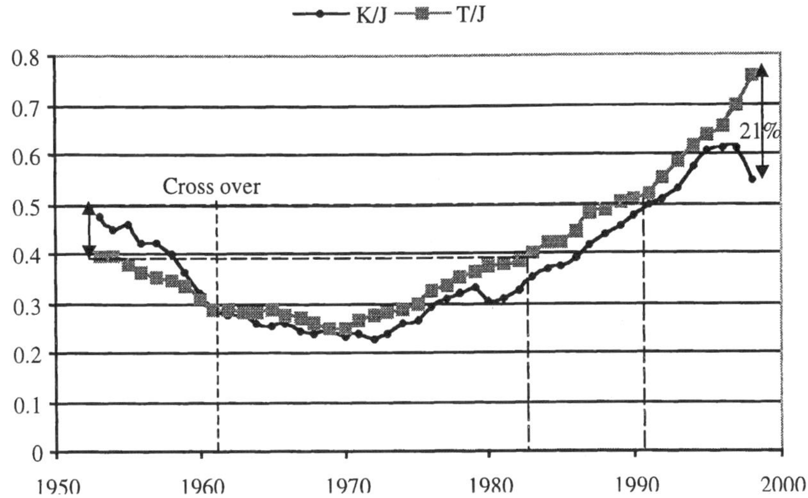

Chart 8.2.2 Per capita real income, Korea and Taiwan, relative to Japan Source: pwt 6.0

The ratio of real per capita income between Korea and Taiwan in Chart 8.2.3 is even more revealing. When combined with historical facts, such information portrays both 'the theme' that reflects the mechanism of the benchmark model in our Chapter 1, and 'the variation' which represents the effect of Korea's industrial policy.

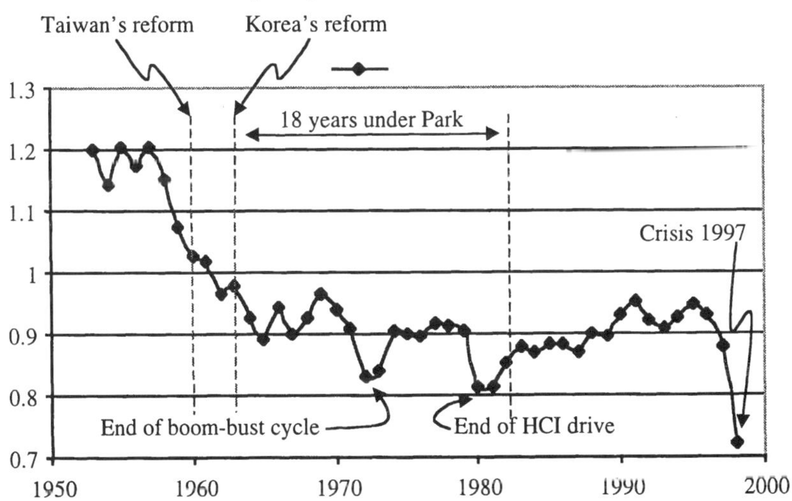

Chart 8.2.3 Per capita real income, Korea relative to Taiwan Source: pwt 6.0

Deregulation of trade and foreign exchange started in 1958 for Taiwan and 1961 for Korea. The four years' early lead allowed Taiwan to catch up with Korea in per capita real income. Moreover, according to the benchmark model in Chapter 1, between similar economies, the phenomenon of 'trend acceleration' allows the 'first mover' to increase the lead for some time. This is seen in Figure 8.2.1. This conclusion is consistent with the observations in Chart 8.2.2, between Japan on one side and Korea and Taiwan on the other. By analogy, it is only fair to conclude that even with the deregulation of President Park, the Korea-Taiwan gap in per capita real income, once opened in favor of the latter, might not close over the 18 years under Park.

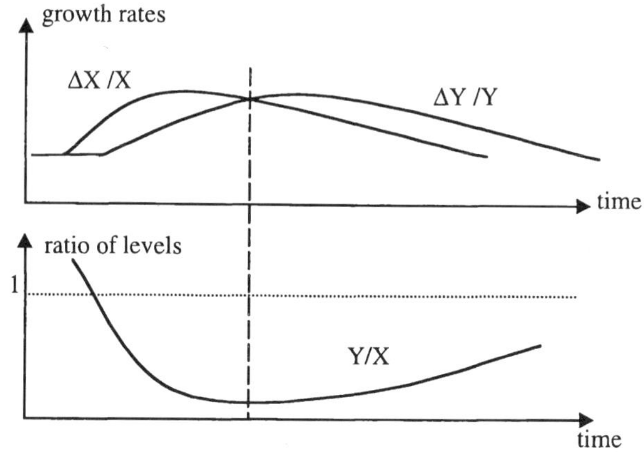

Figure 8.2.1 An idealized pattern

On the other hand, the merit of Taiwan's industrial policy is its stable growth rate, as seen in Chart 8.2.1. This is further confirmed in Chart 8.2.3.

Each major, systematic variation of the Korea/Taiwan locus, away from its 'smoothed theme' is attributable to some event in Korea, typically with several years' growth at rates higher than the Taiwanese, only to be followed by a sudden sharp drop. Thus, although in the literature, most researchers maintain that Korea has grown at a faster pace than Taiwan, Ranis (1999) would state that the reverse is true. One must note that the 1997 setback was very transient for Korea. For reasons to be discussed in Chapter 12, during 2001, Korea maintained positive growth but Taiwan experienced its first output contraction over the decades.

Based upon our theory, one may conclude that both economies are growing as fast as one can expect. Given the long term convergence of both economies, Korea will grow faster than Taiwan in the future, because they are to approach the same limit path, emulating Japan and America. But for now, Taiwan enjoys both a higher income level and a smoother growth path.

All East Asian economies are catching up with the United States. The peak rate for catching up arrives in due time. This peak rate comes earlier for an economy with a higher initial level of GDP than one with a lower initial level (For Korea and Taiwan, the initial date is mid-1960s when both became outward oriented). This is idealized in Figure 8.2.1: X stands for the first-mover and Y, for the latecomer. The upper panel shows the growth rates $\Delta X/X$ and $\Delta Y/Y$ and the lower panel, Y/X. See Lau and Wan (1994).

The macro-economic indicators

In financial aspects, there is marked difference between Korea and Taiwan over the decades. For our purpose, three points need be mentioned.

First, over the 18 years 1981-1998, the balances of current account are shown in Table 8.2.1.

Year	Korea	Taiwan
1981	-	+
1982	-	+
1983	-	+
1984	-	+
1985	-	+
1986	+	+
1987	+	+
1988	+	+
1989	+	+
1990	+	+
1991	-	+
1992	-	+
1993	-	+
1994	+	+
1995	-	+
1996	-	+
1997	-	+
1998	+	+

Table 8.2.1 Balance of trade: Korea and Taiwan (- deficit; + surplus)
Sources: WDI.; Taiwan Statistical Books

Second, the debt service ratio over the three years 1994, 1995 and 1996 are respectively 6%, 5% and 6% for Korea and insignificant for Taiwan.

Third, for the past decades, Taiwan has consistently kept a higher stock of foreign exchange reserve than Korea, even though it has a far smaller population and total GDP than the latter.

The most dramatic difference between these two economies came during Crisis 1997. Korea had to ask the IMF for a bailout, but Taiwan weathered the storm.

Thus, relative to Korea, the higher level of living standards in Taiwan is neither the result of living beyond one's means over the 18 years we considered, nor the outcome of mortgaging one's birthright. The keeping of a larger foreign exchange reserve may be prudent for Taiwan since it can never appeal to the International Monetary Fund or the World Bank for succor in times of trouble.

Various socio-economic indicators

The above comparison rests on aggregate measurements of a decade ago. We supplement it with additional microeconomic data, over the most recent period. Chart 8.2.4 is based upon information on twelve aspects, covering:

- The health aspects: male and female life expectancy, infant mortality and hospital beds;
- The education aspect: expenditure on schooling;
- The consumption aspects: housing and electricity usage;
- Aspects of consumer durables ownership: motor vehicles, fax machines, cellular phones and personal computers.

As the 'radar chart' of Chart 8.2.4 indicates, Taiwan is ahead of Korea in every aspect, with the exception of the ownership of personal computers.

Next, for what it is worth, one may take note that, based upon available recent information, the income distribution of Korea and Taiwan are both reasonably equitable and quite similar to each other. Based on the incomes received by the top 10% and bottom 20%, one may display the information as a pair of rough approximation of Lorenz curves in Chart 8.2.5.

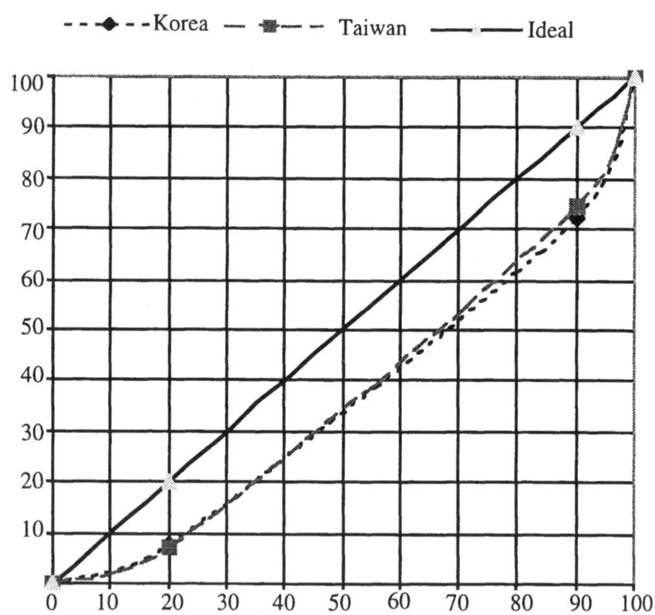

Chart 8.2.5 Lorenz curves Source: Britannica Book of the Year 2000

More on this topic will be said in Chapter 12.

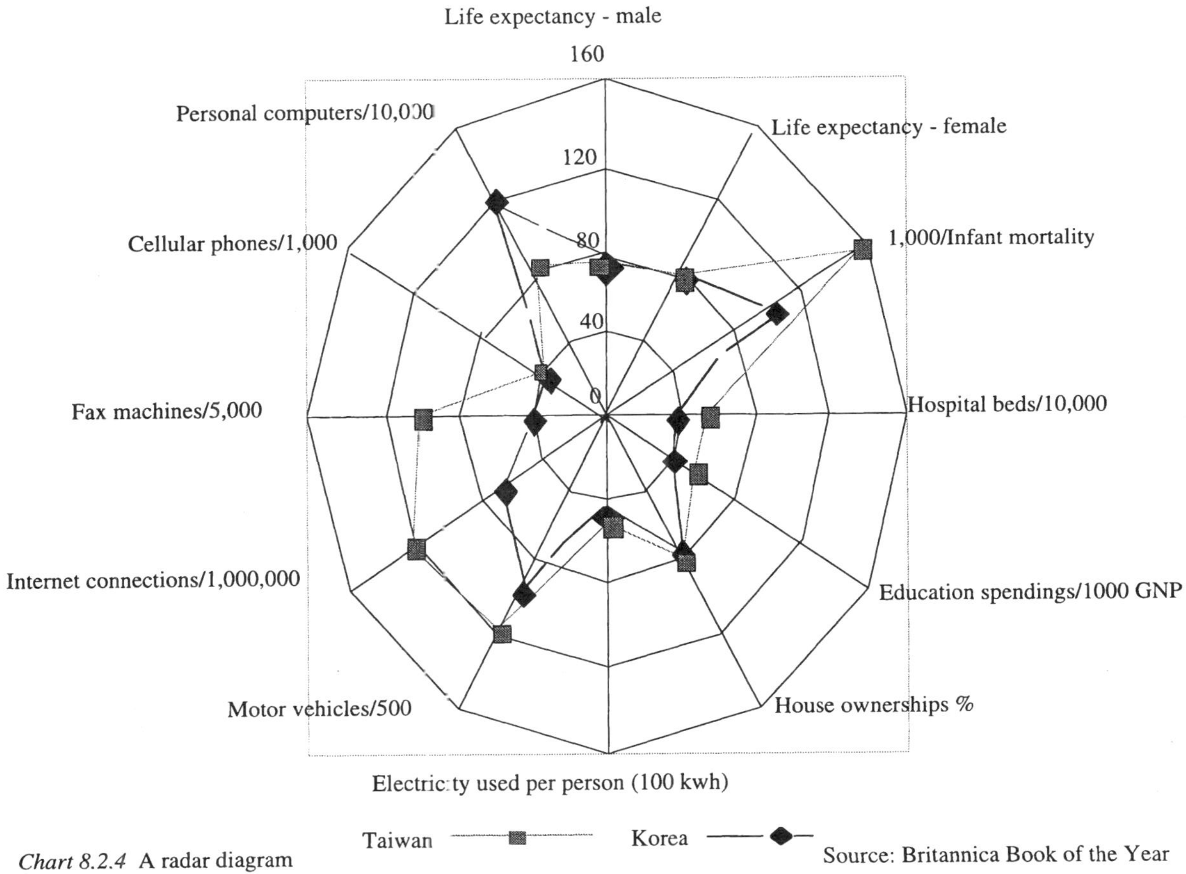

Chart 8.2.4 A radar diagram

Technological strength

Relative to Korea, Taiwan has maintained both a higher living standard and a larger foreign exchange reserve. In addition, as we shall discuss later, firms and business groups in Taiwan are smaller and the government policy seems to be less resolute in pursuing industry targeting. One may suspect that Taiwan has invested less adequately for the future. There is no easy answer to this question. Instead, one may search for some indices of relative technological strength.

First, in the *Technology Review* (May 2001: 48), the Patent Scorecard listed the top 150 firms throughout the world by the quality of their patents. These are classified into 8 industries. The economy-by-economy breakdown is as follows:

United States	86
Japan	32
Germany	8
France	5
United Kingdom	4
Taiwan	4
Switzerland	2
Netherlands	2
Korea	2
Italy	1
Denmark	1
Sweden	1
Finland	1
Singapore	1

For the NIEs, the names of such firms, listed by industries are as follows:

	Electric/Electronics	Computer	Semiconductor
Korea	Samsung		Hyundai
Singapore			Chartered
Taiwan		Hon Hai	TSMC,UMC,Vanguard

Next, *Business Week* (June 18, 2001) listed the Top 100 Information Technology firms, with 15 from East Asia, in the following breakdown:

Taiwan	7
Japan	6
Hong Kong	1
Singapore	1

Judging from the above information, Taiwan has not suffered in innovativeness relative to Korea, as Mody predicted, at least up this point.

Comparative advantage as revealed in the world market

To balance the above discussion, which is focused on some derived measures of 'innovativeness,' we now turn to the market acceptance of the exports of an economy. It is generally agreed that the Korean development strategy relies on both economy of scale and vertical integration, seeking market share for its products. Taiwanese businesses are concerned with current profit and operate in niche markets. We now study the efficacy of the Taiwanese economy in two aspects.

First, an economy with successful products should enjoy favorable terms of trade. The terms of trade indices for both Korea and Taiwan at selected points of time over 1988-1998 have been displayed in Smith (2000: 66). The contrast is striking. The terms of trade index for Korea both gyrated wildly and declined significantly. The similar index for Taiwan improved gradually over time with minor fluctuations.

Second, an economy with successful products should experience enthusiastic clientele. At the product level, according to Chen and Liu (2000), Taiwan's world market share of nine information technology products are as follows:

Palmtop scanner	95%
Motherboard	74
Mouse	65
Keyboard	61
Video card	55
Switching board supply	55
Monitor	53
Desktop scanner	52
Audio card	50

At the firm level, according to Tung (2001), TSMC was the first firm in the world to operate as a pure chip foundry. Between it and its Taiwanese competitor, UMC, they held 52% of the world market share in such trade. TSMC often earns a gross profit rate of 30-50%. Due to their success, small high tech firms have managed to win foreign partners in strategic alliances and to induce Taiwanese business groups to invest in the information technology sector. In addition, the stock market also has become a source of investment funds. Thus the perceived handicaps noted by previous observers have been largely ameliorated.

Summing up, Taiwan industrialized before Korea. Over the decades, it managed to stay ahead of Korea in both consumption and assets ownership. Taiwan's growth performance is smoother and at least not much slower than Korea's. Judging from the resilience of the economy during Crisis 1997, Taiwan's development clearly differs in major ways from that of Korea.

Such difference in performance must reflect differences in both economic structure and government policy. These are matters to be studied next.

3. THE ECONOMIC STRUCTURE

We now start with the industrial structure. Taiwan has four major types of firms: (a) foreign owned, (b) government owned, (c) large, private domestic firms, and (d) small and medium enterprises (SMEs). The importance of the first two types in Taiwan is more than their counterparts in Korea but much less than in Singapore. Large, private domestic firms are the key to success for Korea (also Japan) but not for Taiwan. The type crucial to Taiwan's development is the SMEs, a feature similar to the economy of Hong Kong. As a fabricator in the world market, the distinct feature of the Taiwan economy is its vibrant SMEs in the manufacturing sector. According to Yang (2000), for the period 1990-1995 the average share of SMEs was 80% in manufacturing employment and 58% in manufacturing export.

In Taiwan, with its heavy export dependence, the relationship among these four types of firms is perhaps even more important than their relative weights. This is highlighted in Chart 8.3.1.

After the late 1950s, when the 'first stage import substitution' period ended, foreign firms regarded the newly opened economy as a supply base for manufacture, not an important outlet for their produce. The local market was limited in size and purchasing power. Subsidiaries of multinational firms started to conduct labor-intensive operations on the island, or to place orders with local SMEs as subcontractors. Since the foreign firms came for the hardy and inexpensive workers, it was obviously more cost effective to have local firms recruiting and supervising the local labor force.

Most local firms were very small then. To take large foreign orders, arriving with short notice, they often formed ad hoc coalitions to share orders. To assure acceptable quality and punctual delivery, the manufacturing process was broken into standardized segments, with intensified division of labor. Thus foreign demand converted the local SMEs from perfectly competitive firms producing 'more of the same' to monopolistically competitive firms, each with some specialized expertise. See Kato and Wan (2001) for further discussion.

Initially, the value added margin was small relative to product value. To save shipping cost and utilize inexpensive local inputs, backward integration took place. Sometimes public firms spearheaded the risky process. Local private firms would join the operation later, once the risks became better known. This is referred to as Second Stage Import Substitution, or Taiwan's Heavy Chemical Industry Drive, by Chen and Ku (1999). At all times, the production process was not vertically integrated, and the SMEs remained

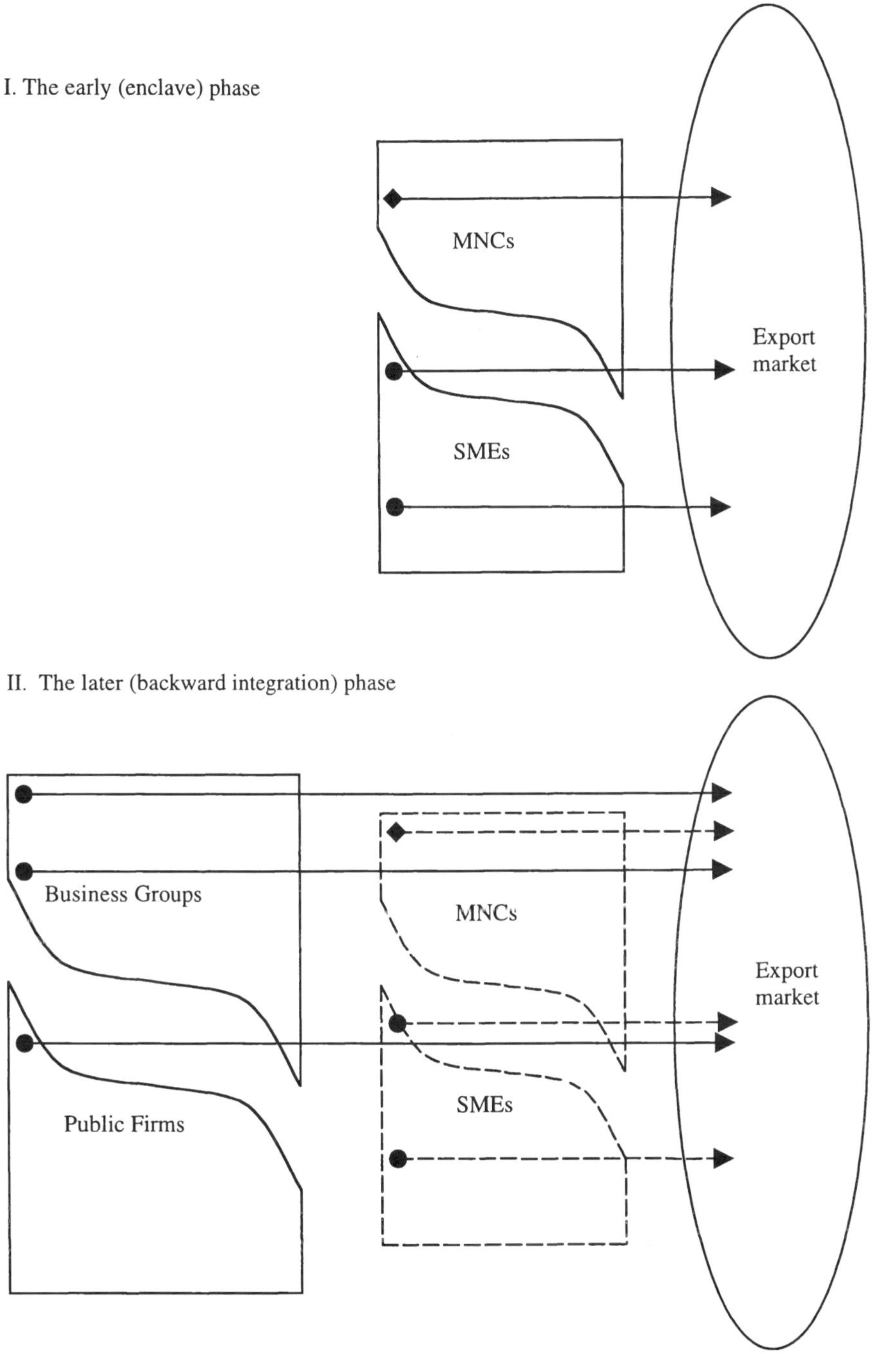

Chart 8.3.1 Taiwan's changing industrial structure

responsible for exports. Given the small domestic market and the scanty resource base, export is the lifeblood of the Taiwanese economy. The upstream firms, be they public or private, must submit to the market discipline, lest they kill the goose that lays the golden egg. The survival of the exporting SMEs is always the supreme concern. Eventually the less bureaucratic private firms tend to edge out the public enterprises, once they are permitted to enter the field. As free agents, the SMEs associate with foreign clients and acquire technology. The high rate of employee turnover facilitates the spread of production skill.

This situation is in sharp contrast to the Korean scene. There, organized in business groups, the large, private domestic firms receive support inside the groups, through cross-subsidization or from government controlled banks. They enter targeted industries with vertically integrated operations, crowding out SMEs in the more traditional sectors, or reducing them to sub-contractors for their own operation. The situation is depicted in Chart 8.3.2.

As we have seen in Chapter 7, it is the GTC system in Korea which made the Korean SMEs dependent upon the business groups for market access. Thus, as we shall see in the next section, Taiwan's failure to nourish its Large Trading Companies seems to be a blessing in disguise.

What distinguishes the large, private domestic firms of Taiwan from their counterparts of Korea are therefore:

1. Their position in the supply chain as upstream producers, rather than vertically integrated producers;
2. Their position relative to the SMEs as trading partners rather than dominant players;
3. Their relatively modest size in the economy rather than being entities 'too big to fail';
4. Their position with the government-controlled banks as merely favorite business clients rather than the recipients of loans as part of state policy.

Table 8.3.1 gives some indication of the situation.

Share of large business groups	Korean top 43, 1989	Taiwan Top 80, 1994
In sales of mfg.	40.7%	16.4%
In value added of mfg.	15%	6.7%

Table 8.3.1 Size comparison of business groups Source: Yang (2000)

According to Woo-Cumings (2001), Korean business groups form integrated and self-contained systems. Before Crisis 1997, the top five employed 600,000 workers between them, so that government-controlled banks had to think twice before forcing any of them into bankruptcy. No Taiwanese firm or business group is in that league.

The distinction in industrial structure has both its effect on the export mix and its cause in government policy. Leaving policy issues to the next section, we focus now on the export mix. According to Chen and Ku (2000),

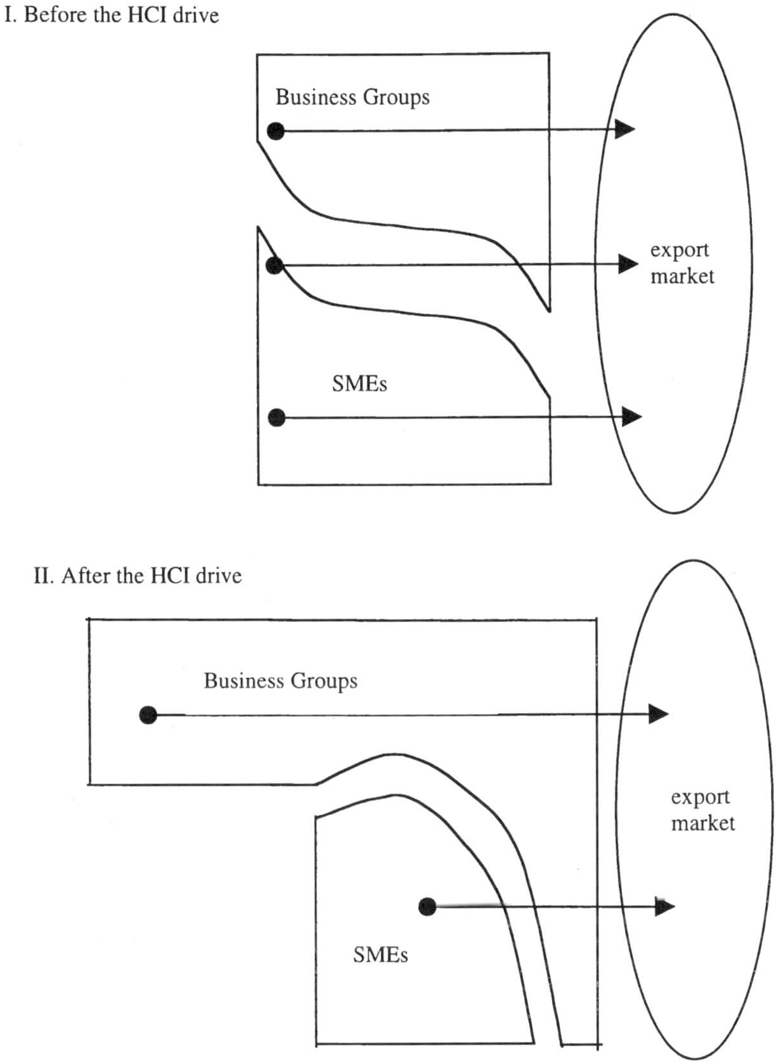

Chart 8.3.2 Korea's changing industrial structure

the export comparison between these two economies in 1982 and 1992 is quite illuminating. The export shares in 'heavy chemicals' are given in Table 8.3.2.

	Korea	Taiwan
1982	44%	32%
1992	51%	47%

Table 8.3.2 The export shares of Heavy Chemical outputs Source: Chen and Ku (2000)

Hidden behind the apparent similarity between these two economies are subtler distinctions. Industry by industry, Korea and Taiwan specialize in different products. Chen and Ku cited the following examples (Table 8.3.3):

Specialized by	Chemicals	Iron and steel	Electronics
Korea	Petrochemicals	Plates, coils	Semiconductors
Taiwan	Synthetic fiber	Pipes, sections	Computer peripherals

Table 8.3.3 Pattern of specialization

What lies behind such differences is the Korean preference to challenge the market leader (Japan) on capital intensive, upstream products and the Taiwanese predilection to enter in joint ventures with partners from advanced economies on labor intensive, downstream products. The scale economy is crucial for Korean efforts. The niche market is the attraction for Taiwanese firms.

An in-depth comparison may be found in Smith (2000: 74-5) regarding the electronics industry of Korea and Taiwan. To acquire foreign technology, Korea mainly relies on licensing and the purchase of new equipment. In contrast, Taiwan exploits the technology spillover from direct foreign investment (DFI) and the experienced personnel returning from foreign firms and universities. Korea has to seek market share to realize scale economy. In contrast, Taiwan's skill in product design and anticipating customers' needs improves automatically with practice. This explains why, in 1997, the terms of trade declined sharply for Korea but not for Taiwan.

4. INDUSTRIAL POLICY – TAIWANESE VERSION

Evidence presented in the previous two sections suggests that Taiwan's growth is about as rapid as Korea's, but is much more stable in its pattern. The performance difference between these two showcase economies may be traced to the differences in their market concentration and export mix. The last chapter shows that Korea's industrial policy has decisively shaped the structure of the economy: in particular, the dominance of the business groups and the importance of the heavy and chemical industries. Is Taiwan's industrial policy equally influential in Taiwan's economic structure? If not, why? These are controversial topics with complex answers. The subtlety at issue is such that, to gain a deeper understanding into these questions, it is best to clarify the nature of industrial policy itself. In addition, a satisfactory analysis of the Taiwanese case would gain us much insight about the interactions between market and government elsewhere.

We shall present in turn: first, a chronological summary of Taiwan's development; second, the questions economists usually ask about Taiwan's industrial policy; third, a digression into the nature of industrial policy; and finally, our interpretation and assessment of Taiwan's record.

Taiwan's Development Record in a Nutshell

The Taiwanese economy was heavily damaged by aerial bombing in World War II. The end of World War II in 1945 was followed by the end of the Chinese Civil War in 1949. Taiwan was initially cut off from its protected markets – first Japan and then Mainland China. The heavy inflow of evacuated soldiers and civilians needed sustenance, and the warlike preparations against a possible attack could not be relaxed. There were deficits in the government budget as well as the balance of trade. Under hyper-inflation, exchange control and import control were imposed to preserve the lifeblood of foreign exchange and stop the hemorrhage of capital flight.

The Korean War in 1951 brought the renewal of U.S. aid, which arrested the inflation and restored the import of the direst needs under a state trade agency. Under the powerful influence of the U.S. advisers at the aid agency, funds were allocated to set up factories managed by selected private individuals, to meet local needs and save foreign exchange. Meanwhile, land reform and rural reconstruction had raised farm productivity and supplied the export staples of rice and sugar for Japan. This was called the first stage import substitution.

The Japanese Miracle raised Japanese wages and caused a Japanese labor shortage. The outward-oriented reform of Taiwan in the late 1950s made it possible to fill the needs of the U.S. market, replacing Japanese supply, often under Japanese intermediation, but also occasionally under the U.S. initiative. To take full advantage of the opportunity and to short-circuit the slow regulatory reform in Taiwan, the Kaohsiung Export Processing Zone was launched in 1965, with instant success. The export boom brought along many labor-intensive industries that relied upon Japanese-supplied intermediate goods. Much direct foreign investment came, under government licensing. The emphasis was on selecting projects that would help technology transfer.

The quickly improved government finance and trade balance provided the government with the wherewithal to finance development. The oil crisis and the U.S. retreat from Vietnam provided the stimulus to pursue industrialization through backward linkage. Steel, petrochemicals and electronics became targeted industries. Public firms played a leading role when private firms showed reluctance to join government-led consortia. This was called the second stage import substitution.

The 1980s started with a huge export surplus that caused U.S. pressure and massive exchange revaluation. The result was the exodus of labor-intensive industries to Mainland China, after the outward-oriented reform under Deng. At the same time, government efforts to enhance the science and technology base began to yield fruits. The Industrial Technology Research Institute was founded, and the Hsinchu Science-based Industrial Park was launched, attracting high tech industries. Vain efforts were made to launch aerospace industries by acquisition.

The 1990s was largely a continuation of the earlier trends. High tech industries blossomed and Crisis 1997 was weathered with only minor damage.

Questions Pertaining to Taiwan's Development

In the literature, Taiwan's economic development has attracted attention to a sequence of overlapping issues:

- the role of the first stage import-substitution program in industrialization;
- the role of the second stage import-substitution in industrial upgrading;
- differences with the industrial policies of Korea; and
- differences with the industrial policies of Hong Kong.

It is generally acknowledged that, first, Hong Kong has never practiced import substitution, but Korea has a government that micromanages the economy from time to time. Second, in Taiwan's development, the State is more interventionist than in Hong Kong but the intervention is less pervasive than in Korea. It is also a matter of record that Taiwan shares *both* the market structure of Hong Kong, with vibrant SMEs, *and* the export mix of Korea, where the high tech sector is prominent. If in terms of performance, Taiwan's development is comparable to that of Hong Kong, then Taiwan's industrial policy is superfluous and the State is not very relevant. Alternatively, if Taiwan's development more closely resembles Korea, then the role of industrial policy is crucial. Therefore, evidence from Taiwan is critically important to the debate in the development literature about the role of the government. This significance increases further with the massive de-industrialization of Hong Kong[2] and the debt crisis suffered by Korea in 1997-98.

There are contrafactual questions that can be raised: Would industrialization have happened without the first stage import substitution? Would the industrial structure have been different without the second stage import substitution? The answers must be speculative by nature.

---

[2] See next chapter.

There are also serious issues in evidence assessment. On record, there are a host of laws, regulations, government programs and official exhortations (like the once widely posted signs on buses encouraging private saving) over the five decades of rule by the Chinese Nationalists (KMT). These are documented by Wade (1990) and held to be important by Rodrik (1995), but their relevance is questioned by Hobday (1995). In interviews, typically, the Mainland-born current and former officials would emphasize the benefits of such initiatives, and the Taiwanese-born entrepreneurs dominant in business would regard them as not very significant. In the development literature, the liberal and 'revisionist' economists draw opposite conclusions. See Bhagwati (1999) and Amsden (1999).

To sum up, even though the facts about Taiwan are important, their study is not simple, using *either* macroeconomic data *or* the documented laws and regulations. Sustained rapid growth has been achieved by both Hong Kong under *laissez faire* and by Korea practicing government intervention. Thus, from macroeconomic performance alone one can hardly decide what has contributed to Taiwan's development. It is also known that in Taiwan, the relationship between the government and the SMEs is, in general, wary and distant.[3] The impact of the government is mostly through the state-owned sector, which has had declining importance over time. Moreover, many government initiatives (like the development of the aerospace industry) did not bear any fruits. Yet, the positive role of government initiatives in the electronics sector seems to be generally accepted. So from case studies, the record again appears mixed.

To gain further headway, we find it necessary to reconsider industrial policy at a conceptual level.

The Concept of Industrial Policy Reconsidered

In the particular case of Taiwan, one should cite Kuo (1999: 44): "[G]overnment policies in Taiwan over the past 50 years were, in general, case by case innovations instituted in response to impending economic problems. Yet when we look back, we see them as if they were systematically designed, since they seem to form a consistent long term package."

Further, she documented that "[N]egative effects generated by previous policies were however dealt with by remedial policies later on. . . . [P]olicies adopted in response to impending problems were quietly abandoned or retained in name only after the problems disappeared."

---

[3] See for example, Hobday (1995).

Evidence shows that in Japan,[4] Korea,[5] and Singapore,[6] industrial policy has been practiced in approximately the same fashion. Therefore, what is important for us is to discover the nature and content of that *consistent long-term package*. In addition, unlike the case of Korea, the same KMT ruled Taiwan for fifty years, *both* during Taiwan's industrialization *and* before it. This offers researchers the opportunity to tackle this problem.

We shall begin our discussion with a very simple example.

Example: Funding the research for a particular discovery

Let,

t be time, with the research already started at $0 \leq t$,

d(t) stand for the decision to continue at t, with two possible choices: 0 for abandoning the project and 1 for continuing it,

c(t) stand for the cost estimate for the entire project at time t,

a(t) stand for the rate actual cost has been incurred per unit of time,

b stand for the value of the expected benefit.

For simplicity, we assume that $a(t) = \alpha$ is constant and there is no discount.

Since the cumulated sunk cost is αt, the expected future cost is $c(t) - \alpha t$, to be compared against the benefit b. To maximize the expected net benefit, the *optimal decision rule* is shown in Figure 8.4.1.

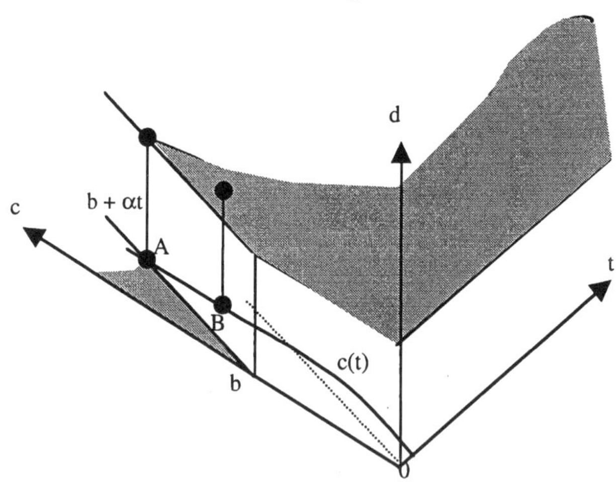

Figure 8.4.1 Policy function for funding research

---

[4] Kikkawa and Hikino (1999: 24).

[5] Jones and Sakong (1980: 63).

[6] Huff (1994: 340).

$d(t) = 1$ if and only if $b \geq c(t) - \alpha t$, or $c(t) \leq b + \alpha t$.

In Figure 8.4.1, the above policy prescribes 'to continue the construction' at time t', when the situation is B = (t', c(t')), but 'to drop the project' when at time t" > t', the situation becomes A = (t", c(t")).

The crucial point here is that a public policy is a contingent plan. The decision depends upon both time t and some 'state variable.' This is the cost estimate in this example. This fact is represented as a shaded surface over the two dimensional domain of (t, c). In real life, the record observable by an economist is most likely the time path d(t): when a project is suddenly stopped, t units of time after its launching, with all the previously committed cost lost. At most, besides d(t) one observes also c(t), the sequence of total cost estimates, depicted in dotted line, as shown in Figure 8.4.2. *Both* the decision rule *and* its justifications are usually hidden from the observer. What an economist might surmise about the appropriateness of the decision function is necessarily guesswork.

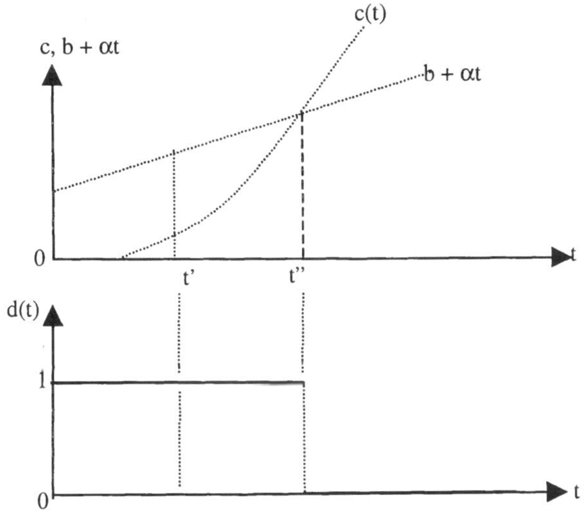

Figure 8.4.2 Time paths for c(t), and d(t)

However, the above discussion provides a useful conceptual perspective. By analogy with the format of dynamic programming, we regard government action as decided by the following elements: (a) information about the state, that in itself depends upon (a') the true state and (a") the information about it; (b) the set of available instruments, which may depend in turn on (b') past government actions; and (c) the political agenda of those in power, which is colored by (c') past events. This is schematically shown in Chart 8.4.1.

For illustration, a sequence of cases are considered below.

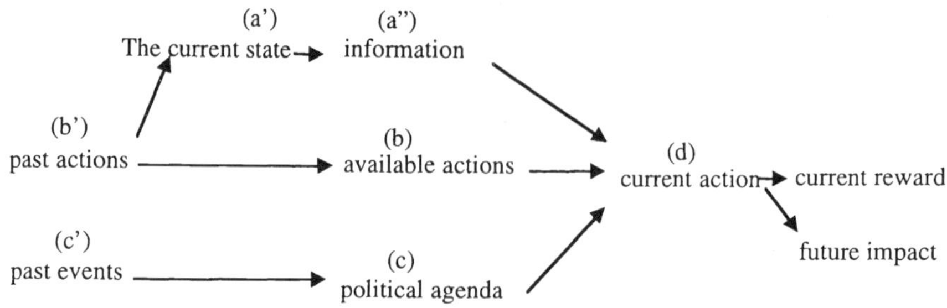

Chart 8.4.1 Government decision making

First, Taiwan's style of decision-making: Over time, Taiwan negotiated a sequence of high-profile projects with foreign firms, from a mass-producing automobile plant with Toyota, to the planned takeover of McDowell, to the projected launching of the aerospace industry. After much publicity and heated debates, most of these projects ended in stillbirth. An exception is the spectacular success of the founding of the Taiwan Semiconductor Corporation (TSMC) with Philips. These frequent false starts are often held as signs that Taiwan lacked resolve (Wade, 1990: 101). But according to Chart 8.4.1, foreign firms' evolving positions or other new information form the '*states*' facing Taiwan's policy makers, and lie beyond the latter's control. Thus, these negotiation failures do not constitute a basis to judge the quality of decision-making. Korea under Park might appear more decisive. "[D]uring this period, a great deal . . . of advice . . . of the EPB [Economic Planning Board] was overruled by policymakers . . . bent on . . . accelerating . . . Korea's heavy and chemical industries regardless of cost." (Kim, 1991: xv). But with the hindsight after Crisis 1997, such decisiveness may be a dubious virtue.

Second, Taiwan's first stage import-substitution: Some economists regard this period as instrumental to the subsequent industrialization. Yet, Hong Kong industrialized without such an interlude. The more interesting question concerns the nature of the reform that ended this phase. According to Tsiang (1984), what caused the reform was the acceptance of his assessment against the view of export pessimism. Thus, what was changed was the *perception of the 'state,'* and not the 'state' itself. The reform brought new policy measures, but not a new policy.

Third, the ineffectual promotion of the large trading companies ('LTCs'): According to Fields (1995), in order to end the reliance on Japanese general trading companies ('GTCs'), Korea successfully adopted measures to nurture Korean GTCs, but Taiwan vainly took measures to create the Taiwanese LTCs. The assessment of Fields is that Taiwan lacked the powerful incentives used by Korea, such as directed credit at a negative real interest rate. As seen in Chart 8.4.1, the difference between Korea and Taiwan lies both in the set of *available actions*, shaped by the economic structure, and also in *past policy actions* that gave Korea the industrial concentration absent in Taiwan.[7] This will be elaborated below.

Fourth, the constrained industrial policy: In launching its own heavy chemical industries, whether in steel mills or in petrochemicals factories, the government in Taiwan always tried to organize a consortium, with the participation of both private firms and the public sector. Repeatedly, the local businesses showed scant interest. In comparison with the Korea of President Park, the principal distinction is the presence of heavily leveraged giant business groups present in Korea but absent in Taiwan. With their multisectoral reach, Korean business groups could cross-subsidize a less profitable emerging sector from their oligopolistic profits in more established industries.[8] Because of their heavy, short-term borrowing from government banks, the Korean government could command the giant business groups into action, like urging circus lions through a flaming hoop.[9] The Korean heavily leveraged giant business groups were the personal creation of President Park. Their effectiveness was well observed by the policy makers in Taiwan. The fact is not that Taiwan tried and failed to emulate policies so effective in Korea: instead, there was never any attempt to try. That deserves analysis.

In Taiwan, when the chips are down, the government is both willing and capable of reining in business interest. For example, early on, the Formosa Plastics Group abandoned an investment plan in the Peoples' Republic of China because of government opposition. But it is one thing to force a firm to cease and desist, and quite another to ask private interest to invest wholeheartedly according to government plans. Repeatedly, the same Formosa Plastics Group was most reluctant toward such government initiatives, because the government was never willing to deploy the carrots and sticks, Korean fashion.

The apparent constraints are of two kinds, financial and political. Industrialization was credit-financed in Korea[10] and equity-financed in Taiwan. To make directed credit part of the command and control mechanism for industrial targeting would further require not only the control

---

[7] Fields (1995) observed thoughtfully that the advantages of the Japanese GTCs arise from their scale economy rather than monopolistic power. Thus, Taiwan would not have to supplant them altogether, as Korea did.

[8] In fact, according to Stern et al. (1995), the Korean government guided business groups to enter paired industries, one being currently profitable and the other being favored by the government.

[9] The threat President Park used to prod Hyundai's entry into shipbuilding is mentioned in Jones and Sakong (1980).

[10] As well as in Japan.

of banks by the government[11] but also significant interest rate differentials on policy loans.[12] This tends to involve either domestic inflation or foreign loans (under government guarantees) or both. Such measures were adopted by Korea but eschewed in Taiwan. In Taiwan, loans of government banks were viewed as government property. The incurrence of bad debt was thus equivalent to public property loss, with comparable penalties for the loan officers.[13] Judging from the differential impact of Crisis 1997 on these two economies, and given that Korea has access to IMF and the World Bank in emergencies but Taiwan does not, the cautious policy stance and the pawn-shop attitude of government banks in Taiwan appear quite justifiable in hindsight.

Fifth, the political agenda of the Chinese Nationalist Party (KMT), which was in power in Taiwan during the industrialization: The seat of the government was relocated to Taiwan in 1949 with a large military force. The principal threat to the regime has been from the Chinese Communist Party, through military attack, and also through political agitation. With the Korean War, the U.S. 7th Fleet could prevent the former but not the latter. It was the popular belief that the KMT lost its mandate in the Civil War because of the hyperinflation and the illicit profiteering of the well connected. In Taiwan, the corruption and economic dislocation after World War II had already caused one general uprising against the KMT in 1947.

At the same time, the heavy Chinese loss during the Korean War and the serious famine after the failed Great Leap Movement led the KMT to hope that they might still have some chance to recover the Mainland.

This explains the KMT's priorities. Only when military spending made little difference to the future on both shores of the Taiwan Strait would economic development be the objective. The process of development could not be allowed to destabilize its political base. For a long time, the local Taiwanese population could neither participate meaningfully in the exiled 'central government,' nor hope to seize power through another uprising. Instead, those in power were most concerned about loyalty among the ranks of their fellow exiles. Some of these were believers of the moderate socialist ideal of Dr. Sun Yat-sen, the founder of the party. Others were homesick and poorly paid soldiers with dimming hopes for return.[14] To forestall their alienation, inflation and income polarization had to be avoided like the plague.

---

[11] This is the case for Korea as well as Taiwan, but not for Japan.

[12] This is true only in Korea, not in Taiwan or Japan.

[13] See Cheng (1993).

[14] As in the General Sun Li-jen Incident, the KMT was most concerned about a coup.

This gives the background of the 'growth within stability' principle, referred to by Kuo (1999). It also explains why the Korean policy under Park was never seriously considered in Taiwan. On the one hand, the KMT had no need to seek legitimacy through ambitious expansion, since in those years there was no election to contest. On the other hand, inflationary finance and the enrichment of business leaders, be they Mainlanders or local Taiwanese, would be equally dangerous, not because there may appear a center for dissent, but because it may alienate the base of support of the regime.[15]

Finally, the second stage import substitution. By 1970, the decade of trade liberalization, the labor-intensive industries had brought to Taiwan both rising income and a trade surplus. Yet labor shortage boosted wage levels and industries depended heavily on imported intermediate goods. As a remedy, policy makers increasingly argued for the deepening and upgrading of the industrial structure. Taiwan's second stage import substitution had arrived. Industrial priorities were declared, and government banks granted loans to targeted industries at concession rates. But according to Cheng (1993) and Chen and Ku (1999), the resemblance to the Korean HCI drive is only skin deep. Their distinct features are: (a) For lack of interest from private firms, the government-proposed consortia often became fully public owned or joint ventures with foreign firms; (b) both the interest concession and the total of such loans were rather minimal; (c) the targeted industries were mostly those supplying downstream local exporters; (d) Taiwan's industry targeting went on until the mid 1980s, much later than Korea's HCI drive; (e) the instruments used included the training of a skilled labor force, the setting up of industrial parks, the supported research and the public owned firms that provided pioneering information for late-coming private firms. These public firms were allowed to be out-competed by their private competitors or to be privatized for more independent management.

An interesting comparison is between government initiatives of this type and the *laissez faire* regime of Hong Kong. By 1990s, the de-industrialization of Hong Kong had proceeded much farther than that of Taiwan, with falling wages and polarizing income distribution as consequences. In fact, given its larger labor force and the reluctance of the Taiwanese to be absorbed into the Mainland polity, an evolution like Hong Kong would have been unsupportable for the Taiwanese economy. Despite the prominence of the labor-intensive SMEs in both economies, the difference in economic structure between Taiwan and Hong Kong today is significant. Furthermore, this difference clearly is the result of the differences in government policy.

---

[15] To wit, the temporary eclipse of K. Y. Yin in 1955 was on a charge of cronyism.

As a first approximation, we have left out an important element in our discussion of policy making, namely, the competence of policy makers. It is a stressful fact of real life that policy makers are like clinical physicians. Formally, in playing the incomplete-information game of decision making, their knowledge about 'the rules of the game' vary too widely for comfort. To wit, in the 1950s, Taiwan's policy makers underrated the capability of Taiwan's SMEs and underestimated the export opportunities. Some argued that every commodity deserves a distinct exchange rate, thus, comparative advantage would count for nothing in resource allocation. Others insisted to raise cotton crops under protection, thus, Taiwan's absolute disadvantages in cotton were blithely ignored (Thorbecke, et al., 2002). They were ignorant about both elementary economic principles and the twin sources of Taiwan's eventual economic success: the vibrant SMEs serving as the foundation of Taiwan's export prowess. Their *modus operandi* is certainly a far cry from the sophisticated analysis, with which Taiwan managed the First Oil Crisis in the early 1970s. How and why Taiwan successfully deployed a 'cold turkey defense' is described in Kuo (1999), although she modestly left her own decisive role out of that case of decision making.

Of course, surviving an oil crisis is no standard fare for economic development. Nonetheless, two related issues are relevant here.

First, it is all important for a society to train and retain competent economic policy makers. Second, in the absence of competent policy makers, it may well be more prudent to live with market failures than to court government failures, in trusting vital decisions to sorcerer's apprentices.

5. POSSIBILITY OF REPLICATION

By casting industrial policy in the fashion discussed above, we can address the often-asked question of replication from a fresh angle. The initial condition of every economy is unique, so that the total replication of the performance of another economy appears impossible by definition. Yet, one can adopt from another economy the entire policy program or specific policy instruments.

From that perspective, many policy instruments of Taiwan have been adopted in other economies, such as the export zones and the industrial parks. From the Masan Export Zone of Korea, to the Export Zone Industries in Mauritius to the numerous Special Economic Zones in the PRC today, the lessons of Taiwan have been emulated with various degrees of success.

On the other hand, the overall policy program under the KMT has rarely been replicated. Under the guiding principle of growth within equity, Taiwan's industrial base has been emerging steadily in the form of a host of vibrant and resilient SMEs. Under an autocratic ('alien') regime, economic leadership – even before political control – was quietly and gradually transferred to the hands of the capable, hardy ethnic majority. Opportunities were seized and over-ambitious projects were given up. The end result is a growth path that is more stable than Korea's but not slower in pace. It has nurtured an industry with more technical depth than Hong Kong and an indigenous entrepreneurial class more independent than its counterpart in Singapore. All this came about, not due to any visionary design but through sensible adaptation.

Presiding over Taiwan's industrialization was Generalissimo Chiang Kaishek, who led China through World War II, only to lose the Civil War through his flawed leadership. In Taiwan, he was ready to listen to whatever economic advisors he could find, from the very mixed group in the National Taiwan University in the early 1950s, the competent advisers in the U.S. Aid program, to distinguished scholars like T. C. Liu and S. C. Tsiang in the 1960s. Aided by dedicated technocrats and cautious financiers, he set the economy on its growth path.

It is interesting that neither the economists, nor the technocrats, nor the financiers, let alone the businessmen and the political opponents of KMT were entirely happy about the eventual outcome. The government is free from neither inefficiency nor corruption. The environment is somewhat polluted. The industries are still dependent on foreign technology. The list of possible complaints can go on. On the other hand, given the objective conditions, it is not clear how much better Taiwan's development could have been, either.

Perhaps it is precisely its imperfection that makes Taiwan's record interesting, since the record appears achievable by many other economies, if one makes a serious try.

CHAPTER SUMMARY

- Taiwan's economy bears some resemblance to Korea's, but differs in several respects. The similarities may support conclusions drawn from Korea; the differences offer policy makers diverse options and researchers clues with which to rank alternative strategies.
- Both economies have high population density, scant natural resources, initially modest human capital and a war-ravaged infrastructure. With a homogeneous labor force of Confucian heritage, and as former Japanese colonies, both were positioned to export labor-intensive goods formerly supplied by Japan, especially in joint ventures with Japanese firms, after Japanese wages rose.
- Foreign exchange shortages persuaded both economies to adopt policies conducive to this type of development: this occurred in Korea after Park's coup, and in Taiwan when the KMT adopted an economic reform. Learning-by-exporting improves the skill of the current workers; education upgraded the new entrants to the labor market.
- Over four decades, Taiwan's slightly earlier start may account for the higher relative per capita real GDP, and higher social and economic indicators in almost all categories. But the growth-with-stability policy of Taiwan may also have paid off in comparison with the Korean policy goal of becoming 'the New Japan,' with market share of products being taken as a symbol of national strength. Taiwan's better macro-economic performance has also been matched with credible showing in terms of the quantity and quality of patents registered, notwithstanding the small scale of Taiwan's firms.
- In Taiwan, most private firms start small, and the private sector has outgrown the public sector. Beside the high tech firms, which are spin-offs of government laboratories, small firms receive no special regard from government banks, with their pawnshop mentality. Their vitality owes much to their free association with other domestic or foreign firms, unlike their Korean and Japanese counterparts, which operate in 'closed systems.'
- Taiwan's chemical and electronics industries were initially launched by government-sponsored consortia. These have either been privatized through public stock offerings or attracted private competitors with better performance. Irrespective of their eventual performance, they served useful roles in launching industries that are very successful today.
- Taiwan's industrial policy has often been criticized as desultory and hesitant, especially in comparison with that of Korea under President Park. High profile projects of acquisition were often given up. This evidence can be misleading: in industrial acquisitions, the final decision to

go ahead cannot be independent of the negotiation positions offered by one's negotiation partners.

- The Taiwanese economy is imperfect, as all opinions agree. However, given the political and historical constraints faced by the economy, it is not easy to see how much more successful it could have been. From the viewpoint of replication, its imperfection is an indication of the accessibility of its path.

QUESTIONS AND EXERCISES

1. Given the international political reality, Taiwan's policy makers can never hope for the kind of external support in a crisis that Korea received in 1997. Can this fact explain the differences in government policies between these two economies? If so, how?
2. Korean economists believe that SMEs prosper in Taiwan due to supportive government measures (Hong, 1994). Comment.
3. According to Kuo, the case-by-case policy innovations in Taiwan are policy responses to impending economic problems. Then why is it that, looking back, these policies appear to be systematically designed and to fall into a consistent package? Where does the policy consistency come from?
4. Under Taiwan's Second Stage Import Substitution, Taiwan's upstream producers of petrochemicals and steel are supposed to supply Taiwan's downstream users, provided that they can match the quality and price of imports. How does this differ from the practice in other import substitution programs, say in South America? Why does it matter whether the final goods are sold on the world market or in the home market?
5. Regarding the interrelationships between the big businesses and the SMEs in Taiwan, compare on the one hand, the views of Amsden (1991) and on the other hand, the industry studies by Chu and Li (1996) on bicycles, Fransman (1986) on machine tools, Hobday (1995) on electronics, Levy (1990) on footware, and Shieh (1992) on garments.
6. Besides Levy (1990), study further (a) the historical narrative by Cheng (2001) which traces the roots of the current Taiwanese footwear industry to the 18th century peasant females' productive activities in Taiwanese villages, and (b) the global perspective of Meyanathan and Munter (1994). With this literature as background, comment on the views of Young (1994) and Rodrik (1995) about the role of trade on East Asian growth.

Chapter 9

HONG KONG

1. INTRODUCTORY REMARKS

Hong Kong is atypical. Without either a large home market or any natural resource, it has now a real per capita income comparable to Japan's, but with better recent growth. While it is certainly true that Hong Kong's development depends on its idiosyncrasies, it is perhaps no more so than for any other developing economy. Valuable lessons may be learned from Hong Kong,[1] especially when placed in perspective – in contrast to Singapore, Macao and Mauritius, and perhaps also Taiwan and Shanghai.[2]

Consider population size. Think about the following group of twelve economies around the world: Denmark, Finland, Norway, and Ireland in Europe, Israel, Jordan and Lebanon in Asia, Costa Rica, Paraguay and Uruguay in Latin America, Libya and Liberia in Africa. Few would want to rule these twelve economies out from study. At seven million people, Hong Kong is more populous than any of these twelve.

Consider history. Among economies with a Chinese majority once under European rule, there is Macao (once Portuguese), Taiwan (once Dutch and Spanish), as well as Singapore (once British) and Shanghai (part of the

---

[1] After all, should one ignore an economy because it has performed atypically well?

[2] Or the PRC as a whole.

former international settlements), besides Hong Kong (currently part of the PRC, like Shanghai). Each has its own development trajectory.

The smallness of the home market makes tariff protection not very meaningful, but that does not stop Singapore from adopting an effective industrial policy, in contrast to Hong Kong. A hands-off (or *laissez faire*) European administration seemed to work much less well for Macao than for Hong Kong. The vibrant SME sector evolved into a Silicon Valley clone in Hsinchu, Taiwan, but not anywhere in Hong Kong. Before Pearl Harbor, the former International Settlement of Shanghai and Hong Kong were the twin anchors of British commerce in East Asia. Although both now are part of the PRC, there is still a great deal of difference between these two. As these comparisons illustrate, one might gain much insight into various development issues through a careful study of Hong Kong.

At a more aggregate level, both the rapid industrialization and precipitous de-industrialization of Hong Kong provide precious information about the two-phase nature of East Asian development: first trade expansion and then sectoral transformation. In contrast to Japan, Korea, Taiwan and Singapore where sectoral transformation took the form of industrial upgrading, with much government involvement, the Hong Kong economy was transformed by shifting massively into such service sectors like insurance and finance, away from manufacturing (thus becoming *de-industrialized*), with minimum State participation.

The fact that Hong Kong is more populous than Singapore but much less populous than the other three economies clinches the issue: in sectoral transformation, Hong Kong is the 'odd economy out' not due to its size, but as the result of its political economy. Apparently, in the political agenda of those ruling British Hong Kong, what might happen to the Hong Kong economy in the future did not matter much.[3] Thus, the effect and cause of Hong Kong's de-industrialization bring out the proper roles between the market and the government for an economy in the modern era.

Our discussion of the economy of Hong Kong follows the natural sequence. After the general observations here, we devote the next two sections to Hong Kong's industrialization and de-industrialization. Actually, both of these phases were triggered by China-related events. The sanctions against China in the Korean War left Hong Kong no choice but to industrialize; the outward reform of China induced the exodus of industries from Hong Kong to the Pearl River delta. Therefore, before offering some concluding remarks, we present some thoughts on the Hong Kong-PRC nexus.

---

[3] Quite early, Hopkins (1971) wrote about Hong Kong, "In 1997, the greater part . . . is due to be handed back to China. . . . It is highly unlikely that the remainder will be politically, or economically viable as a separate unit."

2. HONG KONG – THE HIGHLY INDUSTRIALIZED PHASE

During Crisis 1997, Hong Kong experienced some recession, but survived with *neither* an unemployment rate much higher than that of the U.S. *nor* any devaluation against the dollar. Its massive foreign reserve of US$ 90 billion remained intact. Such an achievement reflects the economic strength amassed during Hong Kong's highly industrialized phase.

The following short recapitulation helps to place matters in perspective:

A General Sketch

Some wars may appear just. Yet such wars can still be lost. Hong Kong became British when Manchu China lost the Opium War in 1842. Except for the four World War II years, it remained British until June 30 1997, when Prince Charles' royal yacht sailed into midnight's darkness. Before the Korean War, Hong Kong was an entrepôt for the China trade. Meanwhile, the British rule brought about (a) infrastructure to complement the excellent harbor (b) a stable British administrative and legal framework, well understood in world commerce and trusted locally, (c) some trade and financial institutions, including the Hong Kong-Shanghai Banking Corporation that remains today a power house in worldwide finance, and (d) a class of largely Chinese 'compradors'[4] to intermediate between the British and the Chinese community, in and outside that crown colony.

According to Phelps-Brown (1971), over long decades, industries arose in Hong Kong largely to meet local needs. When Japan occupied South China, some industries did move to Hong Kong and exported to Southeast Asia, but the scale was not significant. Two decisive events ushered in Hong Kong's industrialization in mid-20th century. The first was the 1949 victory of Communists in the Chinese Civil War. This brought to Hong Kong both half a million refugees[5] as potential labor, and Shanghai capitalists with capital, technology and enterprise.[6] Second, the 1952 U.S. and U.N. embargoes against China in the Korean War forced Hong Kong to shift from entrepôt trade to manufacturing. With their global reach, the existing merchant houses in Hong Kong placed orders with local manufacturers for goods the world market needed. Still another element in this picture is that

---

[4] That is, indigenous managers.

[5] According to Chau (1993: 1), they came from mid-1949 to mid-1954, increasing the population by 27%.

[6] According to England (1971), they also brought 'American market outlet.'

China supplied foodstuff at low and stable prices. One can depict, in Chart 9.2.1, this early appearance of the global supply chain.

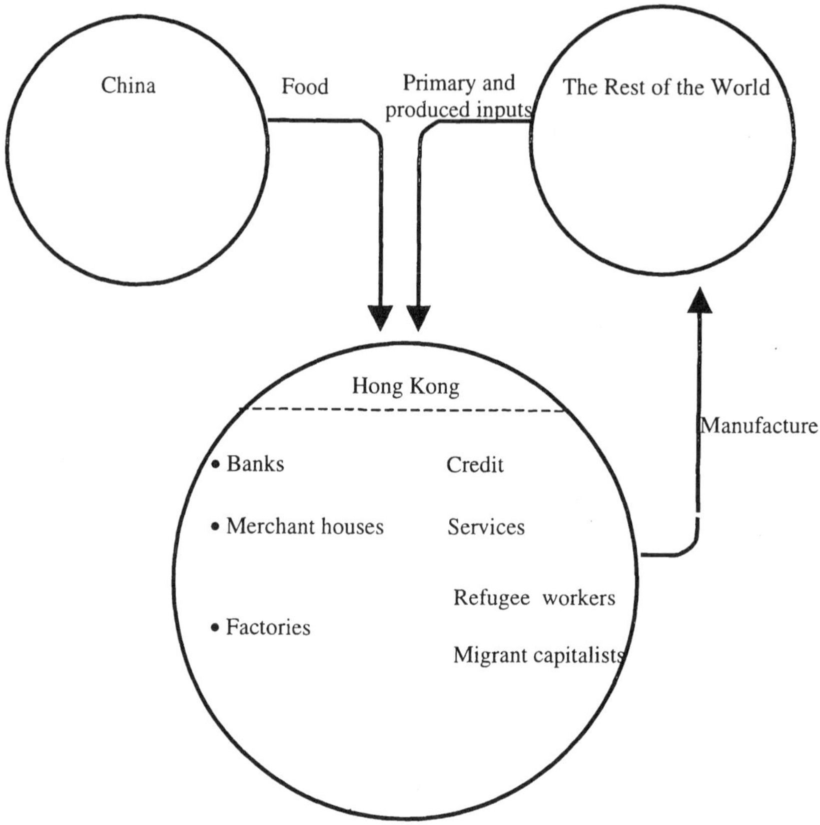

Chart 9.2.1 What Hong Kong brought to the supply chain

In 1966, 40% of the labor force was in manufacturing. During this period, 95% of the output was exported, while China took less than 1% of that. The dynamics of the economy were also remarkable. A British governor wrote, "Initially, it was the Shanghai-Chinese, with their capital and industrial know-how who were largely the salvation of Hong Kong." But eventually, the other Hong Kong residents also set up many firms.[7] Firms were small and ready to rush headlong into profitable ventures. Initially, the export houses placed orders with the manufacturers, and then overseas buyers came to deal directly with the manufacturers. It was said that some of the bigger British buyers of textiles spent considerable time, effort and money in assisting Hong Kong factories to develop their

[7] According to the careful estimate of Wong (1988), the total of Shanghai-Chinese in Hong Kong numbered around 100,000. In 1968, they hired 20% of manufacturing workers. In contrast, the Cantonese owned firms hired 54%.

productive capacity and improve quality. Initially, Shanghai businessmen introduced the textile industry to Hong Kong; the production of metal, plastics, clothing, and electronics followed. At first, foreign firms placed orders; later they set up their own branches. The SMEs ploughed back much of their profit into investment.

Economic Performance

Measures of size, efficiency, enterprise and adaptability provide some indication of the economic performance of the highly industrialized Hong Kong.

(a) quantitative importance. According to Hopkins (1971), "China gets somewhat less than half her foreign exchange from goods, mostly food, consumed by Hong Kong." According to Rear (1971: 369), "Hong Kong's reserves. . .represent something between one-quarter and one-third of Britain's gold and foreign exchange reserves."

Regarding trade, Table 9.2.1 is illustrative. It shows the percentage share of four East Asian economies in five commodity groups in U.S. imports during four selected years between 1962 and 1971 (see Wan, 1978).

%	Japan	Korea	Taiwan	Hong Kong
Textile				
1962	35.3	0.3	3.7	27.1
1965	35.3	3.8	3.8	27.4
1968	31.9	5.8	5.3	29.1
1971	21.8	12.9	10.0	28.4
Footwear				
1962	43.0	0	0	0.3
1965	32.5	2.3	0.9	0
1968	20.6	2.5	4.0	0
1971	12.5	3.5	8.7	0
Clothing Accessory, Knitwear				
1962	17.0	0	0.9	11.5
1965	14.9	1.1	1.3	23.0
1968	11.4	10.9	7.9	25.2
1971	13.2	13.5	26.4	20.8
Radio				
1962	71.2	0	0	0.3
1965	74.2	0.8	1.7	9.1
1968	67.6	0.6	5.0	10.0
1971	65.5	0.8	6.8	10.2
Telecommunications				
1962	0	0	0	0
1965	38.1	0	0	4.1
1968	34.0	0	4.7	0
1971	42.4	0	6.6	2.2

Table 9.2.1 Percentage shares in U.S. imports Source: Wan (1978)

Clearly, Hong Kong's exports were concentrated in textiles and radio. They rose to importance after Japan but before Taiwan and Korea, and their shares could be very impressive, considering the size of the Hong Kong economy.

(b) Indications of *efficiency* may be obtained for two important industries. First, with regard to the Asian loom activity in 1965, data cited by Owen (1971) shows that Hong Kong led 11 economies both in the percent of automatic looms and the number of hours worked per loom per year (Chart 9.2.2). In Hong Kong, 100% of looms were automatic, and they operated 24 hours per day and 360 days per year.

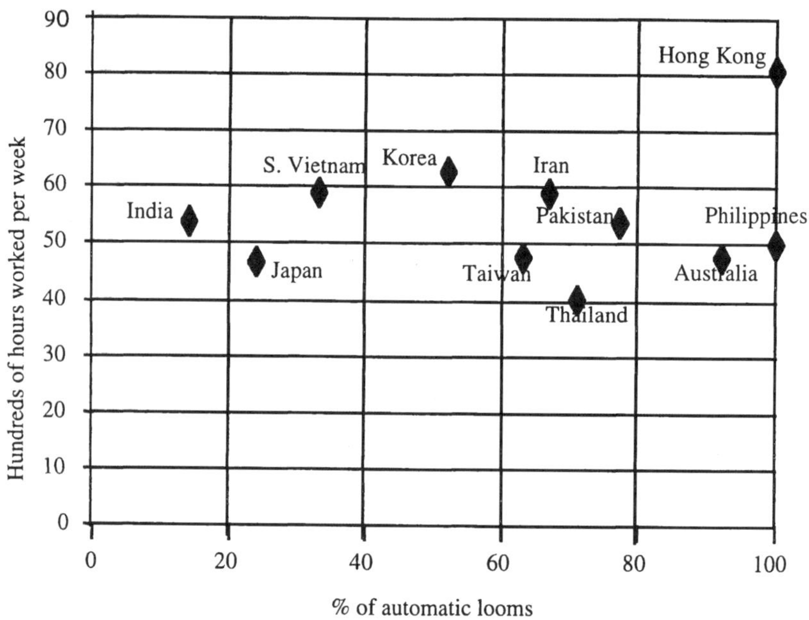

Chart 9.2.2 Asian loom activity, 1965 Source: Owen (1971)

Second, for the electronics industry, in 1973, Arthur D. Little estimated the productivity of female semiskilled workers of various Asian economies, and the result is shown in Table 9.2.2, where Hong Kong ranks with Japan at the top.

(c) *Enterprise and adaptability.* Various pieces of folklore discuss the astuteness of Hong Kong's businessmen in spotting and seizing opportunities and the resilience of Hong Kong's economy in adapting to market exigencies. First, at an individual level, Chau (1993: 26.) cited the rise of the self-made shipping magnate Y. K. Pao. Although he was unfamiliar with shipping, he took advantage of his non-Japanese identity to benefit from Japan's policies in promoting shipbuilding and export. He bought ships at Japanese shipyards cheap, used them as collateral to get mortgage loans from Japanese banks at favorable terms, and leased the ships back to Japanese shipping companies, before he started his own shipping company. After becoming a shipping tycoon, he shifted to real estate, just before the shipping glut.

Economy	Productivity rating
Japan	1
Hong Kong	1
Taiwan	.8 - 1
Korea	.7 - 1
Philippines	.8
Singapore	.7 - .8
Indonesia-Malaysia	.65 - .8
Thailand	.65 - .8

Table 9.2.2 Productivity of female electronics workers Source: Arthur D. Little

Second, at the economy-wide level, Findlay and Wellisz (1993: 21) documented how Hong Kong benefited from the meteoritic rise of the wig industry (from a single factory in 1961 to 39,000 workers in 1970), but escaped relatively unscathed during that industry's catastrophic demise due to fashion change (with only 77 employees left in 1977). Even owners of the wig-making machines found a new use for them in scaling fish.

Industrial Policy in British Hong Kong

Three questions must be pursued. First, the remarkable industrialization occurred under *what* public policy? Second, *how* did growth occur under such a policy environment? Finally, *whether* Hong Kong's lessons are relevant elsewhere? We consider these in turn.

(a) As Financial Secretary of Hong Kong, both Cowperthwaite and Haddon-Cave had written about the guiding principles of Hong Kong's public policy. (See Chau, 1993: 9-11). They maintain that *laissez faire* is best for a small, open economy like Hong Kong. Specifically, they advocate:

- No counter-cyclical policy. The effect of any public spending would be dissipated into the world market, and would hence be ineffective against recession.
- No redistributive fiscal policy, lest it weaken the work ethic.
- No subsidy in publicly provided service. Tax collection is wasteful.
- No bailout for firms that are inefficient or mistaken.
- No industry targeting. Predicting the market is futile and damaging to growth.
- The public sector must be kept small.
- Deficit financing must be avoided.

(b) Hong Kong's growth under such a policy regime is succinctly explained in Owen (1971). In the absence of government intervention, the refugee workers produced labor-intensive manufactured goods for export, with the intermediation of the merchant houses that were already in place. Three elements are important. Unlike in other developing economies, the refugees-as-workers were cut off from their rural, traditional background, and unlike in developed economies, the ease in changing jobs and in starting a small firm of one's own made the workers uninterested in management-union conflicts. The export market provided the market discipline. The manufacturing industry provided a stable outlet but also rapid fashion changes and the chance for rising quality and reward. This is the process of 'manufacturing up.'

Hong Kong's success certainly owes nothing to any (non-existing) government intervention. Nor is its progress based on the economy to scale, at the firm level. According to Chau (1993), the average size of Hong Kong firms was always small, and was getting smaller, as shown in Chart 9.2.3.

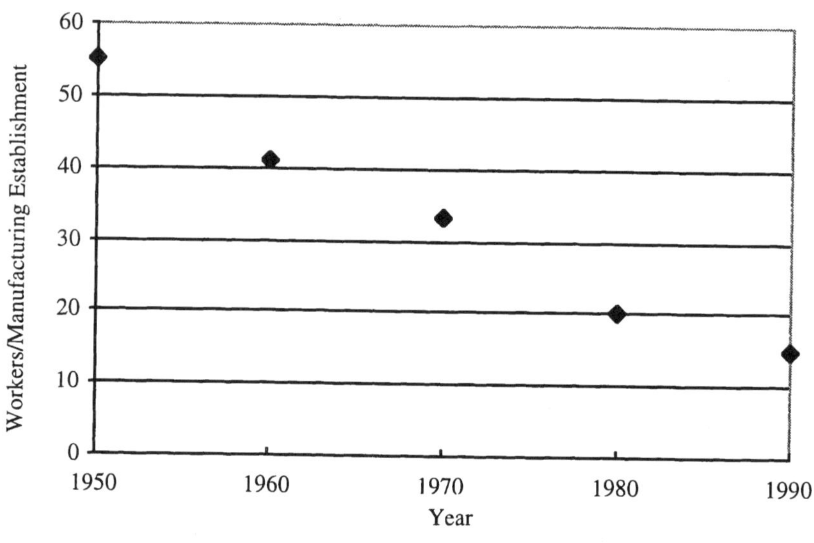

Chart 9.2.3 Employment at Hong Kong manufacturing firms Source: Chau (1993)

There remains the British Commonwealth connection to consider. The fact is, the share of the U.S. and Japanese markets in Hong Kong's domestic exports went from 8% in 1954 to 46% in 1970. It was important enough for England (1971) to regard 'American market outlet' as a strength brought to Hong Kong by the Shanghai migrant capitalists.

Manufacturing earning (hence labor cost) in Hong Kong rate was low by the standard of Japan or Singapore, but not in contrast to Korea, Taiwan or Philippines. According to the 1966 data from Phelps-Brown (1971), one can construct Chart 9.2.4.

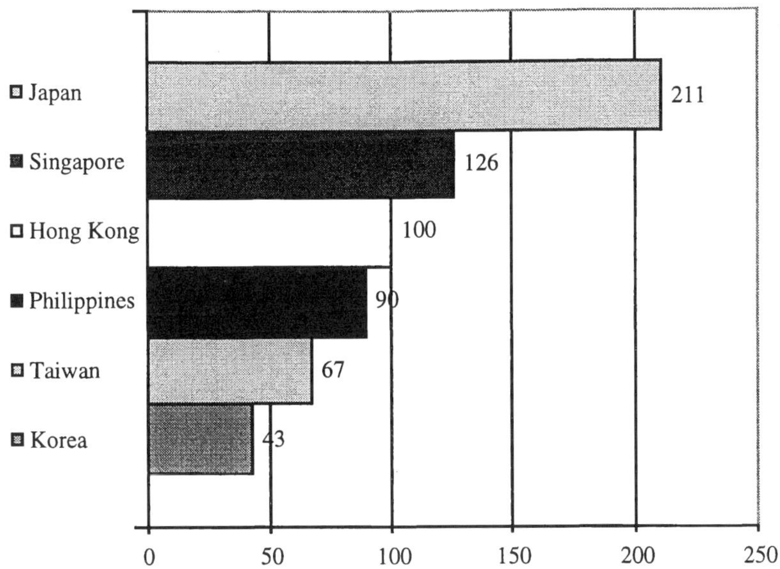

Chart 9.2.4 Manufacturing earnings in 5 Asian economies, 1966 (Hong Kong = 100)
Source: Phelps-Brown (1971)

(c) Hong Kong's lesson is relevant for evaluating Taiwan's industrialization, both in its first phase of import substitution and its outward oriented reform.

To begin with, both economies received large immigrant populations at the end of the Chinese Civil War. The migrant capitalists from Shanghai were present in Taiwan as well as Hong Kong. In fact, some business groups (like the Far East) had been active in both locations. Taiwan had an agricultural sector producing exportable sugar and rice for the world market; Hong Kong did not. Taiwan was the recipient of U.S. aid; Hong Kong was not. It might be true that importing inexpensive Chinese food was an advantage only Hong Kong enjoyed. Yet, as shown in Chart 9.2.4, manufacturing earning (according to the prevailing exchange rate) was 50% higher in Hong Kong than Taiwan. Additionally, Hong Kong practiced *laissez faire*, but Taiwan adopted import-substitution measures, and the textile industry was one sector selected for protection in Taiwan. In a nutshell, one would expect that the Taiwanese textile industry should be stronger than its counterpart in Hong Kong. Nonetheless, as Table 9.2.1 shows, as late as the 1960s, Hong Kong dominated Taiwan in total textile exports to the U.S., despite the difference in the size of labor force.

Although it may be hard to pinpoint what exactly has led to Hong Kong's superior position, some intriguing evidence is available. First, Taiwan's protectionist policy appears to be ill designed. For example, against all technical considerations, cotton was singled out to be a protected crop. Second, ultimately the vibrant SME sector was recognized as a tower of strength for the economies of both Hong Kong and Taiwan. Yet during the phase of import substitution, K. Y. Yin, the architect of Taiwan's import substitution program, was scathing about the quality of the indigenous SMEs. Third, Y. C. Shu, a well-respected industrialist for the textile sector in Mainland China, complained bitterly that the bureaucratic system of state trading (under Yin) had prevented Taiwan from exporting shirts to the U.S. and U.K., as Hong Kong did at that time. Ultimately, Taiwan's industrialization relied upon the export of labor-intensive manufacture, intermediated by foreign firms, just as Hong Kong's did. Therefore, one cannot be at all sure that the import substitution phase during the 1950s was in any sense valuable for Taiwan in the long term.[8]

Ultimately, in 1958, Taiwan's outward-oriented reform was launched because Taiwan failed in its competition against Hong Kong to attract investment from among the overseas Chinese. Consequently, efforts were made to emulate Hong Kong, so as to improve Taiwan's environment for investors. Since a wholesale adoption of Hong Kong's institutions was not feasible, the export zones were designed to be mini-Hong Kongs. The development of export zones in Mauritius was patterned after those in Taiwan, but spearheaded by businessmen from Hong Kong.[9]

3. HONG KONG – THE DE-INDUSTRIALIZING PHASE

The development of Hong Kong over the last quarter of a century is interesting for various reasons. First, it illuminates the relationship between the government and the market. The de-industrialization of Hong Kong may be viewed as a cautionary tale against the lack of a proper industrial policy. Second, in contrast to the German unification, the linked development of Hong Kong and China may be considered as a case study of successful economic integration. Finally, how Hong Kong develops in the near future may influence the successful development of the Chinese economy.

Too Little, Too Late for an Industrial Policy?

In the name of *diversification*, the Hong Kong government realized in the 1970s that the rise of wages and land rents would make the economy vulnerable to competitors in the world market, so something had to be done in response. The transformation of Hong Kong into a regional financial

[8] See Wan and Thorbecke (1999); also Thorbecke, Tung and Wan (2002).

[9] See for example, Wellisz and Shin (1993).

center was a successful step emulating Singapore, and the strengthening of technical education was a visionary measure for the long term. Other plans were also made to keep the manufacturing sector thriving, but these were overtaken by events. By late 1978, the outward reform of the PRC was launched, with special economic zones (SEZs) set up near the border with Hong Kong. Soon the exodus of manufacturing activities was on. A major portion of Hong Kong's manufacturing jobs had gone over to the Peoples' Republic.

The Chinese reform has caused great expansion of its export sector. In export operations, Hong Kong plays an essential role in facilitating such trade. For example, today, 70% of the Chinese export to the U.S. goes through Hong Kong. In addition, reform in China attracted a great deal of foreign investment, and foreign investors rely upon the expertise of people in Hong Kong for such operations. In addition, Hong Kong is a city with adequate facilities to support regional headquarters, so that the development of China created a great need for Hong Kong's service industry. As a consequence, Hong Kong's growth has continued even with the loss of manufacturing jobs. One might believe then that the planned (but never implemented) diversification of Hong Kong's economic base is superfluous after all.

However, even after 1997, both public and private circles in Hong Kong remain interested in 're-industrialization.' Their reasoning is two-fold.

First, from the viewpoint of income distribution, the lost factory jobs require relatively little education, while employment in insurance and finance needs a different type of background. The labor market in Hong Kong has always been extremely flexible. According to Phelps-Brown (1971: 4), wage cuts are not unheard of. According to England (1971. 231), until 1968, even permanent workers could be fired with 30 minutes' notice. Thus de-industrialization incurs hardship for the relatively poor, worsens the income distribution,[10] and ultimately threatens social stability.

Secondly, the manufacturing jobs in Korea, Singapore and Taiwan are associated with specialized skills in demand worldwide. The service sectors in which Hong Kong specializes are mostly China-oriented. They are in high demand today; whether they will remain so after Shanghai becomes fully ready to play a similar role, we do not know. At any rate, part of the transactions taking place in Hong Kong today relate to the relocation of the footloose industries, and the support of the relocated factories, before their local supply chains are in place. The outlook is thus uncertain.

---

[10] According to a survey by the Confederation of Trade Unions, the wealthiest people earn 20 times more than the poorest. Ten years ago, the richest earned 11 times as much (Reuters, 1 September, 2001).

The lack of industrial upgrading and the exodus of manufacturing are particularly pronounced in Hong Kong, in contrast to Singapore, Taiwan and Korea. Moreover, the outcome is not the chosen course of development for Hong Kong. It is something people in Hong Kong, in both private and public circles, tried to prevent, but in vain. Given the fact that effective remedies tend to be costly and time consuming, and the benefit has the nature of a public good, one cannot avoid the conclusion that the culprit responsible for Hong Kong's current predicament was the lack of any industrial policy during the 1970s. Given the size of the economy, one might argue that the strategy pursued by Korea and Taiwan lies out of Hong Kong's reach. Yet, as we shall see in the next chapter, with only half of Hong Kong's population, and coming at least a decade later than Hong Kong, Singapore has succeeded where Hong Kong has failed.

The Gradual Economic Re-integration of Hong Kong and the PRC

Hong Kong was part of the Guangdong Province of Manchu China. The great majority of the Hong Kong residents are speakers of Cantonese, the major dialect in Guangdong. The economic development of Guangdong and Hong Kong is the result of the Chinese policy.

At the beginning of the 1978 reform, the Chinese leadership took a cautious view about the entire process. Among the different possibilities it considered – decentralized control (as practiced in the town and village cooperatives), or private ownership, or foreign investment (as in the SEZs) – it was not sure which one or what combination of these would provide the conditions necessary or sufficient to revitalize the economy. In addition, it was not sure what reform would be compatible with the preservation of the communist system. Shanghai, the industrial magnet of China and a major source of government revenue, was held back for the moment, so that any setback would not affect unduly the foundation of the nation. To see how imperfect was the information at that time, one may note that among the four SEZs, Zhuhai was set up near Macao, just as Shenzhen was set up near Hong Kong, in order to encourage foreign investment. It turned out that Hong Kong is the only fountainhead for foreign trade and investment. Both Zhuhai and Macao itself eventually became satellites of Hong Kong, as did Shenzhen. Because of its proximity to Hong Kong, Shenzhen expanded rapidly in relation to all the other three SEZs. According to Naughton (1997: 94), it became an important bridge between Hong Kong and the Pearl River Delta of Guangdong.

Overall, the re-orientation of the Hong Kong economy toward China is remarkable. The benefit to the Chinese economy is substantial at many levels: in the stimulation of growth through a deeper division of labor, in encouraging foreign investment and in the transfer of technology and experience. The impact on the Hong Kong economy is somewhat mixed. The pace of the re-orientation bears the mark of Chinese policy-making, and the prudence and common sense shown on the part of the Chinese government should be recognized. The essence of the economic re-integration is that even after 1997, for the time being, Hong Kong keeps its monetary system, its legal framework, and its economic institutions. The movement of goods, capital, and labor are all strictly controlled. Enough firewalls are in place, not only between Hong Kong and the PRC, but also between the SEZs (like Shengzhen) of the PRC and points north. The overall process stands in sharp contrast to the traumatic economic impact of the German reunification.

Actually, the political event of the Handover in 1997 had an insignificant impact in comparison with the financial crisis that swept over East Asia, which impacted on Russia, Brazil, etc. We shall focus more on what happened before 1997, in order not to be distracted by the consequence of the financial crisis and, subsequently, the U.S. recession. In consequence, we focus attention on what happened to the economies of China and Hong Kong at the eve of 1997 and not the more turbulent years after that.

Three sets of data indicate how the economic integration proceeded. First, based on Sung et al. (1995, 9), Chart 9.3.1 shows the different per capita GDP levels (in yuan, renminbi) in 1993 for four 'nested' regions in China. Shenzhen – the Special Economic Zone (SEZ) closest to Hong Kong – grew the fastest, next comes the Pearl River Delta – a region of Guandong Province which forms the immediate hinterland of Hong Kong and includes Shenzhen, after that the entire Guangdong Province, and finally China as a whole. Next, in Chart 9.3.2, we see that, according to Sung (1997), over the period 1979-1995, Hong Kong had the lion's share of investment in China.

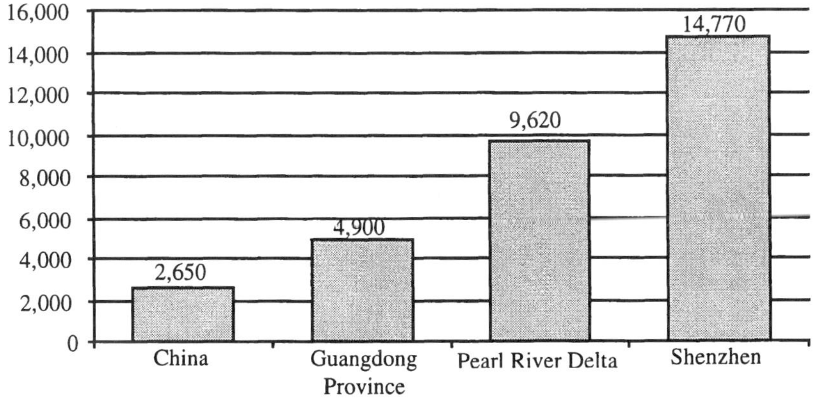

Chart 9.3.1 Hong Kong: growth pole for China: p.c GDP, 1993
Source: Sung et al. (1995)

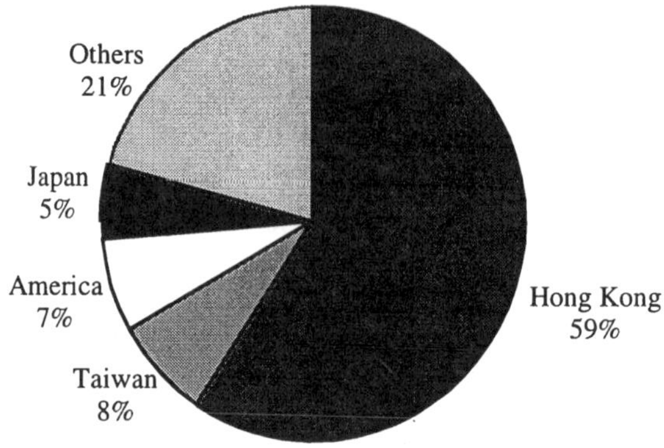

Chart 9.3.2 Cumulative investment in China, 1979–95 Source: Sung (1997)

Finally, again from Sung, in Hong Kong, manufacturing employment went from 905,000 in 1984 to 386,000 in 1995; by then, three million Chinese worked in Hong Kong-owned firms.[11] With cheaper labor available, the relocated Hong Kong firms often expanded. The headquarters, sales and design operations often stayed in Hong Kong; the supervisory personnel went to China with added responsibility. But for older and less educated workers in Hong Kong, it is now harder to find a job once they become unemployed. So income inequality worsens.

The fact is, a well thought-out program, coordinated between Hong Kong and Mainland Chinese authorities, and carried out for the long haul, may provide a win-win solution. This will be discussed below.

The Long View

At present, international trade is essential to the Chinese economy for three reasons. First, the export sector provides precious foreign exchange that is needed for purchasing machinery and equipment that cannot be produced at home. Second, through interactions with the outside world, China can acquire technology and information in a relatively inexpensive manner. Finally, the export sector creates jobs for a country facing serious challenges regarding employment. The key issue is, in what way Hong Kong can help.

For China today, the per capita real and nominal incomes are about U.S. $3,000 and U.S. $750. This means on the average, Chinese products are sold at only 1/4 of their value. Since much of the Chinese exports are sold in the U.S., the above fact might be regarded to be the result of cultural differences. Yet, the situation for Japan suggests this explanation is false. In

[11] By now, the numbers are respectively, 200,000 and eleven million.

real per capita income, the Japanese have always been poorer than the Americans. Yet, in nominal income, the Japanese have been richer than the Americans for quite some time. In the case of Hong Kong, the nominal income and the real income are not far from each other. Thus, the critical question is whether the exports of an economy can win acceptance in the foreign market. To date, the Japanese can and the Chinese cannot.

Among all economies with a Chinese majority, Hong Kong's indigenous entrepreneurs are the most cosmopolitan, bar none. In principle, the economic integration between China and Hong Kong may lend China the help it needs most: intermediation by Hong Kong businessmen. However, some more discussion is needed.

First, Japanese firms are strong in market research. They design new products meeting consumers' desires. Examples include the Walkman and Nintendo. Taiwanese firms improve parts to suit better the needs of producers. An example is the motherboard for personal computers. Korean firms have both these two types of capabilities. Samsung electronics is a good example. The high margin of value added represents innovative rent. In comparison, where Hong Kong has excelled is mainly in making sure that overseas orders are fulfilled to their clients' satisfaction, by identifying and managing reliable and inexpensive sources for the supply chain. Casual empirical investigation suggests that the Japanese or Taiwanese approach may be more rewarding in the long term than the approach favored in Hong Kong, because there seems to be more valuable human capital formation. Moreover, the available skill and talents in Hong Kong suggest that given the opportunities, the Japanese approach can be adopted by the China-Hong Kong coalition.

Second, the re-integration of Hong Kong into the Chinese fold also opens the door to a different line of development. Hong Kong businesses formerly enjoyed two types of comparative advantage: intermediating the China trade and managing the hospitality industries, such as hotels, restaurants, tourism, and various leisure-related activities. The first line of activities is likely to encounter the competition from Shanghai, while the second is an area where Hong Kong enjoys tremendous advantage, due to experience, connections and reputation. Yet, the second line is likely to turn Hong Kong inward, reducing its long-term value to China, as a whole. After all, until China is farther along in acquiring modern technology, export-related skills such as product design and market research are far more important than international tourism.

4. FINAL REMARKS

Under the British rule, the economy of Hong Kong had several special features worth mentioning. Most of these features are still in force after the 1997 Handover. First, all land is owned by the government. Public land was used to construct public housing for refugees in early years. Furthermore, the selling of the users' right was a significant source of government revenue. Second, labor is the mainstay of the economy. It could also pose a serious challenge, as when the unemployment rate was at its peak of 15% during 1954. When light industries absorbed the labor surplus, wages began to rise. Since the jobs Hong Kong offered were better-paid than those in China, the government exercised some control over the size of the population, and hence the labor force, by varying its aggressiveness in prosecuting illegal immigrants. Third, Hong Kong's monetary system is quite unique. Under the institution of the 'currency board,' each Hong Kong dollar is backed with 100% reserve in foreign currency. This means the government refrains from the use of monetary policy for macro-economic stabilization. However, this did not prevent the currency being raided by speculators during Crisis 1997. Finally, in emulating Singapore, the Independent Commission for Anti-Corruption has achieved remarkable success in improving the investment and operational environment.

In retrospect, British Hong Kong appears to be highly efficient. The source of efficiency seems to be three-fold. First, over all, with a 'small government,' partly supported by revenues from land sales, Hong Kong avoided much of the costly and often corrupting process of tax collection. Second, as a freewheeling society in a dynamic world economy, market discipline preserved social mobility and, hence, the selection by fitness. Over the half-century after World War II, the British merchant houses lost their dominance over Chinese wealth.[12] The early prominence of the migrant capitalists from Shanghai became diluted by tycoons originating from Canton or Swatow. Third, any government taking relatively few initiatives has less opportunity to commit major errors due to incompetence.

However, the last point may be a mixed blessing. One might argue that such efficiency is more apparent than real. Alternatively, such efficiency may prove to have been merely static, disappearing when examined within a longer time frame. The eventual pace of de-industrialization suggests that, relative to the other NIEs, Hong Kong was deficient in human capital formation with regard to industrial technology. Such errors of omission may be just as serious as errors of commission. On the other hand, it is not a surprise that, perceiving accurately the imminent end of the British rule,

---

[12] The dramatic change came between 1976 and 1986, according to Lever-Tracy, Ip and Tracy (1996: 26).

those in power in British Hong Kong did not take timely measures against de-industrialization.

In the final analysis, public policy is undertaken by those in power. Those in power care less for matters unrelated to the continuation of their power. Since government failure is inherently possible, public policy is by no means a panacea against market failure.

APPENDIX 9.1 THE ROLES OF HONG KONG: ENTREPÔT, CENTRAL PLACE, AND INTERMEDIARY

In the 1950s, Hong Kong emerged successfully from an economy based upon entrepôt activities, into a major exporter of manufacture. Facts in Chart 9.2.1 make it clear that this metamorphosis did not happen in a vacuum. With its former role as the pre-eminent entrepôt on the South China Coast, Hong Kong had the banks and the merchant houses to lend a helping hand to the migrant capitalists from Shanghai and the refugee workers from Guangdong. They financed the industrial expansion and marketed the output through their worldwide business connections. Several questions suggest themselves.

First, without its past history, could Hong Kong have ever entered the market for light industries? This point is very important. If the answer is 'definitely not', then Hong Kong's success is not replicable. Thus, to development economists in general, Hong Kong's fine record would be welcome, but not very interesting. However, subsequent events suggest that Hong Kong's past history should not be overemphasized. Those same export markets of Hong Kong in the 1950s were later entered by Taiwan, Mauritius, as well as Shenzhen – right across the border. None of these has ever been an entrepôt. What difference Hong Kong's past history makes seems to be the pace at which the inmates of the UN – supported refugee camps were absorbed into the labor force of Hong Kong.

Second, in its own right, the economics of entrepôt is interesting. One must ask what is the economic cause for an entrepôt? After all, besides Hong Kong, Singapore also earns an important portion of its revenue from such a role. To some extent, today Shanghai and Malaysia are contesting Hong Kong and Singapore, respectively, in their niches. For illustration, we examine the following.

Example.

Six ports on the two shores of an ocean are engaged in the trade of a particular commodity. On one side, sources A, B, and C each supplies 1 unit of the good; on the opposite side, markets X, Y and Z each requires 1 unit. The shortest ocean crossing from A to X (or B to Y, C to Z) covers 12 units of distance; any two adjacent ports on the same shore are 1 unit of distance apart. The modal choice of transportation is between shipping by container carrier and by tugboat, with carrying capacities of 3 and 1 units, respectively. The cost for each vessel to cover 1 unit of distance is 12 for the container carrier and 5 for the tugboat.

In general, efficient solutions of such problems are solved by combinatorial optimization, in particular, integer programming.[13] In this example, the plan for the transport cost minimization is described by both (1) a 'matching solution' that assigns which source to which market, forming three ordered pairs of source and market, and (2) a 'shipping plan' that specifies for each source and market pair a connecting route (that is a 'supply chain', made of ports and links in between), as well as the mode of shipping for every link of each route.

Chart A9.1.1 displays the ports on the map and the solution for cost minimization. Tables A9.1.1 and A9.1.2 provide the details.

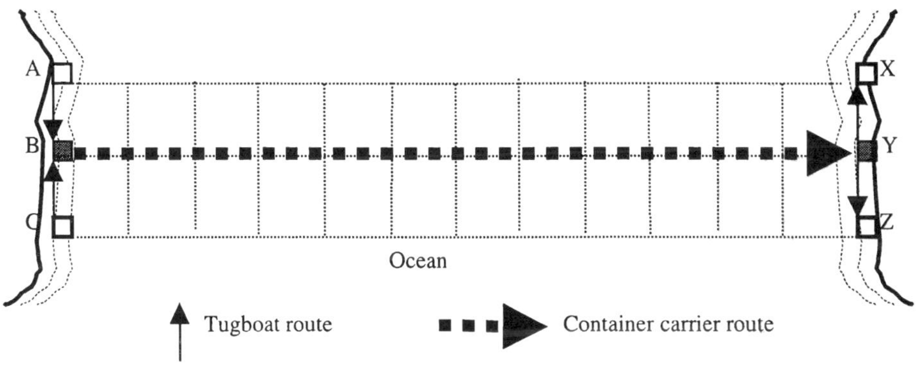

Chart A9.1.1 The economics of entrepôts

		Market		
		X	Y	Z
Source	A	1		
	B		1	
	C			1

Table A9.1.1 Assignment for total transportation cost minimization

Source – market pair	Routing	Cost
A-X	Tugboat-Container carrier- Tugboat	2(5) + 48 = 58
B-Y	Container carrier	48
C-Z	Tugboat-Container carrier- Tugboat	2(5) + 48 = 58

Table A9.1.2 Shipping plan for total transportation cost minimization

Here, the A-X (C-Z) pair uses the supply route of A-B-Y-X (C-B-Y-Z). Note in this example:

- A container carrier will only be used to carry goods from all three sources to all three markets. This is because for each unit of distance traveled, the

[13] An expository discussion may be found in Baumol (1965).

unit cost by container carrier is 12/n when n units of good are shipped. Set n equals 1, 2 and 3, and we have:

$$12/1 = 12 > 12/2 = 6 > 5 > 4 = 12/3$$

(5 being the unit cost by tugboat)

Thus any coastal link must use tugboat.

- The container carrier will be used for cross-ocean traffic if it provides the minimum cost for all three source – market pairs. Thus, if the distance between adjacent ports on each ocean shore is $q > 1.2$, then there is no gain for goods to be shipped in any supply chain which includes both a cross ocean link by container carrier (where the minimum cost is 48) and two or more coastal link by tugboat where the minimum cost is $(2)(1.2)(5) = 12$). Otherwise the cost over the chain exceeds 6o, the cost of crossing the ocean by tugboat. Because the requirement of the assignment problem (one source for one market, no more and no less), a chain with one container carrier link and a single tugboat link makes no sense. Therefore, the container carrier offers no benefit.
- Over the entire cross-ocean stretch, the use of the container carrier, instead of the tugboat, generates at most a saving of $12 (5 - 4) = 12$. This means in using the container carrier, the entire route cannot include more than two coastal links using tugboat shipping of 1 unit distance each.
- Thus, only ports B and Y, by their central-place location, can become entrepôts.
- The status of entrepôts confers cost advantages to B and Y in that the supply pair from B to Y requires no coastal link.
- When ports operate under decentralized control, the savings from the use of container carrier and the status of entrepôts depend on the coordination of all six adjacent ports, which might give rise to bargaining and side payments.
- The presence of additional ports (say, 4 on each shore) would complicate the situation. Which ports can have access to the efficient 'entrepôt' system and which ports qualify as entrepôts become contestable.
- In an intertemporal framework, the sunk cost in infrastructure, or network advantages tend to perpetuate the entrepôt status of the incumbents, making the development process 'path dependent.'

So far we have abstracted from the fact that shipping cost depends upon whether the vessels are loaded on round trip basis. This has been explored in Hadley and Kemp (1966).

Third, the cost advantages of an entrepôt may make such locations into 'central places' that offer a wider range of services than its neighbors. This is illustrated in Chart A9.1.2. One example is the service of the 'insurance adjuster' who decides which insurance company for what ship should pay how much compensation to whom, when two ships collide on the high sea. Historically, over a large part of the Asia-Pacific region, this type of highly specialized expertise is provided by a single person with an office in Hong Kong. In turn, the better access to various professional services becomes an attraction to multinational corporations as sites for regional headquarters.

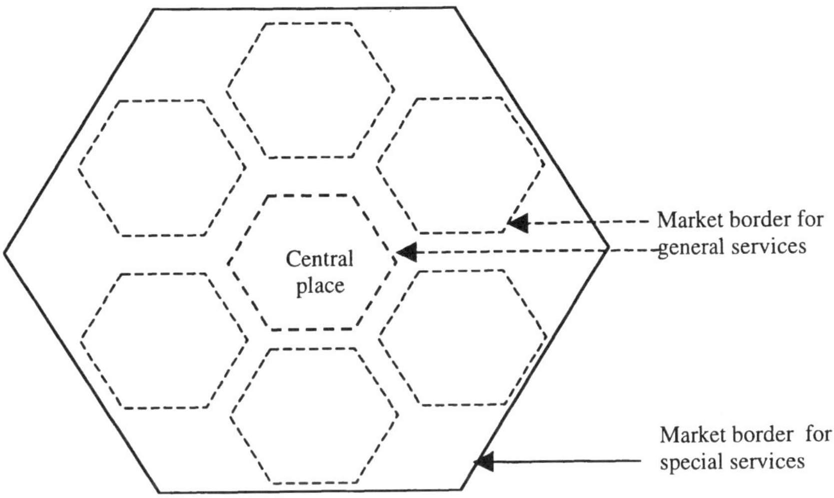

Chart A9.1.2 A hierarchy of locations

Clearly, this advantageous position of an entrenched entrepôt explains at least in part the observed income differentials between an entrepôt and its neighbors. The incentives for the latter to 'join the game' and the former to forestall it are understandable.

Finally, perhaps one of the most important services for the entrepôt location is that the emergence of 'intermediating activities' at such a location, due to information asymmetry. This has been discussed in detail in Wan and Weisman (1999), regarding the future of Hong Kong. In that discussion, there are three locations: the source (PRC), the intermediary (Hong Kong) and the market (America). Product quality is the result of costly action chosen by agents at the source, hidden from agents at the market, but not to the intermediary. Under competitive environment, the latter can offer their (imperfect) truth-revealing services for a fee, allowing agents in the market to enjoy product of higher quality and agents at the source to earn higher rewards by investing in quality-improving activities. This ideal situation can be perturbed if agents at the market are led to believe that some institutional change has allowed the intermediaries to be 'co-opted', so that the 'co-opted' intermediaries would make their service deliberately even less perfect than before, at the consideration of some side-payment.

CHAPTER SUMMARY

- Hong Kong is atypical in a number of ways. However, every country is unique, and Hong Kong offers lessons to learn – both in spite of and because of its distinctive situation.
- Among Japan and the four NIEs, Hong Kong is the second smallest in population and the only one with no industrial policy. Like the other four, Hong Kong industrialized; unlike the others, Hong Kong subsequently de-industrialized. Among the five, Singapore is the least populous but has not de-industrialized to date. This suggests that industrial policy is crucial for keeping industries, but not for attracting them.
- The end of Chinese Civil War brought Hong Kong half a million refugees as well as 100,000 migrants from Shanghai, who brought with them capital, textile equipment, and U.S. connections. Under the U.N. embargo of the PRC, Hong Kong industrialized with refugee labor, migrant capital and technology and orders by local merchants from the entrepôt trade. Textile export boomed.
- With Hong Kong being industrialized, U.S. firms came to procure electric and electronics products, etc. SMEs blossomed, increasing the resilience of the economy.
- Later, East Asian prosperity induced the government to attract foreign capital with tax law revision and make Hong Kong a regional financial center.
- Realizing that their rule probably would end in 1997, the British government of Hong Kong made little attempt to upgrade industry, beside taking some education initiatives. Although in the 1950s, the *laissez faire* regime of British Hong Kong was far more efficient than the interventionist Taiwan, by 1970s and 1980s, Taiwan had gained a better industrial structure, even though SMEs played important role in both economies.
- Once the PRC launched its economic reform in 1978, Hong Kong industries started to migrate to Special Economic Zones across the border to reduce production costs. Half a million manufacturing jobs were eliminated in Hong Kong, but the Hong Kong-managed firms recruited several million new workers in the Pearl River Delta in the PRC proper.
- With de-industrialization, Hong Kong faces rising unemployment and increased income inequality.

QUESTIONS AND EXERCISES

1. In the theory of international trade, factor price equalization is a trend among economies sharing the same technology. Both Hong Kong and part of the PRC across the border have produced textiles for export. Explain why is it that (a) there was no sign of wage convergence before 1978, (b) Hong Kong faced little competitive pressure in the 1980s, and (c) currently an exodus of industry poses a serious threat to Hong Kong employment. Also, (d) does trade play any role in the transition from (b) to (c)?

2. Compare the situation facing Korea, Taiwan and Hong Kong, with the accession of the PRC to the World Trade Organization. What is the common trend, and what explains the differences?

3. In Taiwan, there has been some opposition to allowing electronics firms to invest in the PRC, but no one has made such argument for the textile industry. Can you explain these differences in terms of the role of Hong Kong within the mutual interaction of these three economies?

4. Historically, industries in different economies have acquired technology by different channels, for example:
   (a) The textile and railroad industries in 18th century America benefited from migrant technicians from the culturally related society of Britain (Jeremy and Stapleton, 1991).
   (b) The electric equipment industry of late 19th century Japan benefited from the directed foreign investment in joint venture from America (Uchida, 1991).
   (c) The footwear industry of the middle 20th century Taiwan benefited from producing for export on subcontracts from Japan and America (Cheng, 2001).

   Describe the sources of technology of the textile industry in Hong Kong around the 1950s, in analogy to (a), (b) and (c).

Chapter 10

SINGAPORE

1. INTRODUCTION

We studied Korea, Taiwan and Hong Kong in the last three chapters. The principal purpose was to compare their record, seeking common themes, and looking for such differences among them that illuminate the catching up process. For example, Taiwan has achieved a growth record comparable to Korea in pace but more stable in profile, with no foreign debt but vibrant SMEs. Hong Kong industrialized under *laissez faire*, without starting with an import-substituting regime as Korea and Taiwan did. Both Hong Kong and Taiwan have indigenous SMEs free to operate with any domestic or foreign firms, while the basic premise of the Korean development strategy is that the State must nurture giant business groups to compete in the world market. We now study Singapore in the same spirit.

Like the other three NIEs, Singapore (a) has a majority population with Confucian ethos, (b) relies on education to compensate for its scarcity of natural resources, (c) has a colonial past, (d) enjoys sustained rapid growth, low inflation, and low unemployment, and (e) participates actively in international trade.

Singapore's distinct features become evident in a three-fold comparison. First, compared with Hong Kong, Singapore enjoys higher per capita GDP, and retains more manufacturing jobs, at the cost of an authoritarian society and the shortage of vibrant, indigenous entrepreneurs in the private sector. Second, compared with Taiwan, Singapore has both a higher living standard and a more cosmopolitan society, but it lacks a dense network of high tech SMEs. Finally, compared with Korea, Singapore industrialized without incurring foreign debt, albeit with a heavy reliance on multinational corporations (MNCs).

Singapore's present is influenced by its past. In turn, its history is shaped by its location. As the choke point facing two busy sea-lanes – north to China and west to the Indian Ocean – it combines a deep harbor for mooring with a well-watered island for defense. To Prince Paramesvara (or Sir Raffles), it was literally a position to kill (or to cheat) for.[1]

The initial conditions of Singapore in 1965 reflected the events in the previous 150 years in its neighborhood. According to Andaya and Andaya (1982), two events had a series of consequences.[2] First, European steam gunboats and cargo ships supplanted indigenous privateers and shipping, and as a result Malay exports shifted from herbs, spices and bird nests destined for the Chinese wealthy, to tin, rubber, and oil palm shipped to the entire world. Second, Chinese rural uprisings loosened Manchu prohibitions against emigration and forced peasants to accept the life of bonded workers abroad. The Malay leaders then recruited Chinese labor to supply products for European demand, and often took loans from Chinese merchants, who intermediated between Malays, Chinese and Europeans. Chinese merchants maintained cross-country links and Chinese labor came with organized secret societies for mutual assistance. Chinese secret societies were hired in Malay conflicts, and the increased violence brought British intervention to protect the commerce that yielded huge profit.

When technical progress displaced the Chinese from tin mining to commerce, they in turn displaced Malays from industry and commerce to the subsistence farm. Rural Malays could perceive little immediate gain from education, while migrant Chinese regarded schooling as the only means of escape from privation in a strange land. It was the Chinese and Indians that prospered under European influence among the rising cities and amid the emerging wealth. After World War II, in the combined area of Singapore and Malaysia, immigrants with more education and wealth outnumbered the Malays in their own homeland.

Singapore became British in 1817. Soon it emerged as the entrepôt for all Southeast Asia, eclipsing other contenders. Within ten years, immigrants from China and India outnumbered its Malay population, while the whole of Malaya had slipped under British 'direct' and 'indirect' rule,[3] providing the

---

[1] An interested reader may consult Andaya and Andaya (1982).

[2] For a somewhat different description of such events, see Mahathir (1970).

[3] Formerly the Portuguese and the Dutch only controlled the Melaka port (the successor of ancient Srivijaya), and the Thais demanded homage and tribute.

British huge profits from the tin mines as well as the rubber and oil palm plantations, with immigrant labor from China and India. As the seat of the governor of the Strait Settlements, Singapore became the core of the entire modern Malay economy, with a Chinese majority, and under British dominance.

The eventual Malay-Chinese rivalry was sharpened by the founding of the communist PRC, a billion-person nation that supported the insurgent Malayan Communist Party, as well as the rise of Malay nationalism, which insisted on Malay privileges and emphasized Islamic consciousness.

To counter the common challenges of the Malayan Communist Party and the confrontation of Sukarno from Indonesia, Singapore joined Malaya at independence. To preserve the Malay character of peninsular Malaya, two North Borneo states were included and Singapore was expelled, and the present political map of Malaysia emerged by 1965.[4]

Inter-communal violence precipitated the political separation. Yet even after separation, both Malaysia and Singapore still had a significant minority that was the majority across the border. Internal conflict in one (as in 1969) would destabilize the other. Thus, Singapore in 1965 faced the threat of becoming a Hong Kong in 1950 – an island economy with no resource base and a former entrepôt cut off from its natural hinterland.

In the next two sections, we shall review how Singapore survived by seeking high employment, and then thrived through industry upgrading. Final comments follow.

2. SURVIVAL THROUGH INDUSTRIALIZATION

In 1965, a three-fold challenge faced Singapore. First, before separation, Singapore hoped to become the industrial center for the federated Malaysia, behind a common tariff wall. Such hope was now dashed. Second, historically, Malaysia relied on Singapore both as the export outlet and the connection between its East and West Coasts. After separation, Malaysia planned to reroute trade at the expense of Singapore in the interest of its own economic autonomy. Finally, the British withdrawal from its base at Singapore was expected to affect 20% of the Singaporean GDP and cause a loss of 70,000 well-paid jobs.[5] In 1961, a United Nations report found that wage was 20% to 30% too high in Singapore, while 400,000 labor hours were lost in work stoppages. By 1966, Singapore had 8.9% of unemployment. The prospect seemed grim and social stability was at stake.

---

[4] See, for example, Lee (1998: 618). In 1965 he listed from census the population mix of Malaysia and Singapore as: Malays 39%; Chinese 42%; Indians/Pakistanis 10%; North Borneo people 7%; others 2%. At most, the 46% Bumiputras was a plurality, but no majority.

[5] See Lee (2000: 69).

A comparison with the other NIEs, in Table 10.2.1, is illustrative.

Values for 1965	Population	'Openness'*	p. c. Real GDP (chain index)
Korea	28530	24.23	1754
Taiwan	12928	41.66	2009
Singapore	1698	269.04	3506
Hong Kong	3692	143.72	5047

*(Import + Export)/GDP

Table 10.2.1 Initial conditions Source: Penn Table 6.0

Korea (also Taiwan), with its large domestic market and its initially low living standard, could nurture local firms with protection until they grew experienced. With 7% of the Korean population and an 80% higher initial per capita income, Singapore had no such luxury. But the success of Hong Kong suggested that openness might help, by drawing on the best performing businesses in the world to employ its workers. The smallness of the economy offered chances for micro-management to facilitate that process.

In the event, once the public was convinced about the seriousness of the outlook, the ruling Peoples' Action Party (PAP) implemented far-reaching policy measures and improvised with pragmatism. Jobs were created through industrialization beyond the traditional entrepôt trade. According to Lee (2000):

- Import substitution industries were launched under protective tariff and quota, but abandoned, one by one, when they turned nonviable. These included shipbuilding, automobile assembly and various assembly operations for consumer electronics.
- Potential investors were attracted with tax holidays, a neat environment, practical programs for training industrial skill, and an absence of either corruption or an 'anti-colonialism' ideological baggage.
- Persistent efforts were made to promote investments from developed economies, on account of their better record of success in investment.
- Massive investment was made in infrastructure (including industrial parks), financed out of the compulsory savings through the contributions to workers' pension fund.
- Labor legislation and tripartite wage negotiation were implemented to prevent strikes and moderate wage changes.

Co-investment by the Singaporean Economic Development Board (EDB) made deals more attractive to the desirable multinational firms. One hundred percent foreign ownership is allowed if that is investors' wish.[6]

---

[6] This is a favor that Korea and Taiwan rarely grant.

Subsequent to these efforts, U.S. investment in electronics finally mopped up Singaporean unemployment around 1980. The following discussion provides some insight into this job-creation process.

Using data from Huff (1994: 323), Chart 10.2.1 shows manufacturing jobs increased rapidly from 1967 to 1973, then to 1980.

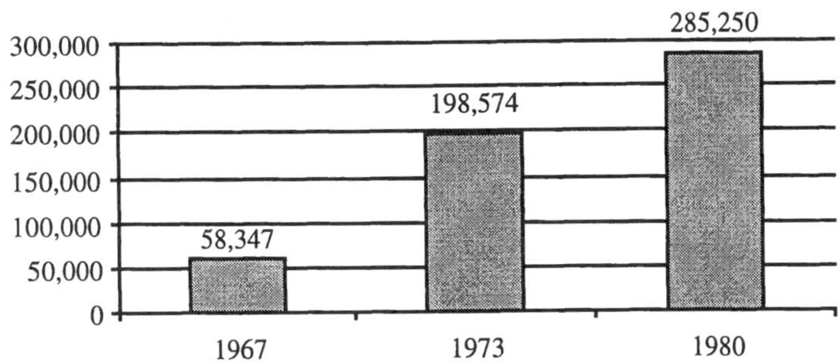

Chart 10.2.1 Manufacturing jobs Source: Huff (1994)

Moreover, Chart 10.2.2 indicates that within the manufacturing sector, the two categories of textiles and garments and electric machines and products doubled their joint weights to 40%. The latter increased especially fast.

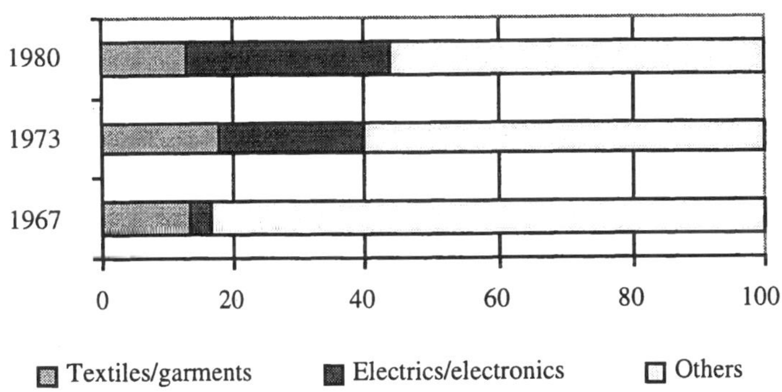

Chart 10.2.2 Manufacturing job-mix Source: Huff (1994)

According to Huff (1994), four factors may explain Singapore's success with U.S. investors in electronics. First, in 1969, Singaporean workers were paid about as low as in any Asian economy and their wages amounted to less than 10% of what their American counterparts received, even though they were about equally efficient. Second, under the new laws, there was almost no work stoppage after 1967. Third, with English being the official language, Singaporean workers could interact with Americans. Finally, the government officials in Singapore were known to be very efficient. According to Lee (2000) and Huff (1994), in 1968, Texas Instruments was the first to go to Singapore, supposedly unhappy with the red tape in

Taiwan, and their factory started operations within 50 days after the investment decision. Soon their competitor, Hewlett-Packard, came, and also enjoyed special treatment.

Because the EDB co-invested in various projects with direct foreign investment, one naturally wonders to what extent the EDB was undertaking industry targeting, and to what extent it was performing the function of investment banks and venture capitalists. According to Lee (2000: 85), "We left most of the picking the winner to the MNCs." The options, however, were rather limited, and included ship repairing, oil refining, petrochemicals, and banking and finance. Each of these is based upon the special geographic advantage Singapore enjoys, namely a world-class harbor on the primary sea-lane for oil tankers and a location between San Francisco and Zurich for 24-hour service in banking.

Policy making in Singapore is based on improvisation. Goh Keng Swee, the architect of the economic policy in this period, mentioned that the First Economic Plan was cooked up during a long weekend to satisfy the World Bank.[7] Therefore, to understand the industrial policy of Singapore, one must seek out guiding principles beyond the published plans.

According to an October 1978 speech of Lee Kuan Yew, Prime Minister of Singapore over that period,[8] the rates of failure in the export business over the period 1960-1978 are as follows:

U.S., European and Japanese firms	6%
Singaporeans joined with the above	7
Singaporeans joined with partners from Hong Kong and Taiwan	17
Singaporeans alone	38

Recently, Lee (2000: 85-6) defended Singapore's choice of relying on investors from the advanced economies, "Had we waited for our traders to learn to be industrialists we would have starved. It is absurd for critics to suggest in the 1990s that had we grown our own entrepreneurs we would have been less at the mercy of the rootless MNCs."[9]

In short, the main concern of Singapore over that period was to create jobs by attracting reliable foreign investors. From that perspective, the policy was a success in the immediate run.

Additionally, after the fall of Sukarno, Indonesian trade resumed. Malaysia reduced its reliance on Singapore, but as long as the entrepôt

---

7 See Lim, Pang and Findlay (1993: 102).

8 From Chia (1986: 102)

9 In his 1978 speech, Lee regarded indigenous merchants as too cautious toward industrial venture to create enough jobs, when the unemployment rate was at 10% in those years. For perspective, David Bonavia suggested (*Far Eastern Economic Review*, 1967: 38) that for the beleaguered, independent Singapore, "the only sensible answer is a fresh accommodation with Malaysia."

service of Singapore is economically advantageous (thanks to massive Singaporean investment), no client can afford to sacrifice the competitive advantage of exporting to the world market by the cheapest means. Thus Singapore remains a top supplier of rubber and palm oil. Moreover, the cluster of oil refining, petrochemical and oil rig industries has become an important extension of Singapore's entrepôt trade for petroleum.

Yet none of these development guarantees the long-term prosperity of the economy. To become 'fully developed' like Japan or the Netherlands remains the unrealized goal.

3. TO THRIVE THROUGH RESTRUCTURING

After achieving full employment in the 1970s, labor shortage spurred Singapore to continuously upgrade its economic structure. This process has secured obvious achievements, but also generated criticisms and controversies. In this section we sketch some highlights of the achievements and outline the major shortcomings suggested by the detractors. Our own assessment is offered in the next section.

Indications of Achievements

In terms of the level of real GDP per capita, Singapore's progress is beyond dispute. By the end of the twentieth century, Singapore had overtaken Japan as well as most of the advanced European economies. To avoid the turbulent record that affects all Asian economies after Crisis 1997, we focus on 1996 data released by the World Bank (1998), in Chart 10.3.1

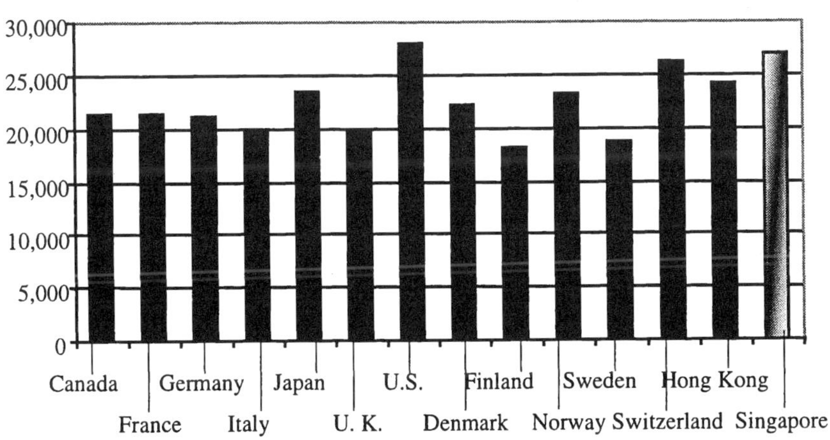

Chart 10.3.1 Real per capita GDP Source: World Bank (1998)

Significantly, this achievement was accompanied by a total re-orientation of trade. This becomes clear from the data in the Yearbook of Statistics, Singapore, various years, and shown in Chart 10.3.2 and Chart 10.3.3. It represents the success of the first part of Lee Kuan-Yew's two-prong strategy (Lee, 2000: 75): *"to leapfrog the region"* (or ASEAN). Between 1965 and 1993, the percentage shares of Singapore's exports and imports expanded dramatically with the developed world of the U.S., Europe

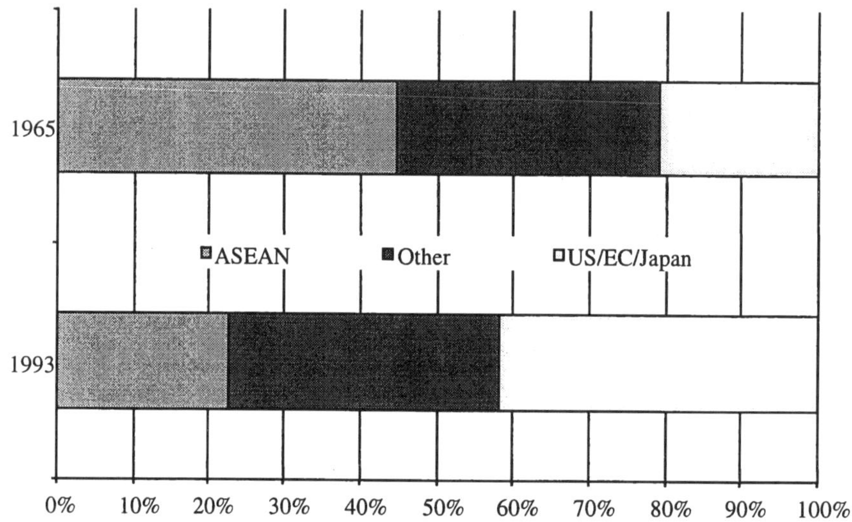

Chart 10.3.2 Percent share of Singaporean export
Source: Yearbook of Statistics, various years

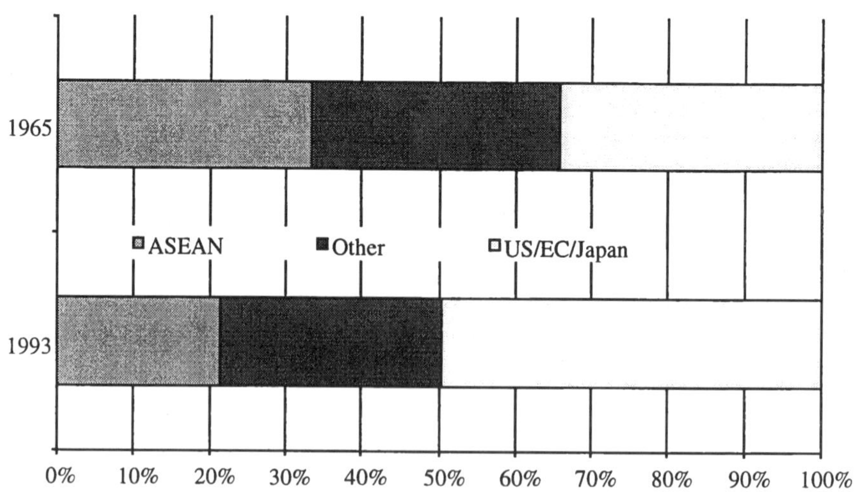

Chart 10.3.3 Percent share of Singaporean import
Source: Yearbook of Statistics, various years

and Japan, but shrunk with the areas directly adjacent to itself. By creating niches for itself within the trading patterns of the developed economies, the real GDP per capita of Singapore has converged toward the developed world at a fast clip. Politically speaking, by now, no one can fairly claim that Singapore is living off the resources of its neighbors by serving as a middleman.

But actually, much more is there than meets the eye. The content of trade between Singapore and its neighbors has also changed. The percentage composition of the Singapore-Malaysia trade has transformed dramatically as well. Using data from Huff (1994: 314-5), we can obtain Chart 10.3.4 and Chart 10.3.5.

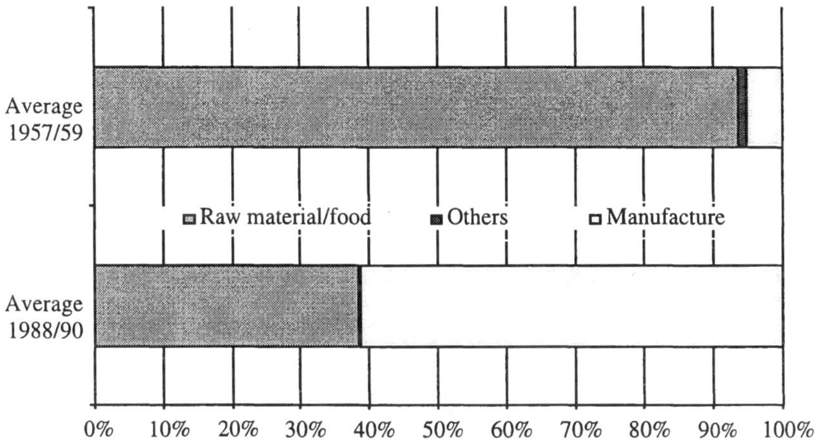

Chart 10.3.4 Percent of trade, Malaysia to Singapore

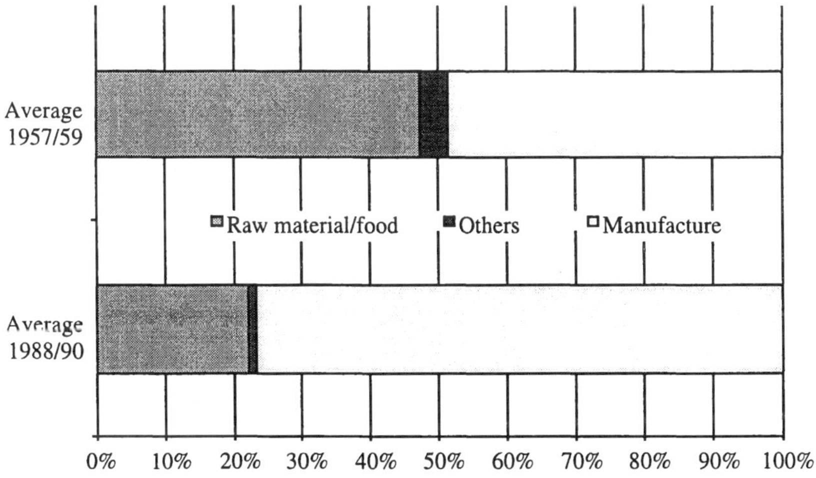

Chart 10.3.5 Percent of trade, Singapore to Malaysia

What these charts reveal is that by 1993, Singapore and Malaysia were mainly joined together in their manufacturing trade, outdistancing their erstwhile entrepôt relationship. The previous entrepôt relationship was resource-based, and the owners of resources would naturally hope to bypass the middleman. The new relationship is a division of labor based on skill. Human capital formation plays a major role, and the objective force of the world market is the arbiter.

The industrialization of Malaysia has been a great success. The inflow of foreign labor is a testimony to its prosperity. But this has worked to the advantage of Singapore as well. The exodus of the labor-intensive industries to Malaysia was the result of the rising wage in Singapore. Instead of relying on immigrant labor alone, Singapore upgraded its industry. The way in which Singaporean firms interact with the other ASEAN firms can be seen below.

According to Itoh (1999), among the eight Sony subsidiaries in the area of Singapore, Malaysia and Indonesia, the Singaporean units include one local headquarters and two firms with very high capital intensity. The local headquarters does planning and coordination for all these eight units. It also provides troubleshooting for all other units. Percentage wise, the other two Singaporean units also have more engineers than the Malaysian and Indonesian subsidiaries.

Thus, Singapore also fulfills the second part of Lee Kuan Yew's strategy: *to be a first world oasis in the third world.* An indication of the degree to which this strategy has succeeded is that, with a population that is only one sixth that of Malaysia, Singapore has a slightly higher total GNP.[10]

We can understand the Singaporean development strategy by considering the top two export items in 1999: electronics, at 57% of the total, and petroleum, at 13%. The petroleum export reflects Singapore's position as the refining center for the Asia-Pacific region, which reaches from the Persian Gulf through Northeast Asia, and from Australia to the U.S. West Coast. As a 'swing' refiner, Singapore complements various national refineries and fills in the deficits of various products. Various major oil companies throughout the world invested in the refinery facilities. They invested in Singapore, not only because of its position astride a major sea-lane, but also because its infrastructure for supertankers has no match in the neighborhood.[11] Likewise, in 1998 and 1999, Singapore was the world

---

[10] For 1997, it was US$10,183,400 for Singapore to US$9,819,500 for Malaysia.

[11] For example, according to Perry, Kong and Yeoh (1997: 175), offshore mooring in Singapore can service tankers above 300,000 tons, but Port Klang and Pasir Gudang in Malaysia cannot handle tankers of more than 80,000 tons.

champion among container ports, and handled 15.3 and 15.9 million TEUs, respectively.[12]

The electronics industry developed because of the technicians trained in skills like precision machining, from the 4-6 month special programs designed and staffed by MNCs but funded by the government. The 4,000 workers trained by the German camera firm Rollei, before its failure, made Singapore the hard disk drive center of the world (Lee, 2000: 84, 88).[13]

The spending on infrastructure lowers the 'distance cost' between Singapore and its trading partners, especially those advanced economies that are located halfway across the globe. The specific form of human capital formation binds Singapore closely to those advanced economies, as their outpost in the middle of the developing economies.

In both aspects, the MNCs have been indispensable partners. There would have been no other way to acquire expertise as fast – not only to achieve full employment but also to join the ranks of the fully developed economies, within one-third of a century after its industrialization.

Singapore did have its own industrial past, the rubber shoe industry before the failure of Tan Kah Kee in the Great Depression.[14] The aftermath was that the overseas Chinese became more interested in commerce, which is more flexible, than industry, which requires long-term commitment.[15] Additionally, the latter requires technical information, the acquisition of which is less a tradition among the overseas Chinese than among families in Hong Kong and Taiwan.[16]

Criticism of Singapore's Development

The arrival of labor-intensive industries, such as textiles from Hong Kong, first mopped up surplus labor and then caused a labor shortage. Gradually, Singapore developed a deep reliance on foreign workers, from Malaysia and elsewhere. To maintain industries from the labor intensive Hong Kong, wage level was trapped at a point below what Hong Kong could support.

This led to the plan for the wage correction of 1979, which was designed to raise wage cost by 40% in three years with a simultaneous

[12] See Tonzon (2002). Here TEU stands for 'twenty foot equivalent unit', a standard measurement used for container capacities in terms of containers of such length.

[13] See Hobday (1995).

[14] See Huff (1994).

[15] See Lee and Low (1990).

[16] For overseas Chinese, see Wang (2000).

increase of the Central Providence Fund (CPF) contributions by both employers and employees. This had several effects at once.

First, from the macroeconomic point of view, this meant workers were provided more generous CPF benefits[17] but not current wage increases. Infrastructure investment would get financed but current prices may not rise with current consumption, as would happen with a simple wage raise. Second, from the microeconomic point of view, raising the labor cost would both make all industries less labor intensive, and cause the less labor-intensive industries to expand at the expense of the more labor-intensive industries. Therefore, the need for foreign labor would be reduced.[18] Third, dynamically, the shift toward the less labor-intensive industries would in all likelihood provide more valuable experience through learning-by-doing. Finally, limiting the use of foreign labor by artificially increasing labor cost would lead to a fall in the current income due to the loss of the trading gains associated with factor movement.

We now discuss the reasons behind the last point, and then the second point. Assume Singapore produces its GDP with three inputs: labor L and capital K which are both internationally mobile and real estate T, which is not. The rewards for L and K on the world market are w and v, the domestic wage rate being $w^* \geq w$. The GDP function, F(K, L, T) exhibits constant returns. Input endowments are, $L^\circ \leq L$ (there is immigrant labor), K°, and $T^\circ = T$:

$$GNP = Max_L\{Max_K[F(K, L, T) - vK] - w^*L\} - w(L - L^\circ) + vK^\circ,$$

where $K = K^*(L)$ depends on the labor force size L, and $L^* = L(w^*)$ is the equilibrium total labor force, decided by the domestic wage, w^*.

Set $f(L, T) = [F(K^*(L), L, T) - vK^*(L)]$. The area below the value of the marginal product of labor curve $\partial f/\partial L$ up to the point L(w) is GDP. Subtracting the wage bill for the foreign workers at the world equilibrium wage w gives GNP - vK°. Raising the unit labor cost to w^* would reduce foreign labor by $L(w) - L^*$, wage bill for foreigners, by $w[L(w) - L^*]$, GDP by the area bLL*c and GNP by the deadweight loss abc. See Figure 10.3.1. This is the current cost paid by Singapore to accelerate 'capital deepening'.

For simplicity, Figure 10.3.1 corresponds to a differentiable aggregate production function. Question 5 below extends the analysis to a two-sector economy producing textiles and garment, as well as electric products.

---

[17] Partly paid for by the employers.

[18] According to Bauer (1996), the government was concerned that foreign labor may have socio-political costs. For example, for unskilled foreign labor, regulations include the immediate sending back of those who failed the 'non-pregnancy' clause in the recruitment contract and the regular stipulated pregnancy test. The same rules in Taiwan, were recently challenged because of the Gender Equality Law (*Taipei Times*, Mach 31 2002).

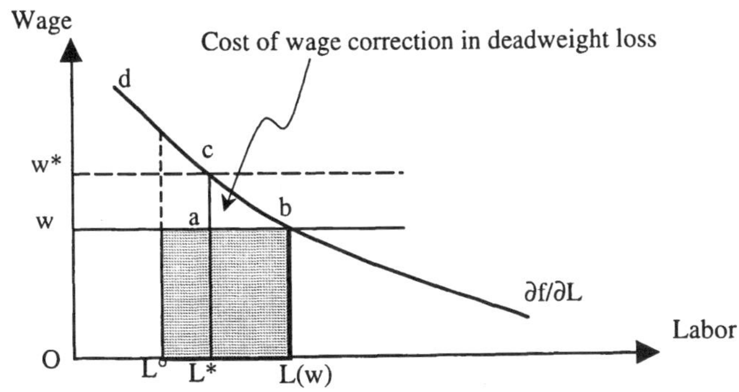

Figure 10.3.1 Deadweight loss

Next, we consider the microeconomic effects. For simplicity, assume every product is produced according to a Cobb-Douglas production function, with the coefficients for K, L, and T as α, β, and γ, regarding to any good, say, good 1. Select output unit to set unit price to 1, the unit cost of capital is $\alpha = vK$, so that the unit usage of capital is always,

$$K = \alpha/v.$$

In the three-dimensional input space for (K, L, T), this plane $K = \alpha/v$ cuts the unit value contour for good 1 and yield a 'partial unit-value isoquant' which is shown in Figure 10.3.2.

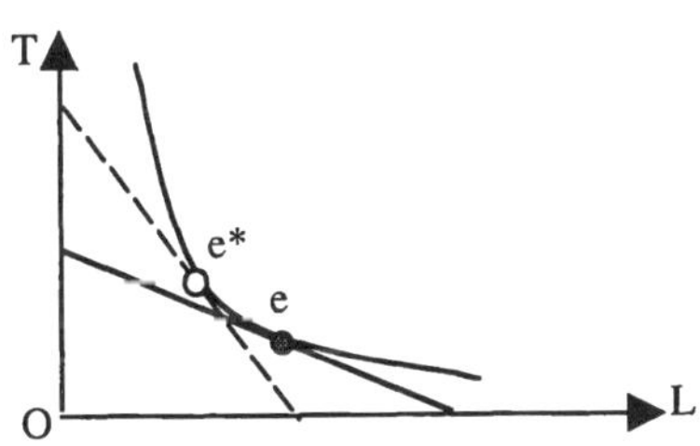

Figure 10.3.2 Partial unit isoquant

Raising labor costs means a shift of the equilibrium position from e to e*, with a reduction of the equilibrium return for T, as well as the unit usage of labor for good 1. The unit labor usage of good 1 is $L = \beta/w$. The value of marginal product curve of T for good 1 is then $Cw^{-\beta}T^{-(1-\gamma)}$, $C > 0$ being a constant. A rise of w by 1% reduces vertically this curve by β%. The larger is β, or the labor coefficient, the larger is vertical shrinkage. Suppose there are two sectors in the economy, the first sector is more labor intensive than the second in that if we introduce a sector subscript, then:

$$\beta_1 > \beta_2.$$

Then the proportional vertical reduction of the value of marginal product curve for good 1 in the more labor-intensive sector must be larger than for good 2 from the less labor-intensive sector. Now the fixed input T is being bidden away in the competitive market. The more labor-intensive sector must give way to the less labor-intensive sector. This is shown in the Jevons diagram in Figure 10.3.3, where the value of marginal product of T for good j = 1, 2 is written as $VMPT_j$, and the equilibrium use of T for j is written as T_j for j = 1, 2. Rising labor cost shifts the equilibrium from E to E*.

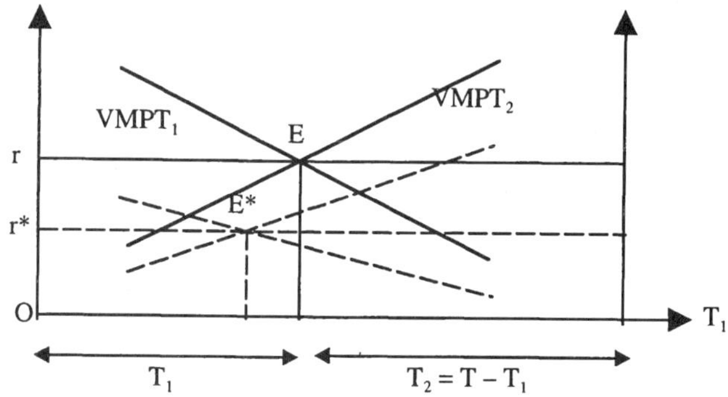

Figure 10.3.3 Jevons diagram

Summing up, to finance the infrastructure investment and to secure the learning effect from the less labor-intensive sector, the Singaporean government raised labor cost through an increased requirement of Central Providence Fund contributions. This led to the shift of the domestic, nontradable input, T, away from the labor-intensive sector, at the cost of incurring the deadweight loss. What happened was a serious recession for Singapore with a sizable exodus of industries. The government rolled back part of the program.[19]

Overall, the restructuring of the manufacturing sector did happen. This can be seen from the following analysis, using Chart 10.3.6, based upon data for 1967, 1973 and 1993 in Table 5.1, Perry et al.(1997).

From this chart, it is clear that the Singaporean economy has gone through a continuous process of concentration. Up to 1973, the three major industries all expanded in both their job shares and output shares against the rest. Among these three, the petroleum industry has the highest output/worker ratio. With less than 2% of the manufacturing labor, it contributed from one-fifth to one-quarter of the output value in manufacturing. Textiles and garments industry was exactly the opposite. The electric products[20] form a group with higher output per worker than the

[19] This took the form of a reduction of the required contribution of the employers to the Central Providence Fund account of the employee.

[20] That is electric machinery (SITC 383) and electronic products (SITC 384).

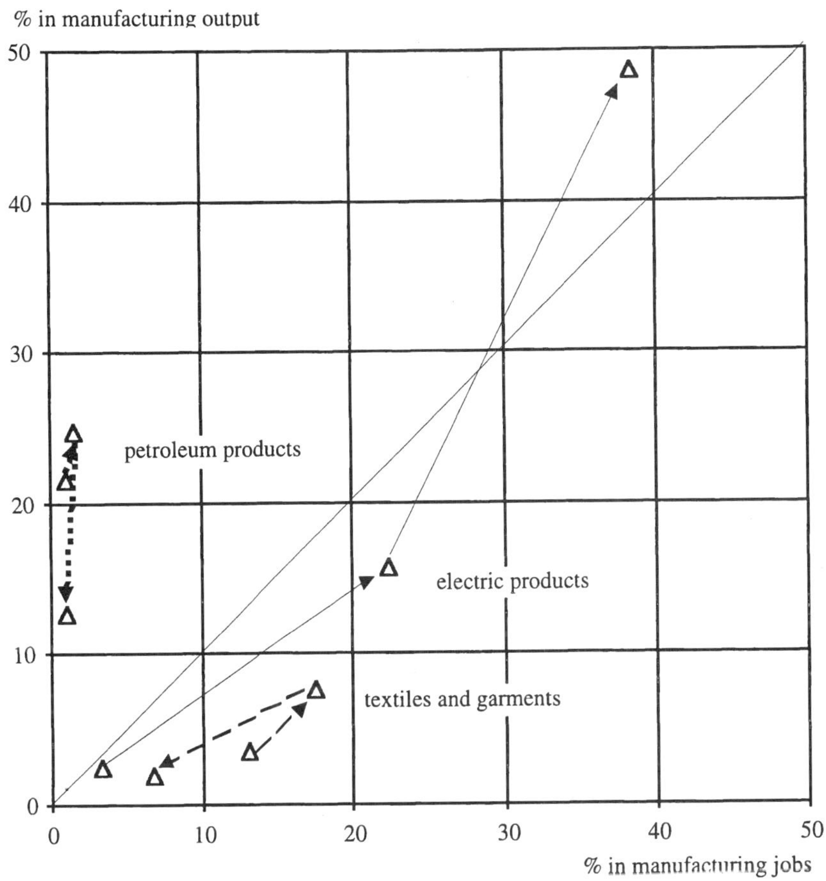

Chart 10.3.6 Jobs and outputs in manufacturing

textiles and garments. Until 1973 its output per worker was still less than the average of the manufacturing sector. This is seen as the triangular mark lying below the 45-degree line. In the next 20 years, the electric product industry gained at the expense of the other two, in both job share and in output share. Its output per worker surpassed that of the manufacturing sector, on average.[21] Almost 40% of the manufacturing workers produced electric products that amounted to almost 50% of the output value. In fact, this trend continues after 1993.

Detractors of Singapore's strategy focus on two points. First, the development process concentrates too much on capital accumulation, and pays little attention to productivity growth. This view is usually associated

---

[21] According to Dr. Soon Tech-Wong, just between 1980 and 1992, net fixed asset per worker increased ten-fold.

with the work of Young (1995) and Krugman (1994). Second, indigenous entrepreneurship gets crowded out by both the MNCs and the government-linked corporations (See Lee and Low, 1990).

From our analysis, conclusive statements are not easy to make. First, we shall address the question of 'ovcr accumulation.' Proceeding from the microeconomic angle, we note that from time to time, heavy one-time spending was made on infrastructure. Such projects are indispensable to reduce the 'distance cost' between Singapore and the advanced economies, and bring long-term benefit. This makes it difficult to conduct growth accounting comparisons between Singapore and other economies.

Next, from the macroeconomic angle, there is no denying that in terms of the level of per capita real GDP, Singapore has advanced very fast in the past one-third of a century. Once an economy has reached such a level – so that Singapore ranks among the richest economies in the world – it is not likely that Singapore can maintain the same pace of growth under *any* policy, judging from all other economies with similar income and wealth.

Again using data from World Bank (1998), we present the information in Table 10.3.1 and then, taking the other thirteen economies beside Singapore to fit a quadratic regression, we get Chart 10.3.7. The data point of Singapore is included for comparison. Clearly in terms of growth rate, Singapore has been an outlier. The continuation of such growth performance may not be in the cards. On the other hand, there is no reason to expect that Singapore's growth will slow down more than that of the other thirteen economies, as a group.

Country	Real per capita Income, '96	Growth Rate, '90–'96
Canada	21,380	0.6
France	21,510	0.7
Germany	21,110	0.7
Italy	19,890	0.9
Japan	23,420	1.2
U.K.	19,960	1.5
U.S.	28,020	1.2
Denmark	22,120	2.1
Finland	18,260	–0.2
Norway	23,320	3.7
Sweden	18,770	–0.2
Switzerland	26,340	–1.0
Hong Kong	24,260	3.7
Singapore	**26,910**	**6.6**

Table 10.3.1 Level and growth of very high income economies Source: World Bank (1998)

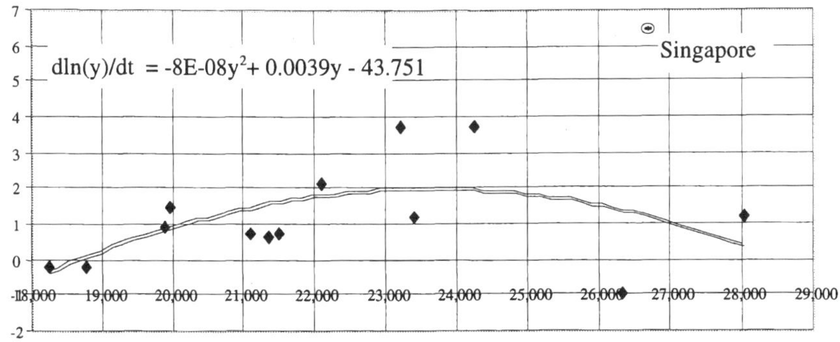

Chart 10.3.7 Singapore's neighborhood

Next, consider the criticism that Singapore's heavy reliance on MNCs has crowded out indigenous entrepreneurship. One reason to believe that this is undesirable is that MNCs are 'rootless,' so that they might abandon Singapore in a pinch. Granted that de-industrialization is undesirable, it is still not clear that if Singapore had followed a purely *laissez faire* strategy like Hong Kong, Singapore would have suffered less de-industrialization than Hong Kong. As seen in Chart 10.3.8, a and b, during the 1990s, Singapore remains favored by international investors, relative to the ASEAN-3, in spite of the differences in area, population, and resource endowments.

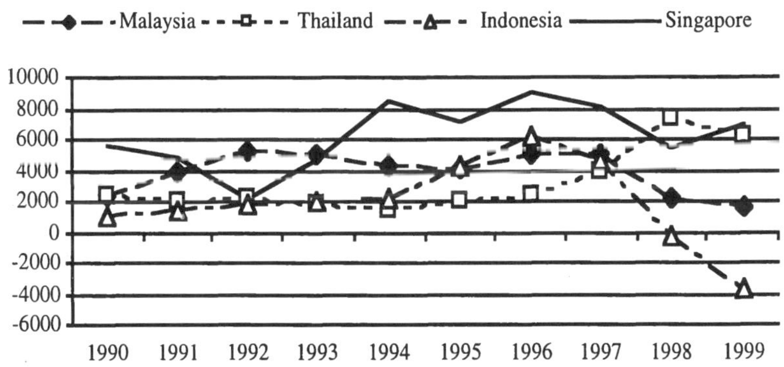

Chart 10.3.8a $ over the decade (units: million U.S. dollars)

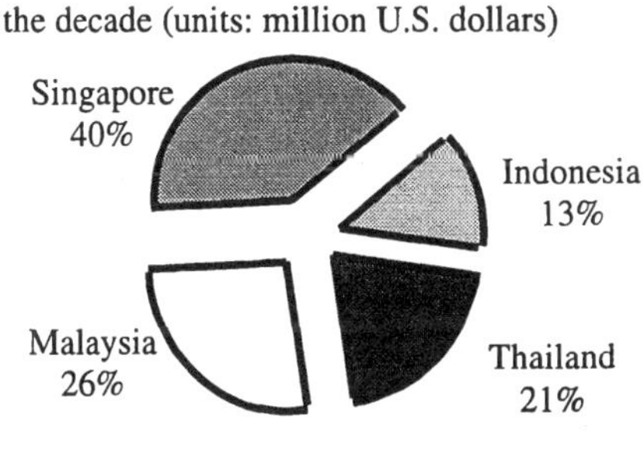

Chart 10.3.8 b Singapore & ASEAN-3: Sum over the 90's

Source: World Development Indicator

Chart 10.3.9 shows that the wholly foreign owned MNCs have a very significant share in jobs (40% to 50%), value added (60% to 72%) and direct export (72% to 80%). By and large, MNCs are more important in direct exports than in value added, and in value added than in jobs. Thus person for person, MNC workers produce more value; dollar for dollar, MNC outputs are more salable abroad. Over time, such distinctions have endured and even strengthened.

In becoming an 'oasis of the first world amid the third world' as Lee Kuan Yew, Singapore's first prime minister had intended, the ownership pattern in Singapore is highly 'globalized'. The booming inward foreign investment happens even when Singapore has no need to tap into foreign savings, thanks to the massive 'forced saving' achieved under the Central Providence Fund. Between 1985 and 1999, the level of gross domestic capital formation is 35.4% of GDP, markedly below the remarkable level of gross national saving, 47.7% of GDP (Koe et al, 2002, xii). In fact, Singaporeans themselves are investing heavily outside that island economy.

Thus, both the level and the rate of change of Singapore's capital/labor ratio are largely shaped by decisions of MNCs, and influenced by such investment inducement like government co-investment. This influence is as tenuous as what a reduction in the current level of auto-insurance premium may contribute to reckless driving on the super highway. As a corollary, such evidence makes it difficult to associate causally the high saving of Singaporeans with low productivity growth in that island economy, whether supposedly observed or predicted.

Remarkably, foreign outfits are far more important in Singapore, as an *independent, developmental state*, than in Hong Kong, when it was a *laissez faire, British colony.* Apparently, foreign investors favor Singapore because Singapore has offered them very favorable terms, in the hope that they will play unusually important roles.

According to former Prime Minister Lee (cited near the end of last section), one can improve the chance of business success by working with foreign investors from the advanced countries. By Chart 10.3.9, foreign investors have repaid Singapore with positive contributions in terms of both productivity and marketability.

Since Singapore could have financed all its own investment needs without foreign investors, yet it invests abroad, and continues to attract foreign investors by offering incentives. Presumably, the government hopes that foreign investors will bring to Singapore both better performance now, and better technology for the future. Technology, and not capital, is what Singapore is after.

To conclude, anticipating benefits from foreign investors, Singapore adopts policies to attract foreign investors. The latter have flocked to Singapore in response, and rendered superior performance as expected.

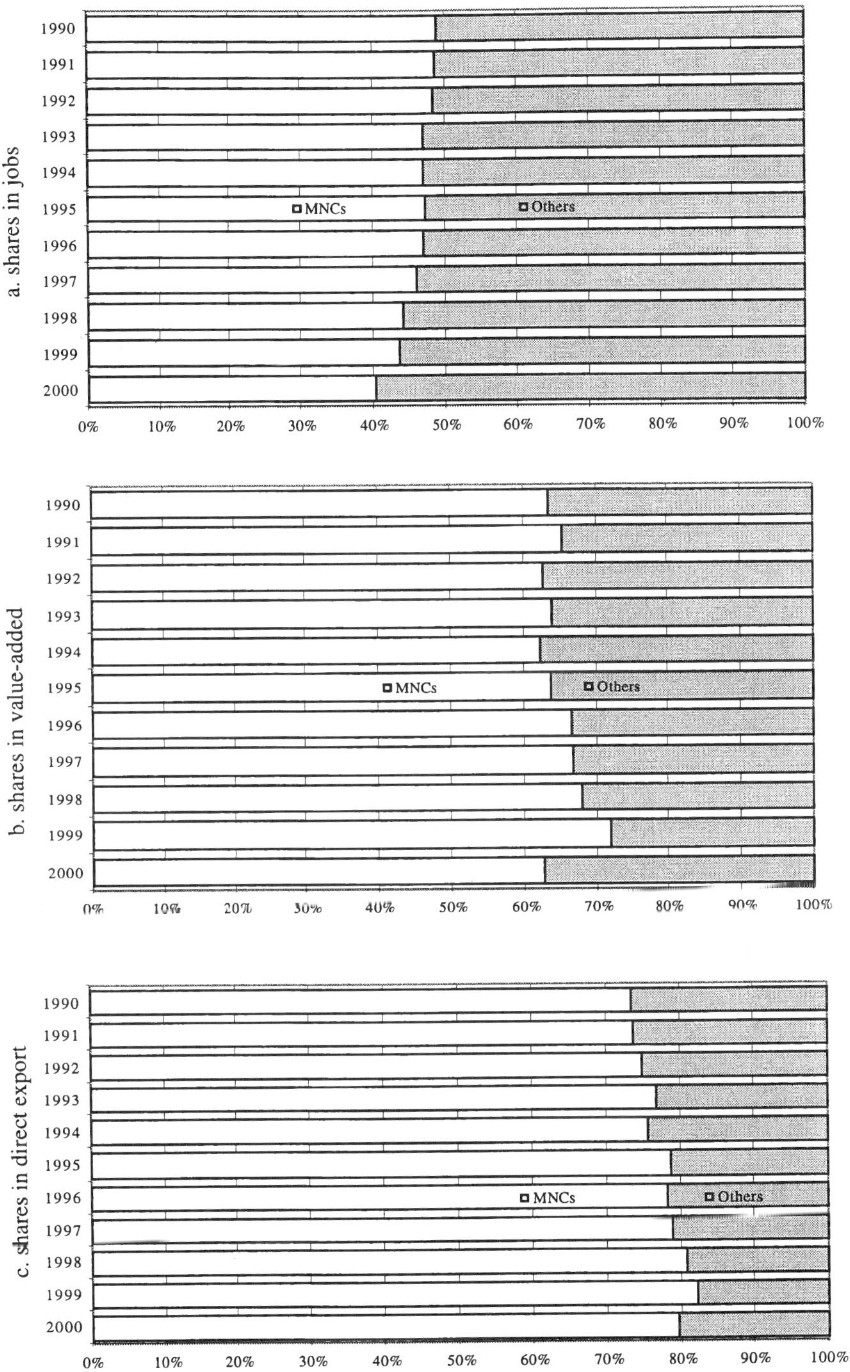

Chart 10.3.9 The shares of MNCs in Singapore

Singapore Department of Statistics (courtesy of Dr. T. W. Soon)

Knowing what one wants and paying for what one gets, Singapore has opted for a policy that may or may not be the best. Nonetheless, its merit cannot be dismissed out of hand by its critics.

4. CONCLUDING REMARKS

We are by no means in agreement with the critics of Singapore's development policy. But there are areas in which that policy may need redirection.[22] Facing the future, new initiatives may be in order for both the product mix and skill mix.

In export, the present concentration in electronics (a 58.6% share) seems risky. First, there are too many contenders competing for the same U.S. market. Outputs become 'commodities,' with little innovative profit left. Second, the electronics market represents increasingly the *replacement demand* rather than the *expansion demand.* Income elasticity becomes high, since potential buyers can easily postpone replacing the durable goods they own, when they feel unsure about their own job and income. Thus, when recession threatens, both export quantity and price fall precipitously. This caused the deep recession in late 2001.

In Singapore, the cluster of chemical industries was promoted as a counterbalance to electronics. Nonetheless, such industries are highly capital intensive. However profitable, they provide few jobs directly. Of course, a country with *stable* and *highly profitable* exports can create jobs for domestic demand, say, in service industries. Still, a more comprehensive solution must be in place.

Next, the unease of the public is not groundless regarding both the heavy reliance on MNCs and the lack of vitality of the manufacturing SMEs. The root cause of apprehension is that the local labor force may lack both the needed skill to afford the present standard of living, in times of change, and any chance to acquire it under the current policy. To understand this issue, let us take a broad perspective of the globalized world economy.

MNCs operate for profit. To manage the global supply chain, they go for the low cost supplier of the goods they need on that day. Cost is low in economies where productivity and quality have risen ahead of reputation. Thus highly productive labor has to accept low pay to join the supply chain. China is displacing the NIEs now like the NIEs had displaced Japan before. To control cost, MNCs often use dual sources. To gain internal and external economy, they purchase in bulk volume. Many MNCs may buy the same

---

[22] Interested readers may also read Soon and Stoever (1996) for a perceptive and independent commentary on Singaporean development policy over time.

good from the same location. For example, once Singapore made about half of the disk drives used worldwide.[23]

When development is successful, wages tend to rise. To offset this, one specializes, using the economy of scale to compete against low wages. As a successful small economy, specialization makes Singapore vulnerable to market volatility.

MNCs also operate as going concerns. New products are continuously developed through market studies and technological research, both to compete against each other in quality and to raise sales through built-in obsolescence. A world market with MNCs is inherently volatile. It is the nature of the beast.

To survive and thrive in a volatile world that they themselves help to produce, MNCs develop the capability for planning and research. These functions are centrally placed in the advanced economies, and not dispersed in regional headquarters in Singapore or Hong Kong. Information is provided on a 'need to know' principle. By association with MNCs, host countries may acquire the skill needed for fabrication, but not for research or overall design.[24]

In short, dealing with the MNCs may provide the NIEs with rising fabrication skill and hence income, but also constant uncertainty. The recent exodus of some producers of hard disk drives has raised such worries in Singapore. As a remedy, Japan and, to a degree, Korea focused on their own product development, through market research. Taiwan emphasized strategic alliances and developed special processes that were valuable to the MNCs. Such activities are based upon the presence of large reservoirs of science and technology manpower. Based on data in Hang (1999), Chart 10.4.1 shows this is a resource relatively scarce for Singapore.

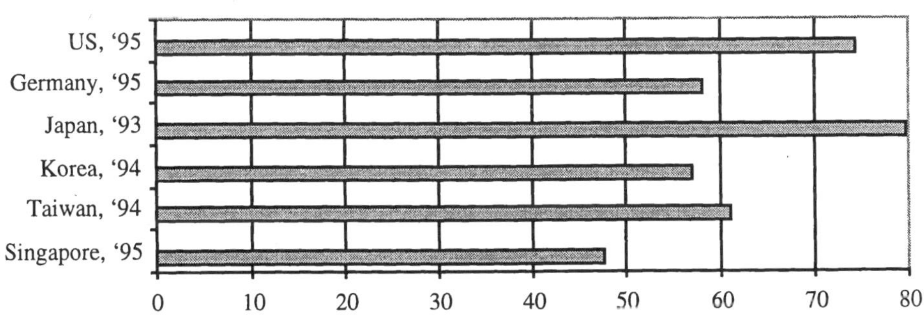

Chart 10.4.1 Research scientists and engineers/10,000 workers Source: Hang (1999)

---

[23] Hobday (1995: 144).

[24] From the technical point of view, foreign investors have no reason to transfer their 'core technology' but the possession of 'core technology' is the basis of flexibility in the face of market change. (Deyo, et al., 2001).

In Singapore today, it is often regarded as desirable to have a vibrant high tech sector like Taiwan. The issues are actually three-fold: (a) there must be enough trained scientists and engineers, (b) a sufficient portion of such personnel must decide to stay in the economy, and (c) such persons in the economy must be ready to organize start-up firms.

Actually, over the years, many young persons in Taiwan decided to study engineering, in order to study abroad later on research assistantships, and perhaps then to stay abroad to work. In 1967, Generalissimo Chiang Kaishek was ready to prevent such potential brain drain, until Dr. Wu Ta-yu talked him out of it.[25] Much later, under various policy initiatives proposed by K. T. Li, a portion of these people returned to Taiwan with their expertise and connections, to organize or join high tech start-up firms. Those who survived the Darwinian process become the high tech SME sector, and made the reverse brain drain a popular notion.

In contrast, the top high school graduates in Singapore are offered the opportunity to be 'bonded scholars.' They study in top U.S. or U. K. schools and then return to Singapore for six years' service, mostly in the government-linked corporations. Besides having the obligation to repay the principal and the interest of the scholarship, those who break the bonds would be 'named and shamed' in newspapers, together with their parents, who must co-sign the bond. The system is designed to minimize the occurrence of brain drain. Yet it also makes 'reverse brain drain' unlikely.

Of course, Singapore also has a program to attract 'foreign talent.' However, this is more for potential employees in Singaporean firms rather than for potential entrepreneurs.

The subsequent reverse brain drain must be balanced against the earlier brain drain. From the viewpoint of cost-benefit analysis, whether Taiwan or Singapore has a better policy depends upon the rate of social discount one applies.

---

[25] See 'The passing of Ta-yu Wu, the physics master of a generation', p.77, *Overseas Scholar*, (Chinese) March 31, 2000, Taipei.

CHAPTER SUMMARY

- ♦ Singapore is located at a strategic position and faces complex inter-ethnic relations. Situated at a choke point of an important seaway, its Chinese majority forms a node in the Overseas Chinese network that plays a major economic role in the Malay world. The separation of Singapore from Malaysia was intended to cool off communal conflicts.
- ♦ After early false steps toward import substitution, Singapore attracted labor-intensive industries from locations like Hong Kong. Double-digit unemployment soon turned into labor shortages that called for foreign workers.
- ♦ To anticipate competition from countries with lower wages, Singapore soon settled on a course of hosting multinational corporations from the advanced countries. This strategy involved massive infrastructure investment for industrial parks, tanker terminals and container ports, compulsory arbitration to eliminate strikes and moderate wage demand, technical training programs tailored to employers' needs, and financial incentives – from tax holidays to 30% co-investment – to attract targeted high tech firms to Singapore.
- ♦ The contributions to workers' pensions through the Central Providence Fund may amount to 50% of workers' wage. Singapore responds to various external shocks by raising or lowering the ratio of contributions by employers and workers to: a) increase labor cost for reducing labor intensive industries in a tight labor market; b) decrease labor cost for retaining foreign investors in recessions so as to avoid deep devaluation; and c) dampen effective demand of households for cooling inflation. In regulating the withdrawals of pensions, the government can practice forced saving or encourage spending on housing to improve the urban environment.
- ♦ Over time, Singapore has lessened its dependence on entrepôt trade with its neighbors and benefited from its role as a supplier for the input needs of Malaysian industrialization. With one-seventh the population of the rapidly growing Malaysia, Singapore managed to have a slightly larger GDP than its neighbor. Thus, the criticism of Young and Krugman about the Singaporean development strategy being 'over-accumulation' has not been proven to date. More serious is the apparent lack of indigenous entrepreneurship in manufacturing. The exodus of industries to low cost sites looms as a nightmare to Singapore because of the perceived footloose nature of multinational corporations.

QUESTIONS AND EXERCISES

1. In a multi-year project, Singapore builds the artificial Jurong Island to house its offshore chemical industries. How would this affect the computed Total Factor Productivity Growth, which forms the base of criticism of Singapore's development strategy? Discuss.
2. In comparison with Hong Kong, the lack of indigenous entrepreneurs in manufacturing is often a criticism of the Singapore development program, and the potential exodus of industry is the *bête noire* in such discussions. How valid is this argument, in view of the recent events of these two island economies?
3. If 'success attracts imitation, and competition from imitators threatens decline,' how would one plan for the future development of Singapore, in the face of the industrialization of Malaysia, Thailand, the PRC, etc.? Consider the interaction between the United States, Japan and Korea in the last dozen years and then comment on the validity of the quoted statement.
4. Compare the implementation of industrial policy between Korea and Singapore (one using directed credit, the other via Central Providence Fund stipulations). Discuss.
5. Define

   $$f(L, T) = \text{Max}_{\lambda, \tau} \{f_1(\lambda, \tau) + f_2(L - \lambda, T-\tau)\}$$

   where

   $$f_1(\lambda, \tau) = \lambda^{2/3}\, \tau^{1/3} \qquad \text{and} \qquad f_2(L-\lambda, T-\tau) = (L-\lambda)^{1/3}\, (T-\tau)^{2/3}$$

   stand respectively for the textiles and garments sector and the electric products sector, with the former much more labor intensive.

   (a) Reconstruct Figure 10. 3. 1 to reflect the facts: (i) before the 'wage correction', *both* sectors were present in Singapore where many migrant workers came on temporary working permits, and (ii) after the 'wage correction', the textiles and garments sector disappeared and the number of migrant workers went down as well.

   (b) Assume that the technology is mature for textiles and garments but not for the electric products. Explain why the 'wage correction' may be justified policy measure to stave off de-industrialization, like what happened in Hong Kong after the 1978 reform of the PRC.

   (c) Could Hong Kong adopt a policy similar to Singapore? (Hint: Hong Kong had refugees; Singapore had temporary, migrant workers).

   (d) Comment on the influential view in Young (1992).

Chapter 11

OUTWARD ORIENTED DEVELOPMENT ELSEWHERE

The Question of Replicability

1. A SEARCH FOR ADDITIONAL EVIDENCE

In **Part 1** we introduced a theory for catching up. This theory has both (a) an aggregate version, which is summarized in the single-variable benchmark model, and (b) the disaggregated version, where structural change is the indispensable feature accompanying the process of catching up. For individual welfare, consumption and income per capita, the one-variable model provides a rough and ready picture of what can be expected, if the functional form $F(\bullet;\alpha)$ is associated with the appropriate value of the parameter, α, which is assumed to be a real number.

This first approximation serves the same function for our theory that a scaffold serves for construction. It is a necessary *means*, but an ultimately unsatisfactory substitute for the desired *end*. In the first place, income must be earned with the value of output. Sustained rapid growth of the output value is achieved not so much by producing more of the same, but by producing more valuable output with the same inputs. This takes almost constant structural upgrading, and requires a particular mix of policy instruments at each point in time. To represent alternative sequences of policy packages at the aggregate level, one might say that the parameter α assumes different values. In the second place, the fall of the Soviet economy represents the most acute form of 'creative destruction,' and a common peril for all those who fail to keep up technologically. Yet in truth, the quantitative output level of the Soviets did not decline until the political institutions unraveled. The nature of such a debacle – namely declining value for a non-decreasing output flow – can never be adequately represented in any single variable model.

The catching up theory is supposedly applicable to all developing economies, as long as they meet some general conditions, such as law and order, or participation in the global economy. It assumes that for a less developed economy, the best course for technology acquisition is through emulation. This is a contact game, for which the access to the world market is a prerequisite. Of course, it takes some minimum level of security for individuals to trade and to emulate. In addition, as pointed out by Kuznets (1982), to successfully carry out such a development agenda, one must successfully overcome objections of the entrenched interest, in one way or another.

Chapters 7 to 10 presented evidence from the four Asian NIEs. Close attention was paid to how their rapid growth episodes began and how their subsequent development evolved. What has happened in the NIEs is that not only (a) no vested interest can hold up the catching up process for ransom, but also (b) the usual 'coordination failure' that blocks progress is often overcome by government initiative.

The four Asian NIEs share both (a) ethnic homogeneity, and (b) Confucian heritage. Singapore may be an exception, but it fits this mold in a functional sense to be explained below. They also share (c) a location at the Asian-Pacific littoral, and (d) a population between three million and fifty million. It is fair to question whether our theory is applicable only to economies having these attributes. To argue that our theory is generally relevant, we supply additional evidence from Malaysia, Mainland China and Mauritius, without delving too deeply into their economic evolution. Each of these three differs from the four NIEs in one or the other of the four attributes, (a) - (d).

Table 11.1.1 relates these three economies to the four attributes listed above. Remarks follow.

	Ethnic homogeneity	Confucian heritage	Asia-Pacific location	Medium population size
Malaysia	No	No	Yes	Yes
Mainland China	Yes	Yes	Yes	No
Mauritius	No	No	No	No

Table 11.1.1 Economies and attributes

The attributes (a)-(d) obviously have some positive or negative impact on development. However, their influence is not strong enough to nullify the economic force that allows a less-developed open economy to catch up. Variation in any of these attributes is a far less decisive factor than those forces that prevent North Korea from developing.

In a sense, the inclusion of Mainland China in our discussion is instructive. Presently, Mainland China and North Korea share a Marxist-Leninist ideology and many political institutions. The principal distinction dividing these two concerns participation in the trading world, and – whatever their cultural or ideological affinities – in terms of growth performance, North Korea resembles neither South Korea nor the Chinese Mainland, but rather Myanmar. This is food for thought for development economists who doubt the potency of trade in episodes of rapid growth.

By and large, Malaysia is certainly not Confucian. In ethnic composition, Malaysia is a mirror image of Singapore.[1] With a majority community that is politically dominant but economically disadvantaged, the leaders have had to adopt affirmative action programs rather than meritocracy. In countries such as Singapore, on the other hand, with a majority community that is economically advantaged, leaders are under no such political pressure, and can pursue affirmative action programs at a more modest pace, if at all. In the short run, affirmative action programs, however morally worthy, do not enhance international competitiveness. Therefore, from this functional viewpoint, Singapore behaves as though it were ethnically homogeneous, while Malaysia does not.

In location, Malaysia is contiguous to Singapore and the Chinese Mainland is contiguous to Hong Kong. The migration of industries across the border involves little cost. Mauritius is a small island in geographic isolation.

2. MALAYSIA

Malaysia is fascinating to us both as a member of the ASEAN-3 (the triumvirate of Malaysia, Thailand and Indonesia) and in comparison with Singapore. The ASEAN-3 may be compared to the four NIEs. The similarities and differences of their evolutionary paths are quite informative to us regarding the roles of manufacturing exports. The comparison between Malaysia and Singapore highlights the issues of managing a multi-ethnic society. We consider these two topics in turn.

---

[1] The ethnic communities, in descending relative proportions are Malay, Chinese, then Indians in Malaysia and Chinese, Malays then Indians in Singapore.

ASEAN-3 Versus the Four NIEs

Both Malaysia and Indonesia are producers of petroleum and Thailand is an important exporter of rice on the world market. In per capita terms, the ASEAN-3 are far better endowed in natural wealth than are the NIEs. Over the four decades 1960-2000, the development of these seven may be summarized in five points:

- In per capita income, these seven economies were roughly comparable around 1960.
- Since then, progress has been made by all seven in catching up with the technological leader, the United States.
- Yet, growth of the NIEs has left the ASEAN-3 definitely behind. A gap equal to 10% of the U.S. per capita real income has opened between the two subgroups.
- Still, unlike the Latin American countries, all the ASEAN-3 are well on the catching up path.
- The ASEAN-3 made structural changes in both globalization and industrialization.

Based upon the Penn World Table, the relative per capita GDP ('repcri' in Chapter 1) of the seven economies in both 1960 and 1996 (at the eve of Crisis 1997) is displayed in Chart 11.2.1. In this chart, the shaded bar represents the repcri, 1960, and the entire bar represents the repcri, 1996, with the increment shown as the white area of the entire bar. We further present the relevant figures in Table 11.2.1.

	repcri,1960	repcri, 1996	increments
Hong Kong	23.87	90.78	66.91
Singapore	19.34	104.39	85.05
Taiwan	11.16	54.03	42.87
Korea	11.44	50.16	38.72
Malaysia	17.66	31.76	14.1
Thailand	9.4	25.54	16.14
Indonesia	5.69	13.65	7.96

Table 11.2.1 ASEAN-3 & the NIEs

To assess how well the ASEAN-3 have performed in catching up with the U.S., we rank in Chart 11.2.2 the 1960-96 increments of all 112 economies with available information from Penn Table 6.0.

How have the NIEs overtaken the ASEAN-3? Many factors may be involved. First of all, there is a purely economic explanation, which combines the theory of 'Dutch disease' and the hypothesis of learning-by-doing for manufacture. By 'Dutch disease' we mean that the ASEAN-3 are rich in natural resources, as was the Netherlands after the discovery of North

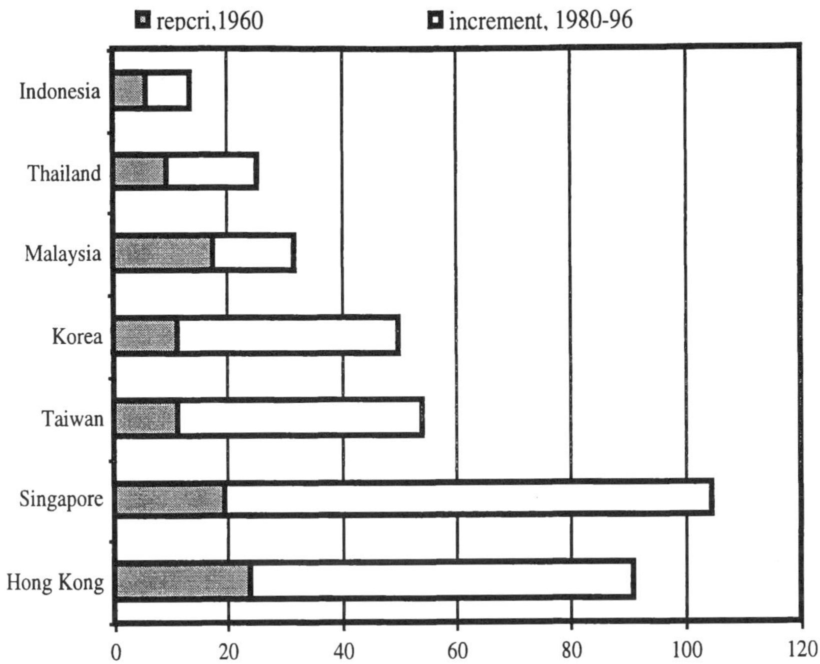

Chart 11.2.1 ASEAN-3 & NIEs: repcri in 1960, 1996 and the increments
Source: Penn World Table 6.0

Sea gas fields. Thus, labor is diverted to the resource-based industries at the expense of the manufacturing output. Assume now that valuable learning can only be obtained through manufacturing activities, then labor skill would rise faster in the resource-poor NIEs, than in the ASEAN-3, which are resource abundant.

Next, one may formulate a cultural explanation. Smith (1983) reported that Japanese managers in Malaysia found their mode of operation more compatible with Chinese workers than with Malay workers. Thus, other things being equal, Japanese firms prefer to invest in Hong Kong and Taiwan rather than in Southeast Asia, bringing along technology diffusion to the NIEs first.

However, the most important fact is not that over those three decades, the catching up process has gone on further and faster in the NIEs than in the ASEAN-3. Sooner or later, that process must taper off by its nature, as has happened in Japan. The main point is that the ASEAN-3 have joined this process, replicating the high-growth episodes of the NIEs, with some time lag.

The way the ASEAN-3 accomplished this feat was through the combination of two tasks at once, namely, globalization and industrialization. The former may be represented by export value as a percentage of GDP. Here export value is a gross figure expressed in market prices and GDP is on a value-

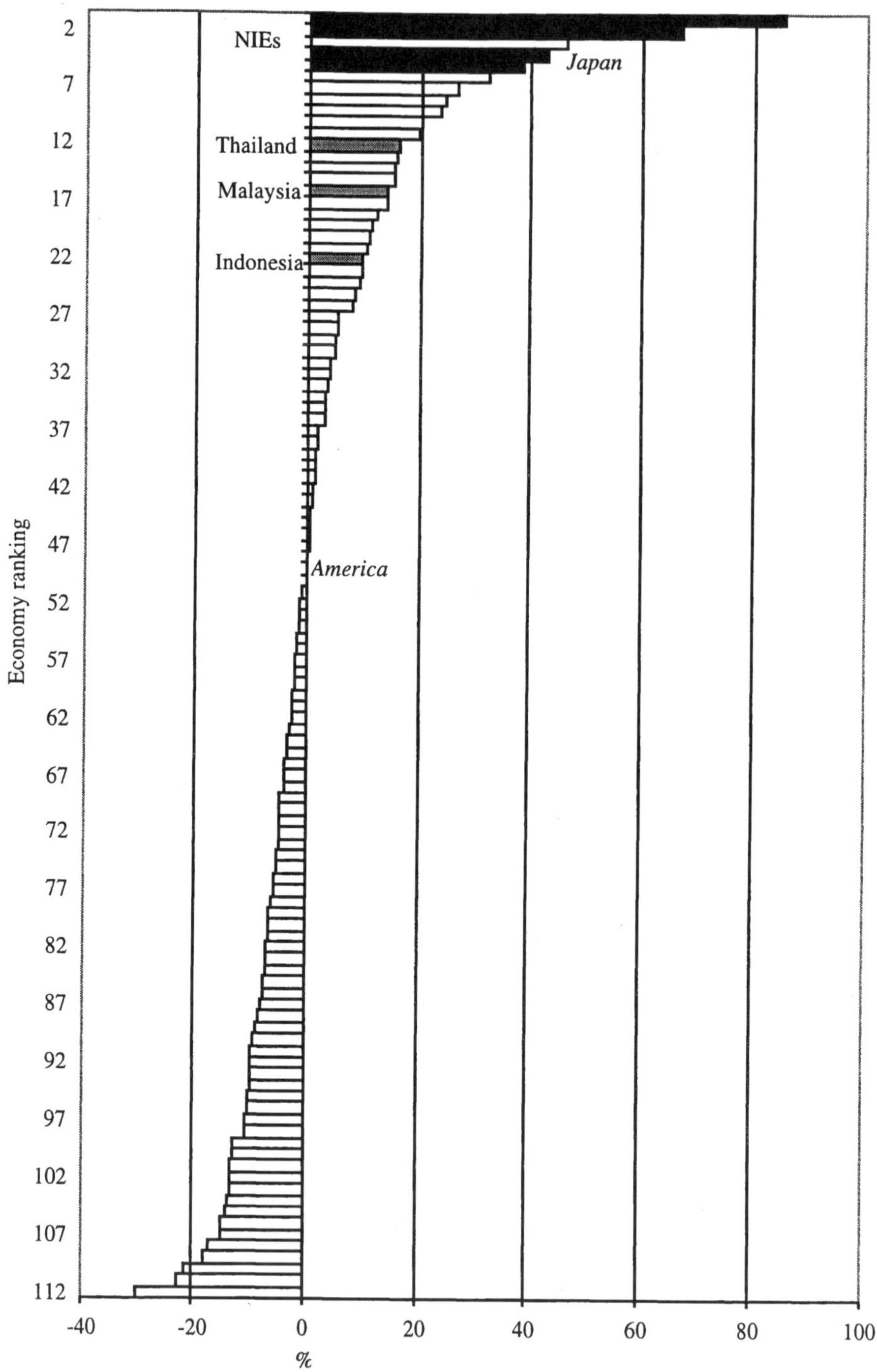

Chart 11.2.2 Catching up of ASEAN – 3, 1960-96 in context Source: Penn Table 6.0

added basis. So what one looks for is only a matter of proportionality. On the other hand, the degree of industrialization is represented by the manufacturing content of the total export. This is a measure of comparative advantage of an economy in the world market.

Charts 11.2.3 and 11.2.4 display the data from the World Development Index (WDI) 2002 and Penn Table 6.0. Note that, among the ASEAN-3, Malaysia is the most globalized as well as industrialized. Reference to Charts 11.2.1 and 11.2.2 above suggests that not only (a) globalization and industrialization are both conducive to growth, but also (b) they reinforce each other in enhancing growth performance.

First, cross region comparison shows that industrialization in a globalized environment, like in the ASEAN-3, is slow in coming, but self-sustained. Industrialization behind protective trade barriers, like in Latin America, may wither away once the protection is withdrawn.

Second, comparison within the ASEAN-3 shows that Malaysia had the highest relative per capita GDP. Thailand is almost as industrialized in export structure but less globalized. Its development is concentrated in the urban core around Bangkok, causing serious regional income polarization.

Finally, comparison over time shows that all the ASEAN-3 have accomplished globalization before industrialization. Significantly, growth after the mid-1980s is more stable than in the previous decade, with boom-bust cycles like the effect of oil shortage, then oil glut.

Worldwide, how general are such regularities deserves future research.

Malaysia in Contrast to Singapore

As shown in Chart 11.2.1 and Chart 11.2.2, over the three decades 1960-1990, Malaysia started at a higher level than the other two members of ASEAN-3, and has progressed faster as well. It is true that similarly, the performance of Malaysia itself is dominated by that of Singapore. However, one must stress that the Malaysian record is quite an achievement, all things considered. Specifically, one must consider its ethnic situation.

Singapore began by the design of Stamford Raffles. He planned it as an entrepôt for the China trade[2] and recruited its population. The Malaysian leaders have always had to play the cards in hand as well as they could, and the Malaysian story illustrates what can be achieved in the face of challenging ethnic issues. The largest three ethnic groups in both Malaysia and Singapore are Malays, Indians and Chinese, in ascending order by edu

---

[2] Ironically for the China trade Singapore was soon supplanted by Hong Kong when the British acquired the latter after the Opium War.

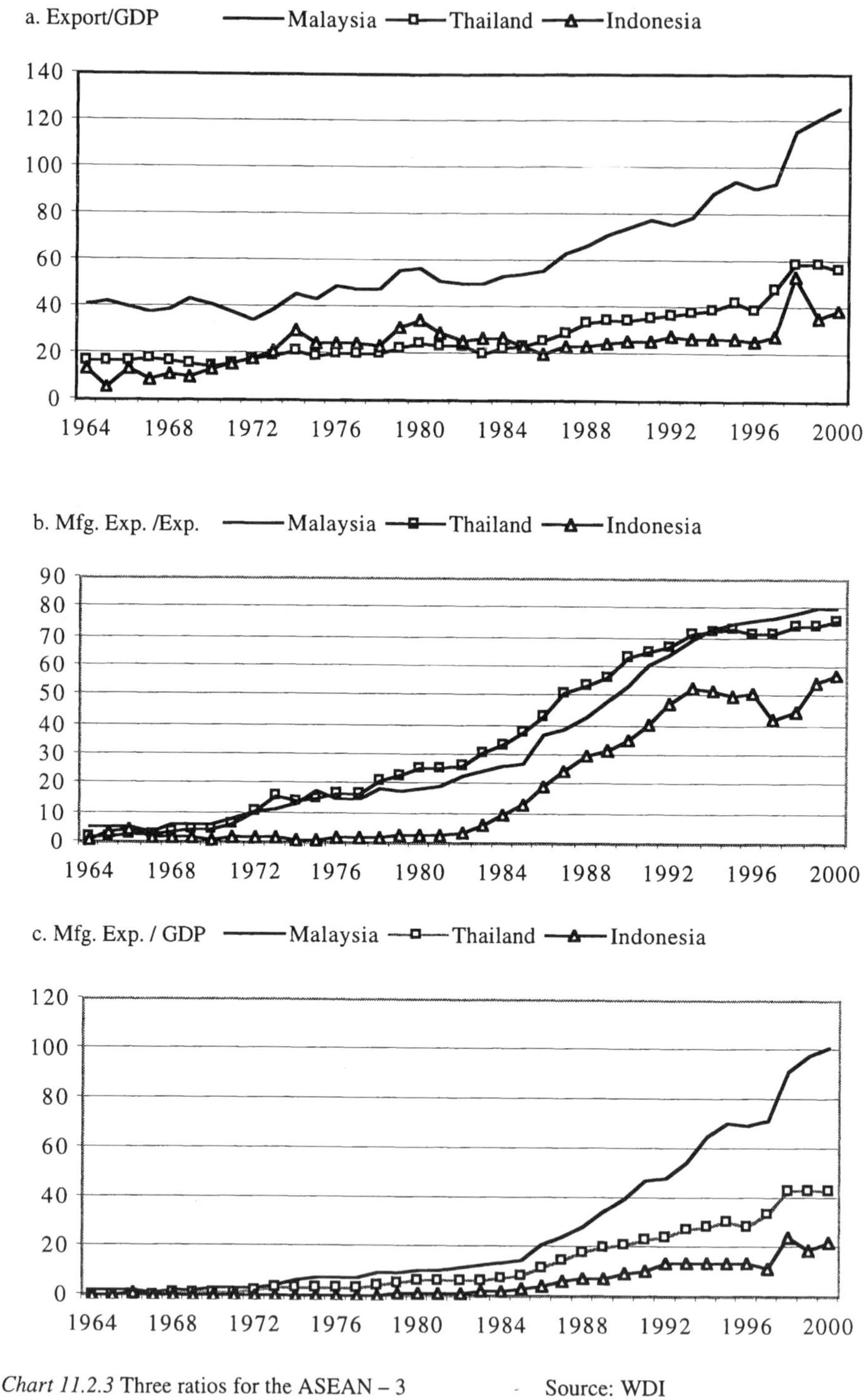

Chart 11.2.3 Three ratios for the ASEAN – 3 Source: WDI

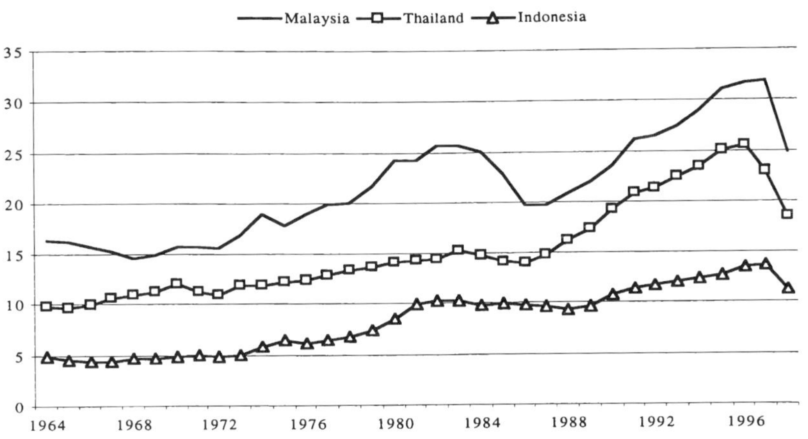

Chart 11.2.4 ASEAN-3 repcri Source: PennTable 6.0

cation and income. By numerical majority, Malays and Chinese respectively are in power in Malaysia and Singapore. Indians form a minority in both.

Indians and Chinese were recruited in the 18th and 19th centuries for the plantations and mines. Those who came, survived and stayed are eager to earn and learn than to enjoy leisure. When World War II ended, the Malays included a small urban elite intermarried with Islamic immigrants from South and West Asia, and a large population of less educated, subsistence farmers. All urban centers had become predominately Chinese, who controlled commerce, crafts, and the professions. Malays and Chinese seldom intermarry because of religion; conversion to Islam is also rare. Both the merger of Malaya with the two Borneo states and its separation from Singapore were designed to prevent Malays to become a minority in their own homeland, overwhelmed by the Chinese.[3]

For the Malay leaders, the first priority is to ameliorate the social and economic position of the Malays, in particular vis-à-vis the Chinese.[4] Economic growth stands as a distinct second. But if the economy is to function smoothly, the Indian and Chinese population at home must be reasonably contented, and the government must not be perceived as being grossly unfair in the eyes of investors and trading partners, many of them from East Asia. This delicate balancing act is carried out on the basis of the initial compromise that granted citizenship to the Chinese and Indians at home and special rights for the *bumiputra* ('sons of the soil'), who include mainly the Malays and other small groups of original settlers.

---

[3] Like their fellow Austronesian speakers in Taiwan.

[4] Both for its own sake, and also as the principal means of drawing support from the rural Malays.

It is the economic content of these special rights that warrants discussion. This includes exclusive ownership of rural land, quotas for government jobs (including teachers), government contracts, admissions to higher education, and various types of assistance to *bumiputra* business.

The immediate result was the significant improvement of the economic status for the Malay elite, but not as much for the rural population, who were less likely to benefit from the special economic rights. The example is the 'Ali-Baba' enterprises that legitimized Chinese owners (the 'Baba' part) with nominal Malay partners (the 'Ali' part) who got paid for their presence. Departure of the British interest after Independence in 1957 was perceived to be likely to benefit the Chinese and Indians more than the Malays.

This was the trigger for the race riot of 1969.[5] The New Economic Policy (NEP), planned for 20 years, was proclaimed to remedy the situation by further measures that were meant to increase Malay ownership of wealth but to still allow the Chinese (and Indians) to get richer at a slower rate. The proclaimed target was very moderate, aiming for the share of the minority Chinese to be 40% of the total wealth, more than the goal of a 30% share for the majority Malays. The wealth share that was to be reduced was foreign ownership.

The high-minded goal was easier set than achieved. Quotas in schools were needed so that the Malay youth could get educated. Since the youth educated under these quotas would be at a disadvantage for employment, government job quotas were to provide partial help. But the limits on the government size implied the solution would have to be found in the industrial sector. To avoid forcing non-Malay business to absorb all Malay job-seekers trained under a quota system, Malay ownership of wealth had to be promoted. Because they lacked managerial experience, shares (from foreign interest) distributed to Malays were likely to be sold out fast and cheap, so these shares had to be placed in Unit Trusts, under government care. To employ the technically educated elites, the government launched heavy industries. Since such industries were not likely to be competitive in the world market, these were placed behind protective trade barriers, justified in the name of infant industry protection. The inefficiency of such industries could not be allowed in the long term; privatization was then carried out with hand-picked Malay owners who could reduce the featherbedding without being 'politically incorrect.' Because of their relative inexperience, and thus dependence on the government, these Malays lost heavily in Crisis 1997 (like Mirzan Mahathir, son of the Prime Minister). See Jomo, 1998: 187ff, also Low, 2000: 114-6. This necessitated a public bailout, using pension funds.

---

[5] With deaths around 200 by official report.

Every measure had its own logic, each brought benefits for the Malay elite. In *The Malay Dilemma*, Mahathir (1970) explained, "At first, this seems grossly unfair. . . . With the existence of the few rich Malays, at least the poor Malays can say that their fate is not entirely to serve the rich non-Malays. From the point of view of racial ego . . . the existence of Malay tycoons is essential."

The discovery of petroleum helped, but petroleum prices fall as well as rise, and the recession of 1985 brought 9% unemployment. Thus, manufactured export had to be promoted. The high tech industry developed in Penang, the only Malaysian state with a Chinese majority, under the advice of international experts. The industry parks were patterned after those of Singapore, originally with ownership limitations. Because of wage advantage, it soon became a favorite location for multinational corporations.

By 1990, the goals of the NEP were only partially reached. The government announced in 1995 the Industrial Coordinating Act, which required firms above a certain size that did not export above a certain limit to sell 30% of their stocks to the government. This had little impact upon the electronics firms, which are export-oriented, but it discouraged many other local firms by Malaysian Chinese from growing big, and join the rank of exporters (Perkins and Woo, 2000: 247). This places a stumbling block against the diversification of the export mix away from electronics.

To make the long story short, we display in Chart 11.2.5 the ownership of share capital of limited companies in 1969 (for Peninsular Malaysia) and 1990 for all Malaysia. Due to the predominant weight of Peninsular Malaysia in Malaysia, the chart presents a fair comparison. In short, the *bumiputras* gained and so did the Chincsc: a win-win solution.

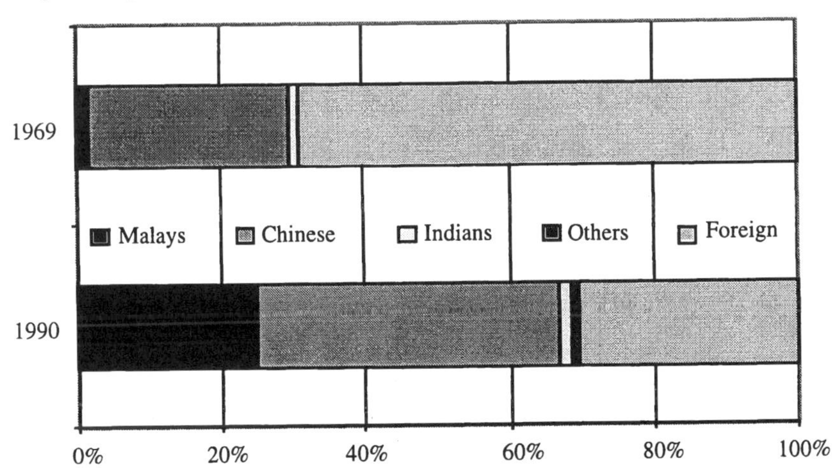

Chart 11.2.5 Ownership of Malaysian wealth, 1969 and 1990 Source: Lim (2001)

The reality is slightly more complex. A large public sector emerged, under the control of the Malay elite. In addition, the foreign ownership represents different things in different times. Early on, foreign interest meant the British; more recently, most foreign investment came from Asia, in particular, societies of Chinese descent: Hong Kong, Singapore and Taiwan. These investors share the same ethos as the Malaysian Chinese.

Chart 11.2.6 presents the direct foreign investment of Malaysia, in 1990, by country of origin. Note that a full 84% is from East Asia, with more than half from the three Sinitic NIEs: Singapore, Taiwan and Hong Kong. Among the Chinese businessmen, a billionaire like Robert Kuok (owner of the Perlis Plantations and the Federal Flour) from Malaysia could stay in Hong Kong, with interest in Singapore. So the interethnic wealth share in Malaysia is to some extent notional.

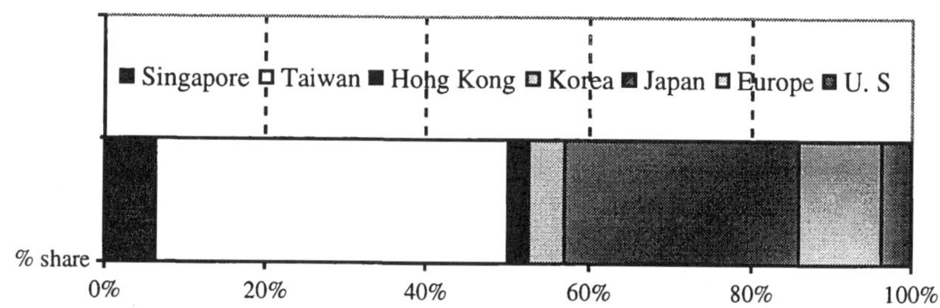

Chart 11.2.6 Direct foreign investment in Malaysia, by economy, 1990

In short, for the Islamic Malay society, the local Chinese can be neither assimilated (as in the Philippines and Thailand), nor successfully competed against without quota protections (as in Korea), nor somehow removed (as was partially done in Vietnam),[6] in view of the international economic and political realities.

Computing the Malay/Chinese ratio of monthly household income in Peninsular Malaysia, we find this rose from 0.463 in 1957-8 to 0.607 in 1987 and then fell back to 0.553 in 1995. There has definitely been improvement for the Malays, but nothing so drastic as to reflect oppression of the Chinese.

On the contrary, it is the perceived widening of the income gap among the Malays that has strengthened the fundamentalist Islam challenge to the Malay leadership. But that has made the Chinese and Indians rally around the latter, consolidating its hold on power.

From the view of development economics, the interest of the Malaysian case is that despite the challenges of a multi-ethnic society, and despite the difficulty of assimilating the immigrant groups (relative to Thailand and the

---

[6] Definitely ethnic cleansing has never been the goal of any Malay leaders.

Philippines), the Malaysian economy has done better than all the other ASEAN members, except for Singapore. The record may not appear perfect to all observers, but it must be counted as an encouraging success.

It is useful to contrast this picture with Singapore, across the causeway. The ruling party there adopts meritocracy[7] as its slogan: "from each his best, to each his worth." Affirmative action programs are rejected because "It would create a crutch mentality, promote communal divisions and undermine the principles of meritocracy," according to Deputy Prime Minister Goh Keng Swee in 1972 (see Rahim, 1998). Goh further stated, "Our main concern was to generate fast economic growth by any and every means ... if unequal income distribution of income generate greater savings and investment . . . then this must be accepted as the price to fight unemployment."

Data do not allow exact comparison. But according to Lim (2001), in terms of mean monthly personal income in Singapore, the Malay/Chinese ratio fell from 0.788 in 1966 to 0.635 in 1972 and then rose to 0.701 in 1990. To Rahim, this record means the policy of meritocracy has failed the Singaporean Malays. The key problem is the lack of successful role models to offset the baggage of a negative identity. The reply of Goh Chok-Tong, the current Prime Minister of Singapore, is that Malays are better educated and proportionately hold more administrative, managerial, professional and technical positions than they do in Malaysia.

As Embong (2000) noted, in the three decades after the 1969 race riot, Malaysia made great progress in reducing poverty (from 51.2% in 1970 to 6.8% in 1997) and creating a middle class, also many entrepreneurs, among Malays in the land of their forefathers. Chinese and Indians also prospered, and continued to earn income higher than the Malay majority. Malaysia has been free from inter ethnic violence even during Crisis 1997, in contrast to Indonesia. Quotas in university admission are recently relaxed. Cronyism exists in the economy, but the public is free to criticize the supposedly autocratic government. The export sector created many jobs and large numbers of foreign workers were employed. They constituted 9.8 % of the work force in 1998. Thus, Crisis 1997 caused more layoffs among the migrants than the locals. Therefore, the unemployment rate rose in Crisis 1997 (from 2.6% to 3.9%) much less than the 4% in 1985.

At the same time, diversification and industrial upgrading proceeded rather slowly. Illegal migrant workers were expelled in 2002 in the hope that the resultant labor shortage would raise wages and force firms to upgrade their outputs. Reform in the PRC has apparently diverted foreign investors

---

[7] The plight of the Malays, as perceived by their leaders, is succinctly put by Mahathir (1970: 25), 'Whatever the Malays could do, the Chinese could do better and more cheaply.' On the eve of the 1997 election, he rejected the pro-meritocracy view of some successful Malays, by repeating his assessment about the ability of the Malays (Perkins and Woo, 2000: 253).

away from Malaysia reccently (See Tan, 1997: 124); this may signal tougher export competition in the future. Malaysia's affirmative action programs might have achieved their laudable goals: helping the poor without harming the rich. Whether the Singaporean focus on meritocracy has tempered a labor force more resilient to survive global competition must be decided by future research.

It seems true that, on average, Malays in both countries have not yet realized their full potential. What is to be done is a different and far harder question. An analogy of some use may be found in Taiwan during the last half of the 20th century. The majority of the population is native Taiwanese,[8] of mainly Chinese descent (but some Austronesian blood). The political power was mostly in the hands of the Mainlander group until the end of the 1980s. Yet economic power gradually shifted to the hands of the native Taiwanese majority even before political power did. Certainly, the native Taiwanese did not benefit from anything like 'affirmative action' programs. If anything, the better-connected Mainlander firms enjoyed official patronage during the earlier years of KMT rule. There were intermarriages, to be sure, but that was not the reason for the shift of economic power. As Johnson (1992) showed, for the largest 100 firms, the Taiwanese firms earned higher and more stable profits throughout the 1980s. Further studies are needed to describe what it took for the native Taiwanese to succeed.

The question for Malaysia or any other multi-ethnic society is not of purely historical interest. If Malaysia has achieved a win-win solution for all communities in the past, whether the process is efficient or otherwise, that may sound fine. But now with the PRC in the WTO, trade competition may be more intense. Facing intense competition, an inefficient economy may have to accept a shrunken pie, and the issue may not be solvable just by sending home immigrant workers from Indonesia, as it was done in the past. The more efficient and mutually understanding is a multi-ethnic society, the better will that society rise to the test.

3. THE PEOPLE'S REPUBLIC OF CHINA

The present volume studies the catching-up process for market economies in a global environment. In the first 60% of its history, the economy of the Peoples' Republic of China (PRC) was an inward-looking, command economy. However interesting and important, that part of the story is beyond the scope of this volume. Yet it is important to ask to what extent

---

[8] 'Native Taiwanese' here means those who arrived before 1949.

our theory, elucidated above, remains valid for an economy like that of the Chinese Mainland economy after 1978, in particular an economy of a billion persons (hence potentially relevant for India) or a government with a Marxist-Leninist ideology (thus, potentially relevant for North Korea). After all, both size and political institutions matter.

With this in view, our brief discussion is not designed to do full justice to the Mainland Chinese economy. All we try to do here is to compare the growth performance of the PRC with two other market economies under private ownership system, namely Malaysia and Argentina, as shown in Chart 11.3.1. The time path of the PRC is credible and stable. Because of its initial modest base, the high proportional growth does not translate into large magnitudes of catching up with the United States. The eve of the reform and 1989-90 (marked with arrow signs) are the only two occasions showing some setbacks. For context, these are less serious than what Malaysia suffered in 1985. In comparison, the Argentina record shows both an unsteady path and a general case of falling behind.

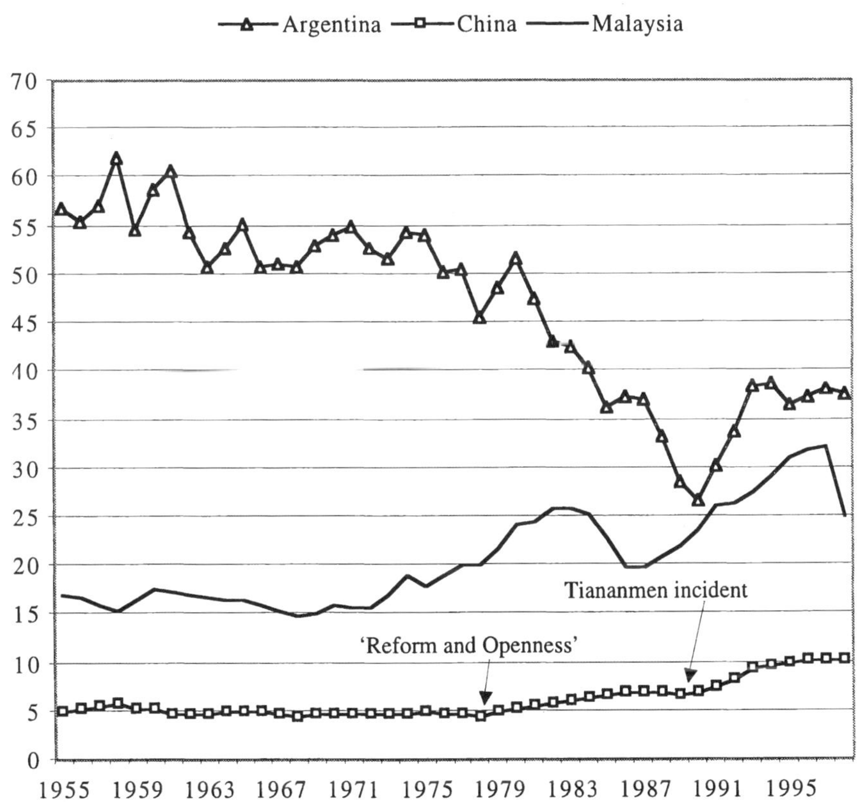

Chart 11.3.1 Repcri: Argentina, Malaysia and the PRC Source: WDI

Next, we would consider the degrees of 'globalization' and 'industrialization,' represented respectively with the ratio of export to GDP and the manufacturing content of the export for the same three economies in Charts 11.3.2 and 11.3.3, respectively.

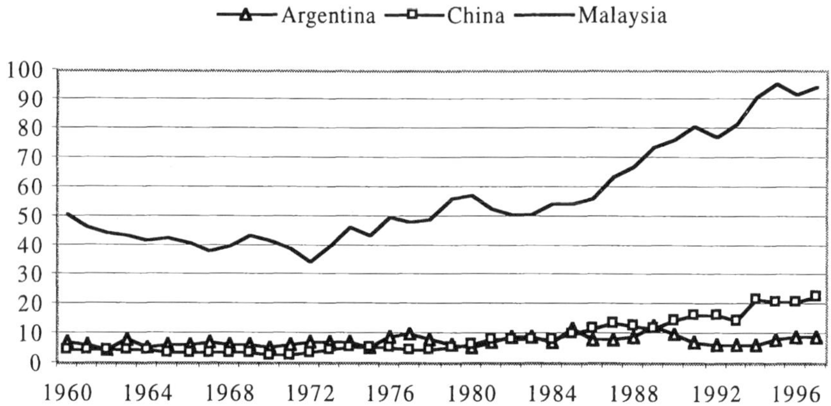

Chart 11.3.2 Export/GDP: Argentina, Malaysia, and the PRC Source: WDI

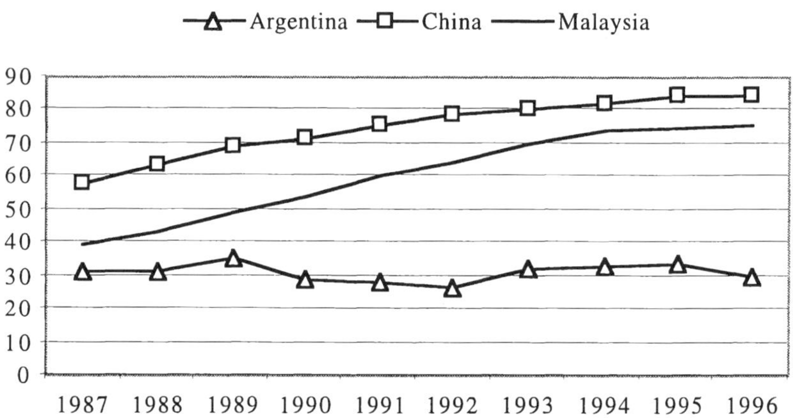

Chart 11.3.3 % of manufacture in total export: Argentina, Malaysia, and PRC Source: WDI

Since the smaller the country, the less self-sufficient it is likely to be, one would expect the export/GDP ratio to be far larger for Malaysia than for the PRC, as it is true in reality. The degree of 'openness' for Argentina is clearly very modest. It has no trend, and gets overtaken by the PRC.

Although for Chart 11.3.3, data for the PRC are only available for more recent years, it is clear that perhaps due to the modest resource endowment per capita, or government policy, the export of the PRC is more concentrated in manufacture even than Malaysia.

We do not deal with here the 're-export' issue, which may overstate (for purposes like summing up the trade of Hong Kong and the PRC) the exports for entrepôt economies like Singapore and Hong Kong, but not Malaysia or the PRC.

From what we discussed earlier, due to the advantage of technology acquisition through learning, the rapid progress of the PRC economy is to be expected. In fact, in policy statements, the leaders of the PRC justify its various measures for 'openness' to the world market in terms of the potential for introducing foreign technology, even at the risk of what they have warned of the ideological disadvantages of 'spiritual pollution.'[9]

In addition, there is still another advantage of market openness for the PRC, namely the consequent application of the market discipline of world trade to convince various entrenched interests at home to adapt to the 'objective laws of economics.' The eagerness for accession to the World Trade Organization is partly motivated by such advantages.

Like Sun Yat-sen[10] previously, the PRC leaders often emphasize in public statements the 'public good' aspect of technology, and identify it as a means for cultural survival,[11] not simply a means to produce goods for consumption. Perhaps history provides the ultimate explanation of why East Asians save proportionally more out of their income than do Latin Americans. The descendants of Cortez and Pizzaro understandably are more confident that the future belongs to them. That is not the view from East Asia, where the ancestors of Montezuma and Atahuallpa set off. Subconsciously, East Asians believe that development is the key to technology, and technology means collective survival. Without technology, it is hard to be accepted as 'civilized'. Without being accepted as part of 'the civilized', conquest and extinction may be their lot.

What does the future hold? As a tentative exercise, we shall search for available data, apply the relevant theory, make computations, and corroborate the result with additional evidence, before we compare the results with qualitative information, all in the hope of distilling some policy-relevant insight out of the exercise.

The available data pertain to the time series of the 'repcri' for the PRC used in Chart 11.3.1, above. From this one can calculate the time series of the growth rate, and regress the latter against the repcri in a polynomial formula. To help decide the form of the polynomial, we do the same for

---

[9] In this context, the observation of Ralph Braibanti is quite appropriate: 'It has long been a theoretical ideal that transnationally induced change should be articulated to the cultural context of the recipient nation. . . . A prerequisite of this is that the recipient nation identify and evaluate its own values and control both the quality and the rate of introduction of outside ideas which will modify these values.'

[10] The founder of the Chinese Nationalist Party and an ally to Chinese Communists.

[11] In a sense familiar to the readers of *Guns, Germs and Steel* (Diamond, 1999).

Malaysia, since both economies pursue an outward oriented policy, so the two economy-specific functions should share some family traits.

The benchmark model in Chapter 1 implies the function form is likely to be quasi-concave in the relevant range, with trend deceleration following trend-acceleration, as well as a partial catching up, according to Lau and Wan (1994).

However, if the polynomial is second degree, then the growth rate of the repcri is a concave parabola for the PRC, but a convex parabola for Malaysia. In addition, the convex formula predicts the Malaysian economy will reach the U.S. level at an accelerating rate. But after fitting instead a cubic parabola, both the PRC and Malaysia have a third degree polynomial with the same sign pattern for the coefficients, that is,

$$y = -415.97x^3 + 59.454x^2 - 1.758x + 0.055 \qquad \text{for the PRC}$$

and

$$y = -141.41x^3 + 93.267x^2 - 20.127x + 1.448 \qquad \text{for Malaysia}$$

where x and y stand for repcri and its growth rate, respectively.

These are shown in Charts 11.3.4 and 11.3.5. One can next compute numerically the limit of catching up:

$$x_\infty = 0.116376 \text{ for the PRC and } x_\infty = 0.293355 \text{ for Malaysia.}$$

These estimates are clearly over-conservative, presumably because the end point of our data coincides with the depth of the financial Crisis 1997, as shown in Chart 11.3.1. Thus, in Charts 11.3.4-5, the sharp downward bend of the regression lines implies that the growth rate of repcri will soon be zero and no more catching up will be possible.

In addition, the above single equation estimation is far from being a good fit, as the scatter diagrams show.

Actually, there are reasons to believe that the regression result is an understatement of the PRC growth potential, that the popular concern of other Asian economies with regard to the threat of Chinese export is overstated, and that the prospect of improving the ordinary life in the PRC may be far better than observers realize, inside and outside the PRC.

First off, we claim that a three- to five-fold improvement of the per capita nominal[12] GDP of the PRC should be achievable, through internal reform, with resultant improvement of the 'terms of trade' (in terms of national accounting) even without much further technical progress. That improvement in international purchasing power should raise the Chinese wage, relative to the foreign wage. It will make the Chinese Mainland an immensely better customer for foreign imports and far less threatening as an export rival. In a second round, the increase in Chinese imports will acceler-

[12] But not real.

ate the modernization of social and institutional aspects and increase Chinese productivity in a gradual manner.

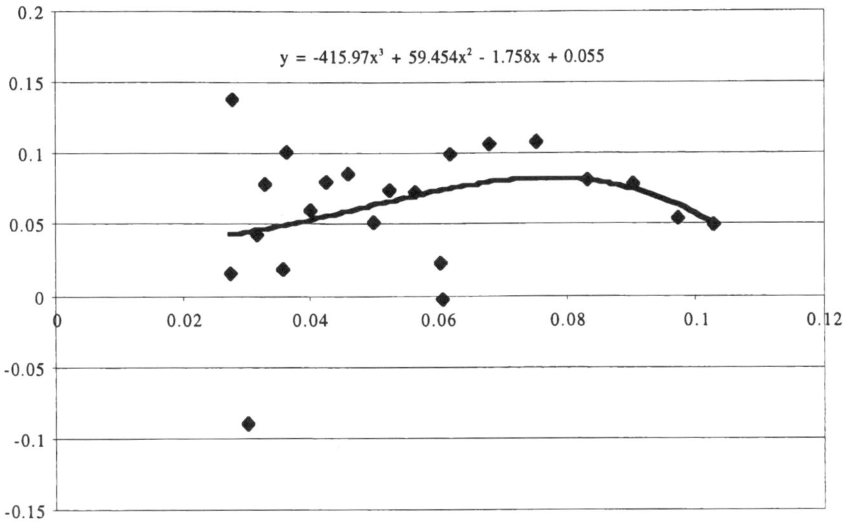

Chart 11.3.4 Growth of repcri as function of repcri: PRC

Source: calculations based on data from WDI

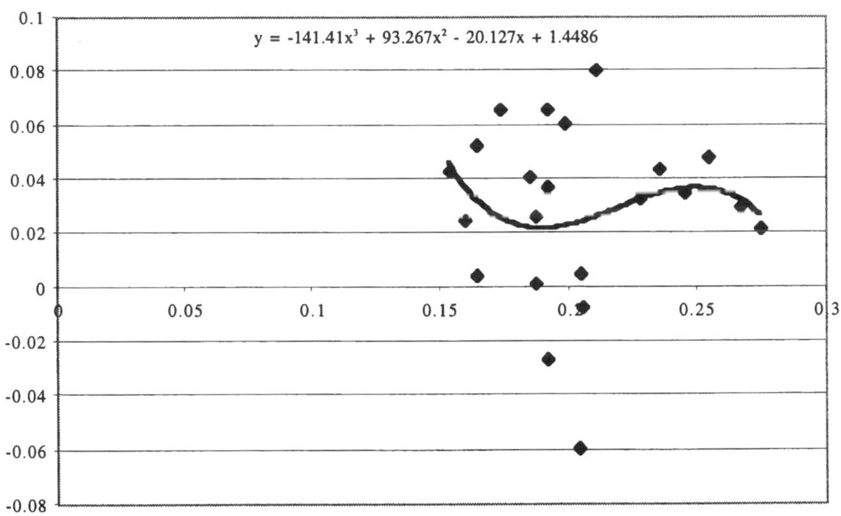

Chart 11.3.5 Growth of repcri as function of repcri: Malaysia

Source: calculations based on data from WDI

The basis of our claim is that Chinese products are heavily under-priced internationally, and that can and ought to be changed. Oddly, the change can come without necessarily costing much to the final customers of Chinese exports overseas. The information in Table 11.3.1 is indicative.

Per capita GNP 1997	Nominal	PPP	Nominal/PPP
PRC, Mainland	860	3,070	28%
Hong Kong	25,200	24,350	103%
Japan	38,160	24,400	156%
USA	29,080	29,080	100%

Table 11.3.1 Nominal/PPP ratio, 1997 Source: WDI

This table shows that an amount of Chinese resources that is worth one dollar to a person in the PRC can produce exports only valued at 28 cents abroad. This does not mean that cultural differences must make export goods under-priced. One dollar's worth of Japanese goods sells for 156 cents; one dollar's worth of Hong Kong goods sells for 103 cents. But why should China differ so much from both Hong Kong and Japan? One possible cause is that in remote areas (which China has in plenty), a person can live well on non-tradable goods. However, this does not appear to be the chief reason. After all, on the world market, a dollar's worth of Chinese goods used to be 'undervalued,' but not by this much.

From the macroeconomic point of view, this increased under-valuation reflects the 1994 Chinese devaluation of the Renminbi, coupled with the attainment of price stability. This led to the expansion of the Chinese export surplus, the rise of foreign investment to China as well as the accumulation of sizable Chinese foreign exchange reserves.

From the microeconomic viewpoint, this is a matter of market channels. Much of Chinese export is accounted for by joint ventures with foreign firms, or subcontracts from multinational corporations. A high profit margin goes to foreign investors or foreign purchasing firms.

In a market economy, the means to rectify the situation is through competition. The case of Hong Kong implies that, in this aspect, no government initiative is needed.

In fact, as Jones and Sakong (1980) have documented, it was the simplification of government regulations that helped in the case of Korea. Under President Rhee, the multiple exchange rate led to high rates of return to those merchants who could lobby and bribe. Under President Park, the exchange rate reform closed such loopholes so that merchants would concentrate on developing new markets, and improve their operations. Their example is the Samsung Group, which shifted its efforts from lobbying for illicit gain to improving management to make honest profits. The moral is, important operations such as improving management or lobbying (whether illegality is involved or not) consumes the attention and effort of the top management. Bureaucratic regulations harm economic development not so much through the diversion of material resources, or the incidence of illegal or immoral practices, but because of the diversion of managerial efforts away from developing new markets and new practices that are so crucial to economic development.

Another useful comparison can be made between Taiwan in the early 1980s and the PRC today. After 20 years of reform (which started in 1958 for Taiwan and in 1978 for the PRC), salesmen representing small, private Taiwanese shoe firms would go abroad to sell their wares in the U.S. and in other countries, but for some reason, no such effort has been launched by small production units in the PRC to date (the equivalent to the Taiwanese small firms presumably would be the town and village enterprises). However directly successful are such small firms,[13] it is this kind of competitive pressure that forces the profit margins of foreign middlemen down.

Presently, according to Dicks (1995), the legal system of the PRC still includes a strong element of the socialistic legal tradition. It is still evolving to adapt to its 'socialistic market economy.' For now, much of the economic activity has to operate under the administrative rulings of the government, which change with the normal changes of government personnel. With or without any corruption, inherently, such 'rule of man,' rather than a 'rule of law,' is not conducive to transparency and constancy. This presumably distracts the managerial efforts of indigenous firms from developing competitive pressure against foreign middlemen, either to displace them or to narrow their profit margin. Reform in the PRC is an ongoing process, and it takes time.

So far we have claimed that in the case of the PRC, an outward orientation helps the economy by stimulating the catching up process. This is so, even though the PRC is in a class by itself, because of its size and its ideology. More discussion is in order.

All our discussions have been conducted as if all that matters is the average individual. In the NIEs, the outward orientation shifts under-employed workers to labor-intensive export trade. The situation is different for the PRC. First, because of its size, the regional income gap is wide, and has gotten wider due to the coastal prosperity under the reform. Second, because of its centrally planned past, a large number of workers are in the large, obsolete state firms threatened by market competition.

Even with such initial conditions, so far the PRC has managed to tame inflation, and to avoid both the serious economic dislocations that ravaged Eastern Europe and the former Soviet economies, and the severe shortages in North Korea and Cuba. Yet selective punishment has not fully restrained widespread corruption, influence peddling and all forms of rent seeking. The government is acutely aware of the risks of massive, open disaffection and

---

[13] Obviously, some firms must be successful for others to participate in such activities.

tries its best to stave off such upheaval. Through deficit financing, public work projects are carried out, not to realize the ambitions of the planners, but to create jobs. Ad hoc relief efforts have been employed to placate laid-off workers, provided they do not attempt organized opposition.

Over the last two decades, the Chinese reform is free from neither inefficiency nor inequity, but the growth of both exports and export surplus, the inflow of sizable foreign investment, and even the fact that so many people can, *somehow,* make a quick fortune indicates that as a whole, the future of the Chinese economy has promise. Given the hardship suffered by Eastern Europe and the successor states of the former Soviet Union in the post-communist transition, a sufficiently large portion of the Chinese population is not ready to risk drastic changes in the current institutions.

For now, improvement in workers' outlook, in equipment, in information, and in institutions would allow China to have further growth. However, for harnessing creative potentials in a world of rapidly changing technology, institutional factors are likely to become increasingly decisive. This is so, especially when the economy is large and complex. It is no accident that, although rent seeking exists in every country, by and large high-income economies operate under the rule of law, and not the rule of man. Japan is an example. Nor is it surprising that both Korea and Taiwan gradually evolved away from authoritarianism.

Only the future can tell what course the Chinese development will take. Nevertheless, some things are broadly predictable. In the long run, people in China would never accept a living standard much lower than that of Japan or Korea, and Chinese institutions will take such forms so as to honor the peoples' wish.

4. MAURITIUS

To appreciate the case of Mauritius, one must keep it in context. This is an island country off the east coast of Africa, settled by South Asians as well as some French-African descendants. First the French and then the British held it as a colony, for a naval coal station, and then for sugar cane.

The population composition by religion in 1983 included:

Hindu	53%
Moslem	13%
Christian	30%
Buddhist	0.4%

By origin, 0.6% of the population was of Chinese descent. This sector of the population never had the economic importance of the Chinese in Southeast Asia. Yet, this small group played a catalytic role, as we shall see.

Chart 11.4.1 shows the repcri of Mauritius compared to South Asian and East African economies. Chart 11.4.2 plots the repcri of Mauritius over time against both that of Malaysia, the highest among the ASEAN-3, and Korea, the lowest among the NIEs.

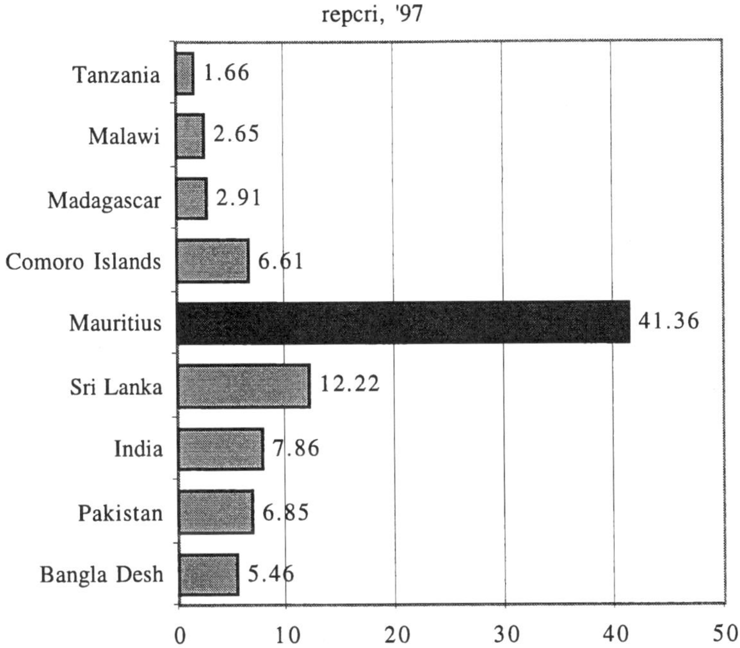

Chart 11.4.1 Repcri, Mauritius and 8 others Source: WDI

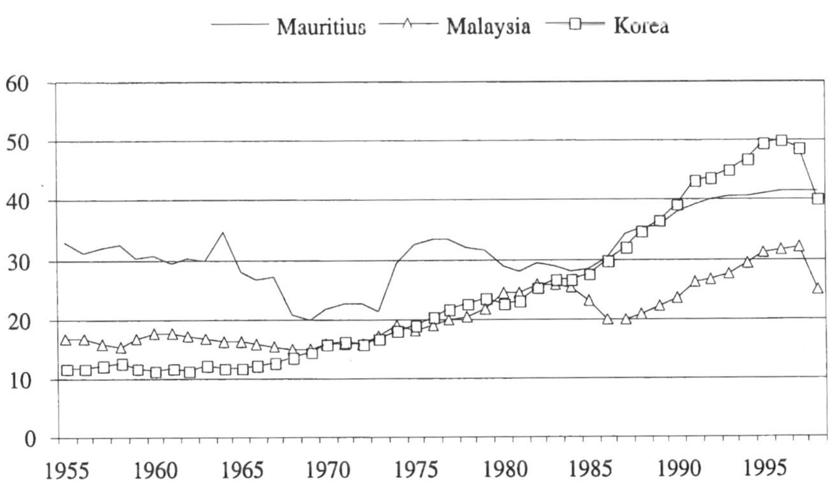

Chart 11.4.2 repcri: Mauritius, Malaysia and Korea Source: WDI

Mauritius has done quite well in performance, on the basis of purchasing power parity.[14] Its history has been described by Findlay and Wellisz (1993). Initially, its grim prospects as an over-populated island dependent on subsistence farming in sugar cane discouraged James Meade, who believed that this would be a classic case of Malthusian tragedy. Population increase would only be stopped by poverty, disease and perhaps famine.

Four factors turned the island's fortune around.

(a) The quota system under the Multi-Fiber Agreement (MFA) forced textile merchants to seek new locales for their investment.

(b) The Lomé Convention granted tariff reduction to former European colonies, including Mauritius.

(c) The local Chinese settlers assured the Hong Kong investors that they could work with Mauritian political leaders.

(d) The Kaohsiung Export Processing Zone of Taiwan provided a viable blueprint to grant foreign invested firms the convenience of a free port, without the complication of an immediate regulatory reform over the rest of the economy.

Unlike the Taiwanese, the Mauritians did not commit the infrastructure investment to locate such export enterprises inside a compact industrial park. Instead, specific firms were granted Export Processing Zone (EPZ) status. Although experts from World Bank regard this practice as second best, still by this means, early unemployment was absorbed, and Mauritius became the world's leading producer of knitted gloves and mittens, even though there was not a single sheep in the economy. More importantly, indigenous entrepreneurs joined the production process, so that the textile industry was no longer exclusively in the hands of Hong Kong businessmen.

According to the Economic Intelligence Unit (EIU), the EPZ exports remain competitive, and they accounted for two-thirds of the exports in 2000, with sugar exports another 20%. Since international quotas will soon be removed and the work force is still not sufficiently well educated (as compared with Korea, for example), the government is launching various projects to improve the productivity of the labor force.

The lessons Mauritius offers are:

(1) With the right policy and institutions, the benefits of export-led development are available to many economies. Confucian ethos, East Asian location, supposed favor of the U.S. during the Cold War, and population size all seem to be irrelevant.

(2) Cultural and historical connections matter, as the presence of the small Chinese community attracted the Hong Kong businessmen, and the Creole-French connection and the Lomé Convention makes France a bridge-

[14] By nominal value, Malaysia does somewhat better.

head for Mauritian exports inside the European Community. But their effect presumably can be overcome with some effort. The Koreans have played a role in Bangladesh similar to that of the Hong Kong merchants in Mauritius, even though there has never been much of a historical Bengali-Korean tie.

(3) Policy does not have to be perfect for the export-led process to take off. Reports from World Bank often note that Mauritian exports could be more competitive if the non-Export Zone factories were also freed from the bureaucratic regime of import substitution, or if all Export Zone factories could be located in a contiguous area to facilitate shipping. Still, the economy prospered regardless.

(4) Education does decide how far and fast an export-led economy can go, and industries like electronics apparently require more skill. The Mauritian attempts to enter the electronics trade have so far not been successful.

(5) Of course, the composition of export alone is only part of the story. Bangladesh has 67% of its export in the two items of garments (56%) and jute manufacture (11%), the former having benefited from Korean and Hong Kong investment. However, Bangladesh has only 11% of its labor force in manufacturing; Mauritius, 36%. One should be encouraged that Bangladesh is already in the process of transforming itself to enjoy the benefits of export-led trade (especially in terms of the declining birth rate), and not be discouraged by its current modest level of income.

Further information on Mauritius can be found in Dabee and Greenaway (2001). Such facts also broadly corroborate our discussion on the NIEs, Malaysia and PRC:

1) Over all, Mauritius enjoys higher per capita income than other African and South Asian economics. Nonetheless, its growth performance is highly uneven, and its long term prospects are quite challenging.

2) Initially, Mauritius practiced import substitution. For some time, the incentives were biased toward these industries against those in the export processing zone, which started in 1970. The boom in the export processing zone industries absorbed the unemployed labor and raised wage cost but not labor productivity, so that investors began to search for other sites. Consequently the Mauritian growth peaked around 1976. At the same time, because the financing of unemployment relief through public projects, deficits developed in both the government budget and the current account, leading to devaluation and double digit inflation.

3) After the crisis developed, The World Bank's Structural Adjustment Program imposed restrictions on both public projects as well as wage increases. This led to another major expansion of business in the Export Processing Zone, over 1983-88.

4) Rising labor costs again induced the exit of investors from Mauritius, this time to nearby East African locations, causing a slowing down of

Mauritian growth, over the period 1989-92. Now the attempt to diversify the economy away from textile exports is in full swing.

Interestingly, wage demand and public spending have been repeatedly the threat of Mauritian economic stability. This has never been the case for any of the NIEs. The recalcitrant protection of the import substitution industries have made the Export Processing Zone industries an enclave, in sharp contrast to Malaysia where backward linkages have spread the prosperity of the electronics sector in the export zone of Bayan Lepas, Penang into the hinterland (Rasiah, 2001). In Mauritius, more than once, the local elections have aroused uncertainty in the mind of investors. Again this has not been the case in Korea and Taiwan, when authoritarian governments were voted out.

The phasing out of the Multi-fiber Agreement is likely to pose a severe challenge to the economy. Again, this has not been much of a factor in NIEs or ASEAN economies.

All these indicate the fragility of the Mauritian economy, even today. Yet, its achievement in comparison with other developing economies suggests how much more can be done in the developing world.

APPENDIX 11.1: ADDITIONAL OBSERVATIONS ON THE CHINESE ECONOMY

In economic development, there are several issues relevant to the PRC (maybe also India) but few other economies, in view of size.

First, trade has brought significant benefit to the NIEs, such as the acquisition of technology, the introduction of (world) market discipline, the opportunity of upgrading output mix in tune with the current skill mix, the tapping into resources not available within one's own boundaries. Most such benefits (such as technology acquisition) increase with the per capita export volume, but are not strictly proportional to it. This suggests that outward orientation may remain crucial to the PRC but benefit it less. Korea, the most populous of the NIEs, had a population of 46.4 million in 1998, which was 1/26.7 of the population of the PRC (1,238.6 million in 1998). For China to match the export per capita of Korea on any item – cars or ships, steel or computer chips - the rest of the world has to absorb 27 times the current Korean total export – a near impossibility.

Second, as a corollary, when the output and export of the PRC expand due to efficient gain, its terms of trade for some specific items may decline so much to cause immiserization: more export implies less rather than more welfare. For Taiwan, the introduction of its asparagus export was monitored to safeguard for adverse terms of trade change.

Third, beside the consideration of 'direct' national advantage, long before immiserization has begun to happen, major price fall of certain exports will cause severe trade friction. Current anxiety among most Asian economies about competition from PRC is a harbinger of how intense such friction can be. For similar reasons, Japan was denied for years the benefit of the most favored nation clause by countries from India to United Kingdom, in the early years under Article 35 of GATT (Komiya, 1990, 8).

Fourth, judging by its population size – four and one half of the American population in 1998 – a more affluent China may develop such import demand for petroleum, or foods with high protein content to cause either changes in world prices which may have severe impact on other economies or environmental pressure. Again one can use the consumption habits of other Chinese communities to predict what Chinese consumption can be. For example, if the ownership of automotive vehicles is about four persons per vehicle in Taiwan (an economy with lower repcri than either Hong Kong or Singapore), one can estimate what new fuel demand the PRC would generate, once its per capita purchasing power has reached what people enjoy in Taiwan today. Judging from the industries migrated from Taiwan to the PRC in recent years, from toys, textiles, to bicycles, and laptops, the rise of per capita income in the PRC is certainly to continue, at a reasonably rapid pace.

One more point to make is that, among many non-Chinese writers, the market potential of China appears like a blessing from heaven – a 'gold mine'. The truth is, China has few mines producing gold. Any sales revenue from China, profit and all, has to be repatriated in the form of commodity exports, and the more marketable are such exports, the more production of the rest of the world is likely to be displaced, the more workers must be reassigned – if ever possible – to other jobs. It would be a Herculean task, at the very best.

Of course, all these discussions do not imply that China cannot, or should not become fully developed. Far from it. But its development ought be approached with great sensitivity. The world market can supply China with technology, experience and market discipline of the most objective type. But the rise of Chinese per capita income is most likely not through massive export, or massive increase of physical volume of production, but in the quality of goods supplied and enjoyed by Chinese themselves, in a form which does not cause havoc on the environment. Better technology and better organization are what can uplift Chinese production in forms Chinese deem enjoyable, but not wasteful in energy or environmental quality.

To accomplish this goal, the policy design for China poses one more challenge. Although coordination and over all consistency are vital, as history has amply shown, rigid central planning would not lead to any growth, let alone sustainable, 'smart growth,' especially in view of the complexity of the Chinese economy, due to its size.

So far we have dealt with the challenges due to 'size'. Does size confer advantages for China? Three points deserve consideration.

The most obvious point is the *economy of scale*, due to either the sharing of overhead, or increasing returns. Two examples illustrate the point. First, suppose technology spreads easier within an economy than across the border, then for the same fixed cost of acquiring certain information, its benefit goes further for China than elsewhere. Next, *other things being equal*, potentially China can mount a larger effort on given important R & D. projects than many other economies. So far, trained and experienced research scientists and engineers remain relatively scarcer in China than in the advanced nations. Moreover, up to now, the PRC has not been as successful as Korea and Taiwan in attracting back from abroad its foreign-trained personnel.

Next in importance is the question whether size may confer bargaining power. From the economic viewpoint, with its potentially vast market, China has the capacity to bargain with individual foreign businesses, trading investment opportunities for technology acquisition. In fact, much more can presumably be done if these foreign businesses can be confident that China does not pose a serious threat to their interest in the world market. Now, on a per capita basis, China can never hope to derive significant gain from deep export market penetration. On the other hand, much benefit can come from some limited export experience. Thus, by logic, there should be great scope for creative negotiation. By the same token, one of the current stumbling blocks against technology transfer to the PRC is the security concerns of America, the European Union and Japan. Presumably such difficulties can be obtained by systematic confidence building.

Finally, the symbiotic transformation of the PRC with the large Chinese Diaspora[15] provides a growth which is quite unique. On one hand, the PRC provided not only such low-priced labor and land, but also an environment of the 'rule of man', under which local cadres can operate with great flexibility. In such an environment, the self-made tycoons from the Diaspora could extend their own activities from commerce and finance to manufacturing. On the other hand, the 'Overseas Chinese' offered organization, market connection, capital and the easy-to-acquire technology to set up Chinese labor-intensive operations for markets in advanced economies. When labor shortages developed in Hong Kong and Taiwan, and the 1978 reform of the PRC made export a national goal, South China experienced explosive growth. The linkages to advanced economies may be more subtle and lie deeper, but the relationship with the global economy remains at the foundation.

Over 1979-2000, 348 billion US$ of direct foreign investment went to the PRC. This fact received much notice in the development literature. Since 48.9% of this came from Hong Kong, and an unknown part of this is disguised investment from China itself ('round tripping'), to gain incentives for foreign investment (EIU, Country Report: China 2002: 32-3), this intrigue often detracts attention from the true significance of such investment. What remains clear is that besides 'round-tripping', the direct foreign investment to the PRC remains sizable. As field reports indicate, much of this direct foreign investment is for export industries. Both the investment amount per project and the employment per firm are quite modest; the output is usually for the advanced economies. In short, what we have seen is that, for the sake of profit (rather than ideology, or ethnic loyalty) Overseas Chinese capital has been financing the migration of export industries from Hong Kong and Taiwan to the PRC. Why does this happen only now but not earlier? The fact is kinship may supply contact. What has currently triggered this investment toward the PRC, away from their present domicile is profit calculation. ASEAN states would have a fair chance to keep such investment fund home, had they matched the PRC in improving the investment environment.

---

[15] Beside the Chinese in Hong Kong and Taiwan, in 1993, the Southeast Asian communities of Chinese descent (Singapore included) were estimated to have a population of 20.05 million. See Lever-Tracy, Ip and Tracy (1996, 15).

However, the investment environment in coastal China may not yet be adequate for industry upgrading, when technological depth is needed for design and R & D. In fact, limitations in the Chinese institutional environment have made it difficult for the PRC to tap senior talents among the Overseas Chinese like those Taiwan had attracted, for example, Morris Chang of Taiwan Semiconductor Corporation. As a former senior executive at Texas Instruments for 20 years, Chang was neither born nor educated in Taiwan, but was attracted there to set up the first 'dedicated chip foundry' of the world, which accelerated the vertical fragmentation of the semiconductor industry. Only after the late 1990s, more senior trained personnel start to return to PRC from abroad, and for now, they focus more on the Chinese, rather than the foreign, market (Saxenian, 2002).

CHAPTER SUMMARY

- So far the evidence for our theoretic discussions comes from the four Asian NIEs. To assess general applicability, we consider three additional economies, each differing from the four NIEs in one or more aspects.
- The first economy to be studied here is Malaysia. As a mirror image to Singapore, the majority of the people are Islamic Malay, not Confucian Chinese, and the country can rely on its rich natural resources instead of its location-based strength. For reasons of equity as well as social stability, Malaysia has programs to grant preferential quotas to *bumiputras* in school admission, government and business employment and government contracts. During periods of high oil prices, the national economy devoted much attention to the energy sector. Nonetheless, the export of manufacture eventually became the leading edge of the economy. Malaysian per capita GDP ranks higher than both Thailand and Indonesia, and electronics is the leading export item. This pattern resembles those of the Asian NIEs.
- The economy of the PRC differs from the four NIEs both because of its state ideology and its size. In its first three decades, the country practiced central planning and placed most businesses under public ownership. Foreign trade and foreign investment were miniscule and development programs were carried out by mass movement. Since 1978, market force has been introduced along with foreign trade and foreign investment. Starting from a low base, sustained growth has been achieved with the introduction of technology from abroad, especially through investment from the Asian NIEs. To this extent, the lessons from the four NIEs appear largely applicable. Because of the PRC's size, its future growth may influence worldwide supply constraints. The main point is, the focus should be to acquire more value for what is produced rather than more of the same.
- Mauritius is an island off the East African coast where the majority of the population is of South Asian descent. Population growth made it difficult for the country to thrive on the sugar cane crop alone. The presence of a small Chinese settlement assured Hong Kong businessmen that, for quota jumping under the Multi-fiber Agreement, Mauritius could serve as an export platform, especially since the Lomé convention provided Mauritius some tariff advantages in European markets. Rather than pursuing wholesale reform of the existing bureaucratic regulations, certain factories were granted an Export Zone status to bypass the regulatory logjam. Business boomed and unemployment disappeared. In addition, indigenous enterprises joined the trade beside Hong Kong investors. Here the main themes are the benefits of regulatory reform and trade as well as the spillover of information and institutions from abroad.

QUESTIONS AND EXERCISES

1. Hong Kong has lost more than half of its manufacturing jobs to its northern neighbor, the PRC proper; Singapore has managed to retain the industrial character of the economy. Can this difference be attributable to certain differences between Malaysia and the PRC? Discuss.
2. For individuals in the PRC today, setting up a startup firm remains more difficult than for individuals in Taiwan. How can this fact influence the pace of technology spillover from foreign invested firms to the host economy? Discuss.
3. Unlike Malaysia, Mauritius has found it very challenging to break into such fields as electronics after scoring its success in the textile sector. Could you venture some guess about the reason?
4. Without alienating entrenched interests to remove all tariffs, an export zone allows the use of local labor with imported inputs to produce outputs sold at world market prices; an industrial park allows the locating of related producers together to realize various agglomerative economies. From this perspective, compare (a) the Export Processing Zones of Taiwan, (b) Export Zone in Mauritius, and (c) the Industrial Estates of Singapore, where there is little tariff lately.
5. Using the information from both Problem 6, Chapter 4, p. 136 and Problem 3, Chapter 12, p. 352, would it be desirable to induce those senior Chinese personnel returning from abroad to redirect their interest from the local market to the world market? Discuss.

Chapter 12

CONCLUSIONS

Managing Globalization

1. AT THE TURN OF THE MILLENNIUM

The new millennium is marked by two events, the attack on the United States on September 11, 2001, and the recession of 2001. Since this volume discusses the catching up process in a world with the U.S. as the technological leader, both events deserve some discussion.

The shifting of world leadership and the conflict between different cultures have been the theme of such well-read works as Kennedy (1987) and Huntington (1996). Their discussion focuses on political and military rivalry, rather than the type of technological and economic evolution by which the U.S. took over leadership from Britain.

September 11, 2001 was both an act of war and a sharp jolt to the world economy. But by the end of 2001, that event did not appear to presage any drastic consequences in the long term. Islamic extremists have neither overwhelmed the rest of the mankind (or 'the West') with force, nor managed thus far to force them to live out their lives in armed fortresses. The challenging party has neither the technological edge nor the industrial muscle to unseat the reigning power, in either a single blow or a sustained contest.

In hindsight, past U.S. retreats from Vietnam, or Lebanon, or Somalia reflected precisely the fact that the American public perceived that their country, or way of life, was secure enough to allow them to yield in minor remote contests. If anything, the events of September 11 seem to confirm the view that no party in today's world can attack the U.S. and escape retaliation. Evolving technology is not likely to change this fact, since the incumbent superpower will mobilize all available modern technology and go to any length to prevent its own demise as a state, due to a surprise attack.

If the world leadership is to pass from the U.S. in some future time, it is going to happen through economic evolution, not an upheaval with violence. Such an event would occur gradually over a long period of time, as happened between the U.S. and Britain over the interval 1900-35 (Jones, 1998: 57). Or else, the U.S. may gradually be integrated into some supra-national entity in an event like the emergence of Switzerland. At the present, it is not useful to speculate about whether, how or when that will come to pass.

To some in the developing world, it is recession 2001 that constitutes a wake up call for the developing lands.

Recession 2001 has brought us face to face to several novel aspects in the catching up process. This time around – unlike Crisis 1997 – every East Asian economy, from Japan to Malaysia, was adversely affected. The following list of the changes in GDP, at the third quarter of 2001, is suggestive:[1]

PRC	7.0%
Hong Kong	-3.0
Indonesia	3.5
Malaysia	-1.3
Singapore	-7.0
Korea	1.8
Taiwan	-4.0
Thailand	1.5

The common thread is the reduced U.S. import of electronics in recession. It is a time for reflection.

By the late 1990s, most electronics in the world market came from East Asia, and most East Asian economies had shifted their specialization in trade from textiles and garments to electronic goods, in order to achieve higher value-added per worker. For example, in Singapore and Malaysia the export share of electronics can be as high as 60%. The major customer for such electronic trade is the U.S., where the demand for electronic products has gravitated from expansionary demand to replacement demand. Buyers tend to postpone their replacement when their job prospects become less

[1] Source: The Economist, January 12-18, 2002. One might note that such figures on percentage change from a year earlier may vary quite a bit from quarter to quarter. They portray general patterns but depend on the particular dates of the onset of a recession or recovery from it. One recent estimate of Singaporean growth for 2001 is –2%. In addition, the positive figures for Indonesia reflect the late recovery from the previous deep crisis. Due to the special nature of the statistical data, different economists also interpret the high growth of the PRC differently.

secure in recession. Thus, electronics has a demand with high income elasticity.

The first implication is that even a mild recession in the U.S. can be transmitted to East Asia as a severe shock.

The second implication is the worsening of income distribution. The electronics industry allows for 'vertically disintegration' across the nations. In recession, firms compete for the dwindling orders and take the *risky* step to search for and develop low cost sources – not yet used to 'quality' and 'punctuality'. Some searchers fail; others succeed. As an alternative to the 'satisficing' view of Simon (1997), Appendix 2 explains both why firms search only in recessions, also the observed failures. Now, the new supply comes from where labor is abundant, inexpensive, but inexperienced. Yet, practice makes perfection. Once the *new*, low-cost source is proven as viable, the end of recession does not restore *old* supply links. Recession thus triggers a permanent switch in the supply chain. This intensifies the drive for global efficiency, but for older supply sites, also inflicts adjustment pains disproportionately on the old and uneducated, than the young and trained.

One example is from Hong Kong. As the development of the Chinese Mainland proceeds, Hong Kong firms relocate their manufacturing operations there. The better workers from Hong Kong are promoted as supervisors in their new factories in China, but the other workers are laid off.

The other example is the electronic industry of Japan, where workers who retired from large firms set up new shops as suppliers of parts and components. In prosperity, large firms would prefer to deal with such suppliers, whom they know well, rather than foreign suppliers who offer lower cost, but also lower reliability. With recession comes intensified competition among the large firms. For survival, they place orders abroad and transfer technology to foreign subcontractors, just to make sure that the latter can meet the quality standard. Their Japanese subcontractors are left out. Currently, the exodus of industries has become a cause for Japanese concern.

The last example is the electronics industry in Penang, Malaysia. After the success of Singapore, the State of Penang (the only one in Malaysia with a Chinese majority) emulated its strategy. Penang attracted enough foreign direct investment to transform the export mix of Malaysia. Presently, the competition from China has made observers uncertain about its future.

The accession of the PRC to the World Trade Organization has quickened the competition among the East Asian economies and offered multinational corporations better opportunities to seek out the minimum cost supplier.

These developments have called into question of the wisdom of both the outward-looking orientation and the heavy concentration on the export outlets with the highest value-added, which often means a high concentration in electronics for the U.S. market.

Underlying these observed events is the mechanism of the product cycle, which causes industries to migrate and economies to evolve. There are winners and losers, good times and times bringing much sorrow, as the juggernaut of globalization proceeds apace. For some people, poverty is overcome and fortunes are made; for others, hope and maybe even life are crushed. This is true in both the developed North and the developing South. The consequences for various individuals are simply too momentous to be trivialized with oversimplified platitudes or exploited for demagoguery.

In approaching such issues, we must emphasize the general trends and not any theoretic lacuna. One can consider either the worldwide welfare implications, or national advantage. Taking the first aspect first, in principle, the product cycle is a process that enhances productivity and disseminates technology. It therefore promises Pareto improvement, that is, potentially it will afford gain to some but loss to none. Of course, the potential best-case outcome is not likely to happen. Governments might try to act to ameliorate undesirable effects on their own citizens (see Kemp and Wan, 1993 and 1995, and Wan, 1997, for discussions of compensation schemes). Should that become impossible for a particular nation, international goodwill and cooperation must be relied upon for remedy. There remains the question of fairness in sharing the gain. Either one leaves it to the market forces, or one makes attempts to arrange cross-border income transfers.

One issue that has received insufficient attention in the theoretic trade literature is the fact that much of the deleterious effect of globalization comes from rapid and unexpected shifts of the trade patterns. As an extreme case, if all the changes in trade patterns are accommodated by natural attrition of the labor force and non-replacement of depreciated facilities, then much of the opposition against freer trade can be deflected. The limited speed of quota adjustments under the Multi-fiber Agreement (MFA) and the system of voluntary export restrictions (VERs) adopted by trading partners of the U.S. are practical means to ameliorate the real costs of changing trade patterns. Apart from some obvious abuses, such arrangements should not be summarily dismissed as rear-guard tactics to defend vested interests. The interested reader may refer to Kemp and Wan (1973) for related theoretic analysis.

As an analogy, the internal combustion engine is a net benefit to mankind, making motorized ambulances and fire trucks possible, among other things. It also causes air pollution and automobile accidents, and thus laws and regulations are devised to counter such undesirable effects. Globalization must be viewed in a similar light. One of its principal consequences is that it facilitates the catching-up process for the developing economies, enabling more economies to narrow their income gaps with the leading economies, at a faster pace. Its negative effects should be countered through coordinated management.

In subsequent sections, we consider the effect of the catching-up process from the viewpoint of national advantage for various economies.

2. THE NORTH AND THE SOUTH IN LITERATURE

On the North-South trade, studies by Grossman and Helpman (1993) deal with a variety of issues about innovation, imitation and trade. For our purpose, the simpler model of Krugman (1979) provides a convenient point of departure. Here all consumers are alike, sharing the love of variety and having the same constant elasticity of substitution preference (of Spence-Dixit-Stiglitz) over infinitely many commodities. There are only two countries, North and South, and two categories of goods, old and new, for each period. Only the North innovates, producing the new goods; after imitation, the South joins the supply of some of the old goods. No input is traded. The model then concludes that (a) by innovation, the North benefits all; (b) with imitation, the South benefits itself and harms the North.

This thought-provoking model captures much valuable truth: both innovation and technology transfer are potentially beneficial, but left by itself, the dynamic process may harm some party. Yet the simplifying assumptions can also lead to a caricature of reality: how a 'villainous' South 'victimizes' the 'virtuous' North (*our* characterization).

We next draw from history cases A, and B which are at variance with (a), and (b), respectively. We then identify the assumptions of such models which lead to these conclusions.

Case A. Industrial revolution allowed Lancashire textile industry to displace the Indian hand-printed cotton fabric in the 19th century, first from the market in the Ottoman Empire and then in India itself (Pacey, 1990: 128-9; Amsden, 2001: 34: Lewis, 1995: 287). In the second phase, some Indians might gain in consumers' surplus. The welfare impact on India depends on (i) can the gain of the users offset the loss to the producers, and (ii) has compensation been made from the former to the latter. But in the first phase, losing the gains from the Ottoman trade must be India's loss.

The principal assumption leading to conclusion (a) is the preference specification, under which the appearance of 'new' good x (the British machine-made textiles) never affects the marginal rate of substitution between good y (the Indian hand–made textiles) and z (Indian imports) that shapes the Indian terms of trade. One remedy is to use a two-level utility function where both kinds of textiles are 'closer substitutes' to each other, and an aggregate 'all-textiles' index is a *milder* substitute for other goods.

Case B. International trade in inputs allowed the American electronics industry to cut production cost against their Japanese competitors in the 1990s. This was done by helping their subcontractors from the 'China Circle' (namely, Hong Kong, Taiwan and southern PRC) in 'imitation': to supply quality parts and components, punctually and cheap (Borrus, 1997).

In contrast, the principal assumption responsible to implication (b) is that only final goods are traded.

The moral is, to deduce valuable conclusions, theorists always have to make simplifying assumptions. But these might lead to some implications at variance with reality. *Caveat emptor*! Apply theoretic analysis with care.

In fact, innovation need not come from the most advanced economies. Taiwanese firms like ASUSTeK can introduce new designs of mother boards for computers. In a technological environment where the only unchangeable truth is constant change, every economy is vulnerable to technological obsolescence. Success implies a high wage relative to neighbors. The best possible defense is through innovation, in product and service for present and potential clientele, and given due weight to benefits and cost, including the avoidance of placing all eggs in the basket of high tech exports.

3. THE NORTH AND THE SOUTH IN PRACTICE

Elsewhere, this volume focuses on the South, for once we now turn more to the North. Qualitatively, one can simplify the analysis of Krugman cited above, and gain insight into what happens. We offer an analytic discussion in five parts, for easy reference, then a policy analysis, before some facts.

(a) Initially, the North can produce goods x, y and z, but the South can produce only x. The opening of trade may benefit both the South and the North. The South gains because without trade, it would be able to consume good x only. Trade allows the South to have a richer menu. The North may also gain because the entry of the South into the trading world may allow the North to acquire good x at more advantageous terms through trading than through production. Neither party can possibly lose.

(b) Next, the North stays the same but the South becomes more productive. Suppose the South only learns how to produce x more efficiently. The South may gain, but also may lose, if the terms of trade worsen too much. That is the case of immiserizing growth in trade theory. The important point here is that the North cannot lose, but may gain from this development if it means cheaper x.

(c) Suppose instead, the South learns how to produce y as well as x, and enters the market. Then the North may lose at least part of its gains from trade, due to competition.

(d) Yet, in the above case, it is conceivable that the North could still gain, and an example can illustrate how this comes about. Note for now, the South still cannot produce z, and let us assume that z is a perfect complement of y. The shift of production of y from the North to the South may reduce the cost of the (y, z) package so much that the market expands tremendously. Hence for the North, the increased trading gain in z may over-compensate the loss of market in y.

(e) Next, suppose the South further learns to produce z as well, and enters the market. It is likely now that the North may lose at least part of its gains from trade. Yet for the North, the outcome must still not be worse than withdrawing from trade. Otherwise, there will be no gains from trade, rather than some reduced gains from trade.

Now we may identify x as natural resource, y as the labor-intensive manufacture and z as parts and components that can be produced only with much human capital.

By (a), one can see it is always to the interest of the North to promote international trade. By (b) the improvement of production technology in resource extraction is always beneficial to the North. This is so especially when there are many national economies in the South, and each is interested in raising its own productivity, even though collectively, the South may face immiserizing growth. By (c), in principle, industrialization in the South may erode the trading gain of the North. By (d), for some time at least, shifting labor-intensive manufacture to the South benefits the North. By (e) the upgrading of technology in the South can eventually threaten the trading gain of the North, but staying away from trade is even worse for the North.

The response in the North to globalization is more or less what would be expected. First, it aims to introduce new products through R&D that may render the competition from the South technologically obsolete, and second, it attempts to tighten up standards that protect intellectual property rights and prevent Southern entry into markets involving 'strategic technology.'

Over all, two points must be made. The main conclusion is that in a globalized environment, growth and development in the world economy represent the general trend – the tide that lifts all boats. Nevertheless, there can be adjustment costs that may have a severe impact on particular economies, or particular segments of the world economy. Through far-sighted policy and appropriate institutions, as well by international cooperation, there is substantial scope to ameliorate the adverse side effects of development.

For illustration, we consider the OECD imports of non-rubber shoes over 1970-1994. Chart 12.3.1 shows a 4.5 times increase of import volume, with a 2.5 times jump over 1981-6.

This is clearly a substitution of imports for domestic production.

Chart 12.3.1 OECD imports of non-rubber shoes, 1970-94. Source: Cheng (2001)

Chart 12.3.2 further displays the substitution of some import (to OECD) source for others. Clearly, in volume (rather than value) terms, first Taiwanese firms and then, after the revaluation of the New Taiwan Dollar in the late 1980s induced them to relocate, the PRC producers have replaced the market shares of their rivals in a dramatic fashion.

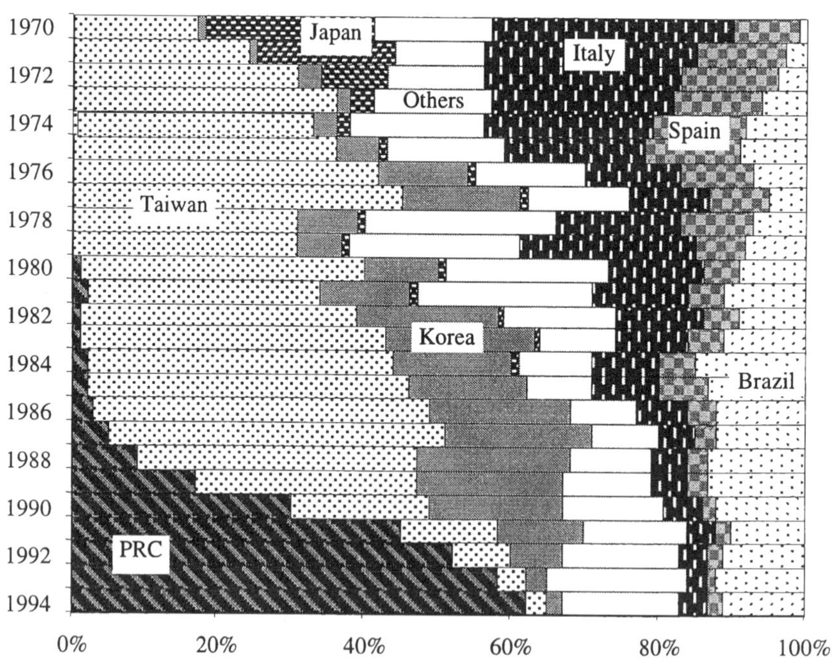

Chsrt 12.3.2 % share in OECD imports of non-rubber shoes Source: Cheng (2001)

Changes like this may improve efficiency, due to international division of labor. At the same time, too rapid a change may also incur much adjustment cost.

4. STUDY OF THE FUTURE AND THE FUTURE OF STUDIES

When Lee Kuan Yew, the Oxford-trained Singaporean senior minister, took a sabbatical at Harvard in 1968, the American specialty that intrigued him most was 'futurology'. At the end of this volume, which is written in the U.S., the future is the topic we turn to.

So what is the world economy turning into? The evidence of this volume suggests the same answer as that of Mencius[2] (390-305 BC): "Matters will settle on unity." For us economists, this means the globalized economy will become ever more homogeneous. In production, the dominance of modern technology is monolithic, even if some holdouts of Neolithic technology remain in the Papua Highland. This does not mean that in politics and culture the world must be unified. In politics, history shows that when cannon became ubiquitous, cannon-using Egyptians repulsed the cannon-using Mongols, saving Islam from the fate of Baghdad. In social behavior, the current percentage of children born out of wedlock can vary from 10% in Switzerland to 55% in Sweden, within the same high-income region, Western Europe.[3] There is no reason that the diversity and plurality of culture and behavior among the fully developed world must wither away.

One example may suffice. In biology, it is Darwinian selection that drives evolution. The economic history of the past 50 years has not shown any competitive advantage to either the legal system of Japan or the legal system of England. There is definitely a high cost involved in uprooting one legal system and adopting the other. Therefore, each system evolves on its own; convergence between these two is not to be expected. This discussion is relevant, because in some countries today (such as Saudi Arabia), there is

---

[2] His context was Chinese politics. His prediction here, made a century before the unification of China in 221 BC, was completely right, just as his answer to the next question, "who would unify [the affairs under the heaven]?" was totally wrong. He answered, "the one who has no taste for killing people." One can defend the humanist Old Master by saying that the answer was morally responsible (as it was addressed to a king, ready for war) though intellectually mistaken. If the recorded history conveys the truth, kindness was not the strength of the first emperor of Qin, who united China. But that illustrates the risks facing a futurologist.

[3] In Japan, it is 1%.

much concern that to develop in a more globalized context may undermine the preservation of traditions the society cherishes.

This volume introduced the topic of development within a globalized environment. Hopefully, a great deal more will be done in the future. A word should be said about how this may be done.

In his theory of models, Thom (1975) favors the use of models fitting each problem, and not a model for all problems. In practice, existing models often have to be modified for our specific use. That is why a number of rightfully renowned models in the literature of development and growth are not mentioned in this volume. Ours is a discussion oriented toward policy relevance. Space is not available to introduce elaborate analytic models and then explain the modifications needed to make them yield results useful for the decision makers.

One example is the analysis of increasing returns by Murphy, Shleifer and Vishney (1989) and Matsuyama (1991). Their elegant results are obtained under the specific assumptions that made the analysis succinct. Now our task is to explain to national policy makers the observed successful development process that is accessible even to small island economies such as Mauritius and Singapore. Increasing returns may be a relevant element both for local infrastructure as well as the R&D of the multinationals. Joining the supply chain of global production remains the key to the observed success. With suitable adaptations, it is quite likely that the 'big push' models may be so adapted in order to explain that the observed episodes in some fashion. But we find it hard to justify to readers why they should join us in such an intellectual exercise.

It is far more important for us to discover from empirical data what are the ingredients for success. The situation is analogous to the notion of Tolstoy on family happiness: "All happy families resemble one another; each unhappy family is unhappy in its own way."[4] The story of Mauritius in the last chapter provides us with some insight. The MFA quotas supplied Hong Kong businessmen the *motive to invest abroad*. The tariff preference of the Lomé Convention gave Mauritius the favorable *investment prospect*. The Mauritian *pragmatic socio-political milieu* enabled the local Chinese to convince Hong Kong investors to select Mauritius rather than other locale nearby. The Taiwanese export zone served as the *institutional template* for investment. Together these brought both *capital* and *technology* to Mauritius as a vibrant export platform. But it takes the policy of *openness toward trade and investment* to allow the other conditions (quota, tariff preference and so on, or their equivalents) to do the work. Back to the Tolstoyan

[4] The opening line of *Anna Karénina*, translated by Nathan H. Dole.

context, it takes a *kind, honest person* and a suitable spouse to make a happy family.

One important step for the study is to establish a criterion for successful performance. As the benchmark model in Chapter 1 suggests, whether a development performance should be judged as satisfactory depends upon the stage of development that an economy has reached. The next step is to explore the common foundation of satisfactory performances. In that exploration, one must not be distracted by the idiosyncrasies of those economies with unsatisfactory performance. We are currently pursuing such a research agenda.

5. A FINAL REMARK: WHAT VALUE IS RAPID GROWTH?

It is time to ask how the less fortunate fare under outward-oriented development. Are the fruits of growth equitably shared? Do the poor get poorer amid the prosperity fueled by growth?

After all, we seek evidence from East Asia, the lands under the influence of Confucius. In Analects, the lasting Confucian injunction is: "worry not about scarcity, but inequity." So it is altogether fitting to ask, assuming sustained rapid growth is attained in a globalized environment, what can be expected in the way of income distribution?

Growth and Equity

To begin with, with or without trade, market forces alone cannot provide any assurance that aggregate growth will bring equal, instant benefit to all the people. Thus, when any particular developing economy adopts an outward orientation, it is an empirical issue what growth pattern and distribution will obtain. How things might have stood had the economy taken any alternative path can be discussed only by making further contra-factual assumptions.[5] Any attempt to quantify the comparison of such alternatives must confront further conceptual challenges, which are not usually dealt with in the voluminous literature on the measurement of poverty and equity. This would be a task well beyond the scope of the current volume. Yet anyone who favors or rejects the outward-oriented strategy must make implicit assumptions on such moral issues of policy

[5] An example is, at the time of Trafalgar, had Napoleon been allowed to land on British shores, he would be immediately arrested, saving Europe a decade and half of warfare.

relevance. Not taking any stand is a choice to endorse the consequence of 'letting things happen.' These are just not matters to keep silent on, however convenient and comfortable is that course.

At this point, it is useful to consider the relationship between equity and growth for a developing economy. This may be depicted schematically in Figure 12. 5.1 where x and y, respectively, are some measure for equity and growth. Denote F(x) as the maximum growth attainable at a given level of equity measure, then an equity-growth frontier can be represented as:

$$y = F(x).$$

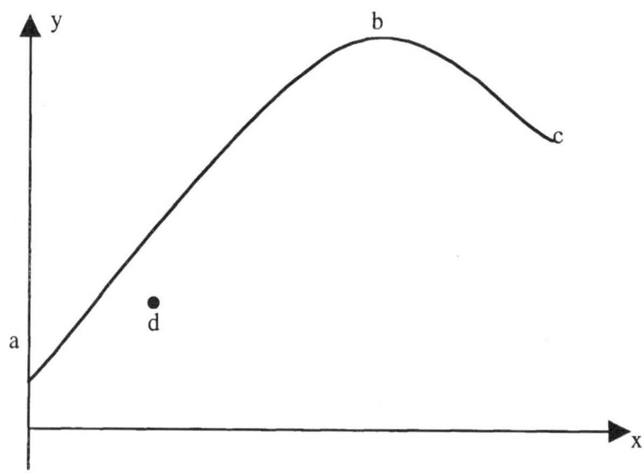

Figure 12.5.1 Equity and growth

Up to point b, a more equitable income distribution means a more productive labor force. Beyond b, there is some trade off between equity and growth.

Most of the time, the NIEs operate along the ab segment of the frontier abc, near b. Healthy, adequate public housing for the employed labor force is productivity-enhancing, and public housing programs were carried out most successfully in both Hong Kong and Singapore. The policy goal of 'seeking growth within stability' in Taiwan also reflects awareness of the fact that economic development requires a healthy, contented labor force. This explains the positive slope of the ab arc. At the same time, the efforts of the government to promote frugality in both Taiwan and Korea also indicates a desire to restrict the economy from going far beyond b down the range bc. Overgenerous welfare goals are usually shunned in these economies.

This is also seen in the case of Singapore. (a) The general political philosophy may be seen in the comments of Senior Minister Lee Kuan Yew (2000: 417) on British society: "[W]elfarism blunted motivation to exert . . . and to excel," and on Hong Kong, "I had seen the advantage of having little or no social safety net. It spurred Hong Kong's people to strive to succeed" (p. 605). (b) More specifically, to promote the growth rate beyond what is attainable with the locally available skill-mix, the government encourages multinationals to bring along expatriate talent without limitation. To enhance the attraction of the country to 'foreign talent,' unskilled domestic help has been recruited from neighboring countries. The presence of both high tech foreign firms and the coming of low skill foreign workers (half a million in total, and amounting to 25% of the labor force) have influence on the income distribution of the local workers as well, making income distribution more unequal than otherwise. The salary ratio between a professor and a secretary (as V. V. Bhanoji Rao observed) is as much as 16: 1 in Singapore. Here, income distribution is part of the development strategy, and not merely its effect. (See Appendix 1.)

It is to be noted that there are developing economies that pursue a quite different type of policy. Oftentimes, as a measure to win the support of the urban, organized labor force, labor legislation is adopted to benefit the unionized workers already on the job, but not 'the reserve army of the unemployed.' For example, a prohibition against the laying off of workers discourages investors and hinders development. This is represented at point d in Figure 12.5.1. One wonders, politics aside, what indeed is the point of reducing the employment opportunities of the mass of surplus rural labor and bestowing generous terms on the relatively lucky few who already have factory jobs. The high-minded 'progressive laws' make the employed complacent with their 'iron rice bowls' and deny the economy the means to invest and create more jobs. Thus, both growth and equity are lost in this one stroke. This is precisely how did India, China and quite a few of the Latin American countries get mired in a low development trap.

This does not mean that, when growth is well under way, a state with full employment should not offer workers fair rewards out of the fruits of growth. Both Korea and Taiwan erred this way until the mid-1980s.

Experience also has shown, for instance in the Korean case, that when an economy depends critically on export success, rampant wage demands and disruptive industrial strikes can be tamed by an alarmed public worrying that export markets might be lost to rivals in an irreversible manner. For an outward-oriented economy, under the (world) market discipline, wandering too far from point b on the bc arc can be constrained more effectively by popular will than the acts of an autocrat.

For a reality check, we turn to data from Low and Ngiam (1999). The household income distribution of selected economies can be displayed in Chart 12.5.1.

Dividing the share of the top 20% by the bottom 20%, one gets a numerical measure for comparison as in Chart 12.5.2.

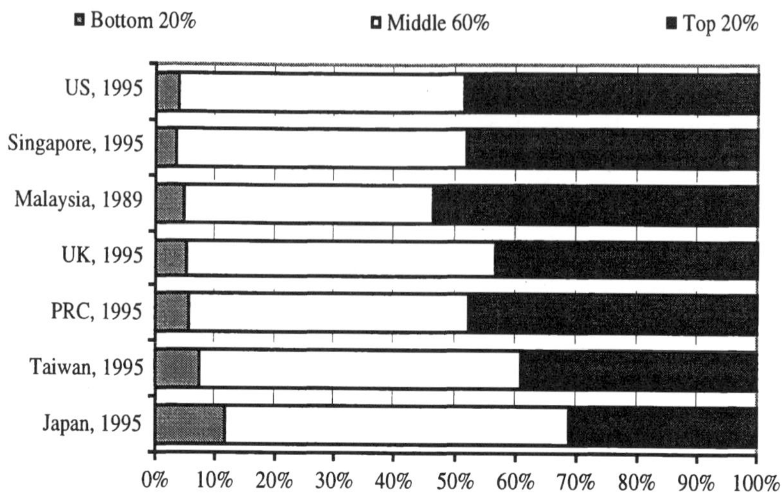

Chart 12.5.1 Income distribution Source: Low and Ngiam (1999)

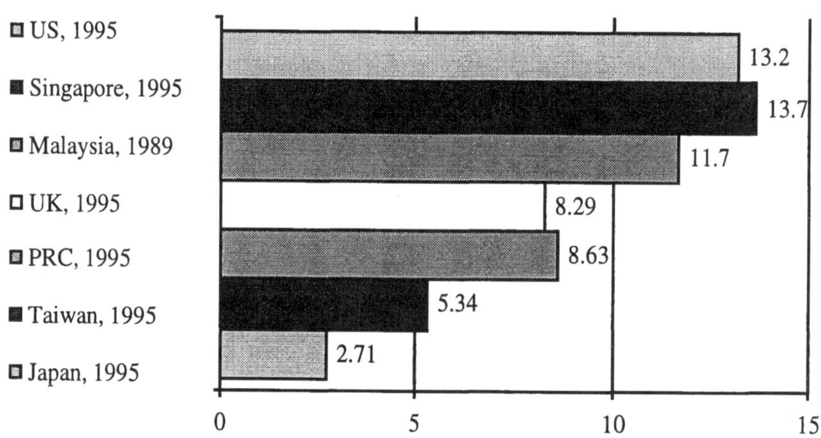

Chart 12.5.2 Top 20% over bottom 20% Source: Low and Ngiam (1999)

Two facts are clear: (a) Between the two NIEs, Singapore and Taiwan, income distribution is more even in the latter than the former. (b) Still, in terms of the Gini coefficient,[6] both Singapore and Taiwan are bracketed by the U.S. and Japan, so that the sustained rapid growth of the NIEs has not caused income distributions that 'extreme,' judging from the patterns of U.S. and Japan.[7]

---

[6] See Low and Ngiam, (1999).

[7] However, according to Rao, Hong Kong's figure is 0.5.

In the historical context, Rao (2001: 40-41) found that in terms of the household Gini coefficient, the East Asian economies do not show any uniform trend. Apparently, as the case of Thailand has shown, other things being equal, measured inequality tends to increase with the size of the country. As Rao noted (pp. 41-2), the Korean data have serious problems.

Three additional considerations would qualify the impression that Singapore has a highly skewed income distribution.

First, income distributions are usually compared against each other among economies *before* or *after* the phase of industrialization. Each distribution observed represents a sort of steady state, in a deterministic or stochastic sense. The NIEs are studied because they are in the process of a rapid transition. For example, Singapore was an economy with one and a half million people and 10,000 cars in 1960, but an economy with three million people and around 300,000 cars today, at the turn of the century. The present life expectancies are 70 for males and 76 for females. This is the kind of archetype economy that is central to the present inquiry. Information in Charts 12.5.1 and 12.5.2 are snap shots of a fast moving object. Conceptually, one ought compare time sequences of income distributions, each for a different economy. In such situations, which is the more desirable sequence, say, between a faster growth with a less equal distribution or the other way round, is not free from value judgment.

Second, to be fully realistic, inter-generational issues are also involved. Two cases may be cited. (a) Demographic force matters. In the case of Taiwan, after detailed analysis Schultz (1999: 196) concluded that economic growth comes with changes in social structure, including a reduction in the number of adults per household. The latter fact accounts for all the increase in inequality of household income over 1976-95 that has caused some concern in various circles. (b) Some results are inevitable side effects of policy. As Low and Ngiam (1999: 239), argued, the recent accelerated industrialization of Singapore has understandably left the less-trained, older workers behind at this stage.[8] The desirability of such policy is again a matter of value judgment.

A rigorous policy critique requires a simulation exercise of a major order, which we are not prepared to conduct here. The conceptual issues regarding the interactions between income inequality, growth, technological transition and demographic transition have been explored recently by Galor (2000), Galor and Weil (2000) as well as Galor and Moav (2000, 2001).

---

[8] By this argument, Taiwan has a more equal income distribution, but also an economy with a more gradual transformation. How valid is this explanation is not considered here.

Outward Orientation and Poverty

So far we have argued in favor of an outward orientation, based upon aggregate or average outputs. It remains important to ask whether distributive concerns (with regard to poverty or inequality) are likely to be so serious as to totally offset the merits of 'openness' for developing economies. We use the word 'likely' because – as we cannot conduct a comprehensive simulation exercise – circumstantial and fragmentary evidence is all that we can use. Thus, as we go along we must be careful to note the inherent complexities that are caused not only by the imperfect data that are available, but also by unresolved conceptual issues.

It is often implicitly assumed, both in Western societies and in many developing lands, that the interests of the poor coincide with those of the working class, which are safeguarded by organized labor in independent unions and parliamentary socialist parties in democratic states (the United States being an obvious exception). Now, in none of the four NIEs used as evidence in this volume did growth episodes start under a government backed by organized labor, or for that matter, facing an effective parliamentary opposition. Accurate or not, some writers like Deyo (1989) have characterized the policy of such governments as 'labor subordination,' in view of the absence of protection for strikers from retaliation by management. As a matter of fact, strikes or independent unions were not favored, if not banned outright by the State during such periods.

Therefore, in the abstract, there is ground to be concerned about inequality, poverty and perhaps democracy under outward-oriented growth. These issues ought be addressed, in a careful manner.

First, with regard to politics, those economic policies that have proven to be effective in the NIEs are compatible with parliamentary democracy with participation by powerful socialist parties. From day one, active opposition parties have always been present in Malaysia. Organized labor is effective in Mauritius. The party in power in Singapore came to power and got re-elected through free and un-rigged votes. After the mid-1980s, parliamentary politics have blossomed in both Korea and Taiwan, with governments changed by ballot.

Second, suppose leaders of authoritarian states are motivated by their personal agenda and not public vision nor historical reputation, they must still balance between growth and equity as long as they intend to preserve political power. In the end, even authoritarian regimes only rule with the acquiescence of the people. Twice in a decade, the Korean Central Intelligence Agency (KCIA) did not protect its masters. Surely the KCIA had guns. But guns were turned against the President in 1979, and thrown down before the mass uprising of Seoul residents in 1987. In the NIEs, the governments would avoid scandalous workplace hazards, because that might destabilize the society. So parliamentary opposition and independent, organized unions may be desirable in their own right, but their roles in preserving income equality can be overstated.

Third, in the beginning, working conditions in some export industries in the NIEs were not ideal and sometimes justifying corrections. Yet the work force came of their own volition, because the alternative options in their life were worse. Some measures popular in advanced economies, such as a high minimum wage, would slow the pace of industrialization, benefiting some of the luckier workers but excluding the rest from jobs they desired.

One would like now to study where matters stand statistically in the outward-oriented developing economies, the NIEs as well as the ASEAN-3. The recent contribution of Rao (2001) is a comprehensive and succinct source for such information.

One might take a broader perspective than GDP growth, and consider the Human Development Index (HDI), which is a weighted average of health, education and purchasing power. The last item is represented by the per capita real GDP. and the first two are associated with poverty reduction. Two points must be made.

First, it is generally agreed now, that for all the outward-oriented NIEs[9]:
(a) Their industrialization is followed by sharp decline in poverty measures.
(b) Their absolute poverty levels are insignificant today.
(c) Their current HDI scores are about as high as the developed countries,
From Rao (1988), absolute poverty fell from 25% in the 1950s to 0.3% in 1982/3 for Singapore, and from 40.9% in 1965 to 4.6% in 1984 for Korea.

Second, Sen (1999) has pointed out that health and *basic* education are necessary (though insufficient) conditions for the sustained, rapid growth of East and Southeast Asia. He further pointed out that although India has six times as many students with college education as China. The literacy of people aged 16 – 24 in 2000 is 97.8% for China, but still only 72.6% for India, a fact which will be a road block to Indian development.

East Asia has not ignored human development, but used it for growth.

6. REPLICABLE ASIAN LESSONS – FIVE PRINCIPLES FROM SEN

Our evidence, however fragmented, suggests that, in the NIEs, the outward-oriented strategy appears to be no worse than any alternatives for poverty and inequality reduction. During industrialization, those in power knew that

---

[9] When data from Taiwan is unavailable for international political reasons, work by Ranis (1999) supplies a reliable estimate, which is in line with the other NIEs.

to preserve their power, people need jobs for now, and hope for the future. Export offers jobs, basic education, a better tomorrow for the children if not the parents. The living and working quarters of the people are often adjacent to the seats of power.[10] Shantytowns must be improved.

Engineering is not physics, though engineers should all have some grasp over the elements of physics. Likewise, in studying the mechanics of catching up, our readers can do well to familiarize themselves with some basics of political economy. Now is the time for the finale of our volume. We find that after marshalling Asian evidence, our purpose is best served by invoking the writings of the first Asian Nobelist in Economics, *Development as Freedom* by Sen (1999). In five principles we deduced:

A. Human potential in health and basic education is necessary for sustained, rapid growth.
B. To realize such growth, the State should supply the basic public goods, and not indulge in bureaucratic intervention.
C. National independence and participatory democracy offer checks against famine from policy failure and debt crisis due to cronyism.
D. Female empowerment through education is proven to be even more effective in population control than authoritarianism.
E. Broad based education can be more effective for industrialization than liberal art education for the elite.

---

[10] Thus the city-state of Singapore is quite different from Mexico, where workers in the export industries live in the Northern Tier, far from the policy makers in the Valley of Mexico.

APPENDIX 12.1: SINGAPORE'S CHOICE

We have emphasized by means of Figure 12.5.1 that for any developmental state, equity and growth are not separable goals. Sometimes, policy makers cannot freely choose one goal, heedless of its consequences due to its impact on the other. In the last two chapters we have seen, that for Malaysia, growth without equity may end in strife and chaos, making growth impossible. It is equally true for Singapore, any single minded pursuit of equality would stunt economic growth and render the society economically nonviable and politically ungovernable.

Moreover, when rapid growth is achievable in a developing economy – as it has been true for the NIEs - then the issue of equity takes an entirely new light. In that dynamic setting, almost all the established tools of analysis for inequality become insufficient to assess how equitable is a growth program. The relevant question is what portion of the population should have the opportunity to have what time profile of income growth. If two income time-profiles share the same mean income over a life-time, but have quite different rates of growth over the same period, there is no objective way to say which path is preferable to another, let alone what criterion to use to rank growth programs with different mixes of two growth profiles for a given population.

But as we shall immediately see – for Singapore – what population should one 'assemble' in a particular economy is also a matter of choice, in the final analysis.

From Wong (2001), Singapore is a producer of hard disk drives, with the highest rent and wages, as shown in table A12.1.1 and Figure A12.1.1.

	Rent, 100 sq. ft.	Operator's pay	Engineer's pay	Manager's pay
Shenzhen, China	90	55	182	302
Thailand	13	105	327	458
Batam, Indonesia	79	138	360	490
Penang, Malaysia	46	232	619	967
Singapore	105	382	1048	1637

Table A12.1.1 Costs in producing had disk drives in 1993 Source: Wong (2001)

Singapore survives as a producer because of its flexible labor force. Multinational corporations operate in Singapore because workers there can shift product mix or produce products of new design faster than workers elsewhere. More interestingly, they favor Singapore because Singaporean workers can serve as trainers to help those corporations relocate their operations to low cost locations in other places. Thus, on the one hand, the presence of their plant in Singapore is crucial for industry upgrading in other economies, but on the other hand, the same possibility of those multinational corporation relocating their plants poses a constant threat to Singapore itself.

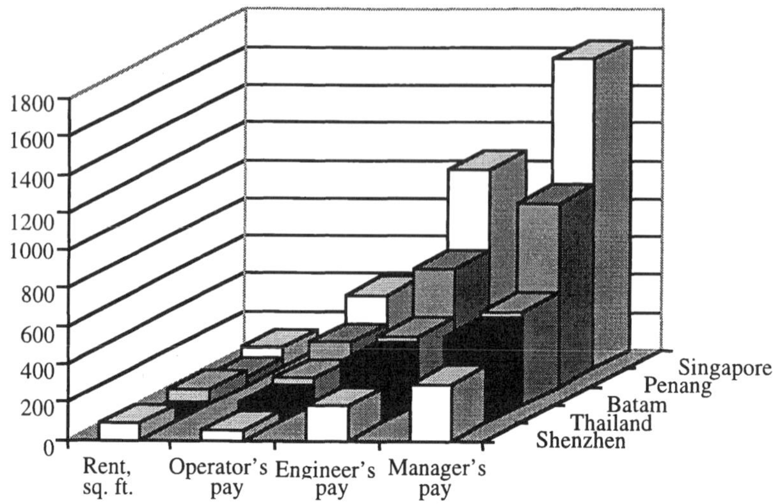

Chart A12.1.1 Wage/rent comparison: Singapore and rival locations   Source: Wong (2001)

Thus, in order to serve its function to both those multinational corporations it hosts and its rival production sites, Singapore must continue to reinvent itself, in more ways than one. It concerns *how* Singaporeans work, *when* Singaporeans get raises, *what* training do Singaporeans receive, *which* jobs Singaporeans fill, and finally, *who* Singaporeans really are.

To track down the metamorphosis of the Singaporean population, the best tool is the Theil measure of inequality, due to its perfect decomposability. In such an inquiry, we turn the usual study of income inequality on its head: instead of asking the desirability of the change in income distribution for a given population, but studying the changing characteristics of a ' design population', the composition of which is itself the result of conscious 'recruitment policy' and so on.

For Singapore, the fascinating study of Mukhopadhaya and Rao (2002) has provided us thought-provoking results regarding what does the usual measurement of income inequality mean for a successful development state. Their results can be listed below:

- The effects of recessions on aggregate inequality in both the short and the long run:
    - (a) Since labor income is more equally distributed than capital income and the latter is reduced in recessions, so the short-term effect improves equality.
    - (b) In recession, firms let temporary migrant workers go and seek more labor intensive methods of production, the end of recession does not return the firm to its old mode operation, so the long-term effect reduces equality.
- Meritocracy has the effect of reducing age premium over time.

- The improvement of general education has the effect of reducing the premium for college education
- The restructuring of industries away from labor intensive operations also has its effect, with larger portion of people now classfied as supervisors.
- The simultaneous recruitment of 'foreign talents' and low-paid temporaty workers from abroad (altogether about half a million in the late 1990s) has understandable 'stretching effect' on the payscale, which increases inequality.

One can moderate the human impact of the relatively high and somewhat increasing level of income inequality (which is at a level in the vicinity of America itself). But since Singapore has chosen to serve as a conduit of technology transfer between the North and the South and to maintain a level of efficiency much higher than its surrounding area, the resultant income distribution is to a great extent the side effect of its economic survival. Its own full employment as well as its ability to assist the industrialization of its neighbors can only be sustained by remaining competitive on the world market.

What does the future hold for Singapore in its constant effort to stay more efficient than its immediate neighbors? The best one can foresee is by analogy - in comparison with countries like the Netherlands. At one time, Amsterdam (and not London) was the financial center for Europe. The efforts of the Dutch to keep abreast of its competitors had benefits for the rest of the industrial world. In the long run, such efforts may not be successful forever. Yet when other countries have caught up, the Netherlands remain to be a highly respected part of industrial Europe, with a secure economic future among its affluent neighbors. For the Singaporean economy, the only necessary measuring rod is to make its income comparable to the rest of the advanced world, and not whether its own income level is higher or equal to its neighbors.

We have mentioned that in the *dynamic* context of Singapore (perhaps true also for any economy gaining sustained, rapid growth), no measure of income inequality can in itself serve as a rigid measure for normative purposes. Moreover, in the case of Singapore, with its 'foreign talent' initiative, who would be tomorrow's typical Singaporean is also an endogenous variable.

Since equity issues are valid concerns, how should one arrive at any normative policy guide? The only possible answer is obviously, 'consult various evidence and then heed one's own conscience.'

APPENDIX 12.2: INDUSTRY EXODUS IN RECESSION

Industries migrated from Japan to the NIEs in the1960s due to the 'cost push' of Japan's labor shortage, and from the NIEs to the PRC, in response to the 'opportunity pull' of the Chinese reform in 1978. The current exodus of Japanese industries to China occurs during Japan's long recession. This third wave of intra-Asia industry relocation deserves some explanation.

Such a movement is an opportunity for the economy of destination, but an operation involving costly search for those initiating the relocation. At the new site, labor is usually abundant, inexpensive but also inexperienced. If the search cost is justifiable by the cost-saving, why should the move be delayed until the recession? The 'satisficing' explanation is not convincing, if those initiating the move are methodical in outlook, like the Japanese firms. An 'option theory' explanation would claim that in recession, agents may make desperate gambles. But why must such gambles take the form of out-sourcing or investing abroad? We offer instead a decision-theoretic explanation, with a simple example for illustration.

There are two states: s = 0 for prosperity and 1 for recession, also two actions for the agent: a = 0 for not out-sourcing and 1 for out-sourcing. There are four outcomes F(s, a) as follows:

F (0,0) is a 'sure event' with profit, A,

F (1,0) is a 'sure event' of bankruptcy, B, due to a depressed sales price,

F (0,1) is a 'lottery': L',

with an even chance of a high profit of amount Q, or bankruptcy,

F(1, 1) is also a 'lottery': L",

with an even chance of a low profit of amount q, or bankruptcy.

This reflects the fact that there is an even chance that the low cost but in-experienced supplier would not be able to deliver the goods on time in acceptable quality, and then the non-performance on a sales contract implies a penalty which causes *bankruptcy*. Yet, if there is no out-sourcing, then the revenue in recession will not cover some fixed cost and result in *bankruptcy*, as well. On the other hand, the cost-saving under successful out - sourcing will result in a profit, even during a recession.

If this agent's preference is:

A is better than L'; and L" is better than B,

then out-sourcing happens only during recession.

The following numerical values may help to illustrate our example. Let sales revenue be 26 during prosperity, and 14 during recession (12 being the price drop); variable cost, be 12 with no out-sourcing, and 7 with successful out-sourcing (5 being the cost-saving of a successful out-sourcing); fixed cost be 5, and bankruptcy be assigned a utility value of –20. Thus,

A = 9, Q = 14, q = 2.

The values for the lotteries L' and L" are then –3 and –9 respectively.

CHAPTER SUMMARY

- ♦ 2001 brought double shocks: September 11 gave a sharp jolt, but soon one becomes sure of its limited consequence: modern life is not to be vanquished by fundamentalism. Recession 2001 became a wake up call in Asia, with the decline in the electronics sector raising doubts about the development strategy, perhaps even about outward orientation itself.
- ♦ By now, demand for electronics is more for replacement than for expansion. Demand declines if consumers feel unsure of their jobs. Thus, recession in the U.S. means severe shock for Asia.
- ♦ Competition intensifies in recession, with firms seeking lower costs by transferring technology to low cost but inexperienced suppliers. Such temporary market shocks may mean permanent displacement of supply chains, and accelerated industry migrations in the product cycle.
- ♦ Overall, product cycle is driven by technical progress that enhances efficiency. But there may be losers beside winners. Like the internal combustion engine that gives us motorized ambulances and fire trucks, but also pollution and traffic accidents. We need management and regulation, not avoidance. Through gradualism, adjustment assistance, and cooperation, the negative aspects of globalization can be moderated to acceptable levels.
- ♦ Although the continued trend for globalized production is to be expected, sweeping predictions regarding who will gain or lose in the North or South is not possible. For the South, technology acquisition is always desirable, but it takes a combination of factors to benefit from the product cycle. For the North, competition from low cost rivals is always the threat, and only innovation offers the opportunity to stay ahead.
- ♦ Further globalization in production need not imply the convergence of taste in consumption, let alone in institutions and life style. A high degree of plurality and diversity survive and thrive today in the developed North. There is no reason that such a state will change.
- ♦ Last but not least is the question of equity in relation to efficiency, and how equity is affected by outward-oriented growth. Here the record of the four Asian NIEs provides some clue. Available data indicates that the income distributions of these four may differ among each other, but they are bracketed by the figures of Japan and the U.S. Over the course of their rapid growth, both equity and efficiency improved hand in hand, even though none of these economies provided European style welfare systems that may slow down growth. Even over a period of authoritarian rule, East Asian growth was launched by labor intensive export and anchored on industrial peace. To maintain their rule, even authoritarian rulers must allow workers ever improving earnings in the face of their steadily improving productivity. With improved income, the human development index also has risen in all the four Asian NIEs.

QUESTIONS AND EXERCISES

1. During their rapid growth, how have the Asian NIEs fared in income distribution relative to advanced economies such as the U.S. and Japan? Why is there reason to believe that even autocratic regimes would not allow their working class to lose ground in terms of living standards during periods of high growth?
2. How can we make the globalization trend more humane?
3. [Korea IV] Describing the challenges facing Korea today, Kim (2000) wrote:

   > Korean firms relied heavily on foreign . . . original equipment manufacturer (OEM) buyers for . . . international marketing . . . [B]uyers provided valuable technical help through interactive tutorial processes to ensure that Korean products met their technical specifications. . . [O]ver the more recent decades. Korean producers . . . lost their market . . . in the United States rapidly when . . . buyers shifted . . . to . . . countries like China. . . Korean firms diverted their export to Third World markets. . . Competitive stimulus, however, is not as strong from these markets . . .

   Actually, in the ASEAN states, Korea also loses market to the PRC, just like in the U. S. (*Korean Chamber of Commerce & Industry* 7 Aug. 2002). 'The Third World markets' cited above mainly means the PRC is now the largest outlet for Korean exports, after the U. S.

   (a) Does this description agree with any of the following views?
      - i) The 'after shocks' of Crisis 1997 remain formidable today.
      - ii) This is a temporary effect of the American economic slump.
      - iii) This may be caused by a foreign recession, yet export need not recover with the recovery of the foreign economy.

   (b) Based upon such observations, comment on
      - i) Krugman's opinion that Korean past growth came from 'perspiration, not inspiraton'.
      - ii) The assessment of Kim and Lau (also Young) that Korea did not achieve productivity gain.
      - iii) Young's conclusion that trade provides only a once-for-all static gain.

   (Compare Chapter 5.)

Appendix

PROBLEMS FOR GENERAL REVIEW

Problem I

(a) Based on the benchmark model, is it likely that Japan will have another high growth period, like the one in the period 1955 - 70? Why?
(b) Why is it so hard for any economy to surpass America in per capita real GDP?
(c) Are the 10 year recession of Japan and the implosion of the Soviet economy similar events? Why?
(d) Latin American economies lost their share in world trade and they did not manage to close the gap between themselves and America. Explain why these facts support the benchmark model.

Problem II

(a) Why is industrialization important for economic development? Illustrate this with the experience of Taiwan and Korea. What did they export in exchange for fuel and raw material before they industrialized?
(b) What elements of Confucianism might have prevented China to launch the Industrial Revolution ahead of Europe? What in Confucianism may be conducive to the catch up process?
(c) Is trade equally helpful to growth for both East Asian economies and America? Why not? Can an average Chinese gain as much from trade as an average Korean has gained?

(d) If imitation is a 'contact sport', allowing the host country to learn from the home country through direct foreign investment, why should foreign investors be so naïve, in exposing their secrets? If the host country cannot learn from the foreign investors, why do developing economies compete among themselves by granting tax holidays?

Problem III

(a) Do trade and foreign investment play the same roles for the developing South as for the developed North? Explain.
(b) Are such roles now the same as the roles in centuries past? If not, what makes the difference.
(c) Can opening to trade affect the rate of saving? If yes, is that effect once for all or long lasting?
(d) If learning is 'bounded', is trade against the interest of the developing South? Why and why not?
(e) Both Korea and Singapore adopted industrial policy, but not similar trade policies? Why?

Problem IV

(a) East Asian economies have gained experience in exporting to the advanced economies, especially America. Would they gain the same benefit by exporting to India and Chinese Mainland instead?
(b) Why were import control and foreign exchange control such stumbling blocks for Korea and Taiwan? How did reform unleash the growth potential of Korea and Taiwan?
(c) Why did Young and Stokey believe that trade harms The South and benefits The North? If you do not agree with them explain why.
(d) In what sense the recent East Asian concentration in electronics export may bring also some undesirable consequences?

Problem V

(a) Is the support of the state necessary for the emergence of large business? Cite evidence.
(b) Is the presence of large business necessary for industrialization? Cite evidence.
(c) What are the influences of big business on product innovation?
(d) What role has large business played in Korea, during the industrialization under President Park, and during Crisis 1997?

Problem VI

(a) Compare the views of Schumpeter and Arrow about the size of the firm and R & D.
(b) What roles have small and medium enterprises played in Japan, Korea and Taiwan?
(c) Why did Korea nurture large business groups and Taiwan not?
(d) How does industrial concentration make financial crisis more intractable?

Problem VII

(a) Japan, Korea and Taiwan did not practice free trade like Hong Kong. Latin American countries keep protective barriers against imports. Why do their growth performance differ so much?
(b) Taiwan and Singapore carried out industrial policy, using instruments quite different from Japan and Korea. Discuss.
(c) Discuss the de-industrialization of Hong Kong.
(d) What is the main concern in Singapore today and how is it handled?

Problem VIII

Compare Japan and Korea regarding:
(a) The role economic planning played
(b) The ownership structure of large business
(c) The relationship between small and large firms
(d) The macro-economic performance over time

Problem IX

Both Thailand and Korea are affected by the Asian financial crisis.
(a) Compare their experiences and those which affected the Latin American economies.
(b) Would such an experience have long term impact on these two economies? Explain.
(c) What growth profiles are expected for Thailand and Korea, respectively? Why?
(d) Discuss the pros and cons of development with borrowed funds.
(e) How can we explain that the difficulties faced by Thailand affect Korea?

Problem X

Compare the economies of Taiwan and Chile regarding:

(a) The initial conditions before the `reform' (Taiwan around 1958; Chile under Pinochet)

(b) The nature of their economic reforms regarding trade, state ownership and labor market

(c) Discuss the current status of these two economies in trade structure, and manpower

(d) Explain the economic prospects of these two economies.

Problem XI

Discuss the economies of Hong Kong and Mauritius

(a) What phase and what aspects of the two economies are comparable?

(b) What are the main differences between these two economies?

(c) Draw whatever inferences you can and discuss the policy implications for Mauritius

(d) Are there any lessons one can draw from these for economies such as Sri Lanka, etc.?

Problem XII

One of the usual goals in economic development is the reduction of income inequality. Discuss this issue in the context of Singapore, where:

(a) There is a sizable foreign population which numbered over 600,000 and formed 18% of the total population in 1998.

(b) This foreign population includes both (i) a large, revolving pool of unskilled workers holding temporary working permits, and (ii) the highly skilled group recruited as 'foreign talents' who may apply for permanent resident status. In 2000 alone, 110,000 came to Singapore. Over the last 20 years, ⅓ of a million became permanent residents. That figure is more than 10% of the resident population.

(c) By the estimation of the government, over the period 1994-96, this 'foreign manpower policy' has allowed the economy to grow at 7.5% instead of 5.3%.

Problem XIII (Institutionism)

A. According to North (1994, 1995, 1998), economic development should be explained in terms of *history* and not *neoclassical theory*. He focuses on institutions, such as laws, custom, and organizations, which form the rules of the game for agents, deciding their actions and effectiveness. Institutions vary not only *among nations*, causing differences in efficiency level and growth, but also *over time,* due to chance, politics, beside economic factors.

B. Many other economists believe, institutions can be either taken as given, or as objects of choice, or in terms of proxies (say, 'social capital') that change as functions of time, noise, or economic variables, toward efficiency.

To assess both the *effect of institutions* and the *cause of institutional change*, one may either compare the performance of entire economies as in North (1990) and various authors in Hayami and Aoki (1998), or proceed issue by issue, as in many chapters in Hariss, Hunter and Collins (1995).

Like North, we wish 'to learn *from* history', beyond 'to learn *about* history'. Discuss with the following sample of 24 issues from this book, *whether* and *how* has position A gone beyond B, to include political and other feedback mechanisms for making predictions or designing policy:

1. The Industrial Revolution is the product of the European university system and the British legislation on patents.
2. History gave Japan the capacity to assimilate foreign technology fast.
3. Historical linkage facilitated industry migration within East Asia.
4. De-colonization after World War II, and the absence of a labor party in America contributed to the rise of the Circa - Pacific supply chain.
5. To defend against American corporate raiders, the Japanese government helped the formation of the *keiretsu* system. Power devolved to the hired managers, with fixed terms, unlike the founders of the Korean *chaebols* who value dynastic pride over efficiency.
6. As wages rise, Europe relies on guest workers for services, and Japan shifts labor intensive industries abroad. Due to learning-by-doing, technology transfer to neighboring lands is easier in the latter case.
7. Korea controlled the heavily indebted *chaebols* with directed credit in short term loans. As the *chaebols* grew, they became 'too big to fail'.
8. In their industrialization, the PRC, Taiwan, South Korea and Vietnam are more or less alike, with North Korea being the 'odd man out'.
9. Relative to America, the difficulty of attracting migrant entrepreneurs in Japan and other East Asian economies makes direct foreign investment important in technology-intensive industries.

10. East Asia exported garment to America and the Colombians exported inside the Andean Group: the former have learned much, and the latter relatively little.
11. From the shoemakers in Taiwan to the Eng Hardware of Malaysia, foreign subcontracts made traditional SMEs into niche-market players.
12. Exchange rate reform unleashed Korean entrepreneurs for growth.
13. To some Korean economists, the political need to legitimize the coup explains the costly promotion of heavy industries by Korea under Park, but not by Taiwan under the KMT.
14. The organization for planning may explain why Korea financed heavy industries with foreign borrowing but Japan did not.
15. Taiwan's consistent industrial development came from improvisation.
16. For economies with surplus labor, setting up export zones meets less resistance from the entrenched interests than liberalized trade.
17. Export Zones were set up in Taiwan to emulate Hong Kong, but they also exhibit the advantages of Industrial Parks.
18. Emulating the system of Taiwan's Kaohsiung Export Processing Zone, Mauritius succeeded to become an export platform for foreign investors.
19. The rule of law made Hong Kong an economy for trusted middlemen; by their intermediation, the PRC's village industries started to export.
20. With their rule ending, the British eschewed industrial policy in Hong Kong, causing now a de-industrialization that Singapore has avoided.
21. Currently, to produce offshore, Hong Kong invests in the PRC, but Korea invests in Vietnam or other non-Chinese economy.
22. For political viability, both Singapore and Malaysia had to adopt their respectively policies: 'meritocracy' for one, 'affirmative action' for the other, with Singapore's per capita income much higher than Malaysia.
23. The employment imperative drives Singapore's search for high growth; Singapore's labor requirement decides its future population mix.
24. Lacking both resources and home market, Singapore persuaded its labor to adopt compulsory arbitration, and keep the economy strike-free.

Problem XIV (A Project on Argentina)

In Chapters 1 and 2, it is explained *how* Argentina lagged behind both America and Japan but not quite *why*, in particular, for the *historical Argentina* (a) what could have been done and (b) what was actually done in outputs, borrowing, investment, and so on. This book supposedly offers principles and evidence relevant for various time and locations. Try to address (a) and (b), based on the short list of facts and events below. [Much of this information came from Cardoso (1987), Diaz-Alejandro (1970, ch. 1; 1988, ch. 12), and di Tella and Dornbusch (1989).]

1. In 1895, Argentinean per capita income was,
   a) at the level of Belgium, Germany and Holland
   b) ahead of Austria, Italy, Norway, Spain, Sweden, and Switzerland
   c) below Australia, America and Canada, among the newly settled countries: the Australian/Argentina ratio was slightly higher than 2:1 in 1895 and slightly lower than 2:1 in 1998 (The ratio of Australia to America was 115.91% in 1895 and 74.24% in 1998).
2. In population, Argentina had 2.47 million in 1880, 4.92 million in 1901 and 36 million in 1998, relative to 2.24 million in 1880, to 3.83 in 1901 and 19 million in 1998 for Australia. Australia has a more restrictive migration policy than Argentina. Weak labor market linkage existed between Argentina and Italy as well as Australia and the British Isles. The average real wage in Northwestern Europe was probably higher than Italy, and Italians migrated to Australia, America, and Argentina.
3. Geographic isolation mattered: the Argentinean debt crisis of 1889 was ended by the invention of refrigerated shipping of beef exports.
4. Up to 1900, Argentinean exports responded quickly to the changing world market: hides in the 1840s, grain in the 1880s and frozen beef in the 1900s.
5. The constant reliance on foreign borrowing often placed the economy in a conundrum. When debt service charges cause massive current account deficit, the government is forced to produce trade surpluses through devaluation. But devaluation raises the foreign debt burden which is denominated in foreign currency and encourages capital flight. To service debt, the government often relies on inflation for financing. But that erodes export competitiveness and hurts people with lower income.
6. With macro-economic instability and stagnation in growth, the impoverished labor turns militant and politicized. Turbulent labor-management relations discouraged investment and technological renewal. The rise of Peronism made reform even more complex.
7. The alienation of the educated youth caused brain drain and urban terrorism and the latter led to right-wing repression, which further complicated development.

I. To economists, 1895 seemed to be a highpoint of the Argentinean economy. Now without either any debt crisis, or a single military junta, Australia could not keep its lead over America over the 20th century, can one seriously expect Argentina to keep step with Germany in per capita income?
   a) Can that be done by producing more of the same, through accumulation?
   b) Can that be done through technical progress spearheaded by home-grown R & D?

c) Can that be done through technology diffusion via trade, in primary exports?
d) Can that be done through technology diffusion via trade, in manufactured exports (like Japan – keeping in mind that Japan surpassed Argentina in GDP per capita only in mid 1960s)?
e) Can that be done through technology diffusion via trade, in location-based manufactured exports (like Singapore which is located astride the sea lane between such and such)?

II. Discuss the following.
a) Primary products were important in the exports of both Taiwan and Malaysia. Compare their development with Argentina.
b) Military coup, foreign borrowing and IMF rescue form the shared experience between Korea and Argentina. Compare the differences between these two economies.
c) The recent financial crisis in Argentina caused 18% unemployment, pushed 15 million people below the poverty line, left some government workers unpaid for five months, and 132 billions of foreign debt delinquent in interest payment. In comparison, after World War II, the Japanese per capita income was at 45% of its pre-war level and Japanese technology lagged behind America and Europe. What does it take for Argentina to have a rapid and full scale recovery and then full fledged growth (like Japan)? Why?

BIBLIOGRAPHY

Aghion, P. and P. Howitt, 1998, *Endogenous Growth Theory,* Cambridge, MA: M.I.T. Press.

Alchian, A. A., 1950, "Uncertainty, Evolution and Economic Theory," *Journal of Political Economy* 58, 211-21.

Allen, F. and D. Gale, 2000, "Financial Contagion," *Journal of Political Economy* 108:1, 1–33.

Amsden, A. H., 1989, *Asia's Next Giant: South Korea and Late Industrialization,* New York: Oxford University Press.

_____, 1991, "Big Business and Urban Congestion in Taiwan: The Origins of Small Enterprise and Regionally Decentralized Industry (Respectively)," *World Development* 19: 9, 1121-35.

_____, 1999, "Taiwan's Industrialization Policies: Two Views, Two Types of Subsidy," in: Thorbecke, E. and Wan, H. Y., Jr. (eds), *Taiwan's Development Experience: Lessons on Roles of Government and Market,* Boston: Kluwer Academic Publishers.

_____, 2001, *The Rise of the Rest: Challenges to the West from Late Industrializing Economies,* New York: Oxford University Press.

Amsden, A. H. and W. W. Chu, 2003, *Beyond Late Development: Taiwan's Upgrading Policies*, Cambridge, MA: M. I. T. Press.

Andaya, B. W. and L. Y. Andaya, 1982, *A History of Malaysia*, London: Macmillan.

Antonio, E. T., Jr., 1997, "Industrial Policy in the Philippines: Growing Reliance on Market Mechanism," in: Masuyama. S., D. Vandenbrink and S. Y. Chia (eds), *Industrial Policy in East Asia*, Singapore: Institute of Southeast Asia Studies.

Applebaum, R. P. and D. A. Smith, 2000, "Governance and Flexibility: The Asian Garment Industry" in Deyo, F. C., R. Doner and E. Hershberg (eds.), *Economic Governance and the Challenge of Flexibillity in East Asia*, New York: Rowman and Littlefield

Arrow, K. J., 1962a, "The Economic Implications of Learning by Doing," *Review of Economic Studies* 29, 155-73.

_____, 1962b, "Economic Welfare and the Allocation of Resources for Invention," in: National Bureau of Economic Research, *The Rate and Direction of Inventive Activity,* Cambridge, MA: National Bureau of Economic Research.

Auerswald, P., S. Kauffman, J. Lobo and K. Shell, 1999, "The Production Recipe Approach to Modeling Technological Innovation: An Application to Learning by Doing," *Journal of Economic Dynamics and Control*, 24(3), 389-450.

Barnes, G. L. (ed.), 1990, *Hoabinhian Jomon, Yayoi Early Korean States: Bibliographical Reviews of Far Eastern Archaeology 1990*, Oxford: Oxbow Books for East Asian Archaeology Network.

Barro, R. and X. Sala – i – Martin, 1995, *Economic Growth,* New York: McGraw-Hill.

Basu, K., 1997, *Analytical Development Economics: the Less Developed Economy Revisited,* Cambridge, MA: MIT Press.

Baumol, W. J., 1965, *Economic Theory and Operations Analysis*, Englewood Cliffs, NJ: Prentice-Hall.

_____, 1986, "Productivity Growth, Convergence and Welfare: What the Long-Run Data Show", *American Economic Review* 76, 1072 – 1085.

Bauer, J., 1996, "Responses to Labor Scarcity and Aging in Singapore" in: Lim, C.-Y. (ed.) *Economic Policy Management in Singapore,* Singapore: Addison Wesley.

Bewley, T. F., 1982, "An Integration of the Equilibrium Theory and the Turnpike Theory," *Journal of Mathematical Economics* 10: 233-68.

Bhagwati, J. 1998, "The Capital Myth: The Difference between Trade in Widgets and Dollars," *Foreign Affairs* 77, 7-12.

_____, 1999, "The `Miracle' Did Happen: Understanding East Asia in Comparative Perspective," in: Thorbecke, E. and H. Y. Wan, Jr. (eds), *Taiwan's Development Experience: Roles of Government and Market*, Boston, MA: Kluwer Academic Publishers, 1999.

Boeker, P. H., 1993, Latin America's Economic Opening and the Rediscovery of Foreign Investment" in: Boeker, P. H. (ed.) *Latin America's Turnaround: Privatization, Foreign investment, and Growth*, San Francisco: ICS Press

Borrus, M., 1997, "Left for Dead: Asian Production Networks and the Revival of the U. S. Electronics," in: B. Naughton (ed.), *The China Circle, Economics and Electronics in the PRC, Taiwan and Hong Kong*, Washington, DC: Brookings Institution Press.

Cardoso E. A., 1987,"Latin American Debt: Which Way Now?", *Challenge*, 30: 2, 11-17.

Chang, H.-J., 1994, *The Political Economy Of Industrial Policy*, New York: St. Martin's Press.

_____, 1998, "South Korea: the Misunderstood Crisis," in: K. S. Jomo (ed.), *Tigers in Trouble: Financial Governance, Liberalization and Crisis in East Asia,* London: Zed Books, Ltd..

Chang, Y. F., 1999, *Tides of fortune: memoirs of Chang Yung-Fa*, Singapore: Times Books International.

Chau, L. C., 1993, *Hong Kong: A Unique Case of Development*, Washington, DC, World Bank.

Chen, S.-H. and D.-N. Liu, 2000, "Taiwan's Active Role in the Global Production Network" in: Chow, P. C. Y. and B. Gills (eds) *Weathering the Storm: Taiwan, Its Neighbors and the Asian Financial Crisis,* Washington, DC: Brookings Institution Press.

Chen, T.-J. and Y.-H. Ku, 1999, "Second-stage Import Substitution: The Taiwan Experience" in: G. Ranis, S.-c. Hu and Y.-P. Chu (eds), *The Political Economy of Taiwan into the 21st Century,* Cheltenham, UK: Edward Elgar.

Cheng, Lu-lin, 2001, "Sources of Success in Uncertain Markets: The Taiwanese Footwear Industry," in Deyo, F. C., R. Doner and E. Hershberg (eds.), *Economic Governance and the Challenge of Flexibillity in East Asia*, New York: Rowman and Littlefield.

Cheng, T.-Y., 1993, "The State as Banker: Guarding the Commanding Heights," in: Haggard, Stephan et al (eds.), *The Policy of Finance in Developing Countries*, Ithaca, NY: Cornell University Press.

Chia, S.-Y., 1986, "Direct Investment and the Industrialization Process of Singapore," in: Lim, C.-Y. and P. Lloyd (eds.), *Singapore: Resources and Growth*, New York: Oxford University Press.

Choi, B.-S., 1993, "Financial Policy and Big Business in Korea: The Perils of Financial Regulation," in Haggard, S., C., H. Lee, and S. Maxfield (eds), *The Politics of Finance in Developing Countries*, Ithaca NY: Cornell University Press.

Chu, W. W. and J. J. Li , 1996, "Growth and Industrial Organization: a Comparative Study of the Bicycle Industry in Taiwan and South Korea", *Journal of Industrial Studies*, 3(1), 35-52.

Clark, Carol, 1993, "Relative Backwardness in Eastern Europe: an Application of the Technological Gap Hypothesis', *Economic Systems* 17, 167-193.

Clemhout, S. and H. Y. Wan, Jr., 1970, "Learning-by-doing and Infant Industry Protection," *Review of Economic Studies*, 37: 33-56.

Coe, D. T., E. Helpman and A. W. Hoffmaister, 1997, "North-South Spillovers," *Economic Journal* 107: 134 – 49.

Confucius, 1997, *The Analects of Confucius.* Trans. and notes by Simon Leys, New York: W.W. Norton.

Crown, J. and G. Coleman, 1996, *No Hands: The Rise and Fall of The Schwinn Bicycle Company, An American Institution*, New York: Henry Holt.

Cyert, R. M. and J. G. March, 1963, *Behavioral Theory of the Firm*, Englewood Cliffs, NJ: Prentice-Hall.

Dabee, R. and D. Greenaway (eds.), 2001, *The Mauritian Economy: A Reade,* Houndmills, Basingstoke, Hampshire, UK: Palgrave.

David, P. A., 1985, "Clio and the Economics of QWERTY", *American Economic Review* 75: 2, 332-7.

DeLong, J. B. and L. H. Summers, 1991, "Equipment Investment and Economic Growth," *Quarterly Journal of Economics* 106:2, 445-502.

Deyo, F. C., 1989, *The Political Economy of the New Asian Industrialism*, Ithaca, NY: Cornell University Press.

Deyo, F. C., R. Doner and E. Hershberg (eds), 2001, *Economic Governance and the Challenge of Flexibillity in East Asia,* New York: Rowman and Littlefield.

di Tella, G. and R. Dornbusch (eds), 1989, *The Political economy of Argentina, 1946-83*, Pittsburgh PA: University of Pittsburgh Press.

Diamond, J., 1997, *Guns, Germs and Steel, The Fate of Human Societies* (New York: Norton).

Diaz-Alejandro, C. F., 1970, *Essays in the Economic History of the Argentine Republic*, New Haven, CN: Yale University Press.

_____, *Trade, Development and the World Economy/* Velasco, A. (eds) Oxford: Blackwell.

Dicks, A. R., 1995, "Compartmentalized Law And Judicial Restraint: An Inductive View Of Some Jurisdictional Barriers To Reform," *The China Quarterly* 141, 82-109.

Dornbusch, R., S. Fischer and P. A. Samuelson, 1977, "Comparative Advantage, Trade, and Payments in a Ricardian Model with a Continuum of Goods," *American Economic Review* 67:5, 823-39.

Doshi, T., 1988, "Singapore", *Asia Pacific Energy Series*, Honolulu: Resource Systems Institute, East-West Center.

Embong, A., 2000, "The Political Dimensions of the Economic Crisis in Malaysia" in: Embong, A. R. and J. Rudolph (eds.), *Southeast Asia into the Twenty First Century: Crisis and Beyond*, Bangi, Selangor, Malaysia: Penerbit UKM.

Engels, F., 1934, *Herr Eugen Dühring's Revolution in Science* [anti-Dühring], Moscow: Co-operative Publishing Society of Foreign Workers in the USSR.

England, J., 1971, "Industrial Relations in Hong Kong" in: K. Hopkins (ed.) *Hong Kong: The Industrial Colony*, Hong Kong: Oxford University Press.

Enos, J. L. and W. H. Park, 1988, *The adoption and Diffusion of Imported Technology: The case of Korea*, Beckenham, UK: Croom Helm Ltd..

Ericson, R., 1991, "The Classical Soviet-Type Economy: Nature of the System and Implications for Reform" *Journal of Economic Perspectives*, 5: 4, 11-27.

Ernst, D., 2001, "Catching Up and Post-Crisis Industrial Upgrading: Searching for New Sources of Growth in Korea's Electronics Industry," in F. C. Deyo, R. F. Doner, and Eric Hershberg (eds) *Economic Governance and the Challenge of Flexibility in East Asia*, Lanham, MD: Rowman & Littlefield.

Fei, J. C. H. and Y.-P. Chu, 1999. "Liberalization Promotes Development: Evidence from Taiwan," in Thorbecke, E. and H. Wan, Jr. (eds), *Taiwan's Development Experience: Lessons on roles of Government and Market,* Boston: Kluwer Academic Press.

Feldstein, M. and C. Horioka, 1980, "Domestic Savings and International Capital Flows," *Economic Journal* 90, 314 – 29.

Fields, K., 1995, *Enterprise and the State in Korea and Taiwan*, Ithaca, NY: Cornell University Press.

Findlay, R. E., 1978, "Relative Backwardness, Direct Foreign Investment and the Transfer of Technology: A Simple Dynamic Model," *Quarterly Journal of Economics* 92, 1-16.

Findlay, R. E., and S. Wellisz (1993), Hong Kong, in Findlay, R. and S. Wellisz, (eds.), *The Political Economy of Poverty, Equity and Growth: Five Small Open Economies*, New York: Oxford University Press.

Fransman, M. (ed.), 1986, *Machinery and Economic Development*, New York: St. Martin's Press.

Friedman, M., 1953, *Essays in Positive Economics*, Chicago: University of Chicago Press.

Furman, J. and J. E. Stiglitz, 1998, "Economic Crises: Evidence and Insights from East Asia," *Brookings Papers on Economic Activity* v0, n2: 1-114.

Galor, O., 2000, "Income Distribution and the Process of Development," *European Economic Review* v44, S103-17.

Galor, O. and O. Moav, 2000, "Ability-Biased Technological Transition, Wage Inequality, and Economic Growth," *Quarterly Journal of Economics* v115, 469-97.

_____, 2001, "Evolution and Growth", *European Economic Review* 45, 718-29.

Galor, O. and D. N. Weil, 2000, "Population, Technology, and Growth: From Malthusian Stagnation to the Demographic Transition and Beyond," *American Economic Review* v90, 806-28.

Gerschenkron, A., 1952, "Economic Backwardness in Historical Perspective" in: B. F. Hoselitz (ed.) *The Progress of Underdeveloped Areas*, Chicago: Chicago University Press.

Gomulka, S., 1990, *The Theory of Technological Change and Economic Growth*, London: Routledge.

Grossman, G. and E. Helpman, 1993, *Innovation and Growth in the Global Economy*, Cambridge, MA: MIT Press.

Hadley, G. and M. C. Kemp, 1966, "Equilibrium and Efficiency in International Trade", *Metroeconomica* 18: 125-41.

Halberstam, D., 1986, *The Reckoning*, New York: Morrow.

Han, W.-K. , 1970, *The History of Korea*, translated by K.-s. Lee, edited by G. K. Mintz, Seoul: Eul-Yoo Publishing Company.

Hang, C. C., 1999, "What It Takes to Sustain Research and Development in a Small, Developed Nation in the 21st Century?" in: Linda Low (ed.), *Singapore: Toward a Developed Status* (New York: Oxford University Press), 25-36.

Harriss, J., J. Hunter and C. M. Lewis (eds), *The New Institutional Economics and Third World Development*, London: Routledge.

Hayami, Y. and M. Aoki (eds) *The Institutional Foundations of East Asian Development*, New York: St. Martin's Press.

Hobday, Michael, 1995, *Innovation in East Asia: The Challenge to Japan*, Aldershot, Hants, England: Edward Elgar.

Hong, W., 1994, *Trade and Growth: A Korean Perspective*, Seoul: Kudara International.
_____, 2002, Catch-up and Crisis in Korea, Aldershot, Hants, England: Edward Elgar.
Hopkins, K., 1971, "Preface" in: K. Hopkins (ed.), *Hong Kong: The Industrial Colony*, Hong Kong: Oxford University Press.
Huff, W.G., 1994, *The Economic Growth of Singapore: Trade and Development in the Twentieth Century*, New York: Cambridge University Press.
Huntington, S. P., 1996, *The Clash of Civilizations and the Remaking of World Order*, New York: Simon & Schuster.
Itoh, M., 1999, "Foreign Investment, International Trade and Technological Transfer: a Case Study in South-east Asia," in: J. Piggott and Woodland, A. (eds), *International Trade Policy and the Pacific Rim*, Houndmills, Basingstoke, Hampshire: Macmillan Press.
Itoh, M., K. Kiyono, M. Okuno-Fujiwara and K. Suzumura, 1991, *Economic Analysis of Industrial Policy*, San Diego: Academic Press.
Itoh, M. and S. Urata, 1994, *Small and Medium Enterprise Support Policies in Japan*, Policy Research Working Paper 1403, Washington DC: World Bank.
Jeremy, D. and D. H. Stapleton, 1991, "Transfer between Culturally – Related Nations, the Movement of Textile and Railroad Technologies between Britain and the United States, 1780-1940" in Jeremy, D. (ed.), *International Technology Transfer, Europe Japan and the USA 1700-1914*, Aldershot, Hants, England: Edward Elgar.
Johnson, M., 1992, "Classification, Power and Markets: the Waning of the Ethnic Division of Labor" in: Simon, D. F. and M. Y. M. Kau, *Taiwan: Beyond the Economic Miracle*, Almonk N: M. E. Sharpe.
Jomo, K. S., 1998, Malaysia: From Miracle to Debacle" in: K. S. Jomo (eds.), *Tigers in Trouble: Financial Governance, Liberalization and Crisis in East Asia*, London: Zed Books, Ltd.
Jones, C. I., 1998, *Introduction to Growth Theory*, New York: Norton.
Jones, L. P. and I. Sakong, 1980, *Government, Business and Entrepreneurship in Economic Development: the Korean Case*, Cambridge, MA: Harvard University Press.
Jones, R. W. and H. Kierzkowski, 1990, "The Role of Services in Production and International Trade: A Theoretical Framework," in Jones, R. W. and A. O. Krueger (eds.) , *The Political Economy of International Trade: Essays in Honor of Robert E. Baldwin*, Oxford: Blackwell.
Kato, T and H. Wan, Jr., 2001, "Specialization Pattern and Multi-staged Growth: The Korea Taiwan Comparison," *Review of Development Economics* 5:2, 256-61.
Kemp, M. C., 1960, "The Mill-Bastable Dogma," *Journal of Political Economy* 68: 65-7.
_____, 1995, *The Gains from Trade and the Gains from Aid*, London: Routledge.
Kemp, M. and H. Y. Wan, Jr., 1973, "Hystereses of Long-Run Equilibrium from Realistic Adjustment Costs," in Horwich G. and P.A. Samuelson (eds) *Trade, Stability and Macro-Economics*, New York: Academic Press.
_____, 1993, *The Welfare Economics of International Trade*, London: Harwood Academic Press.
Kennedy, P. M., 1987, *Rise and Fall of the Great Powers: Economic Change and Military Conflict from 1500 to 2000*, New York: Random House.
Kikkawa, T. and T. Hikino, 1999, "Industrial Policy and Japan's International Competitiveness: Historical Overview and Assessment" in: H. Miyajima, T. Kikkawa, and T. Hikino (eds.), *Policies for Competitiveness*, Oxford: Oxford University Press.
Kim, J.-I. and L. J. Lau, 1994, "The Source of Economic Growth of the East Asian Newly Industrialized Countries," *Journal of the Japanese and International Economies* 8:3, 235-71.
Kim, K., 1991, "Kim Jae-Ik: His Life and Contributions in: Krause, L. B. and K. Kim (eds.) *Liberalization in the Process of Economic Development*, Berkeley: University of California Press.

Kim, K., and D. Leipziger, 1993, *Korea: A Case of Government-led Development*, Washington DC: The World Bank.

Kim, L. 1997, *Imitation to Innovation: The Dynamics of Korea's Technological Learning*, Boston: Harvard Business School Press.

_____, 2000, "Korea's National Innovation System in Transition" in Kim, L. S. and R. R. Neslson (eds), *Technology, Learning and Innovation*, Cambridge UK: Cambridge University Press.

Kirk, D., 2000, *Korean Crisis: Unraveling of the Miracle in the IMF Era*, New York: St. Martin's Press.

Koe, A. T., Lim, K. L., Hui W. T. Rao, B. and Chng M. K., 2002, *Singapore Economy in the 21st Century: Issues and Strategies*, Singapore: McGraw-Hill.

Kojima, K., 1978, *Direct Foreign Investment: A Japanese Model, Multinational Business Operation*, London: Croom Helm.

Komiya, R., 1972, "Direct Foreign Investment in Post-war Japan," in: P. Drysdale (ed.), *Direct Foreign Investment in Asia and the Pacific*, Toronto: University of Toronto Press.

_____, 1988, "Introduction" in: Komiya, R., M. Okuno, and K. Suzumura (eds.), *Industrial Policy of Japan*; trans. under supervision of K. Sato, San Diego, CA: Academic Press.

_____, 1990, *The Japanese Economy: Trade, Industry, and Government*, Tokyo: University of Tokyo Press.

Koopmans, T. C., 1957, *Three Essays on the State of Economic Science*, New York: McGraw Hill.

Krugman, P. R., 1979, "A Model of Innovation, Technology Transfer and the World Distribution of Income," *Journal of Political Economy*, 87:2, 253-66.

_____, 1987, "The Narrow Moving Band, the Dutch Disease, and the Competitive Consequences of Mrs. Thatcher," *Journal of Development Economics* v27, n1-2, 41-55.

_____, 1994, "The myth of Asia's Miracle," *Foreign Affairs* 73, 62-78.

Kuo, S. W. Y., 1999. "Government Policy in the Taiwanese Development Process: The Past 50 Years," in: Thorbecke, E. and H. Y. Wan, Jr. (eds), *Taiwan's Development Experience: Roles of Government and Market*, Boston, MA: Kluwer Academic Publishers, 1999

Kuznets, S., 1982, "Modern Economic Growth and the Less Developed Countries" in: K.-T. Li and T.-S. Yu (eds.), *Experience and Lessons of Economic Development in Taiwan*, Taipei: Academia Sinica.

Lall, S., 1996, *Learning from the Asian Tigers: Studies in Technology and Industrial Policy*, New York: St. Martin's Press.

Landes, D. S., 1994, "What Room for Accident in History?: Explaining Big Changes by Small Events", *Economic History Review* 47: 4, 637-56.

Lau, M.-L. and Wan, H. Y. Jr., 1991, "The Theory of Growth and Technology Transfer: Experience from East Asian Economies," *The Seoul Journal of Economics* 4, 109–122.

_____, 1994, "On the mechanism of catching-up," *European Economic Review* 38, 952-963.

Lauridsen, L. S. , 1998, "Thailand: Causes, Conduct, Consequences" in: K. S. Jomo (eds.), *Tigers in Trouble: Financial Governance, Liberalization and Crisis in East Asia*, London: Zed Books, Ltd.

Lee, J.-W., 1996, "Government Interventions and Productivity Growth," *Journal of Economic Growth*, vol 1, no. 3, 391-414.

Lee, K. Y., 1998, *The Singapore Story: Memoirs of Lee Kuan Yew*, Singapore: Singapore Press Holdings, Times Editions.

_____, 2000, *From Third World to First: The Singapore Story, 1965-2000*, New York: Harper Collins Publishers.

Lee, T. Y. and L. Low, 1990, *Local Entrepreneurship in Singapore, Private and State.* Singapore: Time Academic Press.

Lever-Tracy, C., D. Ip, and N. Tracy, 1996, *The Chinese Diaspora and Mainland China,* London: Edward Elgar.

Levy, B., 1990, "Transactions Costs, the Size of Firms and Industrial Policy: Lessons from a Comparative Case Study of the Footwear Industry in Korea and Taiwan," *Journal of Development Economics*, v34, n1-2, 151-78.

Lewis, B., 1995, *The Middle East, A Brief History of the Last 2000 Years*, New York: Simon and Schuster.

Liang, C-Y., and D. W. Jorgenson, 1999, "Productivity Growth in Taiwan's Manufacturing Industry, 1961-1993," in: Fu, T.-T.; C. J. Huang, and C. A. K. Lovell, (eds) *Economic Efficiency And Productivity Growth in the Asia-Pacific Region*, Northampton, MA: Edward Elgar.

Lim, Y. Y., 2001, *Malaysia's New Economic Policy and ts effects on Ethnic Malays*, Honors Thesis, Cornell University.

Lim, L., E. F. Pang; and R. Findlay, 1993, "Five Small Open Economies: Singapore" in: Findlay, R. and S. Wellisz (eds.), *The Political Economy of Poverty, Equity and Growth: Five Small Open Economies*, New York: Oxford University Press.

Low, L., 2000, The Politics of Corporate and Financial Restructuring in: Embong, A. R. and J. Rudolph (eds.), *Southeast Asia into the Twenty First Century: Crisis and Beyond*, Bangi, Selangor, Malaysia: Penerbit UKM.

Low, L., and T. L. Ngiam, 1999 "An Underclass among the Overclass," in: L. Low (ed.), *Singapore: Toward a Developed Status*, Singapore: Oxford University Press.

Lucas, R. E., Jr., 1976, "Econometric Policy Evaluation: A Critique," *Journal of Monetary Economics*, 1:2, Supplement, 19-46.

_____, 1988, "On the Mechanics of Economic Development," *Journal of Monetary Economics*, 22: 3-42.

_____, 1993, "Making a Miracle", *Econometrica*, 61: 251 - 72.

Mahathir b. M., 1970, *The Malay Dilemma,* Singapore: D. Moore for Asia Pacific Press.

_____, 1999, *A New Deal for Asia,* Selangor: Darul Ehsan: Pelanduk Publications.

Malraux, A., 1953, *The Voices of Silence.* Trans. S. Gilbert, Garden City, NY: Doubleday.

Mansfield, E., J. Rapoport, A. Romero, E. Villani, S. Wagner, and F. Husic, 1977, *The Production and Application of New Industrial Technology*, New York: Norton.

Matsuyama, K., 1991, "Increasing Returns, Industrialization, and Indeterminacy of Equilibrium," *Quarterly Journal of Economics* v106, n2: 617–50.

Meyanathan, S.D. and R. Munter, 1994, "Industrial Structures and the Development of Small and Medium Enterprise Linkages: An Overview" in: S. D. Meyanathan (ed.) *Industrial Structures and the Development of Small and Medium Enterprise Linkages: Examples from East Asia*, Washington, DC: World Bank.

Meyer, W. H., 1986, "Around the World with The Limited," *New York Times Magazine*, June 8, 1986.

Miyajima, H., 1999, "Regulatory Framework in Post-war Japan," in: Miyajima, Hideaki et al. (eds.), *Policies for Competition* New, York: Oxford University Press.

Mody, A., 1990, "Institutions and Dynamic Comparative Advantage: The Electronics Industry in South Korea and Taiwan," *Cambridge Journal of Economics* v14, n3: 291–314.

Morawetz, D., 1981, *Why The Emperor's New Clothes Are Not Made in Colombia: A Case Study In Latin American and East Asian Manufactured Exports*, Washington, DC: Oxford University Press.

Morishima, M., 1982, *Why Has Japan Succeeded?: Western Technology and the Japanese Ethos*, New York: Cambridge University Press.

_____, 2000, *Japan at a Deadlock*, London: Macmillan.

Mukhopadhayya, P. and V.V. Bhanoji Rao, 2002, "Income Inequality in Koh,, A. T. et al. (eds), *Singapore Economy in the 21st Century*, Singapore: McGraw-Hill.
Murphy, K. M., A. Shleifer, and R. W. Vishny, 1989, "Industrialization and the Big Push," *Journal of Political Economy* 97, 1003-26.
Naughton, B., (eds.) 1997, *China Circle: Economics and Electronics in the PRC, Taiwan, and Hong Kong*, Washington, D.C.: Brookings Institution.
Nermuth. M., 1982, "Information Structures in Economics: Studies in the Theory of Markets with Imperfect Information," New York: Springer-Verlag.
Newbery, D. M. G. and J. E. Stiglitz, 1981, *The Theory of Commodity Price Stabilization: A Study in the Economics of Risk,* New York: Oxford University Press.
North, D. C., 1990, Institutions, Institutional Change and Economic Performance, New York: Cambridge University Press.
_____, 1994, "Economic Preference through Time," *American Economic Review* 84:3, 359-68.
_____, 1995, "The New Institutional Economics and Third World Development" in Harriss, J., J. Hunter and C. M. Lewis (eds), *The New Institutional Economics and Third World Development*, London: Routledge.
_____, 1998, "The Institutional Foundations of East Asian Development: A Summary Evaluation" in Hayami, Y. and M. Aoki (eds) *The Institutional Foundations of East Asian Development*, New York: St. Martin's Press.
Ohkawa, K. and H. Rosovsky, 1973, *Japanese Economic Growth: Trend Acceleration in the Twentieth Century*, Stanford: Stanford University Press.
Owen, N., 1971, "Economic Policy" in: Hopkins, K. (eds.), *Hong Kong: The Industrial Colony*, Hong Kong: Oxford University Press.
Ozawa, T., 1979, *Multinationalism, Japanese Style: The Political Economy of Outward Dependency*, Princeton, NJ: Princeton University Press.
Pacey, A., 1990, *Technology in World Civilization,* Cambridge, MA: MIT Press.
Park, C. H., 1962, *Our Nation's Path*, Seoul, Dong-a Pub. Co..
Perkins, D. H. and W. T. Woo, 2000, "Malaysia: Adjusting to the Deep Integration with the World Economy", in: Woo, W. T., J. D. Sachs and K. Schwab (eds), *The Asian Financial Crisis: Lessons for a Resilient Asia,* Cambridge, MA, MIT Press.
Perry, M., L. Kong and B. Yeoh, 1997, *Singapore, A Developmental City State*, New York: Wiley and Sons.
Phelps-Brown, E. H., 1971, "The Hong Kong Economy: Achievements and Prospects" in: Hopkins, K. (eds), *Hong Kong: The Industrial Colony*, Hong Kong: Oxford University Press.
Prebisch, R., 1959, "Commercial Policy in Underdeveloped Countries", *American Economic Review* 49 (papers and proceedings), 252-73.
Prescott, E. C., 1998, "Needed: A Theory of Total Productivity," *International Economic Review*, 39, 525-51.
Radner, R., 1966, "Optimal Growth in a Linear Logarithmic Economy," *International Economic Review* 7, 1-33.
Rahim, L. Z., 1998, *The Singapore Dilemma, The Political and Educational Marginality of the Malay Community*, Kuala Lumpur: Oxford University.
Ramsey, F., 1928, "A Mathematical Theory of Saving," *Economic Journal* 38, 543-559.
Ranis, G., 1999, "Reflections on the Economics and Political Economy of Development at the Turn of the Century", in: Ranis, G.; S. C. Hu, and Y. P. Chu, (eds), *The Political Economy of Taiwan's Development Into the Twenty-first Century: Essays in Memory of John C. H. Fei. Volume* 2, Northampton, MA: Edward Elgar.
_____, 2002, "Lessons from Taiwan's Performance: Neither Miracle Nor Crisis," in: Peter Chow (eds), *Taiwan in the Global Economy: From an Agrarian Economy to an Exporter of High-Tech Products*, Westport, CN: Praeger Publishers.

Rao, V. V .B., 1988, "Income Distribution in East Asian Developing Countries," *Asian-Pacific Economic Literature* v2.

_____, 2001, *East Asian Economies: The Miracle, A Crisis and the Future*, Singapore: McGraw-Hill.

Rasiah, R., 1999, "Government–Business Co-ordination and the Development of Eng Hardware" in Jomo, K. S., G. Felker and R. Rasiah (eds), *Industrial Technology Development: Industry and Firm Studies*, Northampton, MA: Edward Elgar.

_____, 2001, "Politics, Institutions and Flexiblity: Microelectronic Transnationals and Machine Tool Linkages in Malaysia" in Deyo, F. C., R. Doner and E. Hershberg (eds.), *Economic Governance and the Challenge of Flexibility in East Asia*, New York: Rowman and Littlefield.

Ray, D., 1998, *Development Economics*, Princeton: Princeton University Press.

Rear, J., 1971, "One Brand of Politics," in: Hopkins, K. (eds), *Hong Kong: The Industrial Colony*, Hong Kong: Oxford University Press.

Rhee, Y. W., B. Ross-Larson and G. Pursell, 1984, *Korea's Competitive Edge: Managing the Entry into World Markets*, Baltimore: Johns Hopkins University Press.

Rhee, J. C., 1994, *The State and Industry in South Korea: The Limits of the Authoritarian State*, London; New York: Routledge.

Richter, R., 1996, "Bridging Old and New Institutional Economics: Gustav Schmoller, the Leader of the Younger German Historical School, Seen with Neoinstitutionalists' Eyes," *Journal of Institutional and Theoretical Economics* 152, 567-92.

Rodrik, D., 1995, "Getting Interventions Right: How South Korea and Taiwan Grew Rich", *Economic Policy*, April, 53-108.

Romer, P.M., 1986, "Increasing Returns and Long Run Growth," *Journal of Political Economy* 94, 1002-1037.

Roy, J., 1998, "Trade Liberalization: The Road Ahead," in: Kelkar, V. J. and V. V. B. Rao (eds), *India: Development Policy Imperatives*, New Delhi: Tata McGraw-Hill.

Saito, M., 2000, *The Japanese Economy*, River Edge, NJ: World Scientific.

Sakong, I., 1993, *Korea in the World Economy*, Washington, DC: Institute for International Economics.

Samuelson, P.A., 1948, *Foundation of Economic Analysis*, Cambridge, MA: Harvard University Press.

Saxenian, A., 2002, 'Transnational Communities and the Evolution of Global Production Networks: The Cases of Taiwan, China and India," *Industry and Innovation* 9, 183-202.

Schive, Chi, 1990, *The Foreign Factor: The Multinational Corporation's Contribution to the Republic of China*, Stanford, California: Hoover Institution Press.

Schultz, T. P., 1999, "Income Inequality in Taiwan 1976-95: Changing Family Composition, Aging and Female Labor-Force Participation" in: Ranis, G., S.-C. Hu, and Y.-P. Chu, (eds), *Essays in memory of John C. H. Fei. Volume 2. The political economy of Taiwan's development into the twenty-first century*, Northampton, MA: Edward Elgar.

Sen, A. K., 1999, *Development as Freedom*, New York: Alfred Knopf.

Shell, K., 1966, "Toward a Theory of Inventive Activity and Capital Accumulation, *American Economic Review* 56, 62-68.

Shieh, G. S., 1992, *"Boss" Island: the Subcontracting Network and Micro- entrepreneurship in Taiwan's Development*, New York: P. Lang.

Simon, H. A., 1997, "Satisficing" in *Models of Bounded Rationality. Volume 3. Empirically Grounded Economic Reason*, Cambridge MA: MIT Press.

Smith, A., 1776, *An Inquiry into the Nature and Causes of the Wealth of Nations* (London: Printed for W. Strahan and T. Cadell, in the Strand).

Smith, W., 1983, "Japanese Factories, Malaysian Workers", in: Jomo, K. S., (ed.), *The Sun Also Sets*, Petaling Jaya, Selangor: Institute for Social Analysis.

Smith, H., 2000, "The State, Banking and Corporate Relationships in Korea and Taiwan", in: Drysdale, P., (ed.), *Reform and Recovery in East Asia: the Role of the State and Economic Enterprise*, New York: Routledge.

Solow, R. M., 1956, "A Contribution to the Theory of Economic Growth", *Quarterly Journal of Economics*, 70: 5-94.

_____, 1957, "Technical Change and the Aggregate Production Function", *Review of Economic and Statistics*, 39: 312-20.

_____, 1966, "Review" of John R. Hicks, Jr., Capital and Growth, *American Economic Review*, 56: 1257-60.

_____, 2000, *Growth Theory, An Exposition*, 2nd edition, Oxford: Oxford University Press.

_____, 2001, "Applying Growth Theory across Countries" *The World Bank Economic Review* 15:2, 283-8.

Soon, T. W. and W. A. Stoever, 1996, "Foreign Investment and Economic Development in Singapore", *Journal of Development Areas* 30, 317-40.

Stern, J. J., J-H. Kim, D. H. Perkins and J-H. Yoo, 1995, *Industrialization and the State: The Korean Heavy and Chemical Industry Drive*, Cambridge, MA: Harvard University Press.

Stiglitz, J. E., 2002, *Globalization and its Discontents*, New York: Norton.

Stokey, N. L., 1991, "Human Capital, Product Quality and Growth", *Quarterly Journal of Economics*, 106, 587-616.

Sung, Y.-W. 1997, "Hong Kong and the Economic Integration of the China Circle," in: Naughton, B., (ed.), *China Circle: Economics and Technology in the PRC, Taiwan, and Hong Kong*, Washington, DC: Brookings.

Sung, Y.-W., P.-W. Liu, Y.-C. R. Wong and P.-K. Lau, 1995, *The Fifth Dragon: the Emergence of the Pearl River Delta,* Singapore: Addison Wesley.

Suzuki, T., 1999, "Industrial Policy and the Development of the Synthetic Fiber Industry: Industrial Policy as a Means for Promoting Economic Growth," in: Miyajima, H., T. Kikkawa, and T. Hikino, (eds.), *Policies for Competitiveness*, Oxford: Oxford University Press.

Tan, K. Y., 1997, "China and the ASEAN: Competitive Industrialization through Foreign Investment," in: Naughton, B. (ed.), *The China Circle, Economics and Technology in the PRC, Taiwan and Hong Kong*, Washington, DC: Brookings Institution Press.

Tanzer, A., 1992, "Bury Thy Teacher," *Forbes*, 150: 14, 90–4.

Thom, R., 1975, *Structural Stability and Morphogenesis: An Outline of a General Theory of Models*, translated from the French, edited and updated by the author, by D. H. Fowler with a foreword by C. H. Waddington, Reading, MA: W. A. Benjamin.

Thorbecke, E., A.-C. Tung, and H. Y. Wan, Jr., 2002, "Industrial Targeting: Lessons from Past Errors and Successes of Hong Kong and Taiwan," *World Development* 25:8, 1047-61.

Tobin, J., 1980, *Asset Accumulation and Economic Activity: Reflections on Contemporary Macroeconomic Theory*, Chicago: University of Chicago Press.

Tolstoy, L., 1877, *Anna Karénina*. Trans. N. H. Dole, New York: Crowell & Co.

Tonkay, G. L. and K. Knott, 1988, "An Expert System in Welding," in: Kumara, S. T., A. L. Soyster, and R. L. Kashyap, (eds), *Artificial Intelligence: Manufacturing Theory and Practice*, Norcross, GA: Institute of Industrial Engineers, Industrial Engineering and Management Press.

Tonzon, J. L., 2002, "Developments in Sea Transport, Interport Competition and the Singapore Policy Response", in: Koh, A. T., et al. (eds), *Singapore Economy in the 21st Century*, Singapore: McGraw-Hill.

Tsiang, S. C., 1984, "Taiwan's Economic Miracles: Lessons in Economic Development", in: Harberger, A., (ed.), World Economic Growth San Francisco, CA: Institute of Contemporary Studies Press.

Tung, A.-C., 2001, "Taiwan's Semiconductor Industry: What the State Did and Did Not," *Review of Development Economics* 5(2).266-88.

Uchida, H., 1991, "The Transfer of the Electrical Technology from *America and Europe to Japan: 1869-1914," in: Jeremy, D. (ed.), International Technology Transfer: Europe, Japan and the U.S.A.: 1700-1914,* Aldershot, England: Edward Elgar.

Uchupalanun, J., 1999, *A Contribution to the Theory of Real Exchange Rate Fluctuations*, Ithaca, NY, Cornell University, Doctoral Dissertation.

Van, H. P. and H. Y. Wan, Jr., 1997, "Interpreting East Asian Growth," in: Jensen, B. S. and K.-Y. Wong, (eds), *Dynamics, Economic Growth and International Trade*, Ann Arbor MI: Michigan University Press.

_____, 1999, "Emulative Development Through Trade Expansion: East Asian Evidence," in: Piggott, J. and A. Woodland, (eds), *International Trade Policy and the Pacific Rim,* Houndsmill, Basingstoke, Hampshire: Macmillan.

Veblen, T., 1915, *Imperial Germany and the Industrial Revolution*, London: Macmillan.

Wade, R., 1990, *Governing the Market, Economic Theory and the Role of Government in East Asian Industrialization*, Princeton, NJ: Princeton University Press.

Wan, H. Y. Jr., 1978, "Manpower, Export-led Growth and Industrialization: The Taiwan Experience," *Occasional Papers/Reprint Series in Contemporary Asian Studies*, College Park, MD: School of Law, University of Maryland.

_____, 1988, "Nipponized Confucian Ethos or Incentive-Compatible Institutional Design: Notes on Morishima, 'Why has Japan Succeeded?'" *International Economic Journal* 2:1, 101-8, 1988.

_____, 1992, "On Markets, Planning & Market Reform," *Academia Economic Papers*, 20:2, 291-312.

_____, 1993, "Trade, Development and Inventions," in: Herberg, H. and N. V. Long, (eds), Trade, Welfare and Economic Policies, Ann Arbor, MI: University of Michigan Press.

_____, 1994, " Revisitng the Mitra-Wan Tree Farm," *International Economic Review* 35:1 153-8.

_____, 1995, "A Note on Knowledge Capital and the Needham Paradox," *Academic Economic Papers* 23:2, 1-24.

_____, 1997, "A Note on Compensation Schemes," *Japanese Economic Review* 48, 147-55.

_____, 1998, "The Singaporean Economy: Prospects for the 21st Century," *Singapore Economic Review* 43, 1-11.

_____, 2001, "Reflections on Income and Growth Determination in a Globalized Economy", in: Hu, S.-C. and T.-T. Fu, (eds), *Conference Proceeding on Economic Development in Memory of Professor Mo-Huan Hsing*. Nankang, Taiwan, China: Institute of Economics, Academia Sinica.

_____, 2002, "Why Trade Matters to Development: A Learning Model", in: Woodland, A., (ed.) *Economic Theory and International Trade: Essays in Honor of Professor Murray Kemp*, Aldershot, England: Edward Elgar.

_____, 2003, "Reform Unleashes Korean Growth," *German Economic Review* , 4(1), 19-34.

Wan, H. Y. Jr., and E. Thorbecke, 1999, "Some Further Thoughts on Taiwan's Development," in: Thorbecke, E. and H. Y. Wan, Jr., (eds), in *Taiwan's Development Experience: Lessons on Roles of Government and Market*, Boston: Kluwer Academic Press.

Wan, H. Y., and J. Weisman, 1999, Hong Kong: The Fragile Economy of the Middlemen, *Review of International Economics*. 7:3, 410-30.

Wan, H. Y. Jr., and W. K. Wong, 2001, Contagion or Inductance, Crisis 1997 Reconsidered. *Japanese Economic Review*. 52:4, 372-81.

Wang G., 2000, "The Chinese Overseas: From Earthbound China to the Quest for Autonomy," Cambridge, MA: Harvard University Press.

Weber, M., 1930, "The Protestant Ethic and the Spirit of Capitalism" / translated by T. Parsons, with a foreword by R. H. Tawney, New York: Scribner.

_____, 1951, *The Religion of China: Confucianism and Taoism.* Trans. and ed. by H. H. Gerth. Glencoe, IL: Free Press.

Wellisz, S. and S. P. L. Shin, 1993, "Five Small Open Economies: Mauritius," in: Findlay, R. and S. Wellisz, (eds), *The Political Economy of Poverty, Equity and Growth: Five Small Open Economies*, New York: Oxford University Press.

Wong, P.-K., 2001, "Flexible Production, High-Tech Commodities and Public Policies: The Hard Disk Drive Industry in Singapore", in: Deyo, F. C., R. Doner and E. Hershberg, (eds), *Economic Governance and the Challenge of Flexibillity in East Asia*, New York: Rowman and Littlefield.

Wong, S-L., 1988, *Emigrant Entrepreneurs, Shanghai Industrialists in Hong Kong*, New York: Oxford University Press.

Woo-Cummings, M., 2001, "Miracle as Prologue: The State and Corporate Reform in Korea", in Stiglitz, J. E. and S. Yusuf, *Rethinking East Asian Miracle*, New York: Oxford University Press.

World Bank, *World Bank Atlas,* Washington: World Bank.

Wright, P. K. and D. A. Bourne, 1988, *Manufacturing Intelligence*, Reading, MA: Addison-Wesley.

Yang, T.-H., 2000, Industrial Organization and Transaction Costs: A Comparison between South Korea and Taiwan (unpublished manuscript).

Yoo, J. H., 1990, *The Industrial Policy of the 1970s and the Evolution of the Manufacturing Sector in Korea*, Working Paper No. 9017, Seoul: KDI Press.

Young, A., 1991 Learning by Doing and the Dynamic Effect of International trade, *Journal of Political Economy* 101(3), 443-472.

_____, 1992, "A Tale of Two Cities: Factor Accumulation and Technical Change in Hong Kong and Singapore," *NBER Macroeconomics Annal.*

_____, 1993, Invention and Bounded Learning-by-Doing, *Journal of Political Economy*, 101: 443 - 72.

_____, 1994, "Lessons from the East Asian NICs: A Contrarian View," *European Economic Review*, 38, 964-973.

_____, 1995, "The Tyranny of Numbers: Confronting the Statistical Realities of the East Asian Growth Experience," *Quarterly Journal of Economics* 110(3): 641–680.

INDICES

A Note for Users of Our Indices

For the convenience of readers, we have supplied an Author Index beside the Bibliography. Additionally, the subject index is separated into a Subject Index - General and a Subject Index – Structured Comparisons.

This volume is about *facts*, from which *conclusions* are arrived at. *Facts* gain meaning, only when they are selected and arranged in some fashion; *conclusions* emerge, after appealing to certain ‘theories’ (or hypotheses) of various degrees of formality. These *selection* and *theorization* are closely related to binary groupings, between individual or groups of economies; the differences in various aspects shown in the comparisons suggest causes and effects, as perceived by the author. For interested readers, these appear in the Index – Structured Comparison for reference.

This volume discusses the development process, and the East Asian experience. Our book may also be useful to other readers interested only in some particular and related topics, for example, the effect of ‘export zones’. From our Index – General, the entry Export Zones/Industrial Parks then provides not only pages in this book relevant to the topic, but also names of particular economies which are relevant, Taiwan, Hong Kong, Korea, PRC, Malaysia and Mauritius. From this list of six economies, the reader can go to the Index – Structured Comparisons and find the following related items:

A) The Bangladesh-Mauritius comparison: for the economy as a whole, why has Bangladesh gained less than Mauritius?
B) The Malaysia-Mauritius comparison: why has the export zone generated backward linkage in Penang, Malaysia, but become merely an enclave in Mauritius?

C) The Mauritius-Taiwan comparison: why export zones in Taiwan appear to be more valuable to the economy than their counterpart in Mauritius?
D) The Korea-Taiwan comparison: why did export zones play important roles in the development of Taiwan but not Korea?
E) The Hong Kong-Taiwan comparison: if the export zones of Taiwan arose from emulating Hong Kong, why have high tech industries developed better in Taiwan than in Hong Kong itself?
F) The Singapore-Taiwan comparison: if for high tech industries, the advantage of Taiwan over Hong Kong is solely due to the fact that Taiwan's export zones also serve the function of industrial parks, why should Taiwan's Hsingchu Science-based Industrial Park also become a better incubator for start-up firms in high tech than the Singaporean industrial parks?
G) The PRC-Taiwan comparison: with its own industrial parks, is PRC likely to replicate the success of Taiwan in high tech industries?

Author Index

Subject Index—General

A

B

C

F

G

J

L

M

O

P

Q

R

S

T

U

V

W

Y

Z

Subject Index—Structured Comparisons